ESSENTIALS for design

DREAMWEAVER® 8

level one

Julian Rickards

PEARSON
Prentice
Hall

Prentice Hall
Upper Saddle River, New Jersey 07458

Library of Congress Cataloging-in-Publication Data

Rickards, Julian.
   Dreamweaver 8. Level one / Julian Rickards.—2nd ed.
      p. cm. — (Essentials for design)
   Includes index.
   ISBN 0-13-187812-3
   1. Dreamweaver (Computer file) 2. Web site development. 3. Web sites—Design.
4. Web sites—Authoring Programs. I. Title. II. Series
   TK5105.8885.D74R52 2005
   006.7′8—dc22

                                           2005032662

Vice President and Publisher: Natalie E. Anderson
Executive Acquisitions Editor (Print): Stephanie Wall
Acquisitions Editor: Melissa Sabella
Product Development Manager: Eileen Bien Calabro
Editorial Project Manager: Anne Garcia
Editorial Assistants: Brian Hoehl, Alana Meyers, Sandra Bernales, Kaitlin O'Shaughnessy
Senior Media Project Managers: Cathi Profitko, Steve Gagliostro
Marketing Manager: Sarah Davis
Marketing Assistant: Lisa Taylor

Managing Editor: Lynda Castillo
Production Project Manager/Manufacturing Buyer: Vanessa Nuttry
Art Director/Cover Design: Blair Brown
Interior Design: Thistle Hill Publishing Services, LLC.
Cover Illustration/Photo: FoodPix®
Composition/Full-Service Project Management: Progressive Publishing Alternatives
Cover Printer: Coral Graphics
Printer/Binder: Von Hoffman Press

Credits and acknowledgments borrowed from other sources and reproduced, with permission, in this textbook appear on the appropriate page within the text.

A portion of the images supplied in this book are copyright © PhotoDisc, Inc., 201 Fourth Ave., Seattle, WA 98121, or copyright ©PhotoSpin, 4030 Palos Verdes Dr. N., Suite 200, Rollings Hills Estates, CA. These images are the sole property of PhotoDisc or PhotoSpin and are used by Prentice Hall with the permission of the owners. They may not be distributed, copied, transferred, or reproduced by any means whatsoever, other than for the completion of the exercises and projects contained in this book.

Macromedia Flash, Generator, FreeHand, Dreamweaver, Fireworks, and Director are registered trademarks of Macromedia, Inc. Photoshop, PageMaker, Acrobat, Adobe Type Manager, Illustrator, InDesign, Premiere, and PostScript are trademarks of Adobe Systems Incorporated. QuarkXPress is a registered trademark of Quark, Inc. Macintosh is a trademark of Apple Computer, Inc. CorelDRAW!, procreate Painter, and WordPerfect are trademarks of Corel Corporation. FrontPage, Publisher, PowerPoint, Word, Excel, Office, Microsoft, MS-DOS, and Windows are either registered trademarks or trademarks of Microsoft Corporation.

Other product and company names mentioned herein may be the trademarks of their respective owners.

10 9 8 7 6 5 4 3 2 1

ISBN 0-13-187812-3

ABOUT THE AUTHOR

Julian Rickards has been involved in various computer-related fields over the last dozen or so years, including computer instruction, technical illustration and web design, and is always willing to assist someone who is struggling with a project or concept. He is an advocate of web standards and web accessibility and is a member of GAWDS.org. In his employment with the Ontario government, he oversees the database and archives of digital publications and is often called upon to assist with the development of the Internet and Intranet web sites. Julian hails from Canada where he resides with his wonderfully supportive wife, Nanette, and two sons, Sebastian and Graeme.

ACKNOWLEDGMENTS

We would like to thank the professional writers, artists, editors, and educators who have worked long and hard on the *Essentials for Design series.*

And thanks to the dedicated teaching professionals: Kara Hardin, Visual Arts Department, Pensacola Junior College; Scott Springfield; Doug Borton, Kellogg Community College; and David McGill, Azusa Pacific University. Your insightful comments and expertise have certainly contributed to the success of the *Essentials for Design series.*

Thanks to Debbie Davidson for her help in managing the workflow and for her work on the illustrations.

Thank you to Terry Sisk Graybill, copy editor and final link in the chain of production, for her help in making sure that we all said what we meant to say.

And a very special thank you to Erika Kendra, production designer, technical consultant, partner in crime, and friend.

And to Melissa Sabella, Anne Garcia, Eileen Calabro, and Vanessa Nuttry—we appreciate your patience as we begin this new venture together.

CONTENTS AT A GLANCE

TABLE OF CONTENTS

HOW TO USE THIS BOOK

Essentials for Design courseware from Prentice Hall is anchored in the practical and professional needs of all types of students. The *Essentials Series* presents a learning-by-doing approach that encourages you to grasp application-related concepts as you expand your skills through hands-on tutorials. As such, it consists of modular lessons that are built around a series of numbered step-by-step procedures that are clear, concise, and easy to review.

Essentials books are divided into chapters. A chapter covers one area (or a few closely related areas) of application functionality. Each chapter consists of several lessons that are related to that topic. Each lesson presents a specific task or closely related set of tasks in a manageable portion that is easy to assimilate and retain.

Each element in the *Essentials for Design* book is designed to maximize your learning experience. A list of the *Essentials for Design* chapter elements, and a description of how each element can help you, begins on the next page. To find out more about the rationale behind each book element and how to use each to your maximum benefit, take the following walk-through.

WALK-THROUGH

Chapter Objectives.   Starting with an objective gives you short-term, attainable goals. Each chapter begins with a list of objectives that closely match the titles of the step-by-step tutorials. ▶

OBJECTIVES

In this chapter, you learn how to:

- Distinguish between absolute and relative paths
- Use different methods of linking pages
- Use absolute and relative links
- Link to another Web site
- Create an e-mail link
- Create a link from an image
- Create image maps and hotspots
- Create and link to named anchors
- Organize with default page names and subdomains

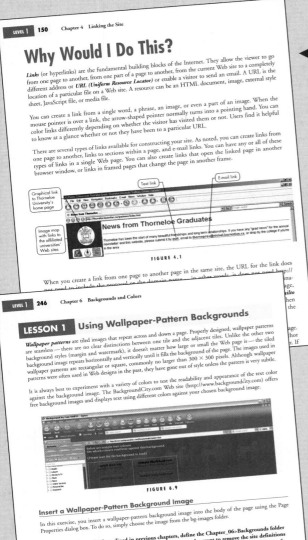

Why Would I Do This?   Introductory material at the beginning of each chapter provides an overview of why these tasks and procedures are important.

Visual Summary.   A series of illustrations introduces the new tools, dialog boxes, and windows you will explore in each chapter. ▼

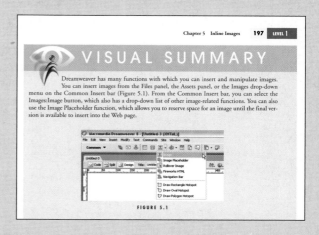

Step-by-Step Tutorials.   Hands-on tutorials let you learn by doing and include numbered, bold, step-by-step instructions.

◄ **If You Have Problems.**   These short troubleshooting notes help you anticipate or solve common problems quickly and effectively.

◄ **To Extend Your Knowledge.**   These features provide extra tips, alternative ways to complete a process, and special hints about using the software.

To Extend Your Knowledge . . .

APPROPRIATE ALTERNATE TEXT FOR IMAGES

All images should have alternate text so users not viewing the images receive the appropriate information about images they encounter. You first categorize the image as decorative, simple, or complex. This categorization helps you determine what amount or type of alternate text is appropriate.

Decorative images provide no content to the Web page. The appropriate alternate text is `alt=""`, which is known as an **empty alt**. In Dreamweaver, the <empty> option in the Alternate text field (or Alt field of the Property inspector) inserts an empty alt.

Simple images include button images or company logos. When these images are simply images of text, make the alternate text the text in the image. Otherwise, keep this text very brief: "Home" for a home page and the company name for a corporate logo such as "IBM Corporation".

Complex images include maps or charts from spreadsheet applications. Since these images convey a large amount of information, explain them briefly. Although there is no limit to how much text you can put in the alternate-text attribute, when a screen reader encounters alternate text, it reads it all to the user who is forced to listen to it all before moving on. The general rule of thumb is to limit alternate text to a few words at most.

Careers in Design.   These features offer advice, tips, and resources that will help you on your path to a successful career. ►

CAREERS IN DESIGN

EXPLORING PROFESSIONAL PORTFOLIO SITES

In the early days of digital publishing technology, imaging and layout software was accepted more by image artists and designers than it was by "niche" professionals — people like photographers, illustrators, painters, and (little wonder) typographers. Although the widespread acceptance of what was then known as "desktop" publishing applications did in fact spell the end of certain specializations (like typesetters), other fields like photography were hardly affected at all.

Why is this important to you as a Web site designer? Because photographers in particular weathered the storm of desktop technology and emerged on the other end, evolved but in many ways exactly the same as they were before. Their ability to see the world through a lens comes through in their Web sites.

Spend time researching how professional photographers display their wares on the Web. They provide some of the best examples of portfolio sites you can imagine. Use Google or Yahoo! to look for photographers in your particular region of the country who show their work on the Web. Call a few of them — particularly those whose sites you find compelling — and interview them about how they view their Web presence. What things are important to them from a design standpoint? Who designed their sites and what software was used? You might be surprised to find that most of them were done using Dreamweaver.

End-of-Chapter Exercises.   Extensive end-of-chapter exercises emphasize hands-on skill development. You'll find two levels of reinforcement: Skill Drill and Challenge. ▼

Chapter 6 Backgrounds and Colors   **273**   LEVEL 1

SKILL DRILL

Skill Drill exercises reinforce project skills. Each skill that is reinforced is the same as, or nearly the same as, a skill we presented in the chapter. We provide detailed instructions in a step-by-step format. You should work through the exercises in order.

1. Choose a Color from an Image

The reach of the eyedropper color picker extends beyond the Color Picker window. You can use it to choose a color from any component in the Dreamweaver application window. If you have a graphic with a color you would like to match, as long as you can see the graphic in the Document window, you can use the color picker to pick up a color from the graphic.

In this exercise you learn to use the eyedropper to obtain a color from a graphic, and then make the chosen color the background color.

Open index.html from the Telescopes site and open the Page Properties dialog box.

1. Drag to select the contents of the Background Image field (images/stars.jpg) and press Delete to remove it.

2. Click Apply to confirm that the starry background is removed.

3. Click the Background Color button.

4. Click the pop-out arrow at the top right of the Color Picker window.

5. If there is a check mark next to Snap to Web Safe, skip to Step 7. If there is no check mark next to Snap to Web Safe, click Snap to Web Safe.

   In the previous exercises, we did not need to worry about whether Snap to Web Safe was enabled or not because the colors in the color palette are all Web-safe. Colors outside of the color palette, however, may not be Web-safe.

6. Move the mouse pointer (eyedropper) over the Telescopes graphic near the top of the Document window. Watch the swatch window and hexadecimal codes change as the mouse pointer moves across the graphic.

   You can see that the hexadecimal codes are always paired triplets, such as 330066 or 003300. The Snap to Web Safe option converts the color at the tip of the eyedropper to the closest Web-safe color.

LEVEL 1   **102**   Chapter 2 Building Your First Web Site

CHALLENGE

Challenge exercises expand on, or are somewhat related to, skills we presented in the lessons. Each exercise provides a brief introduction, followed by numbered-step instructions that are not as detailed as those in the Skill Drill exercises. You should work through the exercises in order.

1. Design Your Family's Web Site

In this Challenge exercise, you create a small Web site about your family. Plan the site on paper, and then construct some of the Web pages. This exercise's purpose is to practice what you learned about planning a Web site, and then putting your plan into action.

1. Before you begin, write the full names of your parents, yourself, and your siblings with several spaces between each on a blank sheet of paper. For each family member, write his or her birth date and birthplace, favorite activity or hobby, and one or two other interesting pieces of information about him or her. Create an e-mail address for each using the format `firstname@lastname.com`.

2. In Dreamweaver, use the Advanced tab of the Site Definition dialog box to define a Web site named with your father's last name. Set the Local Root Folder to Chapter_02>Family.

3. Create a new HTML page with the family's last name at the top and the names of the family members below. Save the page as "home.html".

4. Create a new HTML page. Type your name at the top; in the paragraphs below, type the information you wrote about yourself, and end with your e-mail address.

5. Select your e-mail address and type it in the Property inspector's Link field. Precede the e-mail address with `mailto:` in the Link field.

6. At the bottom of the page, type `Return to our home page`.

7. Select the last paragraph, type `home.html` in the Link field, and then close, saving the Web page using your first name followed by .html as the filename.

8. Repeat Steps 4 to 7 for each family member, using his or her first name as the filename followed by .html.

9. When you have completed all of the individual pages, reopen home.html.

10. One by one, select each person's name and create a link to his or her page.

11. Preview the page in your browser (save when prompted) and test all of the links.

12. Close your browser and return to Dreamweaver. Close home.html.

2. Print a Web Page and Its Source Code

1. Open challenge1.html from the Chapter_02>Challenges folder.

2. Preview the page in your browser.

3. Print the page from your browser.

Portfolio Builder.   At the end of every chapter, these exercises require creative solutions to problems that reinforce the topic of the chapter. ▶

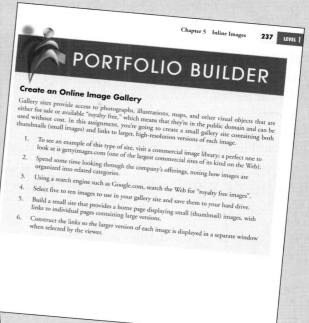

Chapter 5   Inline Images   237   LEVEL 1

PORTFOLIO BUILDER

Create an Online Image Gallery

Gallery sites provide access to photographs, illustrations, maps, and other visual objects that are either for sale or available "royalty free," which means that they're in the public domain and can be used without cost. In this assignment, you're going to create a small gallery site containing both thumbnails (small images) and links to larger, high-resolution versions of each image.

1. To see an example of this type of site, visit a commercial image library; a perfect one to look at is gettyimages.com (one of the largest commercial sites of its kind on the Web).

2. Spend some time looking through the company's offerings, noting how images are organized into related categories.

3. Using a search engine such as Google.com, search the Web for "royalty free images".

4. Select five to ten images to use in your gallery site and save them to your hard drive.

5. Build a small site that provides a home page displaying small (thumbnail) images, with links to individual pages containing large versions.

6. Construct the links so that the larger version of each image is displayed in a separate window when selected by the viewer.

LEVEL 1

INTEGRATING PROJECT

This integrating project reflects a real-world Web site job, drawing on the skills you learned throughout this book. The files you need to complete this project are in the RF_Dreamweaver_L1>IP folder.

Independence Hummer Web Site

The management of Independence Hummer, a car dealership, has hired you to recreate their existing Web site. While this site actually exists (IndependenceHummer.com), graphics and photos used by permission), for the purposes of this project, imagine you are on the Web team creating the site. The client has supplied the information and the images and has approved the design concepts. The team has planned the basic strategy for creating the site and has assembled the components. The final site will feature a frames-based layout that includes tables within the individual pages, as well as text and graphic links.

◀ **Integrating Projects.**   Integrating projects are designed to reflect real-world graphic-design jobs, drawing on the skills you have learned throughout this book.

Task Guides.   These charts, found at the end of each book, list alternative ways to complete common procedures and provide a handy reference tool. ▶

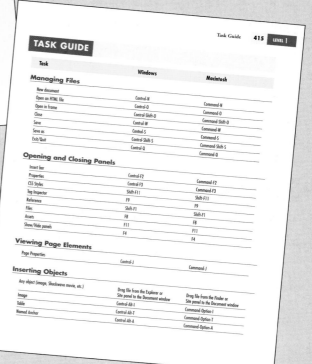

Task Guide   415   LEVEL 1

TASK GUIDE

Task	Windows	Macintosh
Managing Files		
New document		
Open an HTML file	Control-N	Command-N
Open in frame	Control-O	Command-O
Close	Control-Shift-O	Command-Shift-O
Save	Control-W	Command-W
Save as	Control-S	Command-S
Exit/Quit	Control-Shift-S	Command-Shift-S
	Control-Q	Command-Q
Opening and Closing Panels		
Insert bar		
Properties	Control-F2	Command-F2
CSS Styles	Control-F3	Command-F3
Tag Inspector	Shift-F11	Shift-F11
Reference	F9	F9
Files	Shift-F1	Shift-F1
Assets	F8	F8
Show/Hide panels	F11	F11
	F4	F4
Viewing Page Elements		
Page Properties		
	Control-J	Command-J
Inserting Objects		
Any object (image, Shockwave movie, etc.)		
Image	Drag file from the Explorer or Site panel to the Document window	Drag file from the Finder or Site panel to the Document window
Table	Control-Alt-I	Command-Option-I
Named Anchor	Control-Alt-T	Command-Option-T
	Control-Alt-A	Command-Option-A

STUDENT INFORMATION AND RESOURCES

Companion Web Site (www.prenhall.com/essentials).   This text-specific Web site provides students with additional information and exercises to reinforce their learning. Features include: additional end-of-chapter reinforcement material, online Study Guide, easy access to *all* resource files, and much, much more!

Before completing most chapters within this text, you will need to download the Resource files from the Student CD or from Prentice Hall's Companion Website for the Essentials for Design Series. Check with your instructor for the best way to gain access to these files or simply follow these instructions:

If you are going to save these files to an external disk, make sure it is inserted into the appropriate drive before continuing.

1. Start your web browser and go to http://www.prenhall.com/essentials

2. Select your textbook or series to access the Companion Website. We suggest you bookmark this page, as it has links to additional Prentice Hall resources that you may use in class.

3. Click the Student Resources link.

4. Locate the files you need from the list of available resources and then click the link to download.

Moving forward the process will vary depending upon which operating system (OS) you are using. Please select your OS and follow the instructions below:

Windows OS:

5. Locate the files you need from the list of available resources and click the link to download.

6. When the File Download box displays, click the **Save** button.

7. In the Save As dialog box, select the location to which you wish to save the file. We recommend you saving the file to the Windows desktop or TEMP folder so it is easy to locate, but if you are working in a lab environment this may not be possible. To save to an external disk, simply type in or select your disk's corresponding drive. Example: a:\ where "a" designates an external disk drive.

8. Click the **Save** button to begin the downloading process.

9. Once the download is complete, navigate to the file using Windows Explorer.

10. Double click on the file to begin the self extraction process and follow the step-by-step prompts.

Mac OS with Stuffit Expander 8.0.2 or greater:

5. Locate the files you need from the list of available resources and click the link to download.

6. With default settings the file will be downloaded to your desktop.

7. Once Download Manager shows status as "complete", double-click on the file to expand file.

NOTE: Stuffit Expander can be downloaded free at <http://www.stuffit.com/>

Mac OS with Stuffit Expander 8:

5. Locate the files you need from the list of available resources and click the link to download.

6. With default settings the file will be downloaded to your desktop.

7. Once Download Manager shows status as "complete", double-click on the file and choose Stuffit Expander as the application to expand file.

NOTE: Stuffit Expander can be downloaded free at <http://www.stuffit.com/>

Need help? Contact Tech Support Online at <http://247.prenhall.com/>

Resource CD.   If you are using a Resource CD, all the files you need are provided on the CD. Resource files are organized in chapter-specific folders (e.g., Chapter_01, Chapter_02, etc.), which are contained in the RF_Dreamweaver_L1 folder. You can either work directly from the CD, or copy the files onto your hard drive before beginning the exercises.

Before you begin working on the chapters or lessons in this book, you should copy the Work_In_Progress folder from the Resource CD onto your hard drive or a removable disk/drive.

Resource Files.   Resource files are organized in chapter-specific folders, and are named to facilitate cross-platform compatibility. Words are separated by an underscore, and all file names include a lowercase three-letter extension. For example, if you are directed to open the file "graphics.eps" in Chapter 2, the file can be found in the RF_Dreamweaver_L1> Chapter_02 folder. We repeat these directions frequently in the early chapters.

The Work In Progress Folder.   This folder contains individual folders for each chapter in the book (e.g., WIP_01, WIP_02, etc.). When an exercise directs you to save a file, you should save it to the appropriate folder for the chapter in which you are working.

The exercises in this book frequently build upon work that you have already completed. At the end of each exercise, you will be directed to save your work and either close the file or continue to the next exercise. If you are directed to continue but your time is limited, you can stop at a logical point, save the file, and later return to the point at which you stopped. In this case, you will need to open the file from the appropriate WIP folder and continue working on the same file.

Typeface Conventions.   Computer programming code appears in a monospace font that `looks like this`. In many cases, you only need to change or enter specific pieces of code; in these instances, the code you need to type or change appears in a second color and `looks like this`.

INSTRUCTOR'S RESOURCES

Instructor's Resource Center.   This CD-ROM includes the entire Instructor's Manual for each application in Microsoft Word format. Student data files and completed solutions files are also on this CD-ROM. The Instructor's Manual contains a reference guide of these files for the instructor's convenience. PowerPoint slides with more information about each project are also available for classroom use. All instructor resources are also available online via the Companion website at www.prenhall.com/essentials.

TestGen Software.   TestGen is a test generator program that lets you view and easily edit test bank questions, transfer them to tests, and print the tests in a variety of formats suitable to your teaching situation. The program also offers many options for organizing and displaying test banks and tests. A built-in random number and text generator makes it ideal for creating multiple versions of tests. Powerful search and sort functions let you easily locate questions and arrange them in the order you prefer.

QuizMaster, also included in this package, enables students to take tests created with TestGen on a local area network. The QuizMaster utility built into TestGen lets instructors view student records and print a variety of reports. Building tests is easy with TestGen, and exams can be easily uploaded into WebCT, Blackboard, and CourseCompass.

Prentice Hall has formed close alliances with each of the leading online platform providers: WebCT, Blackboard, and our own Pearson CourseCompass.

INTRODUCTION

If you search the Internet for Web-design software, Macromedia's Dreamweaver appears often because of its power, sophistication, and support, not only from Macromedia but also from many user forums. It is therefore not surprising that Dreamweaver is the foremost application for Web design and development. Dreamweaver 8 has great support for Cascading Style Sheets, server-side languages, and databases, such as PHP and MySQL, as well as for accessibility considerations.

Dreamweaver's WYSIWYG (What You See Is What You Get or visual) interface benefits new users who are learning Web design for the first time, graphic designers who are accustomed to creating their designs on screen, and hand-coders for whom some of the tasks are greatly simplified. Although Dreamweaver is primarily a WYSIWYG Web-design application, with the click of a button you can see and work with the code of the Web page you are building. In addition to its functions that enable you to create Web sites, Dreamweaver also has file- and site-management functions, enabling you to manage your Web sites directly from this application. These are only a few of the features that have made Dreamweaver so popular.

This book introduces you to the tools, utilities, and features of Dreamweaver, and gives you hands-on practice so you can apply your new skills to your own design projects. We define many of the terms and concepts that you need to understand when you work in the Web-design field, and explain how those ideas relate to Web-design projects.

Our goal is to show you how to use the software's features so you can implement your own creative ideas. You can apply the skills you learn throughout this book to any Web project, whether a small Web site, a corporate intranet, or a Web site of a large retailer.

We focus on the proper use of Web technologies to help you design and develop Web sites that are accessible by everyone (one of the founding principles of the World Wide Web). You learn how to create properly structured documents, incorporate images, work with colors and backgrounds, present data in tables, and use tables and frames for laying out your Web pages. You learn to use the WYSIWYG interface and to work directly with the code. Armed with the technical knowledge of how to use Dreamweaver, a sound background in the different components of Web design, and an understanding of how those components interact, you will be prepared to design and develop your Web sites comfortably using Dreamweaver.

CHAPTER 1

Taking a Tour of Dreamweaver

OBJECTIVES

In this chapter, you learn how to:

- Launch Dreamweaver on your computer system

- Identify components of the Code view

- Identify components of the Design view

- Recognize features of the Property inspector

- Select HTML tags using the Tag selector

- Insert HTML tags using the Tag chooser

- Modify the Dreamweaver interface

- Obtain help with features and functions

Why Would I Do This?

In this chapter, you explore Dreamweaver and its components. You look at and try out this program's most important features. By examining some Web pages in Dreamweaver, you learn how Web pages are constructed. You also investigate how the Dreamweaver interface allows you to work with the components of a Web page, and you discover how Dreamweaver represents both the design aspect and the underlying code aspect of these pages.

Dreamweaver is a tool that grows with you. Many beginners to Web design prefer to work in a graphical environment. Dreamweaver provides a sophisticated, yet user-friendly *WYSIWYG (What You See Is What You Get)* view called the "Design view." In this view, you can type text, insert images, resize tables, and access many other functions through a click of your mouse.

The appearance of Web pages, however, is created by underlying code called *HTML (Hypertext Markup Language)*, the structural language of Web pages that identifies the graphics, fonts, colors, and more. When you work in the Design view, Dreamweaver creates the HTML for you.

Dreamweaver does not include all HTML code or all options for that code in its interface: there are numerous options and features that require you to manually intervene in the code. When you have enough experience and understanding of HTML, you can add these features manually. Dreamweaver provides a sophisticated interface for doing just this — the Code view. This view provides *code hints* (pop-up menus that offer the options for the current piece of code) and *syntax highlighting* (different parts of the code that are colored differently), both of which greatly assist the novice and the experienced hand-coder. (A *hand-coder* is a person who prefers to create directly from the code rather than through a visual interface.) Many hand-coders also greatly appreciate the sophistication of Dreamweaver's Design view — in a few seconds, they can create a complex table structure that would otherwise take them several minutes or more of hand-coding.

For these reasons, Dreamweaver is the premier Web-page authoring application for Windows and Macintosh systems. It provides you with an abundance of tools, panels, menus, and other means for creating and modifying Web pages. The interface also has many deliberate redundancies, so you have more than one way to accomplish the same task. With such a wealth of tools and other components in Dreamweaver, it is important to learn the locations, names, and functions of the components (as you do in this chapter), so that you can use the program efficiently. Whether you plan to create basic Web sites or manage sites of many thousands of pages, Dreamweaver is a tool that works well for you.

VISUAL SUMMARY

At the top of the Dreamweaver Design view is the familiar Menu bar that provides access to many Web-design functions and to standard document functions, such as opening, closing, and saving documents. Below it, the Insert bar gives you access to many Web-design functions that are collected into groups of related functions. The Start page allows you to continue working on an unfinished recent document or to create a new page from either a blank document or predesigned sample pages.

At the right of the Start page, the panel groups provide access to specific functions, such as Cascading Style Sheets (CSS) from the CSS panel or files in the current Web site from the Files panel. Panel groups can be collapsed (like the CSS panel group) or expanded (like the Files panel group). Panel groups generally consist of multiple panels, such as the Files panel group, which consists of the Files, Assets, and Snippets panels. Other panels, such as the Frames panel, are closed by default. At the bottom of the Dreamweaver interface, the Property inspector displays the properties of a selected item in a Web page, such as an image's height and width.

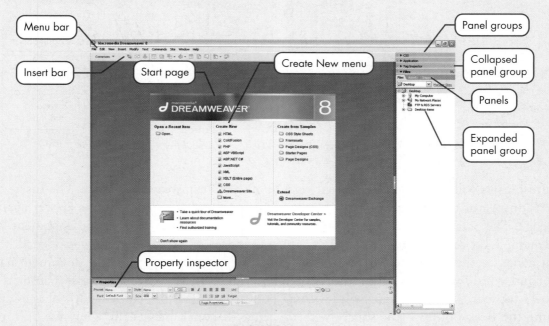

FIGURE 1.1

In this chapter, you learn about and explore the features of the Document window, the working area of the Dreamweaver interface. The following figure shows the Document window in Split view, in which you can see the Code and Design views together; Dreamweaver can fill the Document window with either view. The Code window, the Document window's top portion in this figure, displays the underlying HTML code that is created when you work in the Design window below it. The selected code in the Code window is the code for the figure selected in the Design window.

At the top of the Document window is the Filename tab, which identifies the filename of the page you are editing; if you have multiple documents open at the same time, multiple tabs appear. The Document toolbar allows you to switch between the different views of the current Web page and also provides access to other functions related to the document as a whole. At the bottom of the Document window is the Status bar with the Tag selector on the left; on the right are the Select, Hand, and Zoom tools, the Set Magnification list, and the Window Size and Download Time indicators.

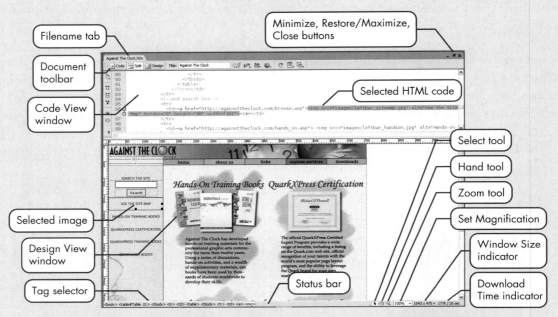

FIGURE 1.2 *(Copyright Against The Clock, Inc. Used by permission of Against the Clock, Inc.)*

Macintosh users will see a slightly different version of the Dreamweaver interface. The Insert bar and Property inspector appear against their screen's left edge, and the panel groups appear against the right edge. The Start page is centered directly beneath the Insert bar. If only one document is open, the filename is centered at the top of the document window. If a second window is opened, the document name for the first window appears in a tab at the window's top left. The document name for the second window appears in another tab to the right of the first, and is also centered in the window's top bar. The document window may be resized to fill the entire width of the screen by dragging the Resize button (the square with the three diagonal lines at the window's bottom-right corner). The window may be closed, minimized, or maximized using the red, yellow, and green buttons in the top-left corner.

The Property inspector below the Document window changes to reflect the current and available properties of the selected item in the Document window. If you select a block of text, the Property inspector shows the format, font list, current style, bold, alignment, and other text and format properties.

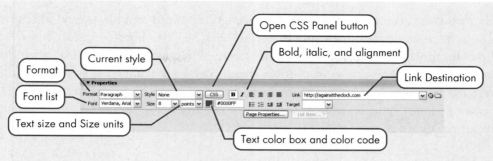

FIGURE 1.3

The Property inspector also shows a selected graphic's properties, such as its height, width, file size, and source. If you have set the graphic as a link to another page, the Property inspector identifies the link's destination. Dreamweaver provides some image-editing functions, which appear in the Property inspector when an image is selected.

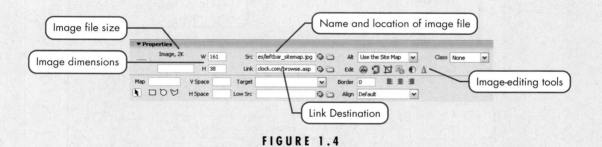

FIGURE 1.4

Tables have very different properties than images, so when you select a table, the Property inspector changes to reflect that table's current and available properties. The Property inspector is an immensely useful feature of Dreamweaver because it displays the properties that are used by and are available for the selected item on the Web page, and it allows you to alter or add properties to the item.

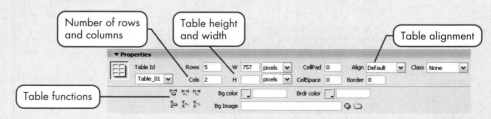

FIGURE 1.5

The Insert bar provides access to many Web-page design functions and has several different forms that you can choose from the drop-down menu on the bar's far left. The Common Insert bar contains many of the common functions that you use to create Web pages. Clicking the appropriate button reveals these functions or presents a drop-down menu that gives you access to related functions. The Layout Insert bar contains features and functions that you can use to lay out Web pages, including tables, layers, and frames. The Text Insert bar offers text-formatting functions and, through the drop-down menu, provides access to special characters.

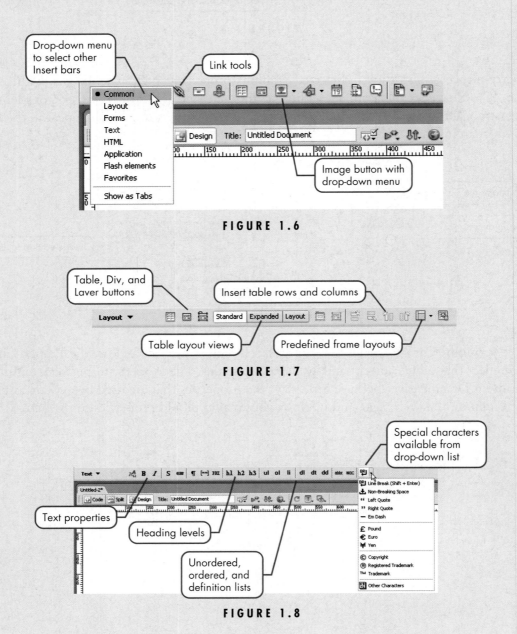

FIGURE 1.6

FIGURE 1.7

FIGURE 1.8

LESSON 1   Launching Dreamweaver for the First Time

The Windows version of Dreamweaver offers a layout option not available in the Macintosh version. In the Windows version, the Designer and Coder workspace layouts contain all toolbars, the Property inspector, and the panels in the Dreamweaver window. In the Macintosh version, components float in the workspace; that is, you can drag and place them separately from one another. Dreamweaver also offers a Dual Screen layout. This layout is like the Macintosh floating layout, enabling Windows users to arrange the components as they wish between two computer monitors.

In the following exercise, you launch Dreamweaver for the first time. Depending on how your system is set up, Dreamweaver may or may not display the Workspace Setup dialog box (Windows) or the Start page. In this exercise, you see these dialog boxes and discover where to enable or disable them.

Because there are some significant differences between the Windows and Macintosh workspace layouts, sometimes users on different platforms must use different methods to perform the same task. Both Windows and Macintosh users can perform all of the exercises in this book; however, in the following exercise, Macintosh users cannot perform one (identified) step but can and should perform all other steps.

Launch Dreamweaver for the First Time

1 **To launch the program, choose Start>Programs>Macromedia>Dreamweaver 8 (Windows) or click the Dreamweaver icon in the Dock or the Applications folder (Macintosh).**

The program launches. If you are working on a Windows system and this is the first time that Dreamweaver has been started, the Workspace Setup dialog box appears, prompting you to choose the Designer or Coder workspace layout. If this is not the first time that Dreamweaver has been started or you are using a Macintosh system, skip to Step 3.

2 **If you are working on a Windows system, choose Designer and click OK.**

Although the Coder workspace layout is available to Windows users, it offers no additional features. This layout simply moves the panel groups to the left and switches the Document window to Code view. Windows users can create this layout manually without using this function. Macintosh users can also create a similar layout by rearranging the panels and switching the Document window to Code view.

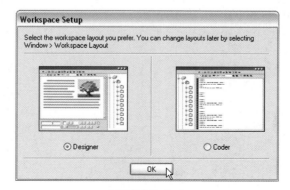

FIGURE 1.9

3 **Choose Create New HTML document from the Dreamweaver Start Page menu.**

The Don't Show Again check box in the lower-left corner of the Start Page menu disables the Start page. Since future exercises require you to choose an option from the Start page, do not select this option.

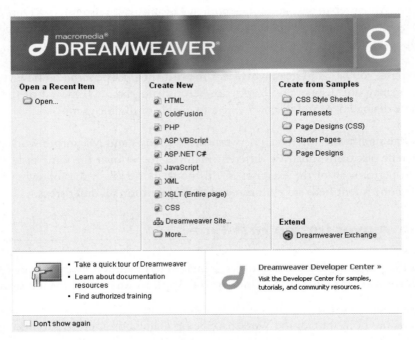

FIGURE 1.10

4 **View the new HTML page in the Design view.**

The Design view is the WYSIWYG view, which is not unlike word-processing software. The white Document window is surrounded by the Menu and Insert bars at the top, the panel groups on the right, and the Property inspector below. The tab at the top of the Document window indicates that the current HTML document is untitled. The only indication of HTML is the **<body>** tag in the Tag selector at the Document window's bottom-left corner. This tag indicates that the insertion point is on the page, ready for you to type in text (body copy).

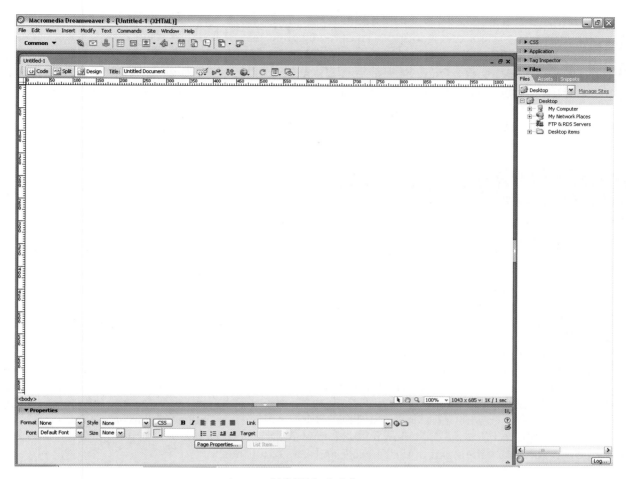

FIGURE 1.11

5 Choose File>Exit to exit Dreamweaver.

To Extend Your Knowledge . . .

WORKSPACE LAYOUTS IN WINDOWS AND MACINTOSH

The workspace layouts are slightly different between Windows and Macintosh systems. Dreamweaver for Windows utilizes an *MDI (Multiple Document Interface)* in which the application encloses all open documents in the application window. Dreamweaver for Macintosh utilizes a floating workspace layout in which the individual document windows and application components float freely in relation to one another. The Dual Screen layout is like the Macintosh floating layout, enabling you to arrange the components as you wish across two computer screens.

The Dreamweaver setups and workspace layouts only affect the application's visual appearance, not its functionality — all functions and features are available to all users from all layouts and setups. Some components of the interface may be visible in one setup but hidden in another. With a click of your mouse, however, you make the hidden component visible.

LESSON 2   Exploring the Code View

Dreamweaver has two basic default document views: the Design view and the Code view. The default is the Design view and is the WYSIWYG interface — the design you create in the Document window is what displays in a Web browser. The Code view displays HTML code in the Document window. A Web graphic designer might prefer the Design view, while a Web programmer might prefer the Code view. At any time, however, you can switch from one setup to the other by selecting the View Select buttons at the Document window's top left.

Hypertext Markup Language (HTML) is the structural language of Web pages. It specifies colors, images, typefaces, and other Web page components. The term "hyper" comes from hyperlink, which is the ability to provide a direct link from one Web page to another. "Text" refers to the fact that the code is written into the document as text characters. An HTML page includes the instructions on how to display the page and the text that appears on the page. Code is differentiated from text content by angle brackets, `<>`, that surround the code. "Markup" indicates that the code is embedded amid the text in much the same way that a teacher or boss might mark up a printed page with instructions, such as "make this bold" or "add a graphic here." The term "language" refers to the fact that the code must follow a standard or it won't work: to make text bold, you use `<b>`, not `<bold>`, because `<b>` is part of the language and `<bold>` is not.

The HTML language consists of HTML tags or just tags. *Tags* are elements surrounded by angle brackets: the bold tag, `<b>`, consists of the bold element, `b`, surrounded by angle brackets. HTML tags come in two forms — container tags and empty tags. *Container tags* surround content and have both an on and an off version. The off tag uses the same element as the on tag except that the element is preceded by a forward slash, such as `</b>` for the closing bold tag. Container tags surround content; for example, to make the word "Tennessee" bold, the HTML would be `<b>Tennessee</b>`. *Empty tags* do not have a closing tag. Examples of empty tags include the `<img />` tag, which is used to insert a graphic, and the `<hr />` tag, which inserts a *horizontal rule* (a horizontal line, hence `hr`).

Tag options are known as *attributes*. With rare exceptions, attributes are paired with attribute values. For example, the `<img />` (image) tag uses the `src` (source) attribute to specify the graphic's filename. The attribute is `src`, and the attribute value may be `red-rose.gif`. You format attributes and attribute values in a standard way as well. You use an equal sign to join an attribute and its attribute value, and you surround the value with quotation marks, such as `src="red-rose.gif"`, which, with the `<img />` tag, results in `<img src="red-rose.gif" />`. Many empty tags, such as the `<img />` tag, specify the content they provide by attributes. Container tags may also use attributes, but the attributes must appear in the opening tag, never in the closing tag. For example, to specify the alignment of a paragraph, you would use `<p align="center">paragraph text</p>`.

To Extend Your Knowledge . . .

HTML STANDARDS

Every computer language follows a particular standard. In some cases, the company that created the language maintains it, as Microsoft Corporation maintains the Active Server Pages language. In other cases, an organization maintains the language, as the **W3C (World Wide Web Consortium)** maintains HTML. The W3C HTML group works to continually improve HTML.

HTML is modified by two means — incorporation of new HTML code developed by browser manufacturers, or code developed by the W3C. For one dark period in the history of HTML, Netscape and Microsoft fought for control over the **WWW (World Wide Web)**, which they saw as an untapped market. In an attempt to improve their browsers' market share, each either created new HTML tags or "improved" upon current HTML, often to the exclusion of other browsers. This led to what is now referred to as the "browser wars." These wars created a huge headache for many corporate Web-site developers who were required to support both browsers for fear of losing a significant portion of their potential customers.

In the end, common sense prevailed; with the aid of the Web-standards advocates, W3C HTML is again the single HTML standard. During the browser wars, the mark of advanced Web developers was to show how far they could push their browser of choice, despite losing others. With the return to Web standards, the mark of advanced developers is to show how similar their Web pages look in all browsers.

Web standards are in; browser wars are out: Web developers are now measured against the W3C code standards, Web-development software is evaluated on the basis of how well it produces standards-compliant code, and browsers are evaluated by how well they display standards-compliant code. Dreamweaver produces good-quality code and, for the most part, displays it as the W3C recommends browsers should display code. Dreamweaver is not a browser, but its Design view is a very good representation of what standards-compliant browsers will display. This is one of the reasons why Dreamweaver has become the premier Web-development software.

To Extend Your Knowledge . . .

XHTML VS. HTML

Dreamweaver 8, by default, creates Web pages using XHTML, not HTML as in previous versions of Dreamweaver. For all intents and purposes, XHTML is simply the next version of HTML. Although future versions of XHTML may become radically different from HTML, XHTML 1.0 (Dreamweaver 8's default), is virtually identical to HTML 4.01, the last version of HTML.

The "X" in XHTML comes from another W3C Web technology called **XML (Extensible Markup Language)**, an extremely strict language in which, if even one component of the language is incorrect, the document does not display. The advantage of such strictness is that if the document meets the standard, it is very easy for browsers to display — guessing is not necessary. The W3C intends, with XHTML, to improve HTML and to increase the strictness of HTML, thereby making it easier for browsers to display.

Dreamweaver supports three subversions of XHTML. By default, Dreamweaver's HTML pages are built against the XHTML 1.0 Transitional **DTD (Document Type Definition)**, (the specification that defines the tags and attributes allowed in each version/subversion of HTML or XHTML). The other versions of XHTML are XHTML 1.0 Strict, XHTML 1.0 Frameset and XHTML 1.1 (Transitional, Strict, or Frameset subversions do not exist for XHTML 1.1). Most standards-aware designers build their pages against XHTML 1.0 Strict or XHTML 1.1: these are the most rigorous versions of XHTML whereas the Transitional subversion is less rigorous and the Frameset subversion is used only when building framed Web pages.

Examples of differences between HTML and XHTML include:

- All code must be lowercase. Whereas HTML treated `<abbr>` and `<ABBR>` equally, only `<abbr>` is allowed in XHTML.

- Empty tags must be closed. Therefore, `<hr>` must be `<hr />`, `<img>` must be `<img />`, and `<br>` must be `<br />`.

- Container tags must be closed. HTML did not require `</p>`, `</li>`, or `</td>`, but XHTML requires that they be used to close paragraphs, lists, and table cells, respectively.

There are other differences between HTML and XHTML but, for the most part, you don't have to worry about any of them, because Dreamweaver creates the code for you and does it very well. However, if you work with the code in Code view, you must be aware of the differences between HTML and XHTML. Read a summary of the differences at http://www.w3.org/TR/xhtml1/#diffs.

Explore the Code View

1   **Launch Dreamweaver.**

2   **Choose HTML from below the Create New heading on the Start page.**

3   **Click the Code button at the top of the Document window and examine the HTML code in the Document window.**

Notice that the Document window contains HTML code that was not visible in the Design view. Different components of HTML are colored differently, which is helpful to a coder looking for an error. Code is blue, whereas text is black, as you can see between the opening and closing `<title>` tags. Displaying different components of code in different colors is called *syntax coloring* and is only available in the better coding applications.

FIGURE 1.12

4   **Click between the "y" and ">" at the end of <body> and press the Spacebar.**

A code prompt appears, listing all options for the **<body>** tag. (You learn more about the **<body>** tag in Lesson 5.)

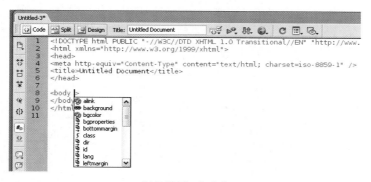

FIGURE 1.13

5   **Move the pointer over the regions of the Document toolbar; note the tool tips that appear.**

The filename displays "Untitled" until you save the file. An asterisk appears by the filename if you have modified the file since you last saved it. The No Browser Check Errors tool tip and the button graphic change when browser-check errors exist.

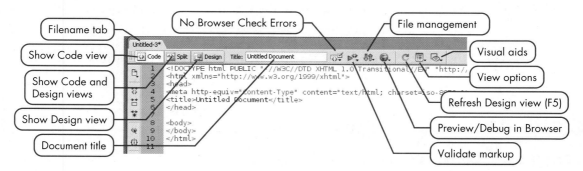

FIGURE 1.14

6 **Move your pointer over the regions of the Common Insert bar; note the tool tips that appear.**

The Insert bar contains many different functions, which are grouped by categories. You can select these categories through the pop-up menu at the bar's left end. By default, you select categories from a pop-up menu, but you can also change its form to a tabbed menu instead.

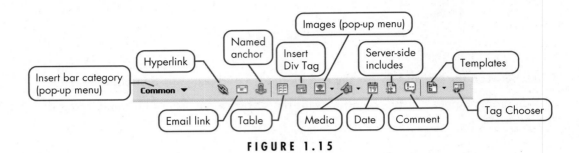

FIGURE 1.15

7 **Click the title of the CSS panel group to expand it.**

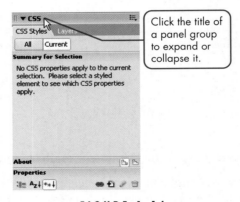

FIGURE 1.16

8 **Click once on the Design button at the top of the Document window to switch to the Design view.**

9 **Choose File>Exit to exit Dreamweaver. Do not save the changes to the untitled document.**

To Extend Your Knowledge . . .

EXPANDED VS. OPEN, COLLAPSED VS. CLOSED

Most Dreamweaver panel groups contain panels; most panel groups are visible on screen by default. For example, by default, the Design panel group is visible, but the Results panel group is not.

Dreamweaver uses "open" and "closed" to describe whether or not the panel groups are visible and available to the user. If a panel-group title is visible, the panel group is open. The Results panel-group title is not visible and is therefore closed. You can open closed panels from the Window menu by choosing Window>Results.

The terms "expanded" and "collapsed" describe whether or not the panels in panel groups are visible. The expander arrow points down if a panel group is expanded and points to the right if collapsed. If the CSS Styles panel tab is visible, the CSS panel group is both open and expanded.

LESSON 3 Exploring the Design View

Dreamweaver's Design view is very beneficial to beginning Web designers — it resembles word-processing software, which is familiar to most people. The common functions and features are available through a keystroke combination or a mouse click. Some people are uncomfortable working with code and naturally prefer the Design view. Furthermore, many Web designers come from a print-design background. Their keen and experienced eyes enable them to create wonderful Web-site designs, but code is unfamiliar to them because it is not part of their print-design work. For all of these individuals, the Design view makes Web design more comfortable and natural.

The Design view permits designers to build a design on-screen while Dreamweaver builds the code in the background. Although many hand-coders may argue that hand-coding gives them greater control over the code, Dreamweaver produces excellent-quality code, and the ease with which it creates tables, for example, can persuade the most ardent hand-coder to try Dreamweaver.

As mentioned before, the Code and Design views provide access to the same functions and features of Web-page design. The primary difference between the views is how users interact with Dreamweaver to create their designs. With the Code view, the user creates the design by keying the code; with the Design view, the user commonly employs the mouse and menus to create the designs.

In the previous lesson, you saw that the Code view is just a click away. When you become more experienced with Web design, you will realize how beneficial it is to know HTML so that you can customize the code that Dreamweaver produces, when necessary. Experienced Web designers are comfortable in both views, switching back and forth as necessary.

Explore the Design View

1   **Start Dreamweaver and choose HTML from the Create New heading on the Start page.**

? If You Have Problems

If you don't see the Start page, choose Edit>Preferences. Click the General tab, and check the Show Start Page option. Click OK to close the Preferences dialog box. The Start page does not appear immediately — you must exit Dreamweaver (File>Exit) and then relaunch it.

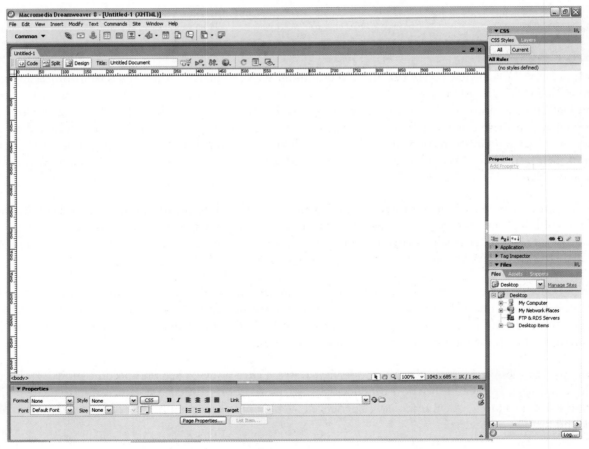

FIGURE 1.17

2   **Click the Code button; notice that the HTML code is visible.**

3   **Click the Split button to see the Code view in the upper portion of the Document window and the Design view in the lower portion.**

At times it is beneficial to see both views simultaneously — the Split button (the tool tip displays Show Code and Design Views) makes this possible.

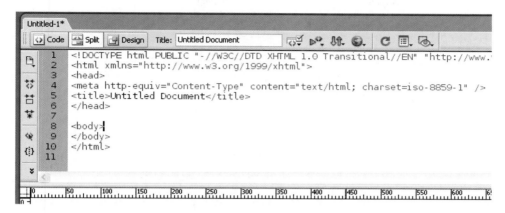

FIGURE 1.18

4   **Move the insertion point to the end of the `<body>` tag in the Code view window; press Enter/Return once, and type your first name.**

Notice that your name does not appear in the Design view window. You must refresh the Design view in order for any code or text typed in the Code view window to be visible in the Design view window. You can also click in the Design window to refresh the Design view.

5   **Click the Refresh Design View button in the Document toolbar.**

Notice that your name now appears in the Design view window.

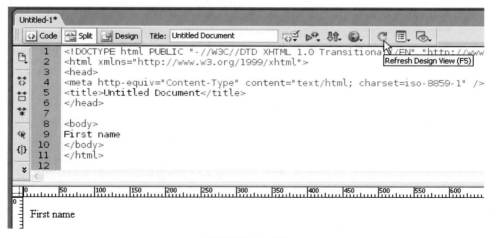

FIGURE 1.19

6   **Click the Design button to close the Code view window.**

7 To change the Insert bar category to Layout, click the Insert bar category pop-up menu and choose Layout from the list.

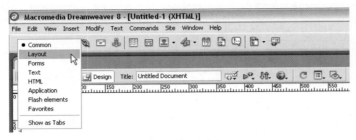

FIGURE 1.20

8 Close the current untitled document (File>Close). When prompted, do not save. Leave Dreamweaver open for the next exercise.

LESSON 4 Exploring the Property Inspector

The Property inspector is the most important panel of the Dreamweaver interface. Its appearance and options change to reflect the properties of the current selected item, such as a paragraph, table, form, or image. You can change the properties of a selected item through the Property inspector.

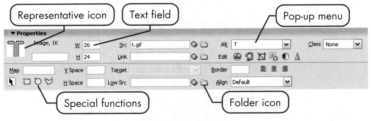

FIGURE 1.21

The Property inspector commonly uses a representative icon to indicate the type of item selected, such as a table-like icon or, in this figure above, a miniature of the selected image. The Property inspector provides different types of methods for changing the selected item's properties, such as text fields in which you type, pop-up menus from which you choose, and folder icons through which you can open a folder and select a file. For some items, the Property inspector provides access to functions that are specific to the item.

In this lesson, you use the Property inspector to explore images, headings, links, and other items; we do not introduce these concepts, as we assume that you have a basic understanding of fundamental components of a Web page, such as images, headings, and links. (We examine all of these items in much greater detail in later chapters.) This lesson focuses on exploring a Web page through the Property inspector. You discover how the Property inspector changes to reflect the properties of different items, how to use the Property inspector to change the item's properties, and how the Property inspector changes to reflect the modifications you make to that item.

You also preview a Web page in your browser. Dreamweaver's Design view is quite like a browser in that, for the most part, what you see in the Design view is what you get in your browser (compare the two following figures). Dreamweaver, however, emphasizes features to make it easier to work with them: black dashed lines surround each cell in a table, and a red dashed line surrounds a form. Dreamweaver's Design view is also static and unresponsive — it does not react to user actions. You must preview your pages in a browser to test these types of effects. A good rule of thumb comes from the programming community: "code a little, test a little," which means test your design frequently. Although you may not be coding while working in the Design view, it is still good practice (especially when you move on to more advanced functions and features) to preview your designs in your browser often.

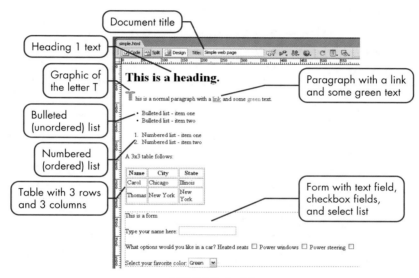

FIGURE 1.22

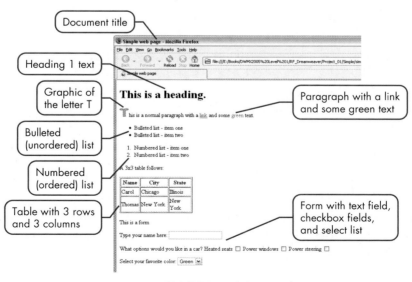

FIGURE 1.23

Explore a Simple Web Page with the Property Inspector

1   **Copy the Chapter_01 folder and all of its contents from the RF_Dreamweaver_L1 folder to your WIP folder.**

This step prepares all of the files you need for Chapter_01.

2   **Choose File>Open, navigate to the Chapter_01>Simple folder, choose the file simple.html, and click Open.**

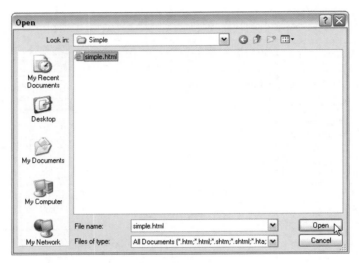

FIGURE 1.24

3   **Click in the first sentence, "This is a heading."**

The Property inspector indicates that this sentence uses Format Heading 1.

FIGURE 1.25

4   **Click the graphic of the red "T."**

The Property inspector changes to display a graphic image's properties, such as its dimensions (26 pixels wide by 24 pixels high) and its source (t.gif). Handles appear around a graphic when it is selected. The *handles* are the three squares that appear in the graphic's bottom-right corner.

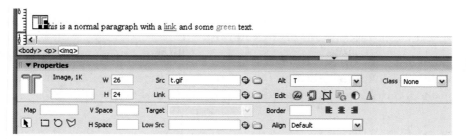

FIGURE 1.26

5   **In the Property inspector, click to the right of the number 26, type the number <0> (making the new number 260), and press Enter/Return.**

The Property inspector displays the selected object's properties and allows the designer to make changes to that object's properties. In this case, you changed the graphic's width from 26 pixels to 260 pixels.

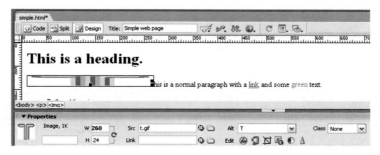

FIGURE 1.27

6   **Click the blue underlined word "link" and observe the Property inspector.**

Blue underlined text is the default appearance of link text. The Link field in the Property inspector shows the destination of the selected link.

FIGURE 1.28

7 If necessary, scroll down so the form section (outlined with a red-dashed line) is visible. Click any of the car check-box options or the color list.

The Property inspector changes to reflect the properties of the information collected by those form controls. However, Dreamweaver is not interactive like a browser: you cannot type into text boxes, check any check boxes, and certain lists do not drop down to show the options.

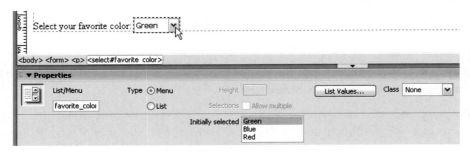

FIGURE 1.29

8 To preview the Web page in your browser, click the Preview/Debug in Browser button on the Document toolbar and choose a browser from the list.

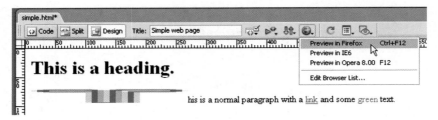

FIGURE 1.30

9 Click Yes to save the changes.

FIGURE 1.31

10 Click any of the car check-box options or the favorite color list; notice that these form controls respond as you would expect them to react to user interaction.

Although the Dreamweaver interface is WYSIWYG, it is not a browser and does not respond to user interaction in the same way a browser does. The WYSIWYG aspect of the Dreamweaver interface is for design only.

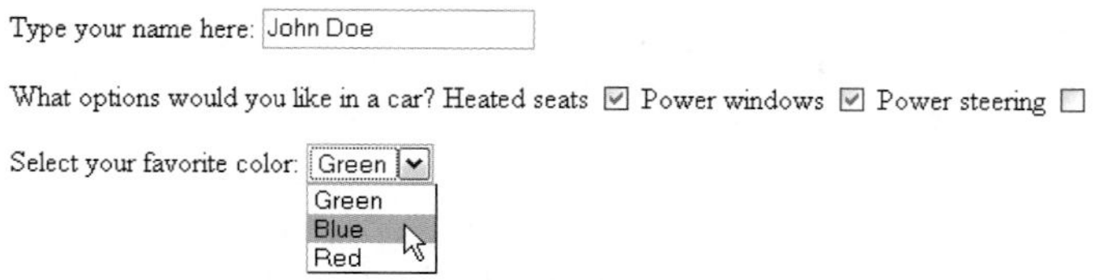

Type your name here: John Doe

What options would you like in a car? Heated seats ☑ Power windows ☑ Power steering ☐

Select your favorite color: Green ▾
Green
Blue
Red

FIGURE 1.32

11   **Close the browser and return to Dreamweaver. Leave simple.html open for the next exercise.**

To Extend Your Knowledge . . .

OTHER BROWSERS

Internet Explorer (IE) is installed on most Windows and Macintosh systems. Although this browser may be the most commonly used browser, other browsers offer different experiences. IE is available at no cost. It comes with the Windows and Macintosh operating systems, and upgrades are free. However, the next version will only be available for Windows.

The Opera browser is a small, fast browser, and is available for Windows, Macintosh, various Unix and Linux operating systems, and, more recently, cell phones and **PDAs (personal digital assistants)**. Previously, this browser was free but had a built-in advertising banner that you could disable for $40. Starting with version 8.5, released in September 2005, the Opera browser is now available for free without advertising. Users have the option of purchasing a support contract for $29.

Unlike Opera, the Netscape/Mozilla browser is entirely free to download and is available for Windows, Macintosh, and Linux/Unix systems. Firefox is the Mozilla browser for Windows, and Camino is the Macintosh version. Netscape, version 6 and later, is built from the Mozilla code — any pages that work in one will work in the other.

The Safari browser will replace IE as the default browser for the Macintosh. Apple adopted KHTML technology from a Linux windowing system called "KDE" and created the Safari browser from it. Other browsers are available for Macintosh systems including iCab and OmniWeb, both for a fee.

The Lynx browser is a text or character-based browser (no graphics). The blind often use it in combination with a text-to-speech or text-to-Braille system to hear or read the Web site. Although it is a good browser with which to test your site for accessibility, the Opera browser (version 7 or higher) can be switched into a text-only mode for the same purposes, reducing the need to install an additional browser.

The BrowserCam.com Web site provides screenshots of your pages in up to 16 browsers. Although this service is primarily available for a fee (a limited trial is available for free), it is much cheaper than purchasing multiple computers to perform the same testing. This service can only show you how your pages look in different browsers; it cannot help you with interactive functionality, such as JavaScript.

LESSON 5   Exploring HTML Using the Tag Selector

Most HTML tags are container tags — they have an opening and closing tag form. What you see in the Document window is content that exists between the **`<body>`** tags, one of the top-level HTML tags. All HTML documents start and end with the topmost **`<html>`** tag in its opening and closing forms. The **`<html>`** tag defines the HTML document's beginning and end. The HTML document has two divisions, the head and the body, which are delimited by the **`<head>`** and **`<body>`** tags, respectively. The head division contains information that is not visible to the end user with one exception — the **`<title>`** tag. The content of the **`<title>`** tag appears at the top of the browser window and also appears as the document's name in a search engine's search-results page. The other tags in the head include **`<meta />`** tags, which are commonly used to contain keywords for search engines; the **`<script>`** tag for JavaScript code; and the **`<style>`** tag for CSS code.

In this lesson, you encounter a heading tag, **`<h1>`**. This tag is the largest and most important heading. The paragraph tag **`<p>`** contains standard paragraph content, which may also include the anchor tag **`<a>`**, which creates links to other documents. The **`<table>`** tag, which you also encounter in this lesson, creates a table. A table consists of rows and cells in each row. Opening and closing **`<tr>`** table-row tags surround each row. Opening and closing **`<td>`** table-data tags, which correspond to table cells, surround the content in each cell. Therefore, a table cell's content is contained by **`<td>`** tags, which are contained by **`<tr>`** tags, which are contained by **`<table>`** tags, making the table one of the most complex structures in HTML. The **`<body>`** tag encloses all content that is visible in the Document window.

The Tag selector enables the designer to view the tags used for a particular block of text and to select a tag and its contents. The Tag selector shows the hierarchy of tags, starting with the left tag. It is not unlike an interactive family tree in which, when you select a particular person, the ancestry of that person is highlighted. For example, if there is an anchor tag **`<a>`** (link) within a paragraph tag **`<p>`** within the document's body, the Tag selector displays **`<body><p><a>`**. However, an anchor tag within a paragraph within a table cell within a table row within a table within the body of the HTML document displays a very different layering of tags: **`<body><table><tr><td><p><a>`**. Clicking a tag in the Tag selector selects the content within the tag. Clicking the **`<a>`** tag selects the link text; clicking the **`<p>`** tag selects the paragraph, including the **`<a>`** within it; and clicking the **`<body>`** tag selects everything in the body of the document.

When you want to select a few words in a sentence, Dreamweaver provides controls similar to those in word-processing software. You can drag to select the words, use a particular key command to select an entire sentence, click several times to select a full paragraph, and so on. Once selected, you may delete, copy, move, or style the selected content.

Although the Code view is useful for coding HTML, CSS, JavaScript, and other Web-scripting languages, Dreamweaver is primarily a WYSIWYG design tool. As mentioned before, when you draw a design in the Design view, Dreamweaver creates the HTML code in the background. Although it might seem that with Dreamweaver, you don't need to understand HTML, in fact, any understanding you can acquire of HTML benefits you, especially when you try to understand messages about the code. Dreamweaver displays code for the user in many ways, such as in the Tag selector. Without understanding HTML, you might not fully comprehend the information that the Tag selector provides. You do not need to be a hand-coder to be a Web-site designer, but if you don't understand HTML, your abilities will be compromised.

To Extend Your Knowledge . . .

CSS AND ECMASCRIPT

HTML is only one of many coding languages used in Web pages. There are numerous others, such as CSS and ECMAScript, which are both text-based coding languages that a knowledgeable user may type into an editor and view in a browser.

CSS (Cascading Style Sheets) is a W3C coding language. CSS, like HTML, is not a true programming language, but CSS is meant to complement HTML as a language of style. HTML was originally designed as the language defining the structure of a Web page, such as paragraphs, headings, and tables. The original intent was not to use HTML for style, such as alignment, color, or typeface options. CSS is the coding language that defines a Web page's style or look and allows "the separation of structure and style." Despite the fact that CSS1 was released with HTML 4 in late 1996, its adoption rate has been very slow. However, Dreamweaver 8, more than any previous version or competitors' products, writes most style changes using CSS rather than the outdated HTML equivalents. For this reason, many Web-standards supporters applaud Dreamweaver 8's adoption of CSS.

ECMAScript, for all intents and purposes, is JavaScript, and both are client-side programming languages. ECMA is the abbreviation for the European Computer Manufacturers Association, an important standards body in Europe. The W3C has adopted their version of JavaScript as the standard for the WWW. A ***client-side*** programming language runs in the browser, whereas a ***server-side*** programming language runs at the server. When you insert JavaScript code or programming instructions into a Web page, it is delivered to the browser along with the page's HTML. The browser then interprets the code and performs the required actions. JavaScript is the most popular client-side programming language, but VBScript (based on Visual Basic) and JScript (a Microsoft proprietary implementation of JavaScript), both of which run only in Internet Explorer, are also available.

Explore HTML Using the Tag Selector

1 In the open document **simple.html,** click in the top paragraph, **"This is a heading." Observe the Tag selector at the Document window's bottom left.**

The Tag selector shows that the insertion point is in a paragraph that uses the **`<h1>`** tag. This heading exists in the body of the HTML document because the **`<h1>`** tag follows the **`<body>`** tag in the Tag selector.

FIGURE 1.33

2   **Click the `<h1>` tag in the Tag selector.**

Notice that the selected tag in the Tag selector is highlighted with a white/gray background, and the content of the tag is selected in the Document window.

FIGURE 1.34

3   **Click the Split button at the top of the Document window.**

When a tag is selected in the Tag selector, the text (enclosed in the tag) in the document and the code in the Code window are also selected. The text "This is a heading." is surrounded by **`<h1>`** and **`</h1>`** tags, indicating that the text is formatted as Heading 1.

FIGURE 1.35

4   **Click in the Carol cell of the 3 × 3 table; notice the string of HTML tags that appear in the Tag selector.**

A table is a complex HTML construct that, in its simplest form, requires a **<table>** tag to denote the table's beginning and end, a table-row (**<tr>**) tag for each row, and a table-data (**<td>**) tag for each data cell.

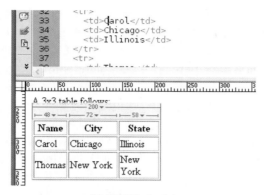

FIGURE 1.36

5   Click the **<table>** tag in the Tag selector and observe the amount of code that is selected in the Code window.

6   To increase the height of the Code window, drag the divider between the Code and Design windows down.

The Code window's height may not be sufficient to see a large block of code, such as you need for this small table. When using the split-window feature, you can raise or lower the divider between the Code and Design windows to increase or decrease the amount of code visible.

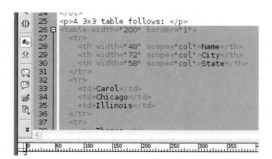

FIGURE 1.37

7   Note the number and variety of tags required to create a table.

The table begins and ends with the **<table>** tag, each row begins and ends with the **<tr>** tag, and each cell begins and ends with either the **<th>** (table header) or the **<td>** (table data) cell. Some tags have additional properties, such as **width**, **border**, and **scope**.

8   Close the Code window by clicking the Design button at the top of the Document window. Leave simple.html open for the next exercise.

To Extend Your Knowledge . . .

THE DTD TAG

You probably noticed that above the opening `<html>` tag is another tag with a rather odd format: `<!DOCTYPE html PUBLIC "-//W3C//DTD XHTML 1.0 Transitional//EN" "http://www.w3.org/TR/xhtml1/DTD/xhtml1-transitional.dtd">`. This is the DTD, the document-type definition tag. There have been different versions of HTML, with each new version introducing new tags and removing others. The DTD identifies the version of HTML used, making it easier for browsers to display the Web page. In the past, many designers and their Web-design software did not insert a DTD at the beginning of the HTML document, forcing browsers to make a best guess at what version was used and, therefore, how to display the Web pages. This was particularly difficult during the time between HTML 2.0 and HTML 4.0, the dark ages of the browser wars, when, even if you specified a DTD, the mixture of tags between the W3C HTML standard and the Netscape and Internet Explorer proprietary tags rendered the DTD essentially useless.

With the return to W3C-standard HTML, the DTD plays an important role. It identifies which version of HTML the document should be measured against. When the HTML in the document meets the standard identified in the DTD, the HTML is said to be "valid" or "compliant with the standard." Dreamweaver 8 has a built-in validator that you can run by selecting File>Check Page>Validate Markup.

LESSON 6　Exploring HTML Using the Tag Chooser

Dreamweaver provides access to its most common functions through buttons and pop-up menus in the application's main window. The most commonly used HTML tags are available from the Insert bar, the Property inspector, or both. Other tags are less prominently displayed but are available. The Tag chooser is the most visible feature that provides access to all HTML tags. Furthermore, the Tag chooser displays the Tag Info window, which provides information about the tag, such as its attributes, attribute values, and use.

The Code window is the obvious place to insert HTML code by hand. However, you must have a basic sense of the tag's name or attribute before you start: is it **q** or **quote**, **b** or **bold**, **abbrev** or **abbr**? The code hints, which are the pop-up menus that appear when you type in the Code window, are helpful, but you may not know, for example, whether the **<q>** (quote) tag or the **<blockquote>** tag is appropriate for your needs, and this type of information is not available from the Code window.

The Tag chooser enables you to choose from all tags that are available to HTML. The tags are organized into categories, and when you click a tag, the lower portion of the Tag Chooser dialog box displays reference information about the selected tag. This reference window, Tag Info, appears in other dialog boxes too. You can learn more about the tags and their uses from the reference information. When you click the Insert button, you open the other component of the Tag chooser — the Tag editor. You use the Tag editor to create the tag and change its attributes.

In addition to HTML, the Tag chooser provides information and assistance with other languages, such as *CFML* (ColdFusion Markup Language, a server-side markup language from Macromedia), *ASP.Net* (the current and more-advanced version of ASP), and *JSP* (Java-servlet pages, another server-side programming language). In all cases, to see the tag categories, click the plus symbol to the language's left, and click the category to see the tags within it. In the HTML language, categories may be further subdivided to show general, browser-specific, deprecated, and obsolete tags. Where possible, avoid deprecated and obsolete tags; look through the deprecated and obsolete tags to see which tags fall in these categories. Unless you select the deprecated or obsolete groups, it is not clear that they are in this category.

In this lesson, you use the Tag chooser to insert the `<sup>` (superscript) tag, which is not available from the other menus or functions. You use the `<sup>` tag to format a block of text that is normally raised above normal text, such as in "1st".

Insert the Sup Tag

1 **In the open simple.html document, click below the form's red dashed line.**

Notice the paragraph about the birthday date.

2 **Click between "1" and the period.**

3 **Click the Tag Chooser button on the right side of the Common Insert bar.**

FIGURE 1.38

4 **Click the plus symbol/triangle to the left of HTML Tags.**

5 **Click the plus symbol/triangle to the left of Formatting and Layout.**

6 **Click General, and then click sup in the right pane.**

The `<sup>` tag is described in the lower window. To read the full content, you may need to drag the bottom of the Tag Chooser dialog box down and drag its sides out.

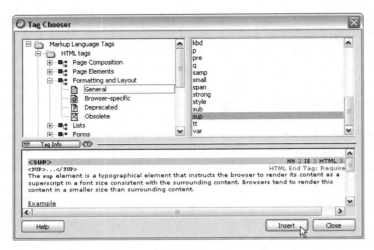

FIGURE 1.39

7 Click the Insert button in the Tag Chooser dialog box's lower-right corner.

8 In the Content field, type `<st>`.

The Tag Editor dialog box provides access to the selected tag's options or attributes, allowing you to apply any attributes available for that particular tag.

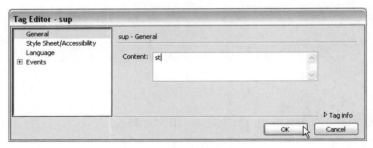

FIGURE 1.40

9 Click OK to insert the `<sup>` tag.

If you are using a Macintosh system, click within the Design window.

10 Click the Close button in the Tag Chooser dialog box.

Examine the Web page and observe that the letters (st) you typed in the Content field are inserted into the page. Notice that the text is small and raised. If you read the description of the `<sup>` tag in the bottom portion of the Tag Chooser dialog box, you see that most browsers display content of the `<sup>` tag smaller than normal text.

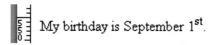

FIGURE 1.41

11   **Look at the Code window at the top of the Document window.**

When you use the Tag chooser, it opens the Document window in Split view. The **<sup>** tag appears in the Code window.

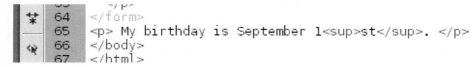

FIGURE 1.42

12   **Click the Design button to close the Code window. Save the changes and leave simple.html open for the next lesson.**

LESSON 7   Configuring the Document Window

No two installations of Dreamweaver or any other computer application look the same after a few hours of use — people have their own preferences for how they want to lay out the application's components. Dreamweaver has many options for personal configuration, such as displaying the download time and resizing the Document window for different browser dimensions.

There are several panel groups, most of which appear on the right side of the Dreamweaver application. You can expand or contract them by clicking the name of the panel group. The Design panel group is often open so that you can work with the CSS Styles panel. Also, the Files panel is almost always open so that you can work with the files in your site.

You can collapse the panel groups as a whole by clicking the Collapse button, thereby giving you more working screen width. Having more screen width is especially beneficial if you are working in code. A Collapse button/triangle also appears between the bottom of the Document window and the Property inspector, allowing you to collapse the Property inspector and work with the additional height of the Document window.

Commonly, the Document window is set to "maximized." However, there are times when you need to ensure that your designs work within specific screen resolutions, such as 1024×768, 800×600, or even 640×480. The Window Size function on the bottom-right side of the Status bar allows you to change the dimensions of the Document window to test different resolutions. There are several preconfigured, common dimensions, but you may also create your own custom dimensions (i.e., for a cell phone or a PDA). You can only set the size of the Document window smaller than your current resolution.

Dreamweaver also has a Download Time indicator next to the document Window Size indicator. This feature enables you to see your current Web page's file size. The distinction made here between an HTML document and a Web page allows for the size of the images (image files are separate from the HTML document but are part of the total download). The Download Time indicator shows both the total size of the Web page and the time it will take to download. The downloading time depends on the speed of the Internet connection. You may change this preference too; however, unless you are depending on a particular audience whose Internet connection speed you know, consider leaving the connection speed set at 56K. A general rule of thumb is to keep the download to less than 30 seconds. Careful use of appropriate image formats, image sizes, and number of images minimizes the download time.

Configure the Document Window

1 | **Click the Restore button in the top-right corner of the Document window's Title bar (Windows). Bypass this step if you are working on a Macintosh.**

The Restore button restores the Document window to its previous dimensions.

FIGURE 1.43

2 | **From the Window Sizes list at the bottom of the Design window, select 760 × 420 (800 × 600, Maximized) to change the window size.**

The Window Size option allows you to change the window's size to mimic different browser dimensions; this shows how your Web-page designs appear to a person using a browser with different dimensions than yours.

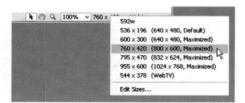

FIGURE 1.44

3 | **Choose Edit>Preferences/Dreamweaver Preferences, then choose the Status Bar category.**

This window of the Preferences dialog box allows you to create new window sizes or modify existing ones. Dreamweaver uses the Connection Speed drop-down list to identify how long a person would have to wait to view the current Web page.

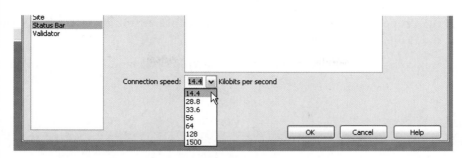

FIGURE 1.45

4   **Change the Connection Speed to 14.4; click OK to accept the change.**

Using a 14.4 Kbps modem, a person would have to wait 2 seconds for this 3-kilobyte page to download. You can find this information through the Download Speed indicator in the bottom-right corner of the Document window.

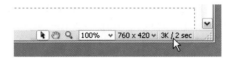

FIGURE 1.46

5   **Reset the Connection Speed to 56 Kbps. From the Window Sizes drop-down list, choose Edit Sizes; then select 56 from the Connection Speed list, and click OK.**

Another path to the Status Bar category of the Preferences dialog box is through the Edit Sizes option at the bottom of the Window Sizes drop-down list.

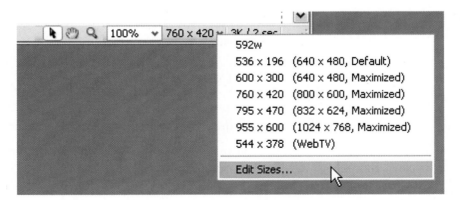

FIGURE 1.47

6   **Reset the Document window to maximum size by clicking the Maximize button, located at the top-right corner of the Document window (Windows); for Macintosh, this button is the rightmost button in the top-left corner.**

7   **Collapse the Property inspector by clicking the Collapse button between the Document window and the Property inspector.**

You can easily collapse and restore the Property inspector to see more of the working document.

FIGURE 1.48

8   **Click the Collapse button to expand the Property inspector.**

9   **Drag the Collapse button to the left to expand the width of the panel groups on the application window's right side. To expand the panel groups on the Macintosh, drag the lower-right corner to the left.**

The panel groups on the right side of the Dreamweaver application are quite narrow and can be awkward to use in the default's limited space. Widening the panel groups makes it easier to work with the panels.

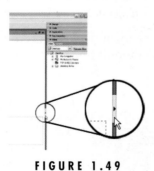

FIGURE 1.49

10   **Drag the Collapse button/Resize button to the right to reset the panel groups' size.**

On a Windows system, you can drag the Collapse button only so far — Dreamweaver has a minimum width for the panel groups beyond which you cannot drag the Collapse button.

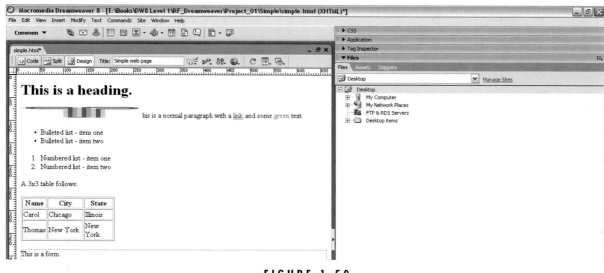

FIGURE 1.50

11   Choose File>Close to close simple.html. Keep Dreamweaver open for the next exercise.

LESSON 8   Exploring the Dreamweaver Help Function

The Help function of any application is very useful. The documentation for many popular computer applications is extensive. It typically includes text documentation, graphics, and annotated screenshots of the application, plus numerous examples and tips on how to use the application, its functions, and its features.

The Dreamweaver Help function uses the standard help format, in which you can read the material like a book organized into chapters, sections, and subsections. You can find this organizational method under the Contents tab of the Help function. The Index tab provides an alphabetical listing of the important symbols, words, and phrases. You may also access the Help documentation by using the Search tab to look for a word or phrase. Dreamweaver's Help function displays in two panes. The Contents, Index, or Search results appear in the left pane, and the selected page displays in the right pane.

In the Contents section, the chapters, sections, and subsections use book icons to indicate that there are multiple pages in the next level. Click a book to open it, and click it again to close it. When you click a page icon, the selected page appears in the right pane. The Index functionality of the Help documentation contains topics ordered alphabetically, starting with numbers, symbols, and then alphabetic characters. A large topic may have subtopics, which are indented under the main topic. Type your topic of interest in the field at the left pane's top; you are then taken to that word in the index. Typing just finds main topics, not subtopics. For example, if you type "extensions", you see that "installing" is a subtopic of "extensions"; but if you type "installing", you don't find "extensions". You can use the Search function to search for a particular word or phrase that doesn't seem to be listed or can't be found in the index. However, the search might identify the word used in any context or as part of a longer word. For example, searching for "point" may lead to "when the insertion point is in the table," and "fonts may be measured in points," and "use your mouse pointer"; so be specific when searching for some terms.

Often, the contents of a particular page may have links to terms or other related pages. These links are identified with blue underlined text, not unlike a link in a Web page. Given that the Help pages are created as part of a chapter, next and previous links (blue triangles pointing to the left and right) appear at the bottom and top right of each page. Use these links to read through the pages in order, according to their organization in the chapters, sections, and subsections.

In this exercise, you explore the Dreamweaver Help documentation. You open a page from the contents, locate a page from the index, and search for a page. The more familiar you are with the Help documentation, the better you will be at using Dreamweaver and resolving problems without purchasing expensive books or spending long hours on the Internet.

Explore the Dreamweaver Help Function

1   **Choose Help>Using Dreamweaver.**

2   **In the left pane of the Dreamweaver Help documentation, click the Dreamweaver Basics book to open it.**

3   **Click Exploring the Workspace, select About the Dreamweaver Workspace, and then click The Workspace Layout.**

On Windows systems, book icons indicate that pages exist within a topic heading, and both the index pane (left) and the information pane (right) appear within the same dialog box; on Macintosh systems, the topics appear as nested bullet items, and the panes float.

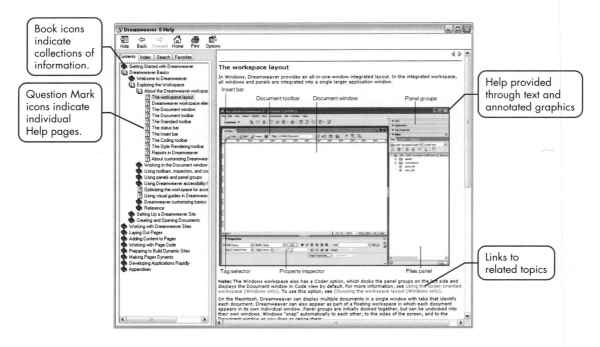

FIGURE 1.51

4   **Click the Index tab at the top of the left pane (Windows) or Back button (Macintosh).**

FIGURE 1.52

5   **Type `<downloading>` in the Keyword/Ask a Question field. Choose "Time" from the list and click the Display button/press Return at the bottom of the left pane.**

The "downloading" topic in the index has four subtopics, which are indented below "downloading". The Display button opens the selected page into the right pane. Alternatively, you can double-click a subtopic to open the page. (Some topics have help content and some do not; however, all subtopics have help content.)

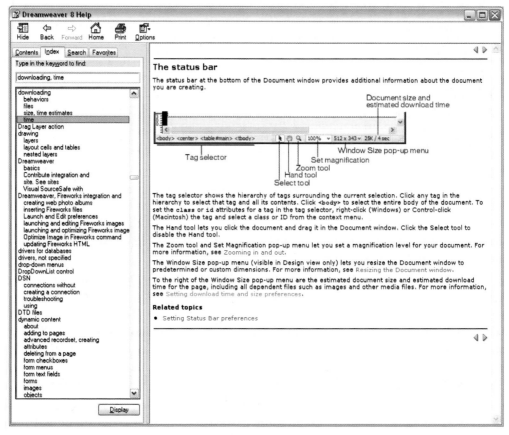

FIGURE 1.53

6 **Click the Contents tab at the top of the Help function.**

Notice where "The status bar" page is in the Contents tab (Figure 1.54). Knowing where the page of interest is located may help you find similar pages another time or may prompt you to explore related pages in the same chapter, section, or subsection of the Contents.

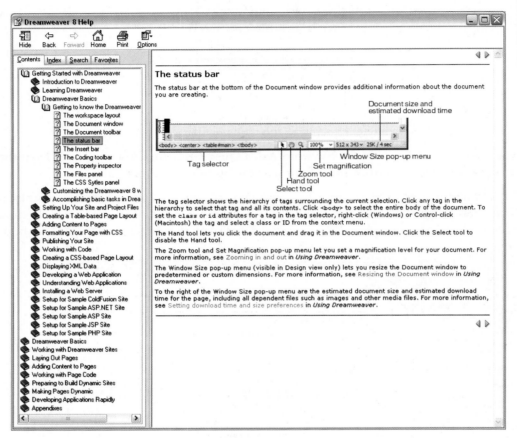

FIGURE 1.54

7 **Return to the Search tab, and type `<experienced>` in the Keyword field. Double-click the Experienced web designers topic.**

The first numbered point refers to a tutorial in the Getting Started help function. This is a second Help file that provides tutorial-style assistance on a variety of topics.

8 **Click the Close button at the top-right corner of the Help window to close the Using Dreamweaver Help function.**

9 **Select Help>Getting Started with Dreamweaver; if necessary, click the Contents tab.**

The contents of this Help file provide tutorial-style assistance on topics ranging from creating simple static pages to understanding Web applications and setting up Web servers, PHP, and MySQL. These tutorials may provide additional insight into how to use Dreamweaver and may also pique your interest in advanced topics, without forcing you to purchase additional books just to explore the topic or methodology.

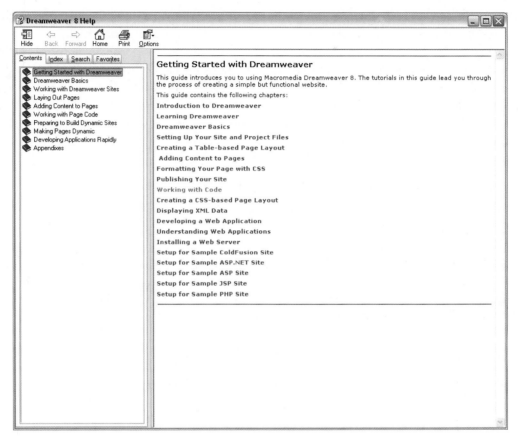

FIGURE 1.55

10 Close the Getting Started Help function by clicking the Close button at the top-right corner of the Help window.

11 Close Dreamweaver (File>Exit/Dreamweaver>Quit).

To Extend Your Knowledge . . .

DREAMWEAVER'S REFERENCE COLLECTION

Help functions tend to focus on aiding the user in working with the application and its functions but not with background or reference material. For example, a word-processing application may teach you how to make text bold or italic, but it won't teach you about proper grammar and sentence structure. The help function for a spreadsheet application may tell you what types of values you need to insert in the PV (Present Value) function, but without an accounting background, you may not realize that you have selected the wrong function.

Despite the availability of help documentation, many users find they need to purchase other books and resources for assistance. Dreamweaver supports many different coding languages, such as HTML, CSS, ColdFusion, ASP, and PHP, all of which require their own reference materials. However, Dreamweaver has somewhat reduced the need to purchase additional reference books by including electronic versions of reference publications within the application. This reference material provides information for the supported languages and for the UsableNet's Accessibility Reference. In fact, the Tag chooser's Tag Info window draws upon these references to provide the information about the selected tag.

SUMMARY

In this chapter, you explored Dreamweaver for the first time. You learned about the organization of the menus, toolbars, and various other features that provide access to Dreamweaver's features and functions. You discovered how to view HTML code in the Code window and saw how the Design window creates code. You learned how to select HTML using the Tag selector and how to insert an HTML tag with the Tag chooser. You saw that as you select different components of a Web page, the Property inspector changes to identify the properties of the selected component. You also learned how to obtain help on Dreamweaver's features.

KEY TERMS

ASP.net

Attributes

CFML (ColdFusion Markup Language)

Client-side

Code hints

Container tags

CSS (Cascading Style Sheets)

Dead link

Empty tags

Forms

Hand-coder

Handles

Horizontal rule

HTML (Hypertext Markup Language)

Image rollover

JSP

Layout

MDI (Multiple Document Interface)

Nesting tables

PDA (personal digital assistant)

Server-side

Spanned cells

Structured query language (SQL)

Syntax coloring

Syntax highlighting

Tags

uniform resource locator (URL)

W3C (World Wide Web Consortium)

WWW (World Wide Web)

WYSIWYG (What You See Is What You Get)

XML (Extensible Markup Language)

CHECKING CONCEPTS AND TERMS

SCREEN ID

Identify the indicated areas from the list below:

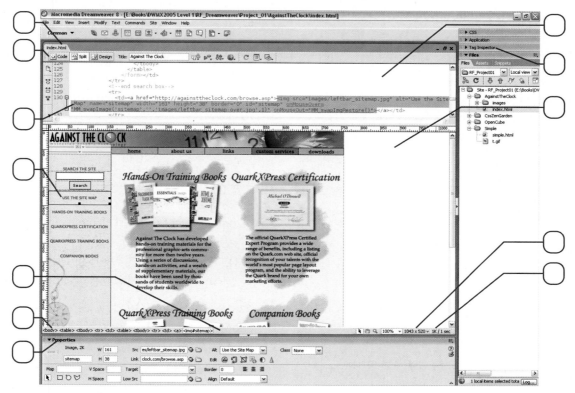

FIGURE 1.56 *(Copyright Against The Clock, Inc. Used by permission of Against the Clock, Inc.)*

a. Filename tab

b. Document toolbar

c. Selected HTML code

d. Selected image

e. Code View window

f. Design View window

g. Status bar

h. Tag selector

i. Window Size indicator

j. Download Time indicator

k. Property inspector

l. Panel groups

MULTIPLE CHOICE

Circle the letter of the correct answer for each of the following:

1. Dreamweaver is the premier _____.
   a. Internet browser
   b. host server
   c. Web-page authoring and site-management application
   d. All of the above

2. What are two document views available in Dreamweaver?
   a. HTML and FTP
   b. Code and Design
   c. Digital and Analog
   d. WYSIWYG and Flash

3. In Dreamweaver, which view is always WYSIWYG?
   a. The Code view
   b. The Design view
   c. All of the above
   d. None of the above

4. HTML is _____.
   a. the structural language of Web pages
   b. Hypertext Markup Language
   c. visible in Dreamweaver's Code view
   d. All of the above

5. In Dreamweaver, it is possible to work in both Code and Design views at the same time.
   a. True
   b. False

6. The Property inspector _____.
   a. is signified by a magnifying-glass icon
   b. changes to reflect the current and available properties of a selected item

   c. can debug HTML code
   d. None of the above

7. Which is not true of the Insert bar?
   a. It provides access to many Web-page design functions.
   b. Common, Layout, Forms, Text, and HTML are forms of the Insert bar.
   c. It is only available when using the Code view.
   d. A drop-down menu can give access to related Insert-bar functions.

8. Tags in HTML are _____.
   a. codes indicating programming errors
   b. attributes of inserted elements for graphical user interfacing
   c. only used to insert a horizontal rule
   d. elements surrounded by angle brackets

9. Which of the following is not true of the Tag chooser?
   a. It provides assistance for HTML only.
   b. It is the most visible feature that provides access to all HTML tags.
   c. It offers the Tag Info window, providing information about the tag.
   d. It provides access to the Tag editor.

10. How can you get the most up-to-date help and support available for Dreamweaver?
    a. Ask a friend who codes HTML.
    b. Choose Using Dreamweaver from the Help menu.
    c. Take an advanced course in Dreamweaver.
    d. Choose Dreamweaver Support Center from the Help menu.

DISCUSSION QUESTIONS

1. You have explored the Code view and the Design view. When would one view be more effective or efficient for developing a Web site? Which view would you find most practical for your work in Web-page design?

2. Even though Dreamweaver writes the XHTML code for you in the background while you work in the Design view, why would it be beneficial to have a fundamental working knowledge of XHTML?

S K I L L   D R I L L

Skill Drills reinforce project skills. Each skill that is reinforced is the same as, or nearly the same as, a skill we presented in the lessons. We provide detailed instructions in a step-by-step format. Work through these exercises in order.

1. Work with Multiple Open Files

It is common to work with multiple files open at the same time. You may need to cut from one and paste to another, or just make comparisons between open files. You must be careful when working with multiple files to ensure that you do not copy from, paste to, or close the wrong file. Windows users see the filenames at the top of the Document window — the active file's tab appears light gray, and all other tabs blend into the background of the Document window. If you do not see the active file's tab at the top of the Document window, click the Maximize button.

1. Launch Dreamweaver if it is not already open.

2. Open index.html from the Chapter_01>CSSZenGarden folder. Open simple.html from the Chapter_01>Simple folder. Windows users: if you do not see a light-gray tab (at the top of the Document window) with simple.html on it, click the Maximize button.

3. In simple.html, move the mouse pointer over the No Browser Check Errors button.

Note the text in the tool-tip message and the green check-mark symbol in the button graphic.

4. Click the index.html tab, which is to the left of the simple.html tab.

5. Move the mouse pointer over the Target Browser Check button.

Note that the tool-tip message has changed and the button graphic contains a yellow warning symbol.

6. Move the mouse pointer over the location of the simple.html tab and Right/Control-click.

7. Close the file simple.html (choose Close from the pop-up menu).

8. Leave index.html open for the next Skill Drill.

2. Explore the Results Panel Group

When you design a Web site for the first time, redesign an existing site, or take over the management of an existing site, you may find that images, pages, and links do not work as they should. You may have an old image that is no longer in use, or you may have prepared an image but not yet incorporated it into the site. In both cases, the image is known as an "orphaned file." Similarly, it is not uncommon for a large Web site to have the occasional **_dead link_** (a link that does not open the page to which it is directed). If the dead link's destination is a page on your site, you must recreate the link, but if the destination is another page was on another Web site and it has been deleted, moved or renamed you must delete the link. When hand-coding a Web site, you perform link management in your mind, which can lead to mistakes; however, with Dreamweaver's coding abilities, dead links and orphaned files can be a thing of the past.

Browser checking is another very practical function. Older browsers do not support the same functions, features, and versions of HTML as do current browsers. For this reason, it is useful to know which features do not work in older browsers or, sometimes, even in current browsers. Netscape 4, for example, does not support many CSS properties, and Internet Explorer 6 for Windows doesn't support the `headers` attribute of the table-data tag. It is helpful to know such information so that if your Web page uses a feature that depends on browser support, you are aware of the issue and may find other techniques for resolving the problem.

The Results panel group is not normally open, which means the Title bar for the Results panel group is not visible. The purpose of the Results panel group is to display the results of various queries, such as the number of dead links, orphaned images, or browser-check errors. Using this information, you can make repairs. Although the Results panel group provides a large amount of functionality, you don't need it constantly. By knowing how to open and close it, you can use it when needed and save the space it takes when you don't need the panel group.

1. Click the Target Browser Check button on the Document toolbar, and choose Show All Errors from the pop-up menu.

   Observe that the Results panel group opens at the screen's bottom, below the Property inspector.

2. Scroll through the browser-check errors (red) and informative messages (white). Read the messages and determine which browsers have the problems.

   A third icon, yellow in color, may appear at times, to warn of unsupported tags or attributes.

3. Click any of the tabs in the Results panel group to explore the other features available from this panel group.

4. Collapse the Results panel group.

5. Right/Control-click the Results panel group Title bar; from the pop-up menu, choose Close Panel Group.

6. Close index.html.

3. Explore a Complex Web Page

Most Web-page designs are complex in structure, employing tables to lay out the page. (**_Layout_** is positioning different blocks of content on a Web page; it has the same meaning as in the print industry.) Tables offer numerous layout options, such as spanned cells and nested tables. Generally, Web pages use a two- or three-column layout. The three rows of a layout table may be the header at the top, the footer at the bottom, and the main content in the middle row. The middle row is commonly divided into two or three columns: the left for the navigation bar, the center for the primary content, and sometimes a right column with either advertising or additional information. **_Spanned cells_** in HTML are the equivalent of merged cells in word-processing or spreadsheet applications — two or more cells in a table or spreadsheet joined into one. Another table technique that you can use for design is **_nesting tables_** — inserting a table in a cell of an outer table. It is easier to nest a table within another than to divide the outer table. Commonly, *forms* that are used to gather information, such as an order form or a username/password login, employ a table to position the input labels and input fields.

In addition to tables, there are other features that create complex Web pages. You can use JavaScript to enhance the page, as with image rollovers. In an *image rollover*, when the user moves the mouse pointer over an image on a Web page, the graphic swaps out with another image; when the user moves the mouse pointer off the graphic, the original image returns. Navigation bars often use this effect to indicate that the mouse pointer is over a particular link. CSS has a similar effect, typically applied to the text of a link: when the mouse pointer moves over a link, the color changes; and when the mouse pointer moves off the link, the text color returns to its original color. You create this effect using the `:hover` property of CSS. You can create both the JavaScript image rollovers and the CSS `:hover` in Dreamweaver, but you cannot view the effects in the application. You must view them in a browser.

Working with complex Web pages can be difficult, even with Dreamweaver. The greater your familiarity with the Tag selector, the easier it is for you to deduce a Web page's layout structure. Once you understand the structure, you can then make modifications or add content to it.

1. Open index.html from the AgainstTheClock folder.

2. Click the top banner logo graphic for Against The Clock.

3. Look at the Tag selector at the bottom of the Document window; numerous tags are visible, and the last one, `<img />`, is selected.

    The Tag selector shows two `<table>` tags (among other tags), which means that the selected image exists within a table that is nested in another table.

4. In the Tag selector, click the first `<table>` tag to the right of the `<body>` tag.

    Observe that a thicker black line appears around the outermost table that has handles around it. You may have to scroll down to see the bottom and bottom-right handles.

5. Click the orange home graphic below the top logo graphic and then click the second `<table>` tag.

    This nested table is used to lay out the horizontal navigation bar at the page's top. A similar layout has been created at the bottom (footer) of the page, again using a table.

6. Click the Search button at the top-left corner of the Web page, and look at the Tag selector.

    This form's text-entry box and Search button are laid out using a nested table in the form. The form on the Web page appears as a red dashed line.

7. Preview this Web page in your primary browser.

    If prompted, do not save changes. Observe that the appearance of the Web site in Dreamweaver is virtually identical to its appearance in your browser.

8. Move your mouse pointer over any of the colored graphic boxes (home, about us, etc.) in the top navigation bar, and note that the graphics change.

    These graphics employ the JavaScript rollover effect, which Dreamweaver does not display.

9. Close your browser and return to Dreamweaver. Leave index.html open for the next Skill Drill.

4. Explore Other Helpful Resources

The Dreamweaver Help system is only one resource for assistance and primarily focuses on using Dreamweaver. However, Web-site design requires more than just using Dreamweaver, and Dreamweaver provides other resources for help.

1. Select Window>Reference to open the Reference panel below the Property inspector.

2. From the pop-up menu of books, choose O'Reilly HTML Reference, if it is not already selected.

3. From the Tag pop-up menu, choose "body".

4. From the secondary pop-up menu to the right of the Tag pop-up menu, select "background".

   The secondary pop-up menu does not have a label beside it, but Dreamweaver Help refers to it as the Attribute pop-up menu—**background** is an attribute of the **<body>** tag.

5. Read through the description of the **background** attribute of the **<body>** tag.

   The top line of the description identifies the attribute's name; browser support and the HTML version in which the **background** attribute was introduced appear on the right. "Optional" indicates that the background attribute is optional.

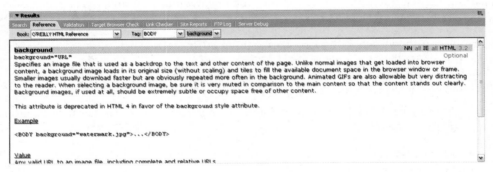

FIGURE 1.57

6. Close the Reference panel group (Window>Reference or press Shift-F1).

7. Open Dreamweaver Help.

8. Choose the Search tab, type **<CSS>** in the Keyword/Ask a Question field, and then click the List Topics button/press Return. Notice that the Search function finds all pages in the Help documentation that contains the phrase "css".

9. Double-click Creating a New CSS Style in the list. The selected page opens in the right pane with all instances of css (in any form of capitalization) highlighted.

10. Close Dreamweaver Help. Close index.html without saving, and then close Dreamweaver.

CHALLENGE

Challenge exercises expand on, or are somewhat related to, skills we presented in the lessons. Each exercise includes a brief introduction, followed by numbered-step instructions that are not as detailed as those in the Skill Drill section. You can work through one or more exercises in any order.

1. Explore Other HTML Reference Web Sites

In addition to the information available through the Reference panel and the Tag Info dialog box, there are many Web sites that contain excellent information on Web-site design topics (such as HTML, JavaScript, ASP, and PHP) that you will want to learn. In this Challenge, you explore two excellent Web sites with reference material about HTML and CSS. You need access to the Internet to view these Web sites.

1. Open your browser and go to the Index Dot HTML Web site at http://www.blooberry.com/indexdot/html/.

2. Click Element Index below the heading "HTML Language".

3. At the bottom of the short page, click the link "All".

4. Find the link to the HTML description and click it.

5. Read the What Is It? paragraph and the Example code block.

6. Go to http://www.htmlhelp.com.

7. Click the heading link "Web Authoring Reference".

8. Click the link "HTML 4.0 Reference".

   Remember that XHTML 1.0 is an upgraded version of HTML 4.01, and although there are some differences between XHTML and HTML, the HTML 4.0 Reference at HTMLHelp.com is still very useful.

9. Click the link "Alphabetical List of HTML 4.0 Elements".

10. Click the link "ABBR" (abbreviation) and read as much of the description as you can understand. Contrast abbreviation with ACRONYM, which is described briefly in the first long paragraph.

11. Move your pointer over SQL or URL, found in the paragraph below the example block. Depending on your browser, you may not see anything happen (see the following To Extend Your Knowledge sidebar).

12. Close your browser.

To Extend Your Knowledge . . .

ABBREVIATIONS, ACRONYMS, AND BROWSERS

Abbreviations, when spoken aloud, are normally spelled, such as HTML and USA. Acronyms, when said aloud, are normally pronounced as a word, such as NATO (North Atlantic Treaty Organization) or MADD (Mothers Against Drunk Driving).

HTMLHelp.com points out that SQL and URL are difficult to categorize as acronyms or abbreviations. The original pronunciation of SQL was the same as the word "sequel", but more recently, it is spelled out as S-Q-L (**SQL** means **Structured Query Language**, used for interacting with databases). **URL (Uniform Resource Locator**, which means the location of a Web page, a Web graphic, or other Web file) is also pronounced similarly to the word Earl or spelled out as in U-R-L.

Still confused about whether a short form is an abbreviation or an acronym? Ian Lloyd of Accessify.com created a tool called the Acrobot. Go to http://www.accessify.com/tools-and-wizards/acrobot/default.asp, type in some text with common short forms, such as "I am learning HTML in NATO", and click the Convert Acronyms button. The code returned includes the proper markup for the abbreviations and acronyms you submitted. There is also a link below the Convert button that displays all acronyms and abbreviations in the database.

When the **title** attribute is used to state the expanded form of an acronym or abbreviation, most browsers display the expanded form as a tool tip. Most browsers also insert a dotted underline below the abbreviation or acronym. However, Microsoft Internet Explorer for Windows does not display either the dotted underline or the tool tip. In the following figure, Mozilla 1.5 (left) and Opera 7.21 (right) both display the dotted underline and the tool tip.

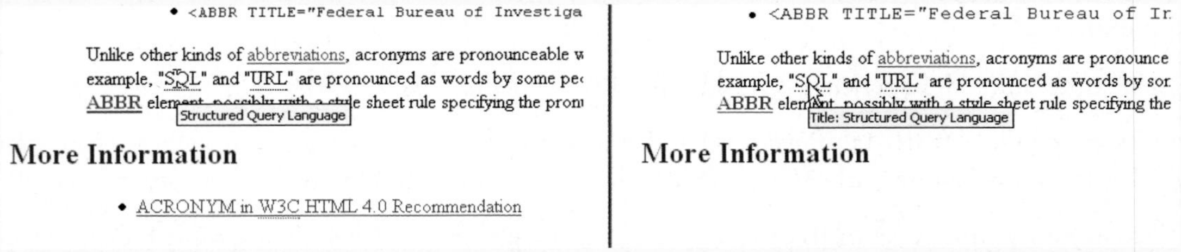

FIGURE 1.58

2. Explore a Web Page Using Tables for Layout

The Chapter_01>OpenCube folder contains the home page of OpenCube.com, a Web site that develops and sells JavaScript and Java technologies. This Web page uses tables for layout. Tables can become quite complex when they are embedded in others, as you see here. OpenCube.com also uses complex JavaScript effects (since the purpose of the Web site is to sell its JavaScript and Java products).

Although at first it may not be apparent, this Web page is full of graphics. Much of the text is actually a text graphic. You learn in a later project about the limits of using fonts in your Web page — if your design uses a typeface that others do not have, they will not see your design exactly as you created and intended it. To counteract this, some designers create text graphics. While using text in graphics allows visitors to see the design exactly as the designers created it, the graphics take longer to download.

1.   Open index.html from the Chapter_01>OpenCube folder.

2.   Observe the number of rectangles created by the dotted lines — the outlines of table cells.

3.   Click the OpenCube logo in the layout's top-left cell; the last item in the Tag selector is the `<img />` image tag. Click any of the menu items down the layout's left side and observe the Tag selector. Note that much of the "text" on the page is graphic text.

4.   Note from the Download Time indicator in the Document window's bottom-right corner that the page weighs in at 84 KB and will take 12 seconds to download.

5.   Preview this page in your browser.

6.   Observe the scrolling text in the bottom-left corner.

7.   Move your pointer over the left navigation-bar graphics (Menu, Products, Downloads, Contact, Order) and across the top menu to the right (same links) to see the drop-down menu system.

8.   Close your browser and return to Dreamweaver.

9.   Close index.html.

3. Exploring a Web Page Using a Table-Free Layout

Both OpenCube.com in the preceding Challenge exercise and index.html in Skill Drill 3 use tables for layout. CSS is another method for laying out Web pages and is commonly used for simple style changes, such as changing colors, typefaces, and font sizes. However, CSS is much more powerful than that — in addition to many other effects, you can use it to style paragraphs to look like lists and lists to look like paragraphs. You can position and size any content with CSS, meaning that it can direct a paragraph to start 10% down from the top of the browser window and to extend 50% of the browser window's width. Advanced CSS can be very tricky, however, and some components have inconsistent support amongst the different browsers.

The Chapter_01>CssZenGarden folder contains a Web page from the CssZenGarden.com experimental Web site. CssZenGarden.com is entirely based on CSS for layout. Graphic artists have contributed their own interpretations of layout and design for the site, and visitors can switch between the different submissions. CssZenGarden.com uses CSS properties without any tables. It also uses no JavaScript; by using the CSS `:hover` property, it enables some links to change in style, thus seeming to mimic JavaScript rollover effects.

JavaScript, particularly complex JavaScript code, can be very long. Tables, especially multiple nested tables, can also add a large quantity of code to a Web page. CSS, however, is much lighter in code and is therefore faster to download. Despite that, it is considered a relatively new concept, partly because many Web-design applications did not provide much support for CSS. Also, many Web designers create pages in other types of applications, such as Photoshop, Illustrator, and CorelDRAW, none of which support CSS well. Creating a Web page using CSS takes great skill, but the benefits are reduced code, faster download, and easier maintenance.

1. Open index.html from the Chapter_01>CssZenGarden folder.

2. Notice there are no dashed lines identifying table borders.

3. Note from the Download Time indicator that this page weighs in at 14 KB and would take only 2 seconds to download.

4. Preview the page in your browser.

5. Click one of the links under the heading "Select a Design". The link moves you to CssZenGarden.com, where the same content is redisplayed using a different design, layout, and graphics. Explore some of the other designs.

6. Close your browser.

7. Return to Dreamweaver and close the application.

To Extend Your Knowledge . . .

TABLE-BASED AND TABLE-FREE LAYOUTS

CssZenGarden.com is an experimental and demonstration Web site whose purpose is to show that, without using tables, CSS can be effectively employed for Web-page layout. Many graphic designers use applications that create table-based layouts. As a result, most graphic designers are not familiar with CSS-based layout options. This Web site demonstrates that with an excellent eye for design and knowledge of CSS, you can use CSS-based layout to produce equal, if not better, design options than table-based designs. At the time of this writing, there are over 600 designs submitted to the CssZenGarden — the content is always the same, but the layout, colors, and graphics are different for each design.

Dreamweaver 8 is much more CSS-aware than previous versions. The projects in this book make use of CSS wherever possible so that you become comfortable with this better method of styling content.

PORTFOLIO BUILDER

Learn to Judge Web Sites

The more you learn about designing Web sites, the easier it becomes to recognize what's good and what's not — and how to incorporate the good and avoid the bad. We're not saying that you should copy the work of others; doing so is illegal and is in very poor taste. That being said, you should still continually search for sites that are considered to be the best of the Web.

1. Launch your browser and go to http://www.webbyawards.com.

2. Look around the site, and pay particular attention to the current picks, which are available from the home page.

3. Make notes about why you feel the sites were chosen; consider the use of images, layout, animations, navigation, and anything else that catches your eye.

4. Check out the "Webby Judging" link, which gives you insight into how the judges select winners.

5. Periodically check this site to view new entries and winners.

CHAPTER 2

Building Your First Web Site

OBJECTIVES

In this chapter, you learn how to:

- Explore the organization of a commercial site

- Use outlines and storyboards to plan a Web site

- Define a site and create its folders

- Build basic Web pages with text and graphics

- Examine Web pages in the Design and Code views

- Apply simple text formatting

- Use an existing page as a template

- Create page-to-page and e-mail links

Why Would I Do This?

In this chapter, you plan and build a few simple pages, the basis for a small Web site. The process is essentially the same whether you're building a site that contains thousands of pages or a site that contains only four or five. Once you've put together a simple site, you'll find it easier to extend the process to larger and larger sites.

This chapter starts off with planning, which takes many forms — gathering the content, collecting related content, establishing relationships between content, and creating a design. Much of this work you will do in consultation with your client, whether in a drawn-out process in the client's office or in your office with various break points along the way requiring the client's signature. Once the client approves the plan, your next step is to commit the plan to Dreamweaver.

You will set up the site in Dreamweaver, which then manages the Web pages that you create in the site and ensures that you do not create any pages outside of the site. You also make the folders for this site so that when you later create Web pages for the client's products or services, the products or services folder is ready for the files.

The next stage is to create the Web site's design. If your design repeats on many pages, you may want to save the design without content so that you can reuse it for other pages. For example, all products pages may have a similar design — you could create the design of the products page and save it. This process is called "templating."

The final stage is to add the content to the pages. At times, you create the content yourself; at other times, the client provides the content. You must insert the content by typing it, copying and pasting it from another document, or importing a word-processing document. You then format the content using headings, lists, and other document structures, and you style the content with colors, typefaces, and other appearances. Next you create links between the Web pages — the links that you planned when you first collected related content.

These efforts essentially complete the process of designing a Web site. You would probably obtain approval from the client before finalizing the Web site, perhaps at various stages along the way. You also need to make the Web site available on the Internet. Generally, the designer creates the design on his or her computer. Making those Web pages available to the public via the Internet is a separate process.

In this chapter, you examine the folder structure of a well-organized Web site. Not all ideas are going to be your own — you may use concepts and ideas inspired by other successful Web sites, as long as you don't copy them directly. (To learn from another site's techniques and organization, Right/Control-click in your browser to examine the ***source code*** [HTML code] of the current page you are viewing.) You then work through the process of planning a Web site on paper, using storyboards and flowcharts. This process starts you thinking about the content, the relationships, and the design. In Dreamweaver, you define a folder on your system as the location in which you will design the Web site, and you create other folders at the same time. You insert content that you type, copy and paste, and import; you also insert images and create Web-page and e-mail links. You will use the Tag editor and the Tag selector to insert and modify HTML tags directly.

This chapter provides a quick overview of many Web-page and Dreamweaver features that you can use as you design your own Web pages. You experience the entire process of creating a Web site, from initial planning to development of the Web pages. The remaining chapters in this book teach you more about the individual components of Web pages and Dreamweaver functions in greater detail.

VISUAL SUMMARY

One of the first steps in designing a Web site is preparing a site definition in Dreamweaver. This process allows you to state the Web site's name. The name does not need to be the Web-site address; it can be any name that helps you remember the project, such as "Laurentian" for Laurentian University's Web site or "IBM Redesign" for the contract you were awarded to redesign IBM's Web site. In addition, you specify the folder (called the "local root folder") in which you will build the Web site. You may also record other information about the Web site, such as the HTTP address (Internet address) and what type of Web-server software you are using to create the Web site. Also, use the Site Definition dialog box in either of its two forms — Basic (on the left in the following figure) and Advanced (on the right). Both forms are suitable for basic Web sites, and the Advanced form of the Site Definition dialog box has some additional options for more advanced users.

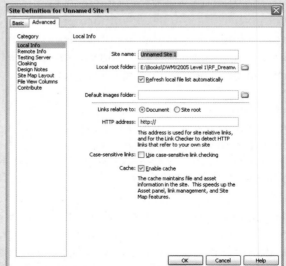

FIGURE 2.1

You create several Web pages in this chapter. Begin by creating blank HTML documents using either the Start Page menu or the New Document dialog box. Through this dialog box, you can create several different types of documents. Dreamweaver groups document types into categories. To create a particular type of document, first choose the category, then choose the particular document type.

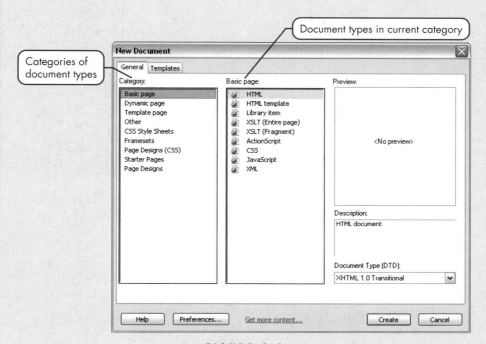

FIGURE 2.2

While you add content to pages, you may want to modify the format, the style, or even some of the HTML code of the text blocks. Use the Property inspector to choose text-block formats, such as paragraph and headings, and to choose font typefaces. Edit code in the Code window at the top of the Document window. To do so, choose the Split view so you can see the Code and the Design views at the same time. Remember, when you make changes to the content in one view, those changes appear in the other view. You can also edit code using the Tag editor, an option of the Tag selector. With the Tag selector, you can choose a tag at the current position of the insertion point. The selected tag then appears with a white background. When you Right/Control-click the Tag selector, the Quick Tag editor appears as one of the options. The Quick Tag editor enables you to edit the selected tag. Both the Code view and the Quick Tag editor provide a Code Hint pop-up window that gives you options for the current tag.

Code window

Design window

Code hint showing attributes of the <h1> tag

Quick Tag editor

Text block formats, such as paragraph and headings

Property inspector

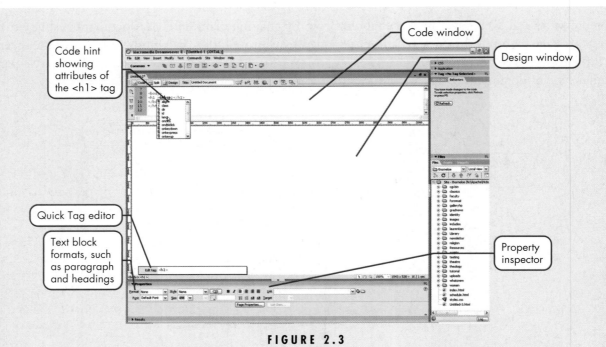

FIGURE 2.3

After creating your Web pages, preview them in your browser. This allows you to test the links you created. Dreamweaver cannot print the Design view of your designs — you must preview your page in a browser to print your design.

Address bar (navigation bar)

Title bar with the document title

Domain name of the Web site

Folder structure in which the current page is located

File name of the current page

Context menu providing the option to view the source code

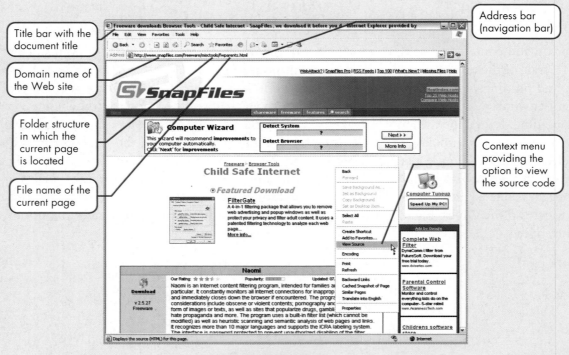

FIGURE 2.4

LESSON 1   Exploring the Folder Structure of a Web Site

When organizing material for a Web site, it is beneficial to think about the content and the various ways of organizing it. Establishing relationships between groups of content in an outline is quite important and can have an impact on the cost of developing and maintaining the Web site, depending on how well (or poorly) you organize the site. Poor organization makes it difficult to find the document for which you are searching and can create additional problems if you try to name a file with a name already in use. The better organized you are, the less work time you waste.

Except for the very elementary sites, most Web sites require some degree of organization. If your site has just a few pages and images, you could probably keep everything in one folder. Add a few hundred pages, 10,000 images, and some *rich media* (such as animations, sounds, and movies), and managing the site takes on a whole new dimension. Managing your site is very difficult without folders to help you organize your work, particularly when you need to make changes later.

The Windows and Macintosh environments commonly use the term "folders." The Unix/Linux environments commonly use the term "directories" for the same concept. Because many Web servers are built on a Unix/Linux operating system, it is important to remember that directories and folders are synonymous.

All Web sites start from a single root folder. The *root folder* (or the *root*) is the starting place of the Web site and is where you keep the site's home page. The *home page* is the front door or opening page to your Web site. You can put other Web pages in the root folder, but the home page must be there. Dreamweaver and your browsers begin looking for links, graphics, objects, and pages from the root folder. Nothing contained in your site can be any higher than the root folder. If it is, the browser won't find it. If images or media are in folders higher than the root folder, they don't appear on your Web pages.

You may create as many folders as you want inside the root folder. If the project calls for it, you can even create folders within folders; the folder structure depends on how you prefer to organize your work. For example, an online gardening store might create a folder for plants and another folder for tools. In the plants folder they could put an indoor folder, an outdoor folder, and a seeds folder. If you make certain that all files you need for the site are in the root folder or below, you can organize the site's resources in any way you want.

If you're using common objects (such as buttons, images, or logos) in several different pages on a site, you can end up with many copies of the same file. For this reason, it is useful to create an images folder where one copy of an image can be used by many Web pages. If the image changes, you have to change only one copy for all the Web pages that use it.

Explore a Commercial Site

In this exercise, you explore a few pages of SnapFiles.com, a Web site of *shareware* (try before you buy) and *freeware* (no cost) software for Windows systems. You examine the content of the pages to see what type of software they present, and you look at the Address bar to see how SnapFiles.com has organized its content. By examining a few types of software, you can determine their organizational pattern.

Web-site organization includes the filename of the Web page. The name should be logical and understandable; for example, you wouldn't name a Web page "word-processing.html" if it was about spreadsheet software, nor would you name a Web page "spreadsheets.html" if it was about word processing. However, you could put both pages (appropriately named) in a folder called "business" for business software. You could also collect antivirus and other security software in another folder named "security." You could then put both the security folder and the business folder in a Windows folder, because the applications contained within it are all used on the Windows operating system. You might also create a corresponding Mac folder for the same types of applications for the Macintosh operating system. Taking it a step further, given that Macintoshes might also require security and business software, including spreadsheets and word processing, you could repeat the names for these folders and filenames in the Mac folder.

When you browse a Web site, you can look at the Address bar of your browser to see the Web page's filename and folder structure. It is often useful to examine the folder structure of Web sites that are similar to yours to see how others approach organization. You might separate security from business software, whereas others might combine them. Examining how others organize their sites may inspire you to do something similar or combine several different techniques you have seen.

1   **Open your browser and navigate to www.snapfiles.com.**

Examine your browser's Address bar; notice that although you are viewing a Web page, no Web-page filename appears in the Address bar — the **URL** or address for the home page is simply shown as the Web site's **domain name** (the base name of a Web site; in this case, www.snapfiles.com).

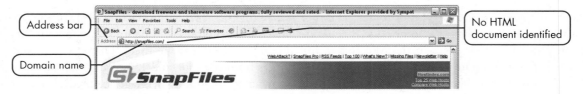

FIGURE 2.5

2   **Below the SnapFiles logo are four green buttons. Click the Shareware button.**

Examine your browser's Address bar; notice that after the domain name, the Web page is shareware.html in the shareware folder.

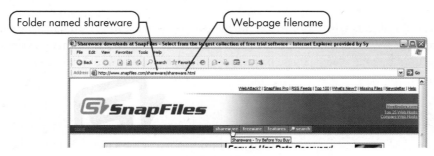

FIGURE 2.6

3   **Click the green Freeware button below the logo.**

Freeware is in a different folder than shareware. The software is separated, right from the outset, based on whether a particular application is shareware or freeware. This is the type of organization you might apply to your Web-site projects. Review all of the content for your Web site and divide it into logical groups. Other people may have different ideas about the divisions to establish. Tucows.com, for example, is another shareware/freeware Web site; they don't separate shareware from freeware but, instead, identify the distribution method only when you read the details about particular software.

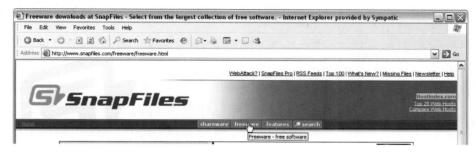

FIGURE 2.7

4 **Click the "Shareware" button again.**

5 **In the Browser Tools category (the top-left category), click Child Safe Internet.**

Notice that the current page, swparents.html, is in the misctools folder in the freeware folder.

FIGURE 2.8

6 **Click your browser's Back button, then click the "Popup Blockers" link (below Child Safe Internet).**

This page's folder structure is the same as the Child Safe Internet page (shareware/misctools), but the filename is different — swpopblock.html. These two pages are in the same folder, but their filenames differentiate the content. In fact, the filenames contain information that identifies the type of software highlighted — swparents.html highlights Child Safe Internet shareware, and swpopblock.html highlights popup blocker shareware.

FIGURE 2.9

7 **Near the bottom of the page, click the link "Switch to Popup Blockers in Freeware".**

The path to the Popup Blockers software in the Freeware category is identical to that of the Shareware category, except for the top-level folder. SnapFiles.com simplifies the software's organization by keeping the folder structure identical after the shareware/freeware split. This consistent and simple organizational structure makes it much easier for the designer to manage this Web site and for users to navigate and know where they are. Another tool that is sometimes used is a ***site map***, where the folder structure is outlined, sometimes with a graphical layout and other times with text. Commonly, the graphics or text identifying folders in the site maps are links to those folders.

FIGURE 2.10

8   **Close your browser.**

To Extend Your Knowledge . . .

DOMAIN NAMES

A domain name is like a business name. It is used to identify a Web site and is commonly the same as or similar to the name of the business that purchased it. Some domain names are long, such as www.websiteoptimization.com, whereas others are short, such as www.ibm.com. Although many Web sites belong to businesses and organizations, many other Web sites exist for other reasons, such as a companion Web site for a book.

Domain names must be purchased. There are many **domain name registrars**, companies from which you can purchase your domain name. Their prices vary from $35 per year to free (as long as you purchase other services from them).

There are six top-level domains: .com (commercial), .org (organization), .mil (military), .gov (government), .edu (educational institution), and .net (originally intended for Internet providers but often used when a company wants to create an online presence). These top-level domains initially suggested that the company or organization that owned the domain be from the United States, but that generalization doesn't seem to apply any longer. One exception to that rule was the .int top-level domain, which was for international organizations such as www.nato.int of the North Atlantic Treaty Organization.

In addition to the preceding domains, there are two-letter country codes, such as .ca for Canada, .uk for the United Kingdom, and .us for the United States, which was rarely used in the past but seems to be gaining popularity. Generally, you must purchase a country-code domain name from a registrar in that country, and many countries do not allow you to purchase one unless you reside in that country. However, some countries have a very useful country code and allow nonresidents to purchase domain names using their country code. Tuvalu has a country code of .tv — you can well imagine what type of business would like to use .tv as part of their domain name. For some small countries, such as Tuvalu, their country code has provided some very beneficial revenue. New domains are developed all the time — .biz is marketed as an alternative to .com (most of the good .com domain names are gone); .info, .museum, and .name are others.

LESSON 2   Planning and Organizing a Web Site

In this lesson and for the next few, you follow some of the steps necessary to create a Web site, such as organizing the content, outlining the site, creating a couple of pages, and adding graphics and links. You do this planning before you begin working in Dreamweaver.

Before you begin creating your pages, you should organize your content. This means working out exactly what you want to say and what you want to include on your pages. You must determine your target audience — who they are and any other information you know about them. The more you understand your users, the better you can plan the site to suit their needs and attract their interest. Consider the purpose of the site. If you want to put up your résumé, assemble your text before you start your pages. If you're designing a business site, consider what the business is looking to achieve through its Web presence. Do you want to provide product information? Give customers access to technical-support information and staff? Allow customers to purchase items from the site? These are just a few of the areas you should think about before you begin designing.

Imagine for the next few exercises that you have been asked to create a Web site for Carver's Store, a department store. Carver's Store wishes to develop an e-commerce Web site. Your first step is to organize the products into categories. These categories are the basis for the site's folder structure.

Sketch a Web-site Folder Layout

Before you begin this exercise, have a sheet of paper and pencil ready. Sketch some ideas on how to organize the Carver's Store Web site before you commit to anything. Pencil and paper are easy to work with, and even if you throw a bad idea into the recycle bin, you can still recover it.

1   **Write "Carver's Store" at the top of the paper; on the line below, write the domain name of Carver's Store's Web site, www.carvers-online.com.**

2   **On the back of the paper, write a list of various products and/or services that the store might sell or provide.**

You may think of clothes for boys, girls, men, women, and babies, as well as shoes. Don't worry about the quantity of detail at this stage.

3   **Continuing on the back of the paper, group similar products and services together, making a list of three or four major categories.**

Using the preceding example, clothes might be listed as a major category with boys, men, girls, women, babies, and shoes as the subcategories.

4   **On the front of the paper, below the domain name, write the major categories across the page. Draw a line from the domain name to each of the category names.**

Use a single word to describe each category. For example, rather than writing "stereos, televisions, and home electronics," write "electronics" or "entertainment."

5   **List the subcategories (from Step 3) below the major categories, and draw lines from the major categories down to their subcategories.**

To Extend Your Knowledge . . .

KEEP IT SIMPLE

Too often, people try to use complex software to solve simple problems. In most cases, they struggle with newfangled software and then return to something simpler and more familiar. Recently, a novice database designer made an inquiry to a discussion group looking for free software tools for database design. Someone replied: "Pen and paper is free, cross-platform, intuitive, and operating-system independent." Animated movies, such as Finding Nemo (by Pixar Animation Studios), start with pencil-and-paper drawings for several iterations of design before they make it into the computer. If Pixar can start their design work with pencil and paper, surely we can too.

Create a Storyboard

Once you've outlined your plan and made some determinations about your audience, start developing ideas by making sketches of your layout. Creating storyboards is an effective way to sketch your layout. (The term "storyboard" was borrowed from the film industry.) Storyboards of your page can be as basic as hand-drawn sketches on scrap paper or as elaborate as complex, computerized minipages that show samples of your chosen graphics, fonts, and page colors.

Creating storyboards doesn't have to be a formal activity. You may want to make storyboards that are simple sets of notes outlining what you think you might put on each page.

When laying out your storyboard pages, use a landscape orientation, since the browser window, as viewed on the typical monitor, is usually wider than it is tall. This is not to suggest that the content of a Web page must fit in the dimensions of a browser window. The reason for the landscape orientation is that studies by the print-publishing industry found that content ***above the fold*** is what attracts buyers. On a Web page, "above the fold" is the browser window before scrolling down.

In addition to determining each page's content, it is useful to organize the proposed pages into a flowchart so that you can sketch which pages relate to each other, which pages can be accessed from one page, and which cannot. It is not necessary that every page be accessible from all other pages on the site, but there must be a means for a visitor to reach other pages in a step or two. The flowcharting process enables you to plan the ***navigation system*** (the links that guide the visitors to other pages on your Web site).

1   **Gather four index cards or cut a sheet of paper into four equal pieces.**

2   **Using these cards, create a four-page storyboard for the Carver's Store Web site.**

3   **Make the first card the home page. This page introduces the store and welcomes viewers. Create a brief introduction to the store and the Web site; include an attractive photograph of the store's interior or exterior, or a product that is currently on sale, and include the store's location, phone number, and other information important to viewers.**

It is essential that visitors know where they are on the Web site and what the site offers. By displaying specials or current products on the home page, you put these products in front of visitors, ensuring that they immediately see these items and, hopefully, investigate further.

4   **On the second card, list the store's categories with a description of each.**

These are the categories that you developed in the previous exercise. Although the categories may be available as links from this page, providing some information about them helps the visitor locate the products they are looking for and might entice them to look at other categories as well: "I didn't know Carver's sells power tools."

5   **Make the third card an outline of the products found in one category. Use this page as a template or model for other categories.**

Consistency is one of the keys to success. By maintaining a common look and feel throughout your site, you ensure that the customers know how to use the pages from one product to another and from one category to another.

6   **Use the last card to represent a contact form that enables visitors to contact Carver's. This form gathers customer information, such as name and phone number, the product they are looking for, and the information that they want to ask the company, such as "Do you carry brand x?" or "When will my order arrive?"**

Visitors to your site must be able to contact you, the person in charge of the Web site, or someone from the business, such as a salesperson, in case they have a problem with your site or want to ask a question. For example, they might be taken to boys' underwear when they choose girls' underwear, or they might be looking for work as a salesperson with the store.

7   **On another sheet of paper, draw a rectangle at the top representing the first card.**

This rectangle represents the site's home page through which people will enter. People may be led to the Web site by radio or television advertising, by print ads, by a friend's recommendation, or by a search engine. In most of these cases, they go to the business's domain name, which brings them to the business's home page.

8   **Below the top rectangle, draw a series of rectangles, which represent the major categories created in the previous exercise. In these rectangles, write the category names, one per rectangle. Join each of them to the top card with a line and to the others with a series of lines.**

From the home page, visitors choose a category to browse but may also want to look at the "home pages" of the other categories to see what is available there. The visitor may be looking for more than one item to purchase.

9 Below each of the category rectangles, draw a series of small rectangles representing the subcategories that you developed in the previous exercise. In these rectangles, write the name of the subcategories, one per rectangle. With lines, join the subcategories to one another, adding a line from each subcategory to the main category above them; also add a series of short lines out from each subcategory representing links to the individual products.

As you can see, the complexity of the linking is growing exponentially. Given the nature of this fictitious Web site, you can create a model page for each level — category, subcategory, and product. Build the links into each model, and copy the model each time.

10 Draw a circle in the center of the top rectangle, representing the area where the featured product would appear. Draw a line from the circle to one of the product lines.

This line represents the link from the featured product on the home page to the detail page for that particular product. Unlike most of the other links you created here, this one will change often with each new special.

11 Lastly, create a rectangle at the page's bottom to represent the contact form you outlined in Step 6 of this exercise. Draw lines from one product line, one subcategory rectangle, one category rectangle, and the home page to this rectangle.

In reality, if you drew these lines from every product line, subcategory, and category; there would be so many lines that the paper would be almost solid black. However, the point is that certain common pages, such as the contact form, the home page, the legal-disclaimer page, the employment page, and several other pages we haven't created or discussed, would be linked from every page on the site.

LESSON 3   Defining the Site and Its Folders

You've organized your content into folders, outlined your basic content on cards, and obtained management's approval of your flowchart. Your next step is to set up your Web site in Dreamweaver. There are two basic steps for configuring the site: first, specify where to store the site's files and folders on your computer; second, create the site's folders.

To use Dreamweaver's site-management functions, you must define your Web site in the application. Do so through the Site Definition dialog box, which asks a series of questions about the Web site, such as the location of the root folder, which you must create before opening the Site Definition dialog box. This root folder does not need to be your computer system's root folder, such as C:\Carvers. It could be much deeper, such as C:\Documents\Websites\Carvers\. For example, you may have the shareware folder on SnapFiles.com as www.snapfiles.com/shareware on the Web site, but you might located in the C:\Documents\Websites\ Snapfiles\shareware folder on your computer.

The Site Definition dialog box uses terms like "local," "remote," and "server technologies." A Web site you are designing on your computer is considered "local." When you put your Web pages on the Web server that is connected to the Internet, that computer is called the "remote" computer. We strongly recommend that you design locally and then put the files on the remote computer when finished. Although most **Web-hosting services** (companies that lease space on their Web servers for Web sites) have rigorous backup procedures, redundant Internet connections, backup generators, and other necessary systems, critical failures do happen. Your local copy may be the only copy that remains of your site. The term "server technologies" refers to special software that you could run on your local computer. Simple Web pages don't require this software, but pages that depend on a database application or server-side programming are difficult to test without it. While not difficult to install and configure, none of these technologies are necessary for this book.

Your final step in defining a Web site in Dreamweaver is creating the folders that exist on the Web site; do this either in or outside of Dreamweaver. In this lesson, you use Dreamweaver's Files panel to create the folders in the defined Web site; the Files panel acts rather like a miniature version of Windows Explorer or the Finder (Macintosh). During your preparation phase, you might not anticipate needing certain folders. Knowing how to create folders from within Dreamweaver can save you a lot of effort in switching back and forth between Explorer/Finder and Dreamweaver.

Create a Site Definition

1   **From the RF_Dreamweaver_L1 folder, copy the Chapter_02 folder and all of its contents to your WIP folder.**

This prepares all of the files you need for Chapter_02.

2   **Launch Dreamweaver.**

3   **Expand the Files panel so that you can see the folders on your computer.**

You can use the Files panel as a file manager, allowing you to view the drives, folders, and files on your system, as well as add, delete, rename, copy, cut, and paste folders and files. You can also use the Files panel to create the site definition.

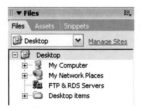

FIGURE 2.11

4   **Click Manage Sites on the top right of the Files panel.**

The Files panel displays all drives on your computer system. You may create, delete, or rename folders and files just as if it were a miniature Explorer/Finder. You may need to do this at times when you want to create the root folder for a new Web site.

FIGURE 2.12

5   **In the Manage Sites dialog box, click the New button and choose Site.**

FTP (File Transfer Protocol) and *RDS (remote data service)* are methods of connecting to a remote Web site so that you can directly edit files on the Web server. Generally we recommend that you do not edit files on the production (Internet-connected) Web server because you could cause a problem that affects the whole site while visitors are browsing and also because you lose the security of a duplicate set of files, development (local) and production (remote). Some corporations, however, provide Web servers for development purposes and a different, final-production Web server that exists on the Internet. In this situation you may use either FTP or RDS as the corporation takes responsibility for maintaining the local Web server.

FIGURE 2.13

6   **Type `Carver's Store` as the site name and click Next.**

In addition to standard *alphanumeric characters* (letters and numbers), Dreamweaver allows some other characters in the site name. The site name is just an internal designation that Dreamweaver uses to store the settings of your Web-site definition. You do not need to enter a HTTP address (URL) for the site.

?   **If You Have Problems**

Ensure that the Basic tab is selected at the top of the Site Definition dialog box.

FIGURE 2.14

7   **Click No, I Do Not Want to Use a Server Technology, then click Next.**

The pages you create in this book do not require Web-server or database software, so you won't need to use any server technology.

FIGURE 2.15

8 **Click Edit Local Copies on My Machine, Then Upload to Server When Ready (Recommended), but do not click Next.**

This means that you will develop locally. To develop remotely, you must choose FTP or RDS servers from the outset.

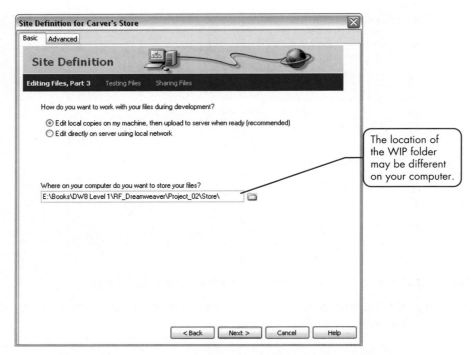

FIGURE 2.16

9 **Click the folder icon to the right of the text field, and then navigate to and open the Chapter_02>Store folder. Click Select/Choose, and then click Next.**

The Store folder, which is the root folder for Carver's, has been created for you. Ordinarily you would have to create the folder before defining the Web site in Dreamweaver.

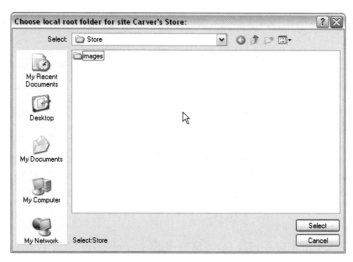

FIGURE 2.17

10 **In response to the question about connection method to your server, choose None; click Next.**

You don't have access to an external (remote) Web server. If you did, then you could specify the settings so that after you finish the design locally, you could copy the files to the remote Web server.

FIGURE 2.18

11 **Click Done and then click Done again. Keep Dreamweaver open for the next lesson.**

You have set up a folder as a site in Dreamweaver. In the next exercise, you create the folders in the Web site using the structure you wrote out previously. You do this using the Files panel, which has much of the functionality of a file manager.

Create Nested Folders

Nested folders are folders within folders. Technically, you have already created a nested folder by creating the root or base folder for your Web site in your Chapter_02 folder, which is nested in your WIP folder. In this exercise, you use the structure that you planned in the earlier exercise (Sketch a Web-Site Folder Layout) to create folders that will exist within your Web site.

1 **Right/Control-click the Site folder for Carver's Store; choose New Folder from the menu.**

FIGURE 2.19

2 **Type the name of your first major category, such as clothes. Use all lowercase characters.**

Although you may name filenames and folders using **mixed-case characters** (both upper- and lowercase characters), Windows systems ignore the character case — the clothes folder is considered the same as Clothes, CLOTHES, and ClOtHeS. However, on Unix and Linux systems, the character case of file and folder names matters, and because more **Web-server software** (software that enables an Internet-connected computer to deliver Web pages) runs on Unix or Linux operating systems than on any other operating system, you should be consistent and use lowercase. Using lowercase characters prevents problems if you have to move your Web site, even temporarily, to a case-sensitive operating system.

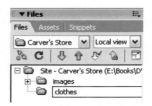

FIGURE 2.20

3   Create the folders for the other major categories that you made in Step 3 of the Sketch a Web-Site Folder Layout exercise.

As you build your Web site in Dreamweaver, use the planning and site organization that you created earlier.

4   Right/Control-click one of the category folders, create a new folder, and name it using one of the subcategory names for that folder.

In this example, "boys" is a subcategory of "clothes."

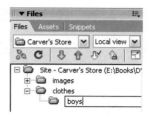

FIGURE 2.21

5   Repeat the process from Step 4 until you have created subfolders for all of your major category folders.

You have now created the folder structure for your Web site. More than this, however, you have begun the process of organizing you site's content.

To Extend Your Knowledge . . .

NAMING CONVENTIONS FOR FILE NAMES AND FOLDERS

When naming files and folders for use on a Web server, certain characters may create problems. Avoid using spaces. Instead, use either the hyphen or the underscore character (i.e., travel-agency.html and travel_agency.html are both easier to read than travelagency.html). Don't start a filename or folder name with a numeral, but use as many numerals as you wish after the first alphabetical character. Finally, restrict the characters to alphanumeric characters (letters of the alphabet and numerals) plus hyphens and underscores. (Windows also allows the # symbol, but that character has special meaning in HTML and CSS, so it is best not to risk confusing your server by using it in a filename or folder name.)

Most current operating systems allow long filenames — up to 255 alphanumeric characters. While you can use this many characters for both filenames and folder names, it's best to keep filenames reasonably short — long enough for clarity but short enough to avoid excessive typing or errors. (Eliminating the eight-character filename and folder name limit that existed in Windows 3.1 and earlier and in

DOS was a welcome enhancement to Windows 95 and later. It allowed travel-agency.html instead of trvagncy.htm. There was also a three-character limit to filename extensions, but that was also eliminated with Windows 95. Web-page filenames may now end with .html instead of the previous .htm.)

LESSON 4   Building Your First Web Page

The next series of exercises shows you some of the functions you use to create Web pages. In these exercises, you create and save a Web page, modify and add more content, and insert a graphic into the Web page. These are many of the types of activities you perform when designing a Web site; although these exercises are quite basic, they give you a sense of what is involved in Web-site design.

Create and Save a New Page

1   Using the Start page, click HTML under the Create New category.

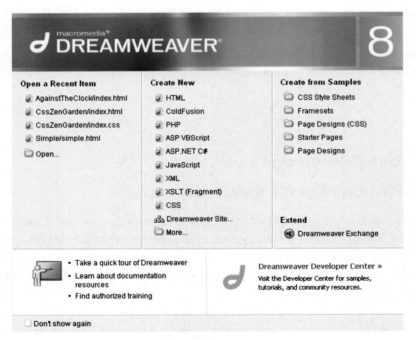

FIGURE 2.22

2   In the document Title field at the top of the Document window, delete Untitled Document, then type Home Page of Carver's Store; press Enter/Return.

The document title appears in a browser window's Title bar and as the document title in search-engine results. Although most people may ignore the text in the Title bar, you want to be sure that when they scan the results of a search, they don't overlook your Web page because the title does not correctly represent your page's content.

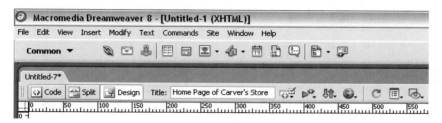

FIGURE 2.23

3 Choose File>Close or press Control/Command-W to close the page.

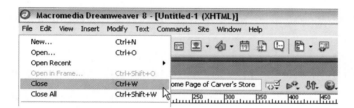

FIGURE 2.24

4 Click Yes to save the changes.

FIGURE 2.25

5 Type `home.html` in the File Name field and click Save.

There are a few different methods for closing and saving a page. You learn other methods in later exercises.

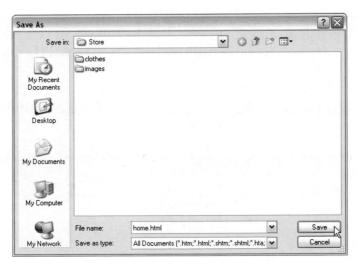

FIGURE 2.26

Add More Text to the Page

In this exercise, you add more content to a page. The process is the same whether you add a brief greeting or more extensive content.

1   **Double-click on home.html in the Files panel to open the this document.**

Double-clicking a file in the Files panel is the easiest method for reopening an existing file; other methods include choosing File>Open or File>Open Recent.

2   **In the body area of the Document window, type** `Carver's Store` **and press Enter/Return.**

3   **Type** `Welcome to our store!` **and press Enter/Return.**

4   **Press Control/Command-S to save the changes made so far. Leave the file open for the next exercise.**

Control/Command-S is a keyboard shortcut for the Save procedure. Learn some of the keyboard shortcuts so you can quickly use those functions. Many of the keyboard shortcuts are common to all applications, making it easy to remember them. It is also a good habit to save often, so you do not lose much of your work in the event of a power failure.

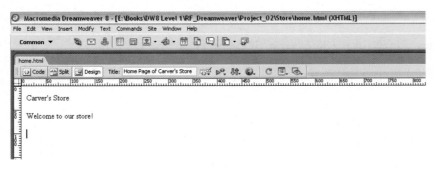

FIGURE 2.27

Insert an Image

1   **In the open home.html file, choose Insert>Image with the insertion point in the empty paragraph.**

This is a simple method for inserting a graphic. In later projects, you learn other methods.

FIGURE 2.28

2   **Double-click the images folder.**

Just as you created folders for the categories of content, you can create folders for other items, such as images and video files. Often, a Web site has many images; storing a large number of these files among the other Web-page files can be confusing.

Note that the path to the images folder on your system may be different from that shown here, depending on which drive and where on that drive you created the Chapter_02 folder. However, from the Chapter_02 folder and down, the structure of the folders is the same from system to system.

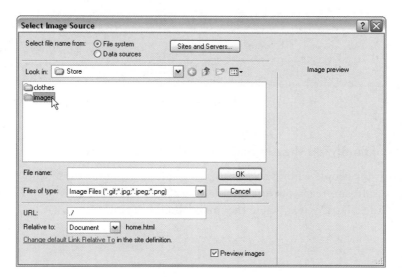

FIGURE 2.29

3   **Click family.jpg to select the image, but do not click OK.**

4   **At the bottom of the Select Image Source dialog box, change the Relative To option to Document.**

You learn more about relative and absolute paths in Chapter 4. For now, consider this example. John lives at 123 Main Street, and you live in the next house. A relative path from your house to John's house is: "he lives next door," whereas an absolute path to John's house is: "123 Main Street." Next door won't take someone to John's house from any house in town, only from your house. But 123 Main Street will always take someone to John's house, no matter where they start from. Relative to Document is like "next door," whereas Relative to Site is like "123 Main Street."

5   **Click OK to insert the image.**

Notice the various properties of the image provided by the Select Image Source dialog box: an image preview, the file format, the dimensions (width, height), the file's size, and how long (11 seconds) it takes to download.

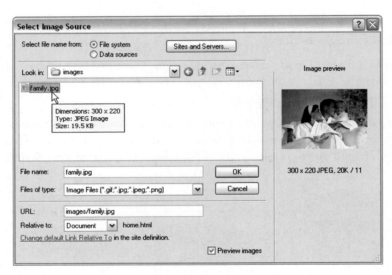

FIGURE 2.30

6   **Type "Photo of family" in the Alternate text field and click OK.**

Alternate text is for people who use screen-reading software and for those who browse with images off: screen-reading software reads out the alternate text, and if an image is not visible on-screen, sighted users can read the alternate text where the image should appear.

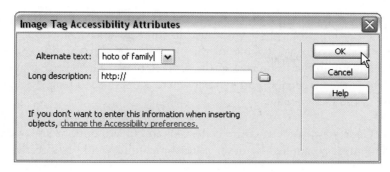

FIGURE 2.31

7   Choose File>Close, and click Yes to save the changes.

To Extend Your Knowledge . . .

DREAMWEAVER DOES THE HARD WORK

Inserting graphics into a Web page is very simple. So simple, in fact, that you don't realize how much other information about the image has been inserted for you. You saw in the preview window that the dimensions of this image are 300 wide by 220 high. The units are *pixels* — (a word created from picture and elements): pixels are the dots on the computer monitor. In fact, Dreamweaver has specified these dimensions in the HTML code. Dreamweaver does a lot in the background when you select one of the HTML options or formats. It creates good HTML code. As you become more comfortable with the program, however, you will learn how (and be expected) to access the HTML code directly to apply options that may not be available from the Design window.

LESSON 5   Working with Views

Most computer applications do not allow you to see or work with the code that is developed when you work with the application. The code produced when you create documents in a word-processing application, for example, is quite complex and not readable by human beings. HTML was originally developed when WYSIWYG applications were just being developed for both the Macintosh and Windows 3.0 — a WYSIWYG application for Web design was not even under consideration at the time. As a result, HTML is not very complex. (Novices may disagree, but look at Java, C++, or another advanced programming language and you will change your mind.) For that reason, all WYSIWYG Web-design applications allow you to view and edit the code.

At times, you may need to examine the code of a particular section of the Web page. When you select a section of the design in the Design view, such as a block of text, the same block of text is selected in the Code view as well. You can then examine the code to correct it or apply something else to it. (Dreamweaver creates good code, but it cannot do everything for you — you must do some advanced functions manually.) Rather than hunt through hundreds of lines of code, looking for the block you need to modify, you can select the block in the Design view, and then look in the Code view at the selected block. The reverse is also true. You may see an unfamiliar block of code in the Code view and wonder where it fits in the Design. Selecting it also selects the related object(s) or text in the Design view.

When you work in the Code view, you can create code. Not all HTML options are available through the buttons and menus — some must be applied by other means, including working directly with the code. As you work in the Code view, Dreamweaver continues to assist you through code hints, a pop-up function that prompts you with options for HTML code.

Your browser uses the code that you create, either through the Design view or by hand-coding in the Code view, to display the Web page you are creating. When you view a Web page on the Internet, the code delivered to you is the same code that the author created. You can examine that code.

In this lesson, you see that the Design view and Code view are linked. You select text in the Design view and find out where it is in the Code view. In addition, you create code in the Code view and see it appear in the Design view. Finally, you examine the code that was sent to your browser to see that it is the same code you created in the Design and Code views.

View Changes in the Code Window

1   **Open home.html in the Files panel by double-clicking it.**

2   **Select "Store" from the first line by double-clicking it.**

3   **Click the Split button at the top of the Document window.**

When you select text in one window, the text is selected in the other window as well. This feature is very useful for showing where you are both in the design and in the code.

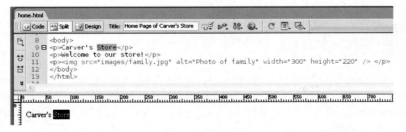

FIGURE 2.32

4   **Press Delete and type** `Online`**. Leave the file open for the next exercise.**

Observe that the changes you made in the Design window are reflected in the Code window.

View Changes in the Design Window

1 In the open home.html file, click to the right of the photo in the Design window.

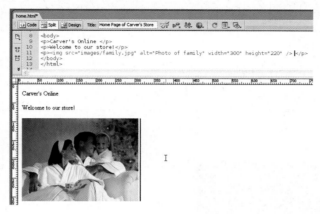

FIGURE 2.33

2 Click in the Code window at the end of the line (to the right of `</p>`) and press Enter/Return.

You added another line of text and code below the graphic.

FIGURE 2.34

3 Type `<p>`.

Notice how Dreamweaver prompts you with options for HTML tags as you type.

FIGURE 2.35

4   **Type** `Your favorite store for all your needs!`

Notice that the Design window below does not reflect the changes you have made (Windows).

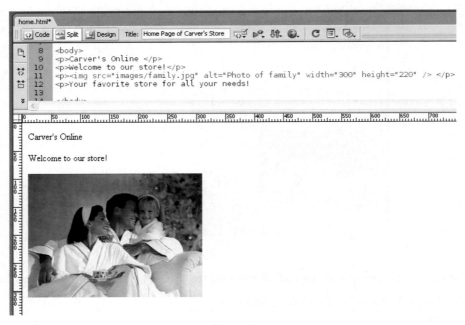

FIGURE 2.36

5   **In the Property inspector, click the Refresh button.**

On a Windows system, the Design window does not dynamically change to reflect the changes in the Code window. You must use the Refresh button to make the changes appear in the Design window.

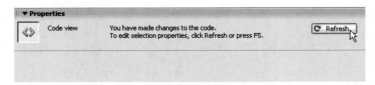

FIGURE 2.37

6   **In the Code window, type "</".**

Note that you don't have to complete the code with **p>**; Dreamweaver recognizes which code is incomplete and automatically completes it for you.

7   **Click the Design button (Show Design View in the tool tip) to close the Code window.**

8   **Press Control/Command-S to save the changes. Leave the file open for the next exercise.**

View Source Code sent to Your Browser

You have made changes to the Web page using both the Design view and Code view. You can examine the code in Dreamweaver, but is it the same code that is delivered to the browser? In this exercise, you examine the code that is delivered to the browser to learn that the code is identical to the code you created.

1 | **In the open home.html file, choose File>Preview in Browser and choose a browser.**

Depending on your computer's setup, you may have only one browser or you may have many. Choose any browser from the list to view the page you created.

2 | **Switch between Dreamweaver and your browser.**

Notice that the Web page you created in Dreamweaver looks the same in the browser window as it does in Dreamweaver's Design view.

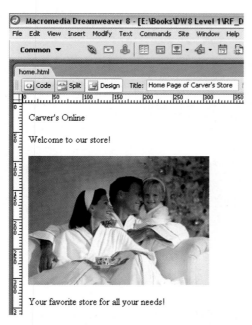 

FIGURE 2.38

3 | **Right/Control-click in your browser window, and choose View Source from the pop-up menu.**

Although all browsers offer this option, different browsers may use slightly different terms for this option, such as View Page Source. Also, different browsers and computer setups display the code using different applications. For example, Internet Explorer for Windows tends to display the code in Notepad, whereas Firefox has its own Code view window.

FIGURE 2.39

4   Examine the Web page's HTML code.

5   Close the application that opened and displayed the HTML code, then close your browser.

6   Switch to Dreamweaver and click the Code button (Show Code View in tool tip).

Notice the code in Dreamweaver is identical to the code the browser received. Dreamweaver uses *syntax coloring*—different parts of the code are given different colors, such as dark blue for tags, purple for attributes, royal blue for attribute values, and black for text. Not all text or HTML editors use syntax coloring; for instance, Firefox's source code viewer (on the right) does, whereas Notepad (on the left) does not. (Notepad is the default source code viewer for Internet Explorer.)

FIGURE 2.40

| **7** | **Click the Design button. Leave home.html open for the next exercise** |

The code you created using Dreamweaver is the same code that the browser uses to display the Web page. You can use this method to examine the code of other Web pages whose style or layout is of interest, so that you can see how they were created. The only instance when the code of the page at the Web server may differ from what the browser receives is when you use a programming language to generate the Web pages. For example, the programming code may use the current time to generate "Good Morning" or "Good Afternoon." Generally, though, whatever code you create is the same code that your browser receives.

LESSON 6   Applying Simple Text Formatting

Although Dreamweaver's focus is on creating Web pages, it also has many text functions similar to those in word-processing software. Many other types of content are available from the Internet, such as graphics, animations, videos, and music, but the primary source of content for Web pages is text. As Patrick Lynch and Sarah Horton wrote in *The Web Style Guide*, "Don't get so lost in the novelty of Web pages that basic standards of editorial and graphic design are tossed aside." HTML has all the basic text structures needed for a text-based document.

The primary structures that are most commonly used are headings, lists, and paragraphs. There are six levels of headings, starting with Heading 1, the most important, down to Heading 6. Headings are formatted with different font sizes, with Heading 1 being the largest and Heading 6 being the smallest. Heading 1 is used just once on a page and identifies the page's basic purpose. The other headings (not all need to be used) divide and subdivide the content into chunks of easily digestible information. One common mistake that novices make is applying Heading 3 as the top heading for the page because they don't like how large Heading 1 appears. In *Essentials for Design: Dreamweaver 8*, you learn how to change the text's default size, including headings, so that you maintain the ***document structure*** (the proper use of headings and other text structures) while creating a pleasing appearance.

Other formatting options include numbered and bulleted lists, which look just like their counterparts in word-processing software. You may change the numbering style from numerals (1, 2, 3) to alphabetic (a, b, c) and other styles, and you can change the bullet characters from a circle (open circle) to a disc (filled circle) or a square bullet character. You can insert a ***horizontal rule*** (line), add an image, or format a quotation.

There are no excuses for not using proper document structure in a Web page. Your Web pages are public documents that may be viewed by thousands, hundreds of thousands, perhaps even millions of people. Using proper document structure ensures that your documents are correctly formatted for easier reading and under-standing. Using proper document structure benefits the blind as well. The blind use the Internet, too, but their experience is very different. They often use screen-reading software, such as JAWS from Freedom Scientific, or devices that convert text characters to Braille on an electronic device in front of their keyboard. Whereas sight-ed people can scan a page visually for large bold blocks of text representing headings, blind people cannot. They depend, instead, on proper document structure to let them know when they have encountered a heading or a list. It is quite possible to fake a heading by taking a standard paragraph and making the text large and bold, but the underlying code remains a paragraph, not a heading. *Accessibility* is the term used to describe methods and procedures for ensuring that your Web pages are just as usable by the blind as they are by sighted persons.

In this exercise, you apply simple text formatting using two different features — the Property inspector and the Tag editor. The Property inspector allows you to apply most text-formatting options by clicking the option or selecting it from a list. In the following figure, you see that the format of the selected text block is Heading 3. The Tag editor is somewhat like the Code view, in that you type your changes in the code. Unlike the Code view, however, only the selected HTML is visible. You first select the HTML block using the Tag selector (a function that appears in the Document window's Status bar). The Tag selector identifies the HTML tags that are in use in the selected text; for example, Heading 3 in the following figure. When you Right/Control-click the tag in the Tag selector and choose Edit tag, a pop-up window appears, showing you the tag and its current options (no options are used in this example). You can then edit the tag in the pop-up window. Just like the Code view, code hints appear to help you select options for the tag.

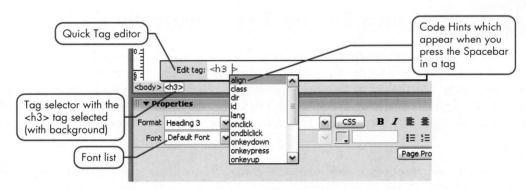

FIGURE 2.41

Format a Heading

1	**In the open home.html file, click in the top line of text.**

2	**Using the Property inspector, choose Heading 1 from the Format list.**

The text becomes large and bold — this is the default appearance of Heading 1 text.

FIGURE 2.42

3   Drag to select the second line of text.

4   Click the Bold button (B) in the Property inspector.

You may notice that the Tag selector displays the `<strong>` tag after you apply bold. The `<strong>` tag is an accessibility feature; when screen readers encounter this tag, their computer-generated voices change to a stronger tone, indicating that the `<strong>` text is emphasized. Read aloud a sentence with bold text in it, and listen to the change in your voice. The bold tag `<b>` is being phased out in favor of `<strong>`. Both blind and sighted users receive the same emphasis when you use the `<strong>` tag.

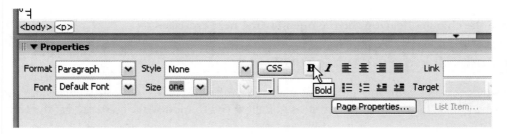

FIGURE 2.43

5   Click in the last line of text.

6   Click the `<p>` in the Tag selector at the bottom of the Document window.

When you click an HTML tag in the Tag selector, all content in that tag is selected.

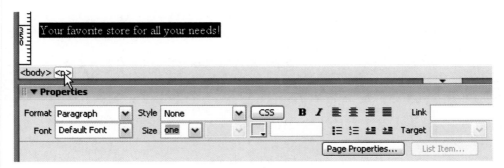

FIGURE 2.44

7   **From the Property inspector, click the Font list and choose the second option: Arial, Helvetica, Sans-Serif.**

Sans serif is French for "without serifs" (*serifs* are the small perpendicular strokes added to parts of letters and numerals in some fonts). For example, compare **T** with T and notice that the first one has additional strokes perpendicular to the top crossbar and the bottom of the upright — these are serifs. Computer screens and, worse yet, television screens display text much more roughly than printers. Serif text is thus more difficult to read on a computer screen because the serifs do not display as clearly due to their small size. Web pages tend to use sans serif fonts because, without the serifs, the fonts appear farther apart and more distinct. Arial and Helvetica are both sans serif fonts.

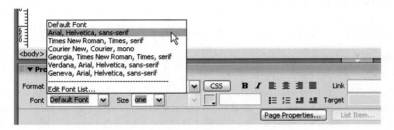

FIGURE 2.45

8   **Save the changes, leaving the file open for the next exercise.**

Modify Code Using the Quick Tag Editor

The Code window is not your only means for making changes to HTML code — you can also use the Quick Tag editor. The Quick Tag editor, however, does not allow you to modify the content, just the code.

1   **In the open home.html file, click to the photo's right.**

2   **Right/Control-click <p> in the Tag selector at the bottom of the Document window.**

When you click or Right/Control-click a tag in the Tag selector, the tag's contents are selected in the Design window. Notice that the photo is selected because it is in the selected paragraph.

3   **Choose Quick Tag Editor from the pop-up menu.**

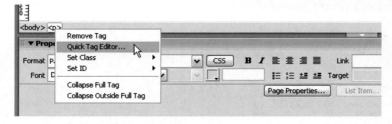

FIGURE 2.46

4 With the insertion point between the p and the >, press the Spacebar once and pause for a moment.

After a moment, a pop-up menu of code hints appears. *Code hints* are options available for the selected HTML tag.

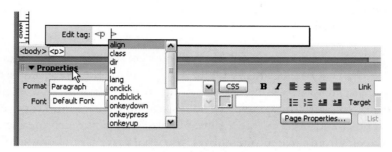

FIGURE 2.47

5 The first option in the list, `align`, is selected. Press Enter/Return to accept it and pause for a moment.

That option — **align** — is an *HTML attribute* (an option) of the paragraph tag (and for numerous other tags too). The **align** attribute has four *values* (attribute options are called *attribute values* or just "values"): **center**, **justify**, **left**, and **right**. After a moment, the four attribute values for **align** appear.

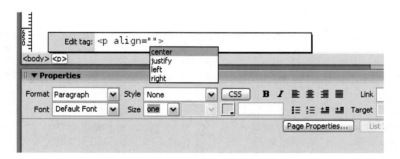

FIGURE 2.48

6 Note that `center`, the first attribute option for `align`, is selected. Press Enter/Return to accept it.

When you choose **center**, the photo centers in the Design view because the photo is in the paragraph whose property you just changed to center alignment.

7 Save the changes, leaving the file open for the next exercise.

LESSON 7 　Using a Web Page as a Template

Designing a Web page can take a lot of time and effort, for you and for others on your team. If you have more than one page that uses the same basic design and differs only in content, there is no need to rebuild the page again. Instead, build a ***template***, a document that contains the common elements you need in multiple other pages. Using the template allows you to efficiently build other similar pages and retain the common look and feel you developed for the original document.

You learned of the need for a template in Lesson 2 when you were sketching some pages at the category, sub-category, and product levels. That type of situation is ideal for templating. In the example of Carver's Store, you may only need three primary templates — one for each of the three levels of detail. Not all pages on a Web site need to tightly adhere to a template; for example, the home page and contact-form page you sketched in Lesson 2 may differ from each other and from the other three templates. However, considering that you could build most of the pages for Carver's from three such templates, you would save a lot of time and effort if you use templates.

Dreamweaver has a very strong templating function with which you can create both simple and complex templates. In this lesson, however, you don't use the Dreamweaver template functionality but something simpler — Save As. You create a document, save it, reopen it, save it as a different name, and make the changes. You then have a new document based on the template of the original document. For basic documents, there is nothing faster or easier than using Save As as a form of templating.

Use Save As to Create Another Web Page

1 | **Open home.html and choose File>Save As.**

2 | **Type** `home-french.html` **in the File Name field; either click the Save button or press Enter/Return.**

You have just built your first page modeled on home.html. The next step is to make the specific content changes to this page.

3 | **Select "Welcome to our store!" and delete it; in its place type** `Bienvenue a votre magasin!`

4 | **Select "Your favorite store for all your needs!"; in its place type** `Votre magasin favori pour tous vos besoins!`

home-french.html*
Code | Split | Design | Title: Home Page of Carver's Store

Carver's Online

Bienvenue a votre magasin!

Votre magasin favori pour tous vos besoins!

FIGURE 2.49

5   **Close the file, saving the changes.**

LESSON 8   Creating Links

Hyperlinks, or links, are an integral part of Web pages. Links are what make the World Wide Web different from any other Internet component. They allow you to go from page to page in a news article; to jump from Web site to Web site; and, to a certain extent, to send an e-mail. Links, whether from one Web page to another or from e-mail links, are very easy to create in Dreamweaver.

There are two basic types of Web-page links. One, you may link from one Web page to another page on the same site. When you create a link to another page in the same site, the domain name remains the same; you need only specify the name of the page to which to send the reader. If the destination page is in another folder, then you must specify the path to the page including the folder (or folders). For example, to link from the home page of Carver's Online to the OshKosh shoes page in the boys' section of the shoes category, the link would be shoes/boys/oshkosh.html.

The second type is a link from one Web page to a page on another Web site. When you link from the oshkosh.html page in Carver's Online to the boys' shoes page on the OshKosh B'Gosh Online Store Web site, the link would be http://www.oshkoshbgosh.com/productselection.asp?did=807. A link to a page on another site must include http://, the domain name (www.oshkosbgosh.com), the Web-page name (productselection.asp?did=807), and the folder path (if applicable). ***HTTP (Hypertext Transfer Protocol)*** is the method by which Web pages are transferred from the Web server to the browser. Browsers can display information from different types of servers — gopher, wais, http, and ftp (the first two are rare these days, but http and ftp are not); to ensure that the browser and server are "speaking the same language," the protocol must be specified. FTP (File Transfer Protocol) is a protocol through which you may view files on a server, not unlike viewing the files on your computer system through Explorer/Finder. Clicking a filename on an ftp site downloads that file. If you are linking to an ftp site, you must add `ftp://` in front of the domain name.

In Chapter 4, you learn more about links and how to create them in Dreamweaver using absolute and relative paths and multiple methods. In this exercise, you create simple links. You type the link destination into the Link field, which means that you must remember to use the protocol, when needed, and check your link's spelling. A link to a misspelled filename takes you either to the wrong page (if the misspelling is the spelling of another page) or to no page at all (otherwise known as a "dead" or "broken" link).

Link Pages to One Another

1   **Open home.html from the Files panel.**

2   **Click at the end of the last paragraph and press Enter/Return.**

When you press Enter/Return at the end of a paragraph, you create a new paragraph block with opening and closing paragraph tags **<p>**. The Tag selector shows a **<p>** at the end of the tags list, indicating that you are working in a paragraph block.

3   **Type** `Cette page en francais.`

You will link this phrase, which means "This page in French", to the French page you created in the previous exercise.

4   **In the Property inspector, click the Style list and choose None.**

The previous paragraph used style1, and the style was carried automatically to the current paragraph. Selecting None removes the style from the current paragraph.

FIGURE 2.50

5   **With the phrase selected,** `type home-french.html` **in the Property inspector's Link field and press Enter/Return.**

You type the link's destination in the Link field. There are other methods for creating a link, but there will still be times when you must type text into the Link field.

Press Enter/Return after typing the link destination into the Link field. At times, Dreamweaver doesn't properly register the link destination typed into the Link field. Pressing Enter/Return forces Dreamweaver to store the value.

FIGURE 2.51

6 Close home.html, saving the changes.

7 Open home-french.html.

8 Click at the end of the last paragraph and press Enter/Return.

9 Type `This page in English.`

10 Set Style to None.

11 Select the paragraph, type `home.html` in the Link field, and press Enter/Return.

You have now created links from home.html to home-french.html and back again.

FIGURE 2.52

12 Close the file, saving the changes.

Create an E-mail Link

In this exercise, you create an e-mail link. Remember that e-mail links require the e-mail protocol **mailto:** in front of the e-mail address.

1 Open home.html.

2 Click to the right of the last paragraph and press Enter/Return.

3 Type `Please contact us if you have any questions.`

4 Select "contact us".

The words "contact us" will be the link to the e-mail address. Often, you see "click here" in a Web page, which is poor form. Click here does not indicate where the link goes — you must read the rest of the phrase or sentence to determine the link's purpose or destination. By contrast, "contact us" clearly indicates the link's purpose. Secondly, some people do not use a mouse with their computer, because they may be blind, visually impaired, or have ***motility challenges*** (such as poor hand-eye coordination, upper-body paralysis, or shakiness, such as from Parkinson's). Commonly, these people use the Tab key on their keyboard to skip from link to link. If they are using a screen reader, the screen reader reads the link text aloud. If these individuals repeatedly hear only "click here" on a page, they become very frustrated, and you can't sell to frustrated clients. However, if your link text is informative, your visitors understand the purpose of your links, navigate your pages with greater ease, and buy more.

5   **In the Link field of the Property inspector, type** `mailto:info@carversonline.com` **and press Enter/Return.**

Do not insert a space between `mailto:` and the e-mail address.

FIGURE 2.53

6   **Save the changes, leaving the file open for the next exercise.**

Test Your Links in a Browser

You can view many features and functions of a Web page in the Design view, but some require a browser to properly test your work. "Code a little, test a little" is a good principle to follow. When you create, add, or modify HTML code by hand, mistakes occasionally creep into your Web pages. Dreamweaver creates excellent-quality HTML code, but you may type an e-mail address incorrectly or link to the wrong page. Whether you create the HTML in the Code view or work in the Design view, you should always test your links.

In this exercise, you test the links in your browser. This is a very important check since Carver's Store does not want their potential customers to be frustrated by dead links.

1   **In the open home.html file, choose File>Preview in Browser; choose a browser.**

2   **Click the link to the French page.**

3   **Click the link to the English page.**

4   **Click the e-mail link.**

If you do not have e-mail software configured on your system, an alert dialog box may appear, warning you that you may need to set up e-mail software. If so, you know that the e-mail link is working fine.

5   Close your browser and return to Dreamweaver.

6   Close home.html.

CAREERS IN DESIGN

DO YOU NEED A WEB SERVER?

Experienced developers may also use a Web server to test their Web sites in a more realistic setting. Advanced Web designers have several options for accessing and using a Web server for development purposes, such as installing Web-server software on their personal computers, setting up a separate computer that has been configured as a Web server, or purchasing Web-hosting services for development purposes only.

Access to a Web server allows you to use server-side programming to create dynamic sites. A **dynamic site** is one that changes regularly, such as a news site or a discussion forum. Commonly, these sites use a database to store the Web site's content. **Server-side programming** is a programming language that runs at the Web server; the results of this programming are returned to the visitor's browser as HTML. A **search engine** is a program that processes your request and returns the results in HTML, which you then see as a Web page. Search engines are dynamic in that the pages they produce are different with every request.

SUMMARY

In this chapter, you learned how to plan and organize the content of a Web site and produce a flowchart from which you could create a navigation system. You learned how to define the site; create folders; and create, modify, and save basic Web pages. You also discovered how to use Save As to make one page serve as a template for another. You learned how to add text and graphics to a simple page and how to use the Design view to create the HTML while you work on the layout. You discovered how to use the Code view to modify the code directly, and use code hints to access a list of attributes appropriate to the selected HTML tag. You learned about HTML tags and attributes. In addition, you discovered how to use the Tag selector to select a text block and how to use the Tag editor to add an attribute to the tag. You explored creating different types of links — to other pages on your site and e-mail links. You also discovered how to test your page in a browser and view the source code.

KEY TERMS

Above the fold

Accessibility

Alphanumeric characters

Attribute values

Code hints

Document structure

Domain name

Domain name registrars

Dynamic site

Freeware

FTP (File Transfer Protocol)

Home page

HTML attribute

HTTP (Hypertext Transfer Protocol)

Horizontal rule

Local computer

Mixed-case characters

Motility challenges

Navigation system

Nested folders

Pixels

RDS (Remote Data Service)

Remote computer

Rich media

Root

Root folder

Sans serif fonts

Search engine

Serif fonts

Server-side programming

Shareware

Site map

Source code

Syntax coloring

Template

URL

Values

Web-hosting services

Web-server software

CHECKING CONCEPTS AND TERMS

SCREEN ID

Identify the indicated areas from the list below:

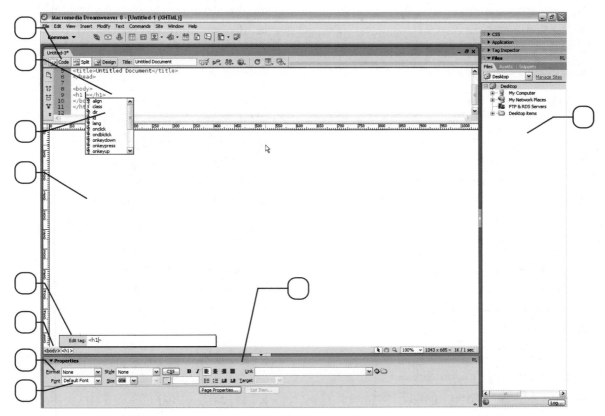

FIGURE 2.54

a. Quick Tag editor

b. Tag selector showing the `<h1>` tag selected

c. Property inspector

d. Files panel

e. Code View window

f. Design View window

g. Code hint showing attributes of the `<h1>` tag

h. Text block formats, such as paragraph and headings

i. Font list

j. Layout View selection buttons

MULTIPLE CHOICE

Circle the letter of the correct answer for each of the following:

1. Which of the following is not part of planning a Web project?
   a. Gathering content
   b. Collecting related content
   c. Writing HTML code for each page
   d. Creating a design concept

2. Storyboarding and flowcharting for a Web site _____ .
   a. require specific HTML coding
   b. begin on paper
   c. have become obsolete in recent years
   d. are only used for Web animation

3. Site definition _____ .
   a. defines thematic site design
   b. establishes the site's working title and root folder
   c. publishes the site on the host server
   d. is a creative brief defining the Web site for client approval

4. Nothing contained in your site can _____ .
   a. have a filename with capital letters
   b. can have more than 256 colors
   c. be higher than the root folder
   d. All of the above

5. In a Web browser, you can view the source code or HTML of a Web page.
   a. True
   b. False

6. The Uniform Resource Locator or URL is _____ .
   a. the filename extension of a Web page
   b. determined by the Web browser
   c. the address of a Web page
   d. only accessible by the host server

7. A domain name _____ .
   a. is always capitalized
   b. must be contained in all filenames of a Web project
   c. can be registered without cost
   d. is like the name of a business

8. When designing a Web site, it is important to _____ .
   a. consider the purpose of the site
   b. determine the target audience
   c. research sites with similar objectives
   d. All of the above

9. FTP and RDS are both _____ .
   a. image-file extensions
   b. HTML tags defining text attributes
   c. alternative programming technologies for Web development
   d. methods of connecting to a remote Web site

10. The primary source of content from Web pages is _____ .
    a. video and animation
    b. music
    c. text
    d. photo images

DISCUSSION QUESTIONS

1. You have learned that good organization and Web-site design begin with planning your content and navigation through outlining, storyboarding, and flowcharting. Why is this process more desirable than simply sitting down at the computer and beginning to design? Are there any disadvantages to working this way?

2. Organizing your content — text, images, videos, and animations — is essential for Web-site management and updating. How would you structure and organize the folders that contain the site content? How would your method of organizing result in more efficient site management and development?

3. Once you have designed the look, why are templates beneficial for Web sites that can grow to hundreds of pages? Which components of a Web page would you put into the template and why?

SKILL DRILL

Skill Drills reinforce project skills. Each skill that is reinforced is the same as, or nearly the same as, a skill we presented in the lesson. We provide detailed instructions in a step-by-step format. You should work through these exercises in order.

The preceding lessons and exercises provide a whirlwind tour of Dreamweaver. In the following Skill Drills, you work through similar steps to define and create Web pages, but at a slower pace so you can learn more detail about the procedures and dialog boxes.

1. Define a Site with the Advanced Tab

In this Skill Drill, you define a new site using the Advanced tab of the Site Definition dialog box. The Advanced tab gives you the same options as the Basic tab but adds many others that are needed for later projects, such as remote access and server technologies.

The site you are creating is called "Tropiflora Online" (hence the abbreviation TO). Tropiflora Online is an actual online retailer of tropical plants and supplies. (Web site content used by permission.)

1. At the top of the Files panel, click the drop-down menu and choose Manage Sites.

2. In the Manage Sites dialog box, choose New, and then choose Site.

3. Click the Advanced tab in the Site Definition dialog box.

4. Type `TO-P2` in the Site Name field.

5. Click the folder icon to the right of the Local Root Folder field.

6. Navigate to Chapter_02>TO-P2 and click Select/Choose.

7. Click OK.

8. Click Done.

Working with the Site Definition dialog box's Advanced tab seems much simpler than using the Basic tab. Unless told otherwise, use the Advanced tab for all future exercises. Refer to this Skill Drill when you need to recall the process for creating a new site.

2. Create a New Page Using the File>New Menu

1. From the Dreamweaver Start page, click HTML from the Create New category.

2. In the Title field of the Document toolbar, type `Home of Tropiflora Online`.

3. In the Document window, type `Tropiflora Online`, and press Return/Enter.

4. Type `Exotic Plants For Your Home and Garden`. Press Return/Enter three times.

5. Type `Home | About Tropiflora | Products | Location | Contact Us`. Type the "|" or pipe character by holding the Shift key and pressing the "\" key.

6. Choose File>Save and save the file as default.html in the Chapter_02>TO-P2 folder.

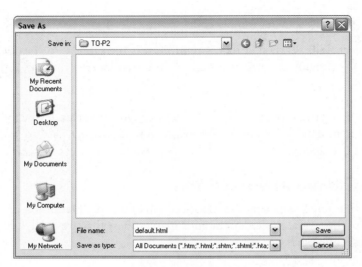

FIGURE 2.55

7. Click the Save button to complete the process.

8. Preview the Web page in your browser.

   Remember the proverb, "A journey of a thousand miles begins with the first step", this basic Web page is the beginning of a Web site.

9. Return to Dreamweaver.

10. Close default.html.

To Extend Your Knowledge . . .

DEFAULT HOME PAGE FILE NAME

Every Web site has a home page. When you go to a Web site, you generally just type the site's domain name (strings of letters used to name organizations, computers, and addresses on the Internet), such as http://www.ibm.com. The Web server then delivers the site's home page to your browser. With many files on a Web server, how does it know which page to deliver when the visitor does not specify the filename? The Web-hosting service configures a filename as the default, commonly either default.html or index.html.

3. Add Another Web Page to Tropiflora Online

Professional Web sites, small or large, consist of multiple pages that describe different aspects of a business, including products, services, and the means by which customers may contact the business. Tropiflora Online is no different, so in this exercise you add pages to the Tropiflora Online site.

1. Choose File>New.

2. From the Category list, choose Basic Page.

3. From the Basic Page category, choose HTML, and then click the Create button.

4. Delete "Untitled Document" from the Title field and replace it with `About Tropiflora Online`.

5. In the Document window, type the following text and then press Return/Enter the number of times indicated:

Type this text	Press Return/Enter
Tropiflora Online	Once
About Tropiflora	Twice
Home | About Tropiflora | Products | Location | Contact Us	None

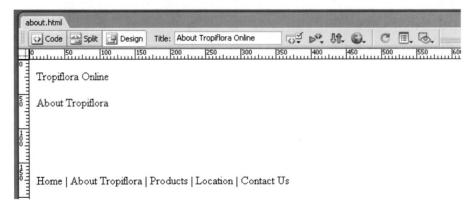

FIGURE 2.56

6. Choose File>Save, type `about.html` in the File Name field, and then click Save.

7. Close about.html (File>Close).

4. Use Copy/Paste to Create New Pages

Web sites generally have a common look and feel throughout so visitors know that they are still in the same site and understand where to find the navigation links. As you create the Tropiflora Online site with this design intent, you use Copy and Paste rather than retyping the common text.

1. Choose File>Open Recent and choose about.html from the list.

2. Choose File>New, and click Create at the bottom of the New Document dialog box.

? **If You Have Problems**

If you are unsure of the New Document dialog box's settings for creating a new HTML page, refer to Steps 2 and 3 of the previous Skill Drill.

---

3. In the Title field, type `Products of Tropiflora Online`.

4. In the Document window, type the following and press Return/Enter as indicated.

Type this text	Press Return/Enter
Tropiflora Online	Once
Products	Twice
Top Sellers	Twice
Descriptions	Twice

5. Click the about.html File name tab to bring the about.html tab in front of the Untitled page tab.

6. Drag to select the bottom line of text.

7. Press Control/Command-C to copy the selected text to the clipboard.

8. Click the filename tab to switch to the Untitled file.

9. Choose Edit>Paste (or press Control/Command-V) to paste the text at the bottom of the current page.

10. Choose File>Close, and choose Yes to save the changes.

FIGURE 2.57

11. Type "products.html" in the File Name field, and click the Save button.

5. Import Content from a Microsoft Word Document

The Web designer does not have to type all content for the Web site — in many organizations, other people are responsible for supplying the content. Knowing how to import content from other program files (such as word-processing documents) saves much typing time.

1. Create a new blank HTML document.

    From the Create New category of the Start page, choose either File>New or HTML.

2. In the Title field, type `Location of Tropiflora Online`, and press Enter/Return.

3. If you are using Windows, choose File>Import>Word Document; select location.doc, then choose Text with structure (paragraphs, lists, tables). Uncheck Clean up Word paragraph spacing, and click Open. Continue with Step 5.

4. If you are using a Macintosh, open location.txt, and select and copy all of the text onto the clipboard. Close locaton.txt. Paste the copied text into the current untitled page. Continue with Step 5.

5. Click the about.html tab at the top of the Document window.

6. If the navigation-bar paragraph at the bottom of the page is not selected, do so.

7. Copy the paragraph into the clipboard.

8. Switch back to the Untitled page.

9. Move the insertion point to the end of the last line and press Enter/Return.

10. Paste the copied text.

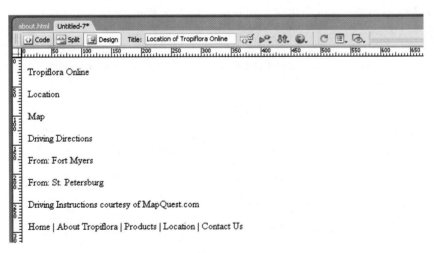

FIGURE 2.58

11. Close, saving the changes as "location.html".

12. Close about.html but do not save the changes if prompted — no changes should have been made.

CHALLENGE

Challenge exercises expand on, or are somewhat related to, skills we presented in the lessons. Each exercise provides a brief introduction, followed by numbered-step instructions that are not as detailed as those in the Skill Drill exercises. You should work through the exercises in order.

1. Design Your Family's Web Site

In this Challenge exercise, you create a small Web site about your family. Plan the site on paper, and then construct some of the Web pages. This exercise's purpose is to practice what you learned about planning a Web site, and then putting your plan into action.

1. Before you begin, write the full names of your parents, yourself, and your siblings with several spaces between each on a blank sheet of paper. For each family member, write his or her birth date and birthplace, favorite activity or hobby, and one or two other interesting pieces of information about him or her. Create an e-mail address for each using the format **firstname@lastname.com**.

2. In Dreamweaver, use the Advanced tab of the Site Definition dialog box to define a Web site named with your father's last name. Set the Local Root Folder to Chapter_02>Family.

3. Create a new HTML page with the family's last name at the top and the names of the family members below. Save the page as "home.html".

4. Create a new HTML page. Type your name at the top; in the paragraphs below, type the information you wrote about yourself, and end with your e-mail address.

5. Select your e-mail address and type it in the Property inspector's Link field. Precede the e-mail address with **mailto:** in the Link field.

6. At the bottom of the page, type `Return to our home page`.

7. Select the last paragraph, type `home.html` in the Link field, and then close, saving the Web page using your first name followed by .html as the filename.

8. Repeat Steps 4 to 7 for each family member, using his or her first name as the filename followed by .html.

9. When you have completed all of the individual pages, reopen home.html.

10. One by one, select each person's name and create a link to his or her page.

11. Preview the page in your browser (save when prompted) and test all of the links.

12. Close your browser and return to Dreamweaver. Close home.html.

2. Print a Web Page and Its Source Code

1. Open challenge1.html from the Chapter_02>Challenges folder.

2. Preview the page in your browser.

3. Print the page from your browser.

4. Right/Control-click and choose View Source (or View Source Code, depending on your browser).

5. Print the source code.

6. Close the application you used to view the source code (unless it's Dreamweaver). Keep both Dreamweaver and your browser open for the next exercise.

3. Learn Techniques from the Code of Another Web Page

As you know, it is beneficial to examine the code of other sites that you admire to see how the designer created them. You can then apply the knowledge to your own work (not just copying and pasting their code into your Web pages). In this Challenge exercise, you compare the printouts of the Web page and the code from the previous exercise to learn how the designer of these pages has constructed different text styles, such as bold, italic, and the large font size.

1. Find three occurrences each of bold and italic in the Web-page printout. Identify, in the code printout, the coding methods used to create each style.

2. Identify the code that makes the text size of the top paragraph larger than the rest.

3. In the code, identify the document title.

4. Determine where the document title appears in the browser and in the printout from the browser.

5. Close your browser.

6. Return to Dreamweaver and close challenge1.html.

PORTFOLIO BUILDER

Recognize How Sites Are Structured

The underlying purpose of all Web sites is the presentation or delivery of information — also known as "content." For information to be useful, it must be easily accessible, which requires that it be broken out into discrete categories. The method employed to categorize the information contained in a site is known as the site's "structure." Your assignment is to create physical flowcharts that reflect how three different Web sites are structured.

1. Select three different sites to use for the assignment.

2. Draw a rectangle at the top of a blank piece of paper and label it "home" or "index".

3. For the first site you selected, determine what major categories fall under the top box. Examples might be "About Us", "Products", "Press Releases", or similar categories.

4. Draw boxes underneath the "home" box and label them appropriately according to the categories you identified in Step 3.

5. Many of these categories offer further information broken into their own individual pages. Continue drawing boxes for each subcategory until you've charted the site's top three levels.

6. Repeat the process for the other two sites you chose.

7. Keep the drawings around for reference when you're designing your own sites.

CHAPTER **3**

Applying Structure to Text

OBJECTIVES

In this chapter, you learn how to:

- Structure a document with headings

- Insert line breaks in a paragraph

- Format quotations with HTML tags

- Separate content with a horizontal rule

- Use ordered and unordered lists

- Change bullet and number styles with CSS

- Create definition lists

Why Would I Do This?

Creating print publications has much in common with creating Web sites — both require good content and effective design. Award-winning children's books, for instance, typically have authors who write the copy and illustrators and publishers who focus on the books' look and feel or design. Similarly, Web sites require quality content and effective layout and design. Quality Web content has two dimensions — it must be meaningful and useful to your visitors, but it must also be structured correctly so that it is understandable and accessible to those same visitors. In this chapter, you learn about the structure that underlies a Web page, why that structure is important, and how to create it.

In Chapter 2, you learned to plan the content of a Web site and to structure the site for easy use by visitors. You must also carefully structure the text that you put into your site, not just type it on a page and style it, as you might do for a print publication. The structure that you use is the initial basis for accessibility, a requirement for many Web sites and a key consideration for others.

Novice Web designers all too often use boldfacing and large-sized letters to indicate that particular text is a *heading* for the paragraphs following it. They may also use distinctive colors, fonts, and other stylistic changes. Blind users who use *screen-reader software* (computer applications that read the content aloud) to browse the Internet cannot see these stylistic changes. Instead they depend on the Web page's author to properly construct the page with headings, paragraphs, and other document structures that their screen readers can understand. Some such applications can be told (via keystrokes) to sound out just the headings, enabling listening users to skim through a document's headings in much the same way that sighted users skip from heading to heading to see if a document or Web page may contain what they are looking for. A lack of proper headings or improper use of headings confuses screen-reader users in the same way that a book without chapter breaks can confuse sighted readers.

Lack of proper document structure negatively impacts not only users of screen-reader software, but others as well. Some visitors use browsers that are character-based, such as the Lynx browser, which does not display styles. For their own needs, other visitors set up their browsers to use their own style settings in place of those of the Web page — paragraphs that the author made large-sized and bold text to suggest a heading would thus be reduced to mere plain-text *paragraphs*. Search engines rate a page's quality on a particular topic based, in part, on the content in headings. It is also just good form to use headings. As Patrick Lynch and Sarah Horton state in the *Web Style Guide,* "Don't get so lost in the novelty of Web pages that basic standards of editorial and graphic design are tossed aside." It is not surprising that some Web-design training organizations even offer courses in writing skills, such as "Business Writing Basics for the Web" by the HTML Writers Guild.

Many tags have *physical appearances*, a particular look or style. In order to differentiate them from body-text paragraphs, headings tend to have larger character sizes and boldfacing. Other tags may include italics or indenting, for example, as part of their physical appearance. However, structural tags, such as headings, paragraphs, lists, and block quotes, also have a *logical significance* — these tags play a role in the document's structure. Headings identify the content in the following paragraphs, *ordered lists* are numbered lists of information, and block quotes contain material quoted from another source. Novice designers commonly use the **\<blockquote\>** tag solely for its physical appearance — left and right indenting — or the **\<address\>** tag because it italicizes the text it encloses, ignoring the intended logical significance they convey. The reverse is also true: Many novice designers apply a larger font size and bold styling to a paragraph tag (**\<p\>**) to make it appear as a heading. It may look like a heading, but, stripped of the style applied to it, the heading is nothing more than a short paragraph, which is all a screen-reader user would "see." Clearly you need to understand the basics of good writing constructs and which *HTML* tags to use, after which you may apply specific style(s) to add more flair to your Web page's appearance.

In this chapter, you learn about block elements and list elements, and then use them to format text. ***Block elements*** are HTML tags that structure a unit (block) of text and separate such units with white space. Included in this group are heading tags, paragraph tags, the **\<blockquote\>** tag, and the horizontal-rule tag. You explore the line-break tag in this chapter. You also learn to use ordered lists, unordered lists, and definition lists.

VISUAL SUMMARY

In this chapter, you use Dreamweaver to format headings, block quotes, and lists. There are different methods for applying functions and features. You explore some of these components while you learn about document structure and its importance to the message that you would like your Web site to convey.

The Insert bar at the top of the Document window has several different modes. From the Insert bar pop-up menu, you may choose the mode that has the functions and features you need to perform the current task. In this chapter, you use the Insert bar's HTML and Text modes.

The Text Insert bar provides access to HTML tags that structure text in a Web page. You use the block-quote function to format large quotations, headings to identify the topics of content paragraphs, and list tags to format ordered (numbered) or unordered (bulleted) lists. While you probably haven't encountered ***definition lists*** outside of Web pages, in Web work you use them for associating a term with its definition or description.

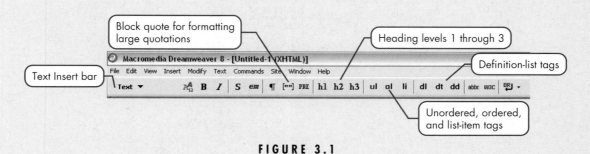

FIGURE 3.1

You use the Other Characters button at the right end of the Text Insert bar to insert characters that are helpful in text but not easily typed. As with most word-processing software, these characters are available from menus or dialog boxes. In Dreamweaver, the drop-down list provides access to the most common characters. The main button on the Text Insert bar displays an icon representing the last-used character. You can insert this character by just clicking the button — you don't need to select it from the list. At the bottom of the list is the Other Characters option, which opens the Insert Other Character dialog box, enabling you to select characters that you may need less frequently than those in the list.

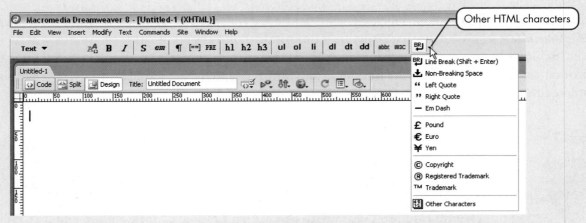

FIGURE 3.2

You use the Property inspector frequently in this and future projects. It may be the most commonly used component of the Dreamweaver interface, as it provides access to the most commonly used functions. The Format menu allows you to format paragraphs or headings. You may create unordered and ordered lists using the appropriate buttons in the Property inspector. Text Outdent and Text Indent buttons perform two functions: You can use them to turn off and on (respectively) the `<blockquote>` tag; when combined with either ordered or unordered lists, the Text Indent button enables you to nest a list in another list.

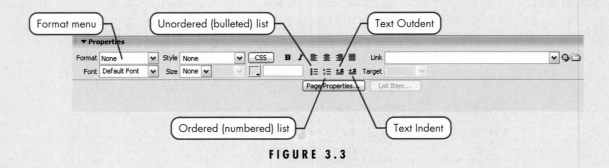

FIGURE 3.3

In addition to mouse-oriented controls (buttons and lists), Dreamweaver provides features for hand-coders in the Code window. This window offers many options for particular HTML tags that are not available from a button or list — all options for all HTML tags are available in the Code window. Dreamweaver also reduces the need to memorize the various options by presenting a Code-Hint pop-up list of valid options for a particular tag. *Valid* means that the code adheres to the standard set by the W3C. For example, <running> is not an HTML tag as defined by the W3C and, therefore, is not valid; neither are the Canadian/British spellings of "colour" and "centre." Although **bgcolor** (background color) may be an attribute of the **<body>** tag in HTML 4 and earlier, **bgcolor** is not an attribute of the **<img />** image tag, so using it in the **<img />** tag is not valid. The **bgcolor** attribute has been removed in XHTML 1.1; therefore, it is not valid even for the **<body>** tag in that version of XHTML. The Code-Hint pop-up list only displays attributes that are valid for the specific tag and HTML version.

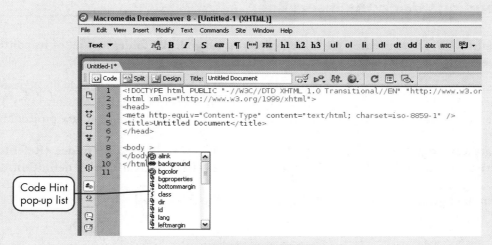

FIGURE 3.4

LESSON 1   Inserting Headings

There are six heading levels — the largest is Heading 1 and the smallest is Heading 6. Heading 4 is the same size as normal paragraph text. Heading tags, in addition to formatting the enclosed text as a block, also boldface the text.

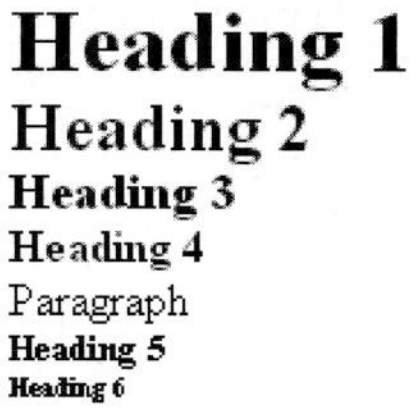

Heading 1
Heading 2
Heading 3
Heading 4
Paragraph
Heading 5
Heading 6

FIGURE 3.5

Every Web page should have a title in the Title bar and in the browser window. The document Title field (in the Document toolbar), which adds the document title to the `<title>` tag, does not produce visible text in the browser window (the area that is normally considered the Web page), but just in the browser's Title bar. The document title is primarily significant to search engines, but its absence from the body of the Web page makes that page harder for viewers to understand. For this reason, you should create a title for each page and use Heading 1 for emphasis. You may use Heading 2 to create either a secondary title or sections in the document. Similarly, you may use Heading 3 and so on to further subdivide the document.

The HTML code for headings is very simple and follows a simple pattern: `<h1>...</h1>` is for Heading 1, `<h2>...</h2>` is for Heading 2, and so on. Alignment (left, center, and right) is a headings attribute option, but the alignment attribute has been deprecated in favor of CSS. ***Deprecated*** means that an item is marked for removal in a future version of HTML; the phrase "in favor of CSS," used in this type of situation, suggests that the CSS property (`text-align`) should be used instead of the HTML (`align`) attribute.

Insert Headings Using the Insert Bar

1 **From the RF_Dreamweaver_L1 folder, copy the Chapter_03 folder and all of its contents and place it in your WIP folder.**

This step prepares all of the files you need for Chapter_03. These instructions do not repeat in any later projects. You may either copy the remaining Chapter folders from the RF_Dreamweaver_L1 folder to your WIP folder now, or you may continue to copy them as you begin each new project in this book.

2 **Create a site definition called "TO-P3" using the Chapter_03>TO-P3 folder. (Refer to the instructions in Skill Drill 1 of Chapter 2 if you need help in creating this definition.)**

3 **Open default.html by double-clicking the file in the Files panel.**

FIGURE 3.6

4 **Click anywhere in the top line of text "Tropiflora Online".**

5   Choose Text from the pop-up menu on the Insert bar.

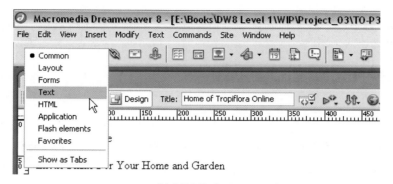

FIGURE 3.7

6   Click the h1 (Heading 1) button in the Insert bar.

Observe that the Tropiflora Online text block is now large and boldfaced. Heading 1 is the most important heading and produces the largest text.

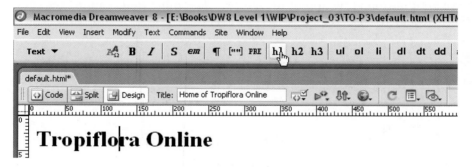

FIGURE 3.8

7   Click the `<h1>` tag in the Tag selector at the bottom of the Document window.

Observe that the whole line is selected. This indicates that the `<h1>` tag is a block tag because Heading 1 has been applied to the entire text block, even though you didn't select the text before applying

Heading 1. (In this figure, the Property inspector has been dragged up closer to the text so that you may easily see both.)

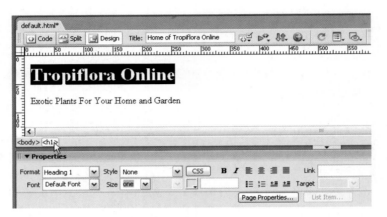

FIGURE 3.9

8 Observe that the Property inspector's Format field shows that the selected text uses the Heading 1 format.

9 Click the Split button at the top of the Document window and examine the code of the selected Heading 1 text.

FIGURE 3.10

10 Close the Code window by clicking the Design button at the Document window's top.

11 Click in the document's second line, "Exotic Plants For Your Home and Garden". Click the h2 button on the Insert bar to format the line as a Heading 2 block.

FIGURE 3.11

12   Choose File>Close to close the document, saving the changes when prompted.

To Extend Your Knowledge . . .

THE HEADINGS ARE TOO LARGE

A common complaint of novice Web designers is that the headings are too large. It is not uncommon to see Heading 3 as the top heading of a page because the designer felt Headings 1 and 2 were too large. Using headings provides structure to the document, but the headings' appearance is a matter of style. You can easily modify the style and preserve the document structure. If it is appropriate to use Heading 2, then use it and style it smaller if it is too large for your design. We discuss creating and modifying styles in *Essentials for Design: Dreamweaver 8 Level 1*.

LESSON 2   Inserting Line Breaks

Paragraphs are large blocks of text with white space between them. When you press the Enter/Return key after typing, you create a new paragraph with white space separating it from what precedes or follows. There are times, however, when you need to keep a block of text together and treat it as a single unit but want parts of it to appear on successive lines. Consider the format of an address, for example — the entire block of text is the full address, but you usually separate the components of an address onto different lines.

Line breaks keep the content in the same paragraph block but force a new line of text to start at the left margin. The line-break code is very useful when you want to separate items but don't want the items to be in different paragraphs. In this lesson, you insert line breaks using two methods. You also examine the line-break tag, `<br />`, in the Code window.

Insert Line Breaks in a Paragraph

1   Right/Control-click contact.html in the Files panel and choose Open.

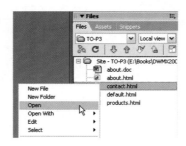

FIGURE 3.12

2   **Click in the empty paragraph space between the Heading 3 lines "Mailing Address:" and "Phone Numbers:".**

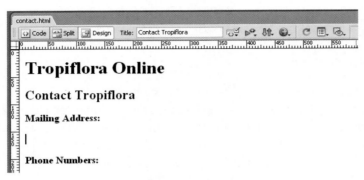

FIGURE 3.13

3   **Type** `Tropiflora`, **press Shift-Enter/Return, and type** `3530 Tallevast Road`.

Observe that the space between the two lines you just typed is smaller than the space between other blocks. A line break just forces text onto another line, but the text remains in the same block.

FIGURE 3.14

4   **Press Shift-Enter/Return, type** `Sarasota, FL`, **press Shift-Enter/Return, and type** `34243-3890` **to complete the address.**

5   **Click the `<p>` paragraph tag from the Tag selector at the bottom of the Document window.**

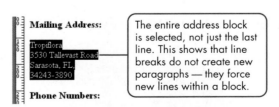

FIGURE 3.15

6 Click the Split button and observe the code in the Code window.

> There is only one paragraph block because there is a single pair of opening (<p>) and closing (</p>) paragraph tags.

```
11    <h3>Mailing Address:</h3>
12    <p>Tropiflora<br />
13        3530 Tallevast Road<br />
14        Sarasota, FL,<br />
15        34243-3890
16    </p>
17    <h3>Phone Numbers:</h3>
```

> Each line (except the last) ends with the line-break (<br />) tag.

FIGURE 3.16

7 Click the Design button to close the Code window.

8 Click in the blank paragraph between "Phone Numbers:" and "Email Address:".

9 Type `Telephone: (941) 351-2267`.

10 Click the drop-down list arrow to the right of the Line Break button (the last button on the Insert bar), and choose Line Break from the list.

This is another method for inserting a line break. You can also use this method to insert other special characters.

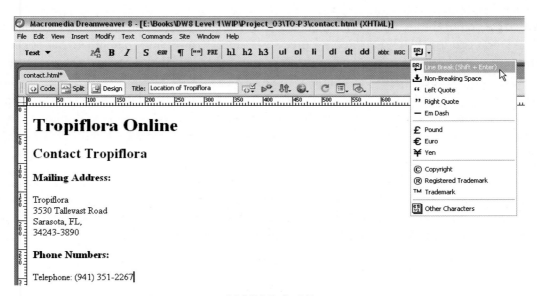

FIGURE 3.17

? If You Have Problems

If the Insert bar does not display the Text options, click the pop-up menu on the left of the Insert bar and choose Text.

---

11   Type `Fax:` `(941) 351-6985` **on the new line.**

12   **Choose File>Close to close contact.html, saving the changes when prompted.**

To Extend Your Knowledge...

OTHER METHODS OF CREATING BREAKS

The break tag (`<br />`) is often used to break a block into separate lines without creating a new paragraph for each line. By default, paragraph tags insert extra white space between the paragraphs, whereas a `<br />` tag simply pushes the text to the next line. When formatting an address, you would commonly use the `<br />` tag to split each part of an address onto different lines. However, you can use the CSS `display` property to create the appearance of breaks in content.

Paragraphs and headings are blocks: The text in each is separated from other blocks by white space above and below. The anchor tag (`<a>`), the `<strong>` tag, and many other tags are inline tags. **Inline tags** do not create blocks from the enclosed content but apply their style or functionality within the blocks. You can use the CSS `display` property to modify the inline content's layout appearance. For example, a paragraph containing only two links, such as `<p><a href="home.html">` Home `</a>` `<a href="about.html">`About Us`</a></p>`, appears as two links on the same line. However, if you add `style="display: block"` to each of the opening anchor tags, you change the default layout of the anchor tag from inline to block, forcing the links to display on separate lines as if they were blocks. In this way, you can create the appearance of line breaks using CSS instead of the `<br />` tag.

You may be thinking that `<br />` is much less to type each time than `style="display: block"`, but there are more efficient and advanced ways of creating and applying CSS to eliminate the duplication and make it simple to change the layout of the anchor tag to a block appearance. We discuss these methods, embedded and external style sheets, in *Essentials for Design: Dreamweaver 8 Level 2.*

LESSON 3 Formatting a Large Quotation on a Web Page

While you or your associates will probably write most of the content on your Web sites, at times you may want to use material written by others. For instance, you might wish to use a quotation from someone else. The block quote is one of two methods you can use to format it.

The block quote, as its name suggests, is meant to format a large quotation, one large enough to warrant its own paragraph. The `<blockquote>` tag may contain one or more paragraphs, and you must surround each paragraph with the `<p>` paragraph tag. The minimum application of the `<blockquote>` tag is `<blockquote>...</blockquote>`. However, Dreamweaver also inserts paragraph tags within the `<blockquote>` tag, which is perfectly valid but not necessary if your quote consists of only one paragraph. If your quote consists of multiple paragraphs, one pair of `<blockquote>` tags surrounds the complete quote and `<p>` tags should surround each paragraph within.

The default appearance of the `<blockquote>` tag indents the paragraph's left and right sides. For this reason, the `<blockquote>` tag is one of the most misused HTML tags. Novice Web designers often use this tag just for its indented appearance. Many Web-design applications must also take the blame for this because they label the On/Off buttons for block quotes with Text Indent and Text Outdent, as if to suggest that only style is affected; in fact, as you have just learned, the tag also has a structural purpose. Dreamweaver uses Text Indent/Outdent buttons and the Block Quote button to provide the block-quote structure.

The quotation's source is known as the *citation*. The `<blockquote>` tag supports this concept with the `cite` attribute. This attribute supports only a Web link as the quotation's source, but the `<blockquote>` tag does not provide a link to the quotation's source. Only the Mozilla browsers allow you to view the citation's source as a property of the `<blockquote>` tag; a visitor using any other browser must view the Web page's source code to find the citation source.

In this lesson, you insert a quotation into a Web page and format the paragraphs as a block quote. You also add the citation source to the `<blockquote>` tag using the Code window.

Insert a Block Quote

1 Open about.html from the Files panel.

2 Click in the empty paragraph space below the About Tropiflora Heading 2 block.

3 If you are using a Windows system, choose File>Import>Word Document, and select about.doc. Then select Text with Structure (Paragraphs, Lists, Tables) at the bottom of the dialog box, uncheck Clean Up Word Paragraph Spacing, and click Open.

FIGURE 3.18

4   If you are using a Macintosh, open about.txt, select all of the text in the file, copy it to the clipboard, and then close about.txt. Paste the text into about.html below the About Tropiflora Heading 2 block.

5   Click in the second inserted paragraph that begins with "Our desire was to make Tropiflora . . .".

6   Click the Text Indent button in the Property inspector.

Observe that the paragraph is indented from both the left and right edges of the Document window.

FIGURE 3.19

7   Click in the following paragraph that begins with "Come visit us online . . .". Click the Block Quote button near the middle of the Text Insert bar.

This is another method for formatting a block as a block quote.

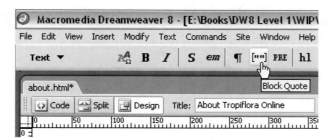

FIGURE 3.20

8   **Click the `<blockquote>` tag from the Tag selector at the bottom of the Document window.**

Observe that both paragraphs are selected. The **`<blockquote>`** tag may contain multiple paragraphs.

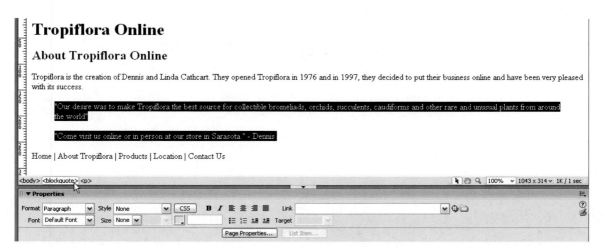

FIGURE 3.21

9   **Click the Split button.**

10   **Move the insertion point inside the `<blockquote>` tag just before the closing angle bracket (>), and press the Spacebar once.**

A pop-up menu of ***attributes*** (options available for tags) appears.

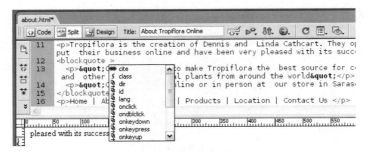

FIGURE 3.22

11   **Press "c" to select the first attribute, `cite`. Press Enter/Return to accept the selection.**

Dreamweaver's HTML editor makes it very simple to choose attributes for each tag — only the appropriate attributes for each tag display in the pop-up menu; typing part of the attribute name selects it from the list.

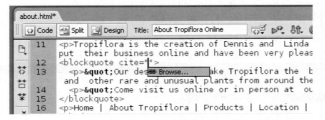

FIGURE 3.23

12   **Type `http://www.tropiflora.com` between the quotation marks.**

The Browse option allows you to select a Web page using the File dialog box. However, if the quotation's source is a remote Web page, you must type its URL between the quotation marks.

FIGURE 3.24

13   **Switch back to the Design view. Press Control/Command-S to save the changes to about.html, leaving it open for the next lesson.**

To Extend Your Knowledge . . .

THE CASE FOR HTML

Do you know the origin of the terms "uppercase" and "lowercase"? When printing-press operators of the nineteenth century and earlier required characters for their presses, they would retrieve the characters from their storage compartments, which were arranged in cases. Capital letters were stored in the upper case, and the smaller letters were stored in the lower case.

All HTML code — tags, attributes, and attribute options — is typed in lowercase characters. Web designers of the 1990s, whether they used a WYSIWYG application or hand-coded the HTML, commonly used uppercase characters for tags, attributes, and attribute options to distinguish them from the mixed-case characters of body text. Beginning with XHTML 1.0, however, it was recommended that all HTML, CSS, and JavaScript code be written in lowercase characters. As you recall, XHTML is an improvement on HTML and brings it closer to **XML** (eXtensible Markup Language). XML requires all tags, attributes, and attribute options to be in lowercase characters. This consistency ensures that an XML or XHTML browser doesn't have to convert uppercase tags to lowercase before interpreting them, thus reducing its processing time.

The only HTML tag that may use uppercase is the **DTD (Document Type Definition)** tag, otherwise known as the "Doctype." This tag precedes the opening `<html>` tag and, for that reason, may be written in uppercase. The Doctype that you commonly use with Dreamweaver is `<!DOCTYPE html PUBLIC "-//W3C//DTD XHTML 1.0 Transitional//EN" "http://www.w3.org /TR/xhtml1/DTD/xhtml1-transitional.dtd">` which is for XHTML 1.0 Transitional.

LESSON 4   Inserting a Short Quotation in a Paragraph

The `<q>` or quote tag is an *inline* tag — its content is contained in a block. You cannot use it by itself to create a block. You must insert an inline quotation into a paragraph or other block. This is different from the block quote, which formats its contents as a paragraph.

The physical appearance of the `<q>` quote tag surrounds the quoted text with quotation marks, although the text itself is not styled any differently than normal paragraph text. While the Opera and Mozilla browsers display the quotation marks, Internet Explorer does not. Given Internet Explorer's dominance in the browser market, it is tempting to counter this deficiency by manually inserting quotation marks in the text. However, the W3C specifically recommends against this to prevent two sets of quotation marks in compliant browsers. Older browsers do not display the quotation marks around text that is marked up with the `<q>` tag; instead they display the text using the default text styles of the surrounding paragraph.

You may use CSS, however, to style the text in the `<q>` tag, such as by using italics or a different color. This provides some indication that the text is a quotation. You should ensure that phraseology of adjacent text makes it clear that the specific text is a quotation, such as, "Queen Elizabeth was heard to say *Two lumps of sugar, please* when she placed her order for tea at Burger King." We use italics here to highlight the quotation, but even without the quotation marks, the quotation is distinct from the surrounding text.

In this lesson, you use the Tag chooser, an excellent utility for inserting HTML tags (and other tags) that are unavailable from the menus. The Tag chooser also enables you to apply the tag's attributes. The `<q>` tag, for example, is not available from any of the menus and must be inserted via the Code window or the Tag chooser.

Insert the Quote Tag

1   **In the open about.html file, move the insertion point to the end of the block quote (to the right of "Dennis").**

2   **Press Enter/Return once, and then click the Text Outdent button in the Property inspector.**

FIGURE 3.25

3   **Type** Linda says These plants bring joy to our lives, let them bring joy to yours.

4   **Drag to select the text from "These" to "yours".**

5   **Click the Tag chooser from the Common Insert bar.**

? If You Have Problems

If the Insert bar shows Text at the left or anything other than Common, click Text (or the other word) and choose Common from the list.

6   **In the top-left window of the Tag Chooser dialog box, click the plus sign/triangle to the left of HTML Tags.**

7   **Click Formatting and Layout, scroll down, and click q, then click Insert.**

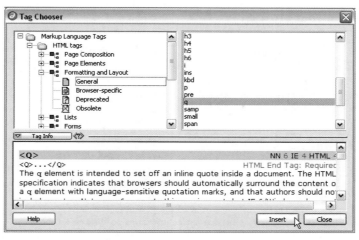

FIGURE 3.26

8 | In the Tag Editor dialog box, type `http://www.tropiflora.com` in the Cite field, click OK, and then click Close.

The first time you clicked Insert in the Tag Chooser dialog box after selecting **q**, the **<q>** tag was inserted into the document. The Tag Editor dialog box allows you to apply some of the attributes available for the **<q>** tag; you don't want to insert another one.

FIGURE 3.27

9   Preview the page in your browser.

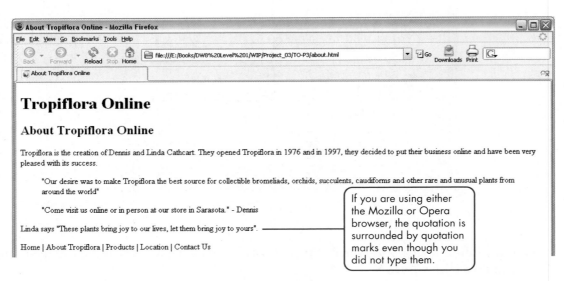

FIGURE 3.28

10   Return to Dreamweaver.

11   Click the Design button and then close about.html.

To Extend Your Knowledge . . .

THE CITE ATTRIBUTE OF <BLOCKQUOTE> AND <Q> TAGS

The primary purpose of the cite attribute is to identify the URL of the quotation's source. However, only the Mozilla-based browsers (Mozilla, Netscape 6+, Firefox, and Camino) actually use this attribute by displaying the URL of the citation in the Element Properties dialog box. When you Right/Command-click the quotation and choose Properties, the citation's URL displays. The URL, however, is not a link; you cannot click the URL in the Element Properties dialog box to go to the citation source.

FIGURE 3.29

LESSON 5 | Separating Content Using a Horizontal Rule

The term *horizontal rule* comes from the print-publishing arena and is simply a horizontal line. Although it is not used to format text, it is considered a block element because it forces apart other blocks when inserted. You cannot have a horizontal rule and a paragraph on the same line; both are blocks, so they separate from each other with white space above or below.

The horizontal-rule tag, `<hr />`, has very few attributes—`width`, `color`, `noshade`, and `size`—but all have been deprecated in favor of CSS. The purpose of the `noshade` attribute is to eliminate the horizontal rule's 3-D default appearance and make it just a flat colored line. Although no CSS property is yet available to replace the horizontal rule's 3-D appearance, you can replace all other attributes of horizontal rules using CSS.

The horizontal rule is one of the few elements of HTML that does not contain content yet behaves like a block element by pushing the following paragraph below it. In this lesson, you insert horizontal rules to divide the main content of Web pages from the text that becomes navigation links in a later chapter.

Insert a Horizontal Rule

1 Open default.html.

2 Click in front of the "H" of Home in the page's bottom paragraph.

3 Choose HTML from the pop-up menu of the Insert bar.

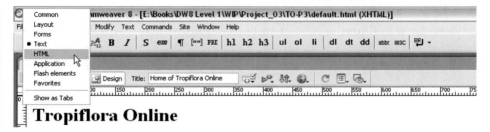

FIGURE 3.30

4 Click the Horizontal Rule button (first button on the left) to insert a horizontal rule.

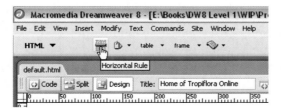

FIGURE 3.31

5 **Click at the end of the bottom line of text to deselect the horizontal rule.**

It is difficult to see the true appearance of the horizontal rule when it is selected.

FIGURE 3.32

6 **Close, saving the changes to default.html.**

7 **Open about.html.**

8 **Click in front of "Home" in the bottom paragraph.**

9 **Choose Insert>HTML>Horizontal Rule to insert a horizontal rule from the menu.**

10 **Close, saving the changes to about.html.**

11 **Open contact.html and products.html and insert a horizontal rule (using either method) at the same position in each page. Close, saving the changes to each when finished.**

To Extend Your Knowledge . . .

STYLING HORIZONTAL RULES

It is possible to apply CSS to horizontal rules to replace the deprecated width, color, and size (height) attributes and to create a style or effect that is not possible without CSS. For example, using CSS, you could create a style for a horizontal rule, such as `style="width: 80%; height: 40px; background-image: url(flowers.gif)"`. This means that the horizontal rule would be 80% of the browser-window width, 40 pixels in height, and have a repeating background of a flowers.gif image. By using this combination of style properties for the horizontal rule, you transform the plain line into a row of flowers, but it remains a horizontal rule structurally for any browser that does not display CSS.

FIGURE 3.33

CSS enables us to create styles and effects that we could not achieve without adding false structure before CSS. You can create many of those effects with CSS and without adding any further structure to the Web page. For example, it was common to place content in a table to achieve a particular visual effect. If the page used CSS instead, a visitor whose browser does not render the stylistic appearances (such as a screen reader or a Braille device) would not have to wade through table structures whose only purpose was to create that particular effect. CSS allows the designer to maintain the structure prepared by the author while permitting freedom to design.

LESSON 6   Creating Ordered and Unordered Lists

Lists might also be considered block structures, since they separate their content from other content; however, they have a special format that affects the individual items they list. Lists also have a more complicated tag structure — two or three different tags are necessary, depending on the list type. There are three types of lists you can use: ordered, unordered, and definition.

The two most common lists are ordered and unordered lists. They look similar except that a number precedes ordered list items and a bullet precedes unordered list items. Other computer applications, such as word-processing or other Web-design software, refer to these types of lists as "numbered" and "bulleted" lists, respectively. Your decision about which list to use depends on whether or not the first item should be done before the second or if the first item is more important than the second. If you don't want to suggest an order of importance or procedure, use an ***unordered list***.

Create an Ordered List

Ordered lists have two tags — the ordered list `<ol>` tag and the list item `<li>` tag. The `<ol>` tag indicates that the list is numbered. The `<li>` tag defines the list item's beginning and ending, just as a paragraph tag defines a paragraph's beginning and ending. If an ordered list has three items, there is one pair of ordered list tags (`<ol>...</ol>`) surrounding three pairs of list-item tags (`<li>...</li>`), each of which surrounds the list-item text.

An ordered list's physical appearances are the number preceding each list item and the indentation of each item (and its number) from the left margin. Dreamweaver simplifies your creation of ordered and unordered lists by reducing the process to clicking a button and pressing Enter/Return.

1 **Open products.html.**

2 **Move the insertion point into the blank line below the "Top Sellers" heading.**

3 **Click the Ordered List button in the Property inspector.**

Notice that Dreamweaver creates the first number for you.

FIGURE 3.34

4 **Type Aechmea fulgens and press Enter/Return.**

Dreamweaver creates the second number.

5 **Type Hernia zebrina, press Enter/Return, and type Tillandsia latifola.**

These are the scientific (Latin) names for three tropical plants.

FIGURE 3.35

6 **Click the <li> tag in the Tag selector.**

Observe that only the last line is selected. The **<li>** tag is the list-item tag and is required for each item in the list.

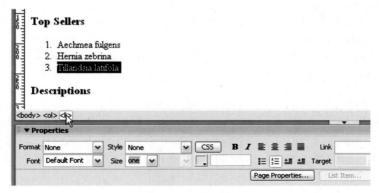

FIGURE 3.36

7   **Click the `<ol>` tag in the Tag selector.**

The `<ol>` tag is the ordered list tag. The entire list is an ordered list, so selecting the `<ol>` tag selects the whole list.

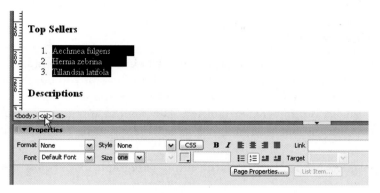

FIGURE 3.37

8   **Switch to the Code and Design view and examine the selected code in the Code window.**

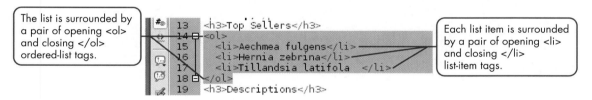

FIGURE 3.38

9   **Switch back to the Design view; to deselect the ordered list, click in the Document window outside the ordered list.**

10   **Choose File>Save to save the changes to the document. Leave the document open for the next exercise.**

To Extend Your Knowledge . . .

EXITING FROM LISTS

In these exercises, you don't ever have to exit a list because the next steps in the exercise ask you to click with the mouse somewhere else in the page, away from the list. However, on your own, you will need to create a list and then, at the end of the list, you may wonder how to exit it. Doing so is very easy: press Enter/Return once more to create another number or bullet and then press Enter/Return again. This removes the empty list item, and the insertion point will be below and outside of the list. This technique works with ordered, unordered, and definition lists.

Create an Unordered List

As discussed earlier, you should use unordered lists if you don't want to imply an order of progression or importance. The tag format is virtually identical to that of ordered lists, except you use a pair of unordered list tags (`<ul>...</ul>`). You use list item tags (`<li>...</li>`) in the same way—the ordered or unordered tags determine whether the list is numbered or bulleted. The physical appearances of an unordered list are the bullet preceding each list item and the indentation of each item (and its bullet) from the left margin.

1   **In the open products.html file, click in the empty paragraph space below the "Products" heading.**

2   **Click the Unordered List button in the Property inspector.**

Notice that Dreamweaver creates a bullet character in preparation for the first list item.

FIGURE 3.39

3   **Type** `Bromeliads` **and press Enter/Return. Type** `Succulents` **and press Enter/Return. Type** `Tillandsias`.

FIGURE 3.40

4   **Click the `<ul>` tag in the Tag selector.**

5   **Switch to the Code and Design view and examine the selected code.**

Notice that the HTML coding for an unordered list is very similar to that of an ordered list, except that the `<ol>` and `</ol>` tags are replaced with `<ul>` and `</ul>`. These tags determine which type of list is created — ordered or unordered.

```
     10    <h1>Tropiflora Online</h1>
     11    <h2>Products</h2>
     12 ⊟  <ul>
     13        <li>Bromeliads</li>
     14        <li>Succulents</li>
     15        <li>Tillandsias</li>
     16 ⊟  </ul>
     17    <h3>Top Sellers</h3>
```

FIGURE 3.41

6 Return to Design view, and click outside the selected text to deselect it.

7 Save the changes, and leave the document open for the next lesson.

To Extend Your Knowledge . . .

NAVIGATION BARS = UNORDERED LISTS

You might think that unordered lists are not used very often. However, the current teaching-by-accessibility and Web-standards advocates is that navigation bars are simply lists of links. You might then think that an unordered list of links would destroy any design ideas you had for the navigation bar.

Not true, because you can use various properties of CSS to style the list of links. For example, `list-style-type:none` removes the bullets, `list-style-image:url(yellow_ball.gif)` adds a custom graphic as the bullet character, and `margin-left:0px` eliminates the left indent of the list items. You can take advantage of many other CSS properties to re-create your design while still using the unordered list as the structure of the navigation-bar list of links. This is an excellent example of the separation of structure from presentation, where you use HTML for the content's structure and CSS for styling the content.

LESSON 7 Styling Lists

Several different styles are available for ordered and unordered lists. The default numbering format of an ordered list is the standard Arabic numerals. With styles, however, you can also have uppercase and lowercase alphabetic characters and uppercase and lowercase Roman numerals (I, II, III and i, ii, iii).

The default style of unordered lists is a solid disc as the bullet character. The other two available styles are the open circle and a solid square. Using styles, you can also replace the bullet characters with a small graphic (even an animated graphic) but not with any other character (unless you have made that character into a graphic).

In the CSS code, you use **`list-style-type:square`** to change a bullet character to a square. The other options are **`disc`** and **`circle`**, but you can also remove a bullet character entirely using `list-style-type:none`. To change a numbered-list counter to uppercase alphabetic characters such as A, B, C, you would use `list-style-type:upper-alpha`. The other options are `upper-roman, lower-alpha, lower-roman`, and `decimal`. It may seem strange to list the default decimal style — why list the decimal style if all you have to do to use that style is make no change to the list style? There are two situations where this may be useful. If you nest lists, generally browsers display a different counter style for each level of nesting. You may want to override the default for a particular nesting level to set the counter style to decimal, or you may prefer to set all levels to decimal. Another situation might be that you set all ordered lists on your Web site to use `upper-roman`, but in one particular case, you want to override the new default and set that list to `decimal`.

You may also replace the bullet character for an unordered list with a small graphic. For example, the style definition `list-style-image: url(star.gif)` inserts a star graphic as the bullet character. However, you cannot add alt text to the graphic, so do not use a graphic that requires reading because this information will not be passed on to screen-reading software.

Change the Bullet Style of an Unordered List

1   **In the open products.html file, click the CSS button to open the CSS Panel from the Property inspector.**

FIGURE 3.42

2   **In the CSS Styles panel, click the All button to switch to All (Document) Mode.**

All (Document) Mode displays all CSS styles created for the current document, whereas Current Selection Mode shows the CSS styles applied to the tag closest to the insertion point. There are no CSS styles for this document at all: both modes are empty.

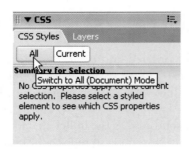

FIGURE 3.43

3   Right/Control-click in the CSS Styles panel and select New . . . from the Context menu.

FIGURE 3.44

4   Choose Tag as the Selector type.

5   Select `ul` from near the bottom of the Tag list.

6   In the Define In section, click This Document Only and click OK.

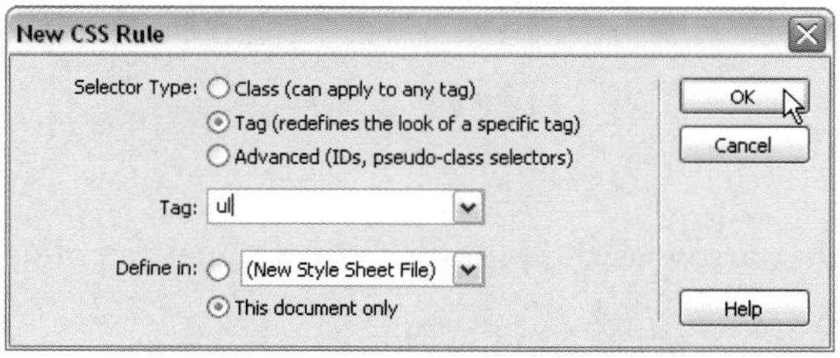

FIGURE 3.45

7   Choose the List category in the CSS Style Definition dialog box.

8   Choose `circle` from the Type list and click OK.

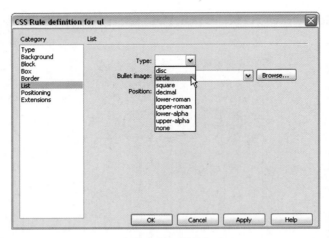

FIGURE 3.46

9 Notice that the bullet characters in front of all list items in the unordered list change to circle characters.

FIGURE 3.47

10 Click the down-pointing arrow at the top of the CSS panel to collapse the panel.

11 Save the changes to products.html, and leave it open for the next lesson.

To Extend Your Knowledge . . .

DREAMWEAVER, HTML STYLES, AND CSS

There are two methods of changing the styles in a page: HTML and CSS. Dreamweaver 8 has reduced support for HTML styles and has increased its support for CSS styles.

HTML styles use presentation tags and attributes to apply styles (which add only appearance). An example of a presentation tag is the `<font>` tag, which enables designers to specify the color and typeface through its attributes (such as `<font face="Arial" color="blue">`). The type attribute of the `<ul>` and `<ol>` tags enables you to change the bullet type, such as `<ul type="square">`, or *counter*, such as `<ol type="lower-alpha">`. (The term "counter" here indicates an incremented value, such as A, B, C; a, b, c; I, II, III; or i, ii, iii.) All of those options are possible counter methods, created respectively by `upper-alpha`, `lower-alpha`, `upper-roman`, and `lower-roman` values of the CSS property `list-style-type`.

HTML did not originally include presentation tags or attributes, but designers requested these options, so they were added in later versions of HTML. Since then, however, the W3C has rethought the purpose of HTML. With the release of HTML 4 in 1997, they also released CSS1 (version 1 of CSS). They intended that CSS would handle presentation and HTML would be reserved for document structure. Web designers commonly use the phrase "separation of structure from presentation" to describe this relationship between HTML and CSS.

Despite the years since the release of HTML 4, there has been very slow readoption of HTML for structure only and CSS for presentation. Web-design software is now making more and more use of CSS for presentation. Dreamweaver 8, for example, primarily uses CSS for presentation — at times without even informing the user that CSS has been applied.

In this book, we deliberately emphasize CSS styles and largely omit HTML styles. There are many more CSS styles than HTML styles, they are much more powerful, and designers who use CSS are much further ahead than those using HTML styles.

LESSON 8   Creating Definition Lists

Definition lists are a bit more complicated structurally than either ordered or unordered lists. Whereas ordered and unordered lists consist of two tags — the tag that defines the list type and the list item tag — the definition list uses three tags.

The definition list has a definition-list tag that defines the list type and indicates where the definition list begins (`<dl>`) and ends (`</dl>`) (like the ordered and unordered lists that use the `<ol>` and `<ul>` tags, respectively). However, the ordered and unordered lists have only one nested tag, the `<li>` tag, whereas the definition list has two. The term or phrase being defined, known as the "definition term," uses the `<dt>...</dt>` pair of tags; the definition or description of the term or phrase, known as the "definition description," uses the `<dd>...</dd>` pair of tags.

Defining words or phrases is not the only way to use definition lists. You may also use them to describe items or concepts. For that reason, it may be easier to think of definition lists as associative lists — the term and the description are associated with each other.

Create a Definition List

1   **In the open products.html file, move the insertion point to the blank paragraph below "Descriptions".**

2 Click the dl (Definition List) button on the Text Insert bar.

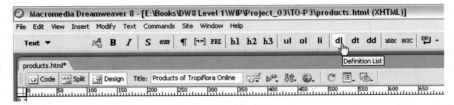

FIGURE 3.48

3 Type `Bromeliads` **and press Enter/Return.**

The insertion point is indented in preparation for the description of the term "Bromeliads".

FIGURE 3.49

4 **Type:** `Bromeliads are excellent indoor plants. They have colorful, long-lasting inflorescences and some have brilliantly colored foliage as well. View our bromeliads.` **Press Enter/Return.**

The insertion point returns to the left margin in preparation for another definition term.

5 **Type** `Succulents` **and press Enter/Return.** `Type Plants that have adjusted to the arid and semi-arid regions of the world are known as cacti and succulents. View our succulents.` **Press Enter/Return.**

6 **Type** `Tillandsias` **and press Enter/Return.** `Type Tillandsias, or airplants, have been called the world's most unusual plants. Tillandsias are very easy to care for, exotic to look at and are a delightful addition to any home. View our tillandsias.`

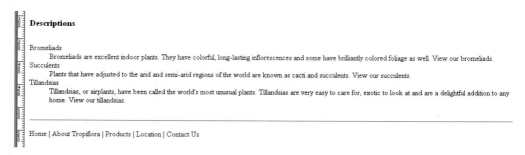

FIGURE 3.50

7 | **Click the definition term "Bromeliads" and observe the Tag selector.**

The Tag selector shows both the `<dl>` and `<dt>` tags, indicating that Bromeliads is text within the definition-term tag within a definition list.

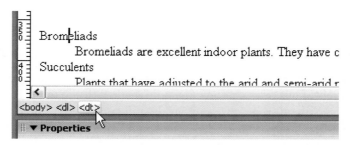

FIGURE 3.51

8 | **Click in the definition description of Bromeliads.**

Note that the Tag selector indicates that the description is in a `<dd>` tag.

9 | **Click the `<dl>` tag in the Tag selector.**

10 | **Switch to Split view and examine the code.**

The definition list begins and ends with the `<dl>` tags. The `<dt>` tags surround the definition terms, and the `<dd>` tags surround the definition descriptions. (You may have to use the scroll bar to the right of the Code window to see all of the definition-list code.)

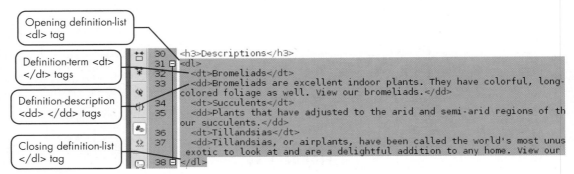

FIGURE 3.52

11   **Return to Design view.**

12   **Close products.html, saving your changes.**

SUMMARY

In this chapter you learned about the importance of structure in text and how to create it in Dreamweaver. You discovered the different levels of headings and how to apply them with the Insert bar and the Property inspector. You became familiar with the distinctions between the different types of block elements, as well as some items that have similar roles but are not block elements. You learned how to insert line breaks and horizontal rules. You now understand the difference between text formatted as paragraphs and text formatted as block quotes. You learned how to create ordered, unordered, and definition lists, and you became familiar with the distinctions between them. You learned how to use CSS to change the bullet and counter type for ordered and unordered lists. You also explored how to use the components of a definition list.

KEY TERMS

Attributes

Block elements

Citation

Counter

Definition list

Deprecated

DTD (Document Type Definition)

Heading

Horizontal rule

Inline

Inline tags

Logical significance

Ordered list

Paragraph

Physical appearances

Presentational HTML

Screen-reader software

Unordered list

Valid

XML

CAREERS IN DESIGN

THE DIFFERENT FACES OF WEB DEVELOPERS

Anyone reading this book who has had experience in the print industry understands the vast difference between the roles of creative personnel and production professionals. In that arena, designers are responsible for developing the look and feel that shapes the perceptions and experiences of the audience. Once the designer has finalized the layout of the piece, the production phase of the workflow begins. Print production professionals are responsible for ensuring the quality of the images, the clarity of the typography, and the other processes required to reproduce the design in quantity.

In the world of Web design, the same situation exists. Web designers are responsible for the look, feel, and effectiveness of the visitor's experience; their responsibility ends there. The next step in the process lies in the hands of Web developers — the programmers, database experts, and site maintenance professionals responsible for the "wiring" of the site.

The skills required for these two types of positions, while equally important, are dramatically different. This holds true in all aspects of professional communication. Creative talent ensures the quality of the user experience, while technical expertise ensures proper preparation and delivery of the content to the end user. As your career matures, it will become apparent on which side of the fence your talents lie — creative or technical.

CHECKING CONCEPTS AND TERMS

SCREEN ID

Identify the indicated areas from the following list:

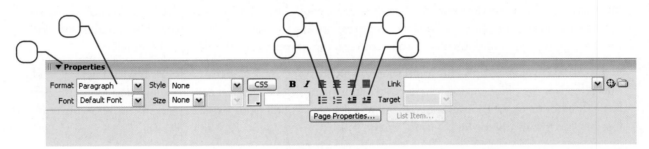

FIGURE 3.53

a. Text Insert bar

b. Text Indent

c. Property inspector

d. Headings

e. Unordered list

f. Definition-list tags

g. Unordered- and Ordered-list tags

h. Block-quote tag

i. Text Outdent

j. Ordered list

k. Format menu

MULTIPLE CHOICE

Circle the letter of the correct answer for each of the following:

1. Information on a Web page must be structured so that it is _____ .
   a. meaningful and useful
   b. understandable and accessible
   c. good content with effective design
   d. All the above

2. The best way to structure text content on a Web page is by using _____ .
   a. boldfacing and large-size letters
   b. distinctive colors, fonts, and stylistic changes
   c. headings, paragraphs, lists, and block quotes
   d. horizontal rules and indented paragraphs

3. Formatting tools similar to those used in word-processing applications can be found in the _____ .
   a. Design panel
   b. Property inspector
   c. Layout Insert bar
   d. Page Properties dialog box

4. Headings identify _____ .
   a. numbered lists of information
   b. material quoted from another source
   c. the content in the following paragraphs
   d. left and right indenting

5. Block elements are _____ .
   a. HTML tags that structure a unit of text
   b. HTML tags that separate blocks of text with white space
   c. paragraph and horizontal-rule tags
   d. All of the above

6. Which text format is the largest on the computer screen?
   a. Heading 6
   b. Heading 2
   c. Paragraph
   d. Heading 1

7. Which of the following is not true of the Text Insert bar?
   a. It provides access to HTML tags that structure text.
   b. It allows text to be inserted from word-processing text files.

   c. It provides access to characters such as a copyright or trademark symbol.
   d. It allows insertion of line breaks.

8. The text in the `<title>` tag appears in the browser window.
   a. True
   b. False

9. In which of the following cases should you use a line break?
   a. Between two paragraphs
   b. After a Heading 1 or 2
   c. Before an ordered or unordered list
   d. Between the text lines of an address

10. The most commonly used component of the Dreamweaver interface is the _____ .
   a. Tag chooser
   b. Help menu
   c. Property inspector
   d. Insert Other Characters dialog box

DISCUSSION QUESTIONS

1. Explain the difference in designing and laying out Web pages, considering logical significance rather than just physical appearance.

2. Pick a recipe from a local newspaper, your favorite cookbook, or any other source. Discuss how you would use at least three HTML document structures to format the recipe as a Web page. Explain why you would choose those document structures and which others you might also consider.

3. Imagine that you have been given a list of courses offered by the Graphic Arts Department of a local school to format for a Web page. Included for each course are the course code, course title, course description, and course prerequisite. Discuss which type of list (or lists) you would choose to present this information, and explain your reasoning.

SKILL DRILL

Skill Drill exercises reinforce project skills. Each skill that is reinforced is the same as, or nearly the same as, a skill we presented in the lessons. We provide detailed instructions in a step-by-step format. You should work through the Skill Drills in order.

In the Skill Drills section of this chapter, you have the responsibility for completing some pages for the Jungle Cat World Web site. The pages are unstructured (all text is plain paragraphs), and some information is missing.

Your job is to add headings and ordered and unordered lists. You must also create a nested list, change the style of an ordered list, and insert some special HTML characters.

1. Create Headings Using the Property Inspector

1. Create a site definition for the folder Chapter_03>JCW-P3 and name it JCW-P3.

2. Open admission.html from the Files panel.

3. Click the top line, "Admission".

4. Choose Heading 1 from the Format menu of the Property inspector.

   This Web page is about admission rates for individuals and groups, so this heading — the main title for the page — must be set to Heading 1.

5. Click the third line, "Day Passes", and set the format to Heading 2.

6. Click the fourth line, "Single Rates", and set the format to Heading 3.

7. Click the fifth line, "Group Rates", and set the format to Heading 3.

   Single Rates and Group Rates are subsections of Day Passes.

8. Click the "Annual Passes" line and set the format to Heading 2.

   Since annual passes allow holders to visit many times during the year, Annual Passes is not a subsection of Day Passes but is parallel to it. Format it with the same heading level.

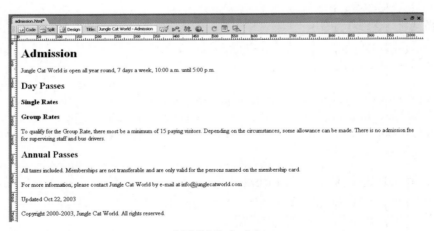

FIGURE 3.54

9. Save the changes to admission.html, and keep it open for the next Skill Drill.

2. Create Unordered Lists

1. In the open admission.html document, click at the end of "Single Rates" and press Enter/Return.

2. Click the Unordered List button in the Property inspector.

3.   Type the following, pressing Enter/Return as indicated:

Text to Type	Press Enter/Return
Adults: $12.00	Once
Teens and Seniors: $9.00	Once
Children: $6.00	Once
Children under 2: Free	None

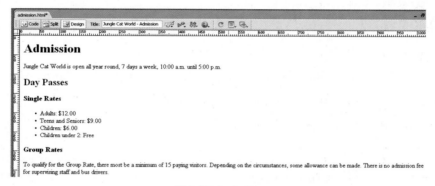

FIGURE 3.55

4.   Click at the end of Group Rates and press Enter/Return.

5.   Click the Unordered List button in the Property inspector.

6.   Type the following, pressing Enter/Return as indicated:

Text to Type	Press Enter/Return
Adults: $8.00	Once
Teens and Seniors: $6.00	Once
Children: $4.00	None

7.   Close admission.html, saving the changes.

3. Create and Modify the Style of an Ordered List

1.   Open family_safari.html.

2.   Below the "Available Dates" heading, drag to select the dates from June 28 to August 24. Click the Ordered List button in the Property inspector.

3.   To change the style of the ordered list, click the CSS button to open the CSS panel. In the CSS Style panel, click the All button.

4. Right/Control-click in the CSS Styles panel and select New from the context menu. Choose Tag as the selector type. Select `ol` from the selector type. In the Define In section, select This Document Only and click OK.

5. Choose the List category in the CSS Style Definition dialog box, then choose **upper-alpha** from the Type menu. Click OK.

   Observe that the numbering style changes to uppercase alphabetic.

6. Close family_safari.html, saving your changes.

4. Create a Nested List

1. Open admission.html.

2. Click at the end of "Annual Passes" and press Enter/Return.

3. Create an unordered list by clicking the Unordered List button in the Property inspector.

4. Type `Family Annual Passes`. Press Enter/Return.

5. Click the Text Indent button in the Property inspector.

Annual Passes

- Family Annual Passes
  - Larger Family (2 adults, up to 4 children): $80.00
  - Smaller Family (1 adult, up to 2 children): $60.00

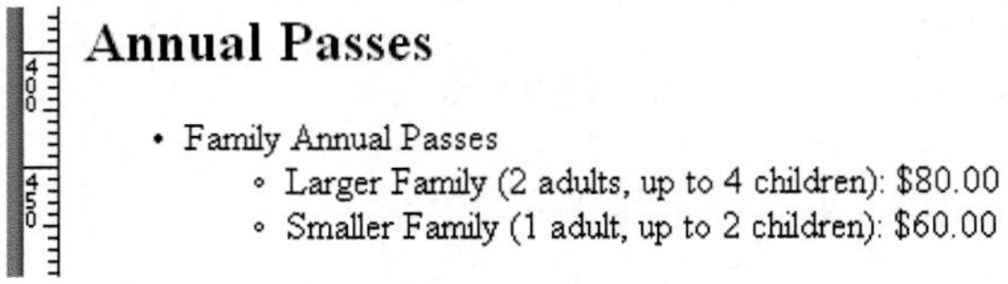

FIGURE 3.56

6. Type `Larger Family (2 adults, up to 4 children): $80.00`. Press Enter/Return. Type `Smaller Family (1 adult, up to 2 children): $60.00.`

   Observe the indented (nested) list. Note also that the bullets are now open circles.

7. Observe the Tag selector at the bottom of the Document window.

   It shows `<ul>` twice. This indicates that one unordered list (the nested list) is contained in another unordered list.

8. Press Enter/Return once more to create a new blank list item.

9. Click the Text Outdent button in the Property inspector.

   The list item shifts from the position of the nested list to the level of the initial list.

10. Type `Individual Annual Passes: $40.00.`

11. Save admission.html, and leave it open for the next Skill Drill.

5. Insert Special HTML Characters

Many special characters are not easy to type. Dreamweaver provides easy access to these characters through the Text Insert bar. In this Skill Drill, you insert copyright and registered-trademark characters in the text.

1. In the open file admission.html, scroll to the page's bottom.

2. Select the word "Copyright" and delete it.

3. At the right end of the Text Insert bar is a drop-down list of special characters. Click the down-pointing arrow to the right of the Characters button to view the list of common special characters.

   The Characters button changes appearance to reflect the last character you chose from this list. If you want to insert the last-selected character, simply click the button; if you prefer to insert a different character, click the down-pointing arrow to display the list of options.

4. Choose © Copyright from the list.

5. Click to the right of "d" in "World".

6. Click the drop-down list of characters, and choose Other Characters at the list's bottom.

7. Click the Registered Trademark character ® at the dialog box's top-right corner.

   At the top-left corner of the Insert Other Character dialog box is an Insert field with **®** in it. Special characters each have a code identifying them. When you click a code from this dialog box or from the Characters pop-up list, Dreamweaver inserts the appropriate code for you. As with all HTML, you can also type the code into the Code window.

8. Click OK to insert the registered-trademark character.

9. Click the Split button at the top of the Document window.

   The code displays as HTML code in the Code view window and as the special character in the Design view.

10. Click the Design button.

11. Close, saving admission.html.

To Extend Your Knowledge . . .

HTML CHARACTERS

HTML and browsers support many special characters — accented characters for French, Spanish, and other Latin-based languages are available through the Insert Other Character dialog box. Different formats of code can create these special characters, such as **®** and **&0174;** both of which produce the registered-trademark character (®). All formats of special HTML characters begin with the ampersand character (&) and end with a semicolon. Most named codes, such as **®** are supported by all browsers. However, the named code for the trademark (™) symbol (**™**) is a problem for several browsers. Dreamweaver wisely uses the numeric-code format (&8482;) for this special character instead of the named code. All current browsers support this numeric-code format for the trademark symbol and all other special HTML characters.

CHALLENGE

Challenge exercises expand on or are somewhat related to skills we presented in the lessons. Each exercise provides a brief narrative introduction, followed by numbered-step instructions that are not as detailed as those in the Skill Drill section. Do these Challenge exercises in order.

For these Challenge exercises, you have acquired a new client, Drummond Reid, a successful small business that sells, restores, and repairs pianos. At times, your client has lots of work for you, such as redesigning their Web site. Today, they just need you to clean up some content and structure. Some pages have no headings: You must format the heading text as proper headings. You must also modify the footers by inserting horizontal rules and converting paragraph breaks into line breaks. You need to apply these changes to all pages to provide a consistent look and feel. You must also format and style some ordered and unordered lists.

1. Format Headings in the Drummond Reid Web Pages

The Web pages presently just contain paragraphs. You need to format some of the paragraphs as headings.

1. From the Chapter_03>DR-P3 folder, create a new site definition and name it DR-P3.

2. Open index.html.

3. Format the top paragraph as Heading 1.

4. Close the file, saving the changes.

5. For each of the following files, repeat Steps 2–4, opening the file, formatting the headings as indicated, then saving and closing the file:

File	Text	Format As
about.html	top paragraph	Heading 1
restoration.html	top paragraph	Heading 1
	Full Rebuilding	Heading 2
	Restoration Costs	Heading 2
	Finishes	Heading 2
	One final word of advice...	Heading 2
location.html	Location	Heading 1
	Directions	Heading 2
	Travel Time: Distance	Heading 2
	four short paragraphs that begin with Coming from...	Heading 3

buying_guide.html	Piano Buying Guide	Heading 1
	Factors to Consider	Heading 2
	Our Advice	Heading 2
	Top Tips	Heading 2
	Never Buy at Auction	Heading 2

2. Insert a Horizontal-Rule Divider above the Footer

1. Open index.html.

2. Click in front of the third paragraph from the bottom that begins with "Home: About".

3. Switch the Insert bar to HTML, and click the Horizontal Rule button.

4. Close, saving the changes.

5. One by one, open the four other Web pages for Drummond Reid, and insert a horizontal rule in the same position. Close the pages, saving the changes for each.

3. Convert a Paragraph Break to a Line Break

1. Open index.html.

2. Move the insertion point to the beginning of the second paragraph, beginning "Japanese" (just below the horizontal rule).

3. Press the Backspace/Delete key once to merge the paragraph with the previous one; then press Shift-Enter/Return to insert a line break separating the two lines.

4. Close, saving the changes.

5. One by one, open the four other Web pages for Drummond Reid. Merge the same two paragraphs in the footer into one, and then separate them by a line break. Close, saving the changes when finished with each Web page.

4. Reformat Text as Unordered and Ordered Lists

1. Open index.html.

2. Select the seven short paragraphs, from "Repairing pianos" to "Supply of piano stools, piano parts and accessories". Format them as an unordered list.

3. Close, saving the changes.

4. Open location.html. Format as an unordered list the three short paragraphs, each starting with "From" (near the bottom of the page and below "Time Travel: Distance"). Close, saving the changes.

5. Open buying_guide.html. Format as an unordered list the four short paragraphs below the heading "Factors to Consider".

6. Format as an ordered list the four paragraphs below the Top Tips heading.

7. Close, saving the changes.

5. Change the Numbering Style of an Ordered List

1. Open buying_guide.html.

2. Click in the ordered list of top tips.

3. Set the style of this ordered list to `lower-roman`.

4. Close, saving the changes.

PORTFOLIO BUILDER

Create an Online Résumé

Regardless of how secure you might feel in your current position, you never know when you'll find yourself seeking new employment. A résumé is a critical component in a job search. The Internet provides a perfect place for you to post your résumé so it can be accessed by potential employers.

1. If you don't already have a résumé, use a word-processing application to write one.

2. Select all the text and copy it to the clipboard.

3. Create a new Dreamweaver document and paste the information into the blank page.

4. Format the résumé so it is attractive when viewed in a browser.

5. Make sure you include an e-mail link so interested parties can easily get in touch with you.

CHAPTER 4

Linking the Site

OBJECTIVES

In this chapter, you learn how to:

- Distinguish between absolute and relative paths

- Use different methods of linking pages

- Use absolute and relative links

- Link to another Web site

- Create an e-mail link

- Create a link from an image

- Create image maps and hotspots

- Create and link to named anchors

- Organize with default page names and subdomains

Why Would I Do This?

Links (or hyperlinks) are the fundamental building blocks of the Internet. They allow the viewer to go from one page to another, from one part of a page to another, from the current Web site to a completely different address or *URL (Uniform Resource Locator)* or enable a visitor to send an email. A URL is the location of a particular file on a Web site. A resource can be an HTML document, image, external style sheet, JavaScript file, or media file.

You can create a link from a single word, a phrase, an image, or even a part of an image. When the mouse pointer is over a link, the arrow-shaped pointer normally turns into a pointing hand. You can color links differently depending on whether the visitor has visited them or not. Users find it helpful to know at a glance whether or not they have been to a particular URL.

There are several types of links available for constructing your site. As noted, you can create links from one page to another, links to sections within a page, and e-mail links. You can have any or all of these types of links in a single Web page. You can also create links that open the linked page in another browser window, or links in framed pages that change the page in another frame.

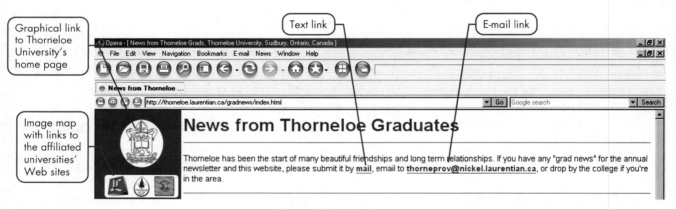

FIGURE 4.1

When you create a link from one page to another page in the same site, the URL for the link does not need to include the protocol or the domain name — in other words, it does not need http:// www.domain_name.com to precede it. *Protocol* identifies how the browser is to handle the destination of the link: *http (HyperText Transfer Protocol)* means that the destination is a Web page, *ftp (File Transfer Protocol)* means that the destination is a file or folder on a file server, and *mailto* means that the destination is an e-mail address and should be handled by an e-mail application. When you create a link to a page on another site, however, you must use the full and complete URL, and the URL must include both the protocol and the domain name.

You can create links from text or images. The anchor tag `<a>` surrounds the link text or the link image. The anchor tag is a container tag that requires its closing `</a>` tag. Unlike many other tags, the anchor tag requires at least one attribute, the `href` attribute, which states where the link is to take the user. If the anchor tag links to products.html, the format is `<a href="products.html">`Tropiflora Products `</a>`, where the phrase "Tropiflora Products" is the link text. If you use an image (products.gif) as the link, the `<img />` tag information appears in place of the text "Tropiflora Products", as in `<a href="products.html"><img src="products.gif" alt="Products" /></a>`.

In addition to the **href** attribute, there is another key anchor-tag option you should know about — the **name** attribute, as in `<a name="location"></a>`. This attribute, which we discuss later in this chapter, creates a named anchor, sometimes referred to as a "bookmark." The **href** attribute, however, is the most commonly used attribute of the anchor tag.

In this chapter, you learn to create links to another page, to another Web site, to an e-mail address, and to a particular section within a page from a block of text, an image, or a region of an image. These functions are essential to building a Web site, as they enable your visitors to access every part of your site. Knowing when and how to create particular types of links will serve you well as you create the numerous links you need for your own Web sites.

VISUAL SUMMARY

The Property inspector provides three common functions for creating links: the Point to File button, the Browse for File button (a folder icon), and the Link field. The browse-for-file function, as the folder icon suggests, opens an Explorer/Finder dialog box, allowing you to choose a file from a folder on your system. The point-to-file method uses a button that you can drag to a file in the Files panel. The Link field allows you to type the file's name, the e-mail address, or the URL of a Web page or select it from the drop-down list.

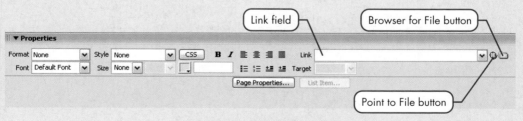

FIGURE 4.2

You can also create links from images. When you click an image in Dreamweaver, the Property inspector changes to reflect an image's properties, including link and target fields similar to those for text, as well as functions for creating an image map with hotspot links. An *image map* is an image in which different regions of the image are links. These linking regions are called *hotspots*, and you use the Hotspot tools to outline the hotspot region. Hotspots can be rectangles, circles (which Dreamweaver erroneously calls "ovals"), or polygons (multisided shapes, such as triangles, stars, or even the outline of a country on a map). You can use multiple image maps on a Web page, but even if you use just one image map, it can contain multiple hotspots. Image maps must be assigned a name so that the code for the image map is associated with the correct image.

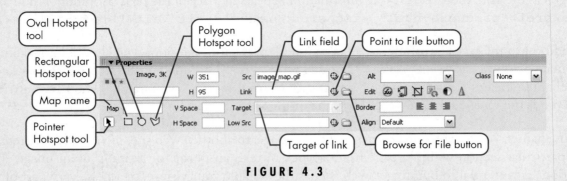

FIGURE 4.3

You can also create links using options available in the Common Insert bar. The Hyperlink, E-mail Link, and Named Anchor buttons open dialog boxes with fields in which you can specify the particulars of these different types of links. The Images drop-down menu offers hotspot options for creating an image map. You can also Right/Control-click selected text in the Document window and choose Make Link from the Context menu.

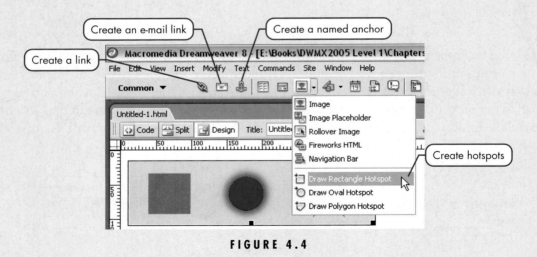

FIGURE 4.4

LESSON 1   Creating Relative vs. Absolute Paths

It is important to know the difference between relative and absolute paths when creating links. Although Dreamweaver creates the link code for you when you define a link, some situations may require you to modify a link or create one by hand. If you create a link incorrectly, you will not get the results you expect.

Relative and absolute paths are two methods for describing the path from the calling page to the destination page. Relative paths use the location of the current page as the starting point. Absolute paths use the site's root folder as the starting point.

For example, let's assume that your office is on the fourth floor of a tower — the third office to the left of the stairs. Someone approaches your desk asking for directions to the ABC Furniture Company, which happens to be the fourth office to the left of the stairs (i.e., next door). Relative directions would be: Go back to the hallway and walk to the next office on the left. Absolute directions to the same destination would be: Go to the front door of the office tower. Take the stairs to the first floor, then to the second floor, then to the third floor, and then to the fourth floor. When you get there, turn left and walk to the fourth office. Both sets of directions would get the person to the same destination, but the absolute directions would always start from the front door of the office tower, or in Web-server terms, from the root folder of the Web site.

Relative directions — go to: the next office on the left

Absolute directions — go to: the front door/second floor/third floor/fourth floor/fourth office on the left

Now imagine that the person is looking for B&L Legal Services, which is located on the second floor, in the first office to the right of the stairs. Relative directions would be: Go back into the hallway. Take the stairs down to the third floor and continue down to the second floor. The office is the first on the right. Absolute directions would be: From the front door, take the stairs to the second floor. Turn to your right and the office is the first on the right.

Relative directions — down to the third floor/down to the second floor/first office to the right

Absolute directions — front door/second floor/first office to the right

Relative Paths in URLS

There are a couple of rules to be aware of when you use relative paths. If the calling and destination pages are in the same folder, you need only to state the destination page's name. For example, consider the folder structure of the fictitious ABC Furniture Company's Web site (Figure 4.5). Linking from bedroom.html to living_room.html in the furniture folder, the URL using a relative path would be **`<a href="living_room.html">`**.

If the destination page is in another folder, you must state the path to the folder. For example, the URL using a relative path from index.html in the root folder to index.html in the contacts folder is **`<a href="contacts/index.html">`**, which means to go down to the contacts folder and open index.html. If you created a link in the reverse direction, the relative path of the link would be **`<a href="../index.html">`**, where **`../`** means go back or up one folder depth. You can use multiple forward or backward paths, if necessary. For example, to link from index.html in the root folder to pots_pans.html in the kitchen folder, you would create the following link path:

```
<a href="products/kitchen/pots_pans.html">
```

The reverse would be `<a href="../../index.html">`. You can combine both forward and backward paths. Linking from bedroom.html in the furniture folder to sm_appliances.html in the kitchen folder would be `<a href="../kitchen/sm_appliances.html">`.

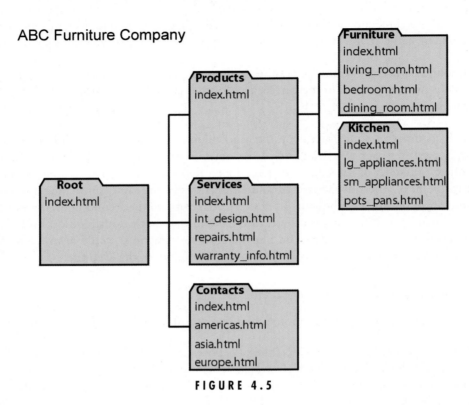

FIGURE 4.5

AbsolutePaths in URLS

When you create absolute paths, you must always create the path from the root — the path must begin with a forward slash `/` to indicate the root folder. It doesn't matter where the calling page is located in the site — the path always begins at the root.

To use an absolute path to link from index.html in the root folder to index.html in the services folder, the link path would be `<a href="/services/index.html">`. To link to the same page from the pots_pans.html page in the kitchen folder, the absolute path would again be `<a href="/services/index.html">`. It doesn't matter where the calling page is in relation to the destination page — the absolute path from the root folder is always the same.

Create Relative and Absolute Paths

In this exercise, you answer questions about relative and absolute links to ensure that you understand the issues involved before you move on. Look closely at Figure 4.5 of ABC Furniture Company's Web site and answer the following questions.

1   What is the relative path of the link from lg_appliances.html to living_room.html? What is the absolute path for the same link?

2   What is the relative path of the link from int_design.html to americas.html? What is the absolute path for the same link?

3   What is the relative path of the link from repairs.html to pots_pans.html? What is the absolute path for the same link?

4   What is the relative path of the link from living_room.html to sm_appliances.html? What is the absolute path for the same link?

5   What is the relative path of the link from asia.html to bedroom.html? What is the absolute path for the same link?

6   Open abc_answers.html from the Chapter_04 folder to view the answers to these questions.

LESSON 2   Linking within Your Web Site

Linking between pages within a Web site is the anchor tag's most common use. You want to keep your visitors in your site and to allow, even promote, access to all public components of your site. Of course, this does not mean that you have to provide links *to* every page *from* every page — a large site would need hundreds or even thousands of links on every page to achieve this! Recall the flowcharting exercise in Chapter 2 in which you drew lines from some pages to other pages. Although you linked the major categories to one another, you did not link every product to one another, just to the category in which the product was found and to other major pages, such as the home page and the contact page.

While there is no limit to the number of links you can build on your site, remember it's best to minimize the amount of clicking and searching your visitors must do to find what they're looking for. Visitors are fickle and impatient — they want what they want, and they want it now. The better you organize the content and the navigation scheme, the easier it is for them to find information quickly and efficiently.

Typically, you might use the same Navigation bar on every page of the site to provide links to the site's major sections. Companies often display their logo prominently at the top of each page, frequently making it a link to the site's home page. Sometimes, breadcrumb navigation may be used to identify the path to the current Web page. For example, you can see Home > Products > Furniture, where Home, Products, and Furniture are individual links to the Web site's home page, the home page of the products category, and the home page of the furniture subcategory. **Breadcrumb navigation** is a feature used on Web pages to show the user where they are relative to the home page of the Web site: its name is reminiscent of *Hansel and Gretel*. You can also provide additional links to pages related to the current page, such as from "bedroom furniture" to "living room furniture". These are all methods that you can use to help your visitors navigate around your site to learn more about your organization's products and services.

Navigation bars, or "navbars" as they're often called, are an excellent means of creating links from every page to the major sections of your Web site. Although you can create text-link Navigation bars, as we do here, you can also create image links. You can even incorporate JavaScript for image rollovers. Dreamweaver has a navigation-bar function for creating dynamic drop-down menus, which, because of the JavaScript component, we discuss in *Essentials for Design: Dreamweaver 8 Level 2*.

Link Pages Using the Browse-for-File Method

1　Using the methods outlined in Chapter 2, define the Chapter_04>TO-P4 folder as a site called "TO-P4".

2　Open default.html from the TO-P4 site.

You will configure the line of text along the page's bottom as a Text Navigation bar. As a general rule, you don't link the current page back to itself.

3　Select "About Tropiflora".

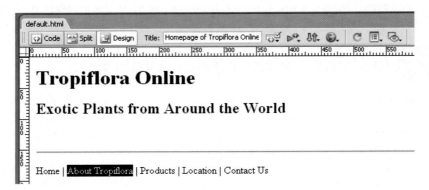

FIGURE 4.6

4　Click the Browse for File button (the folder icon at the right side of the Property inspector).

FIGURE 4.7

5　In the Select File dialog box, choose about.html from the list of files; then choose Document in the Relative To field at the bottom of the dialog box, and click OK/Choose.

The Relative To option creates a relative link if "Document" is selected; it creates an absolute link if Site Root/Site is selected. Unless otherwise told, you use relative links (Relative to Document) in this book.

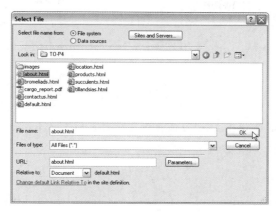

FIGURE 4.8

6   **Preview this page in your browser, choosing Yes to save the changes to default.html when prompted.**

FIGURE 4.9

? If You Have Problems

The dialog box shown in Figure 4.9 appears only when two conditions are met: when you have made changes to the current Web page, which has not been saved, and when you have not set Dreamweaver to display temporary files. The first condition is fairly clear: if you have saved the page, no prompt to save it appears.

The second condition may not be clear if you are new to Dreamweaver. You can set Dreamweaver to display a temporary file when you choose Preview/Debug in Browser. If you have chosen the temporary-file option, Dreamweaver creates a temporary file and sends it to your browser to display. At times, this setting may be preferable, but for this lesson it is unnecessary.

When your page displays in your browser, check the Address bar to ensure that the filename shown is the same filename you are editing. If not, choose Edit>Preferences and choose the Preview in Browser category. Uncheck the Preview Using Temporary File option and click OK. Preview the page in your browser again; this time, the filename in the browser will be correct.

7   Click the "About Tropiflora" link you created, and the about.html page displays in the browser window.

8   Close your browser and return to Dreamweaver.

9   Link "Products" to products.html, "Location" to location.html, and "Contact Us" to contactus.html.

10   Preview the page in your browser (saving if prompted).

11   Click a link and verify that the link takes you to the correct page.

You have not yet created the links in the other pages — you must use your browser's Back button to return to default.html.

12   Close your browser and return to Dreamweaver. Close default.html but keep Dreamweaver open for the next lesson.

To Extend Your Knowledge . . .

CREATE USEFUL LINK TEXT

"I wrote a review of the unauthorized biography of former President Jimmy Carter. Click here to read it." Read what, the biography or the review? Too many links use "here" as the link text, often on the same page. Instead, follow good writing practice by identifying the link's content within the link text, such as: "I wrote a review of the unauthorized biography of former President Jimmy Carter." Now you don't need the words "click here", and the link text clearly identifies to readers what they will see if they click that link.

You can use the anchor tag's *title* attribute to expand on the link-text information. The *title* attribute produces a tool-tip-like pop-up when the mouse pointer hovers over the link. You can use it to expand upon the link text. For the preceding example, the *title* attribute could be: "The Unfinished Presidency: Jimmy Carter's Journey beyond the White House by Douglas Brinkley."

LESSON 3   Exploring Absolute Links to a Local Web Page

Absolute links use an absolute path to the destination. In most circumstances, pages in the same Web site do not require absolute paths, but there are advantages to using them. For example, Web sites commonly use the company logo as a link to the site's home page. Using an absolute link to /index.html works every time, no matter how many folders separate the calling page from the root folder. You may also wish to use the same code for the Navigation bar. If you plan to use the Navigation bar on many pages in many folders, using absolute links ensures that your links always work.

The problem with absolute paths is that they don't work correctly when you test pages located on your computer — your computer operating system interprets the root folder **/** as the root folder of your hard drive, not the root folder of your Web site. Dreamweaver understands where the root of the Web site is, but your browser goes to the root of your hard drive. The only way you can test links that use absolute paths is to either upload your work to a Web server or to run Web-server software on your computer.

Why should you learn absolute paths if relative links work? Some specialized Web-server applications need to know the absolute paths to certain files. When installing some discussion-forum software, for example, you must enter the absolute path to various resources, such as programming scripts or image folders. If you don't understand absolute paths, it would be difficult for you to install this type of software.

Although it may not be easy to use and test absolute paths on your computer, you must use the absolute path when you link to a Web page on another Web site. Whenever you link to another Web site, you always enter the site from its root in the same way that you must always enter a building from its ground-floor entrance — you cannot go from your fourth-floor office directly to the fourth-floor office in the next building.

In this lesson, you create an absolute link to a local Web page. You also explore the problem of testing an absolute link when developing on a local computer.

Create an Absolute Link

1   **Open about.html.**

2   **Drag to select "Home" in the Text Navigation bar at the bottom of the page.**

3   **Click the Browse for File button in the Property inspector.**

4   **Choose default.html from the file list.**

5   **From the Relative To option at the bottom of the Select File dialog box, choose Site Root/Site.**

When you define a site, you have the option of specifying the http address. If this information has not been entered into the site properties, this warning dialog appears when you try to create an absolute link. For the purpose of this lesson, ignore the warning and create an absolute link; normally, however, you would either avoid absolute links or specify the site's http address.

FIGURE 4.10

6 Click OK to close the warning dialog box, then click OK to create the absolute link.

A forward slash (/) precedes default.html, which means that this link's destination is default.html in the root folder of this Web site.

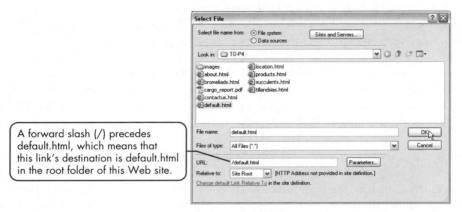

FIGURE 4.11

7 Preview the page in your browser (saving if prompted).

8 Click the newly created link.

The browser tries to find default.html in the root folder of the hard drive. Because this is not in the root folder of the hard drive, the browser displays an error message, indicating that the file does not exist in the specified location.

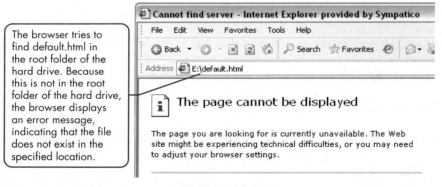

FIGURE 4.12

9 Close your browser and return to Dreamweaver. Keep about.html open for the next exercise.

Reset an Absolute Link to a Relative Link

In the previous exercise, we saw that an absolute link does not work properly on a local computer. In this exercise, we reset the absolute link to a relative link and test it in a browser.

1 In the open about.html file with "Home" still selected, click the Browse for File button in the Property inspector.

2 In the Select File dialog box, change the Relative To option from Site Root/Site to Document and click OK/Choose.

? **If You Have Problems**

Even though you are just modifying the Relative To option for this link, you may still need to choose the link's destination by clicking it. On some systems, the File Name may be cleared, which requires you to reselect the destination file.

3 Preview the page in your browser again (saving if prompted), and retest the "Home" link.

The link correctly opens the default.html page.

4 Close your browser, return to Dreamweaver, and close about.html.

LESSON 4   Linking to Other Web Sites

You must always use absolute links when linking to Web pages on another site. You can think of the domain name of a URL as the Web site's ground-floor entrance, from which you proceed to the final destination. Links to other Web sites must be preceded by the http protocol (`http://`).

It is not necessary to specify a Web-page name when you link to the root of a Web site — the Web server will deliver the default page (the home page). Furthermore, you may not know the name of the home-page file. Is it index.htm, index.html, default.asp, index.php, or even a custom default filename? It doesn't really matter, because you can simply link to the Web site, and the Web server looks after the rest for you.

In this exercise, you create a link to MapQuest.com, a popular site that contains maps for regions in the United States and many other countries. When you create a link to an external Web site, remember to add the protocol at the beginning of the URL. In addition, always test your link soon after you create it, so that you can immediately fix any problems before you forget and leave a dead link.

Create a Link to MapQuest

1 Open location.html.

2 Scroll down to the bottom and select the word "MapQuest" at the end of the last sentence.

3   Type `http://www.mapquest.com` in the Property inspector's Link field.

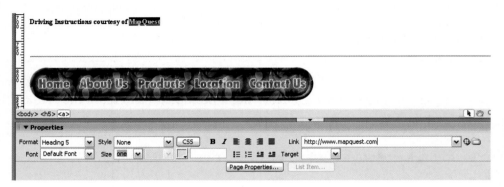

FIGURE 4.13

4   Preview the page in your browser (saving if prompted).

5   Click the link to the MapQuest Web site.

If you created the link correctly, MapQuest.com loads into your browser window. Correct the link if necessary.

FIGURE 4.14

6   Close your browser, return to Dreamweaver, and close location.html.

To Extend Your Knowledge . . .

PREVIEW FREQUENTLY

"Code a little, test a little" is a phrase that makes a lot of sense when building Web pages. Given that Dreamweaver is a WYSIWYG design application, you don't need to check your code quite as frequently as a hand-coder would, because Dreamweaver creates quality code for you. However, always verify links as soon as you create them to ensure that they are correct.

LESSON 5   Creating E-mail Links

E-mail links do not have a path, but they do have a specific protocol; without **mailto:** preceding the e-mail address, the e-mail link does not work. Watch for periods and underscores in e-mail addresses, such as j.smith@domain.com or j_smith@domain.com — these characters may be hard to see.

On most computer systems, an e-mail link opens the user's e-mail application and inserts the e-mail address in the To field. However, not all users visit your Web site using their own computers — they may use Web-based e-mail such as Hotmail or Yahoo! Mail. By not using your e-mail address in the e-mail link — for example: "Send me an e-mail" — you hide your e-mail address from the user. However, most browsers display the link destination (in this case the e-mail address) in the browser's Status bar at the bottom of the browser window (Internet Explorer and Mozilla) or in the form of a tool tip (Opera). Nonetheless, visitors must take the extra step of writing out the e-mail address and then typing it in the To field of their Web-based e-mail application. It is good etiquette (and simpler) to use the actual e-mail address as the e-mail link. If you use an image as a link, it is good etiquette to also provide the e-mail address in text form, so the user can select the link text and copy and paste it into the To field.

In this exercise, you create an e-mail link. The E-mail Link button on the Common Insert bar is simple to use. Just type the link text in the Text field and the e-mail address in the E-Mail field. You don't need to type the **mailto:** protocol — this function automatically inserts it for you. Dreamweaver also remembers the last e-mail address you used with this function. This memory can simplify working with this function if you use the same e-mail address repeatedly, but if you insert different e-mail addresses, you must remember to change the e-mail address each time. You can also create an e-mail link by typing the e-mail link in the Property inspector's Link field. If you do so, however, you must remember to insert the **mailto:** protocol (unlike with the E-mail Link function). Although you can use the Link field for many protocols, it does not automatically insert the protocol for you.

Create an E-mail Link

1 Open contactus.html.

2 Scroll down to the e-mail address (the last paragraph above the horizontal rule).

3 Drag to select "sales@tropiflora.com".

4 **Click the E-mail Link button in the Common Insert bar.**

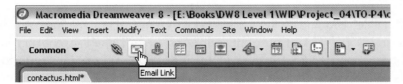

FIGURE 4.15

If You Have Problems

The E-mail Link button appears in the Common Insert bar. If you do not see the envelope icon, click the Insert bar pop-up menu and choose Common from the list.

5 **The E-mail Link dialog box should complete both the Text and E-Mail fields with "sales@tropiflora.com". If it doesn't, type the text into the fields. Click OK.**

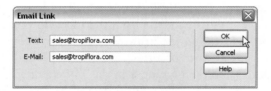

FIGURE 4.16

6 **Preview the page in your browser (saving if prompted).**

7   Move the mouse pointer over the e-mail link; the e-mail address appears in the Status bar (or in the tool tip if you are using Opera).

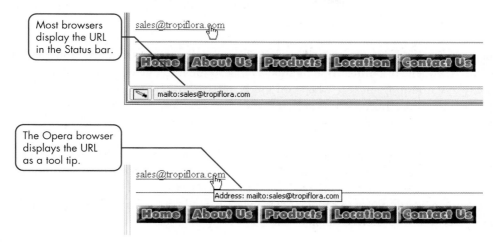

FIGURE 4.17

8   Close your browser and return to Dreamweaver. Leave contactus.html open for the next lesson.

To Extend Your Knowledge . . .

HIDING AN E-MAIL ADDRESS FROM SPAMMERS

Spam or **U.C.E. (unsolicited commercial e-mail)** is a problem for everyone. Many different methods have been attempted to prevent **spammers** (people who send spam) from harvesting your e-mail address from a Web site. The general assumption is that harvesting is done using a computer application that looks for the `mailto:` link and grabs the e-mail address from the link. In response to this, many people have used JavaScript scripts to obscure the e-mail address: your browser then runs the JavaScript code and legibly displays the e-mail address for you. The problem with JavaScript obfuscation is that if a browser can run the JavaScript, so can e-mail-harvesting applications. Other people add obvious nonsense to the e-mail address, assuming the end user will understand and remove it (for example, my.name@nospam.domain.com). Again, this method can be circumvented because certain phrases are commonly used.

The best method for hiding your e-mail address is to use a contact form that sends you the message via a server-side script. The programming code of a server-side script cannot be accessed, so an e-mail address stored in it cannot be harvested.

LESSON 6   Using Images as Links

So far, you have only created text links; but, as you know, you can also use images as links. At this point, we focus on how to set existing images as links.

The process of creating a link from an image is very similar to creating a link from text. You select the image and use either the browse-for-file or point-to-file method to link to the file. There is one attribute that, although an image attribute, plays an important role when you use images as links. Visitors using nonvisual browsers can't see the images or know their purpose unless you use the Alt-text attribute. *Alt-text* is a shortened form of *alternate text*, a text description of the image that is provided as an alternative to the image.

The vision-impaired population may not be the only ones who access your site with nongraphical browsers — other individuals may access the Internet from countries in which computer and telecommunications technology limit browser options to Lynx or other text-based browsers. Furthermore, some users with good vision and good-quality technologies still prefer to browse with images turned off for faster download times. The Alt-text attribute helps make your Web site accessible to all.

In this exercise, you create links from images in the bottom Navigation bar of a Web page and link them to different pages. You also create an e-mail link from an image. Images are often used in Navigation bars to dress up the links and to produce rollover JavaScript effects. You learn more about images in Chapter 5 and about JavaScript in *Essentials for Design: Dreamweaver 8 Level 2*.

Create a Link from an Image

| 1 | In the open contactus.html file, scroll to the Navigation bar images at the page's bottom. |

| 2 | Click the Home image. |

The Property inspector changes significantly to reflect the numerous different properties available for images.

FIGURE 4.18

| 3 | In the Property inspector, click the Browse for File button to the right of the Link field. |

| 4 | Choose default.html and click OK/Choose. |

5 Type Home **in the Alt field.**

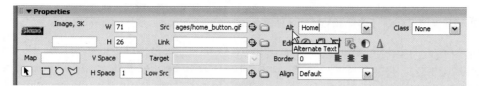

FIGURE 4.19

6 Continue with the rest of the image links, as follows.

Contact Us is not linked, as there is no need to link this page to itself. However, the Contact Us image should have Alternate text.

Button	Link Destination	Alternate Text
About Us	about.html	About Us
Products	products.html	Products
Location	location.html	Location
Contact Us	No Link	Contact us

7 Click the e-mail image above the text "sales@tropiflora.com".

8 In the Link field, type mailto:sales@tropiflora.com.

9 In the Alt field, type Please send us your comments.

FIGURE 4.20

10 Preview the page in your browser (saving if prompted).

From this point forward, if the Save Changes dialog box appears when previewing a page, choose Yes to save.

11 Test all of the links you created.

If your computer does not have an e-mail application, simply move your mouse pointer over the e-mail link image and verify that the e-mail address in the Status bar or tool tip is correct.

12 Close your browser and return to Dreamweaver. Close contactus.html.

To Extend Your Knowledge . . .

APPROPRIATE ALT TEXT FOR IMAGE LINKS

It is tempting to use "Link to Home page of Tropiflora Online" as the alternate text for the Home image link. This elaboration is unnecessary. JAWS and other screen-reader software do indicate to the users that they have encountered a link — it is unnecessary to put "Link to" in the alternate-text description. Furthermore, if the image of the word "Home" makes it clear to sighted users that it links to the current Web site's home page, then "Home" is sufficient alternate text for screen-reader users.

LESSON 7   Creating Image Maps

In the Contact Us page in the previous lesson, you saw that each of the images in the Navigation bar is a separate image. You could also use a single image, in which different regions of the image are links to different pages. In some cases, the image is no more sophisticated than a combination of several simple images. In other cases, it is difficult to separate one region from another. For example, consider a map of the world — the continents are irregular in shape and would be very difficult to divide from one another. As you recall, a single image containing different link regions or hotspots is known as an "image map." As your mouse pointer moves over the different hotspots of an image map, the coordinates of the mouse pointer determine which link is activated.

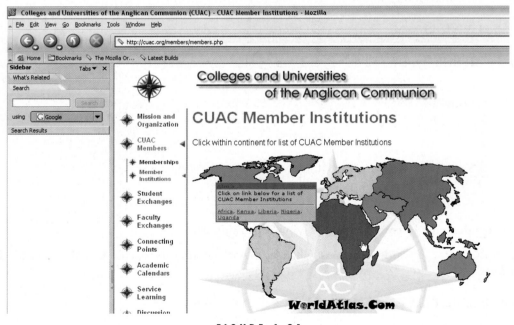

FIGURE 4.21

Furthermore, it is possible to have image-map hotspots tied to **DHTML** or Dynamic HTML (an advanced form of JavaScript that may be used to dynamically create and modify HTML). On a former page of the CUAC

Web site (see Figure 4.21), each region of the world map is a hotspot tied to a pop-up DHTML function that provides links to member countries in each region.

There are two types of image maps: client-side and server-side. The difference between them is whether the Web server (**server-side**) or the browser (**client-side**) processes the mouse-pointer coordinates and delivers the appropriate destination in response. In most cases, client-side image maps are sufficient, but in some specialized cases, where any point in the image may be significant, server-side image maps are used. Server-side image maps require specialized software on the server to process the mouse-pointer coordinate. Unless you are running a Web server, you cannot test the results of a server-side image map on your computer.

MapQuest.com, for example, employs server-side image maps that use the exact position of your mouse click either to zoom into that point or to center the map on that point. Dreamweaver has the tools to create client-side image-map hotspots but not server-side image maps. To create server-side image maps, you must write the appropriate HTML code and server-side programming code yourself.

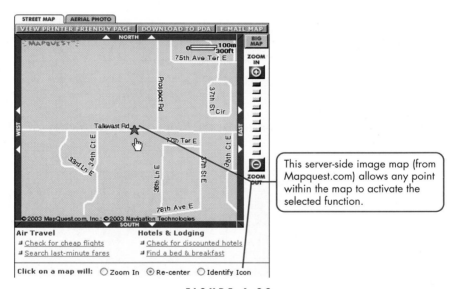

This server-side image map (from Mapquest.com) allows any point within the map to activate the selected function.

FIGURE 4.22

You can use circles, rectangles, and polygons (multisided figures) to create hotspots. Using Dreamweaver, or any other software that allows you to define an image-map's hotspots, you must identify the hotspot's shape, size, and position. Three numbers define the position and size of a circular hotspot: the x-coordinate of the circle's center, the y-coordinate of that center, and the measurement of that circle's radius. All measurements are in pixels. The x- and y-coordinates of a position are measured from the image's top-left corner, where they start at 0,0. Four numbers define the position and size of a rectangular hotspot: the x- and y-coordinates of the rectangle's top-left corner, and the x- and y-coordinates of the bottom-right corner. The quantity of numbers that define a polygonal hotspot's position and size depend on the number of points on the polygon: each point has both an x- and a y-coordinate, and all of these coordinates are needed to define the polygonal hotspot. A triangle, for example, has three points and therefore needs six numbers to define its size and position.

Create Simple Hotspot Shapes

In this exercise, you create image maps in rectangular and circular shapes. You also link the hotspots to movie pages on the Internet Movie Database Web site.

1   **Open image_map.html from the Chapter_04 folder.**

2   **Click the yellow image with the three colored shapes.**

3   **Type `movielinks` in the Map field on the Property inspector's left side.**

Every image map requires a name. This allows the image-map coordinates to be associated with the correct image, which is especially important if there are multiple image maps on the same page.

FIGURE 4.23

4   **Click the Rectangular Hotspot Tool button at the Property inspector's bottom left.**

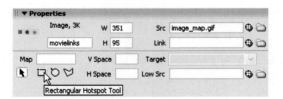

FIGURE 4.24

5   **Drag from one corner of the red square to the diagonally opposite corner.**

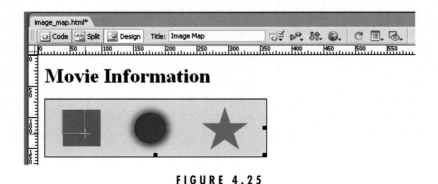

FIGURE 4.25

6   In the Property inspector's Link field, delete the pound symbol (#) and type `http://us.imdb.com/title/tt0220912/`. Type `Arthur and the Square Knights of the Round Table` in the Alt field. Choose `_blank` from the Target list.

7   Click the Oval Hotspot tool in the Property inspector.

8   Drag horizontally across the blue circle until you have created a hotspot circle that is approximately the same size as the blue circle.

Create a circle by dragging at a 45° angle from the circle's top-left edge (the position of the hour hand on a clock at 10:30) to the circle's bottom-right edge (4:30).

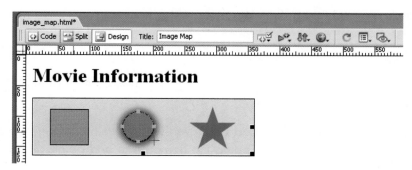

FIGURE 4.26

?   ## If You Have Problems

The Oval Hotspot tool can be difficult to master. If the circle is not the right size, it is actually easier to redraw it than resize it. While it is still selected, press the Delete key to delete it. Click the Oval Hotspot tool in the Property inspector and redraw the circle. If it is simply out of position, click the Pointer Hotspot tool (the arrow tool to the left of the Rectangular Hotspot tool) and drag the circular hotspot into position.

---

9   In the Link field, delete the pound symbol and type `http://us.imdb.com/Title?0286106`. Type `Signs, a movie about crop circles` in the Alt field. Choose `_blank` from the Target list.

10   Save the changes, and leave image_map.html open for the next exercise.

To Extend Your Knowledge . . .

DEEP LINKS

Deep links point to specific content in a site, allowing readers to bypass the site's front page. Many large Web sites, such as CNN.com and search engines, are run by database technology — the content is stored in databases and may be retrieved through queries. As a result, the URLs can be quite long, such as this query for the phrase "deep link" using Google.com:

```
http://www.google.com/search?sourceid=navclient&ie=UTF-8&oe=UTF-8&q=deep+link
```

As another example, this link to the story about Arnold Schwarzenegger's inauguration speech on CNN.com at:

```
http://www.cnn.com/2003/ALLPOLITICS/11/17/arnold.speech/index.html
```

To prevent errors, you should copy and paste (rather than type) long URLs like these into the Link field of the Property inspector.

Some Web sites do not allow deep linking because advertising on the home page generates more revenue than advertising on other pages. Skipping the home page and going directly to a deep link reduces the site's advertising revenue.

Create a Polygonal Hotspot Shape

You have practiced creating some simple-shaped hotspots. In this exercise, you create hotspots from a polygon, a multisided shape that requires that you mark each point of the shape. Remember to name the image map and create alt text for each hotspot; also remember that it is easier to delete and redo than resize a circular hotspot, and if a polygonal hotspot is missing a point, you must redraw the hotspot.

1   In the open image_map.html file, click the Polygon Hotspot Tool button.

2   Going around the star, click each outer and inner point until you have created all 10 points.

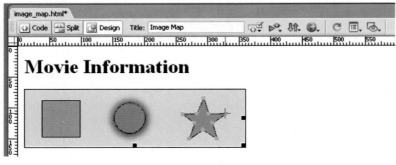

FIGURE 4.27

? **If You Have Problems**

If you have missed a point, you must delete the hotspot and redraw it. If one or more of the points are not positioned to your satisfaction, switch to the Pointer Hotspot Tool (arrow), click the point that is out of position, and drag it into position.

---

3 In the Property inspector's Link field, type `http://us.imdb.com/Title?0121766`. Type `Star Wars, Episode III` in the Alt field. Choose `_blank` from the Target list.

4 Preview the page in your browser. Click any of the shapes to go to the selected movie in another browser window.

The `_blank` target opens the link destination in a new browser window.

5 Close your browser, return to Dreamweaver, and close image_map.html.

To Extend Your Knowledge . . .

LINK TARGETS

Most links open the destination page in the same browser window as the originating page. However, it is possible to open a link in a new browser window by using the anchor tag's target attribute. There are four predefined targets: `_blank`, `_parent`, `_top`, and `_self`; each begins with an underscore. The `_blank` target opens the link in a new browser window and is sometimes used by one Web site to open a link to another Web site in another browser window.

Framed layouts make use of the three other predefined target attributes. You can also assign names to targets; this is another feature of framed layouts, enabling a link to open a page in the named frame. The designer decides the names of the frames, such as bottomFrame, mainFrame, and topFrame.

There are accessibility issues with using targets. The `_blank` target "breaks the Back button," which is a phrase meaning you cannot use the Back button on a browser to return to the originating page because the originating page is in another window. A sighted user can see that a new browser window has opened, but it is more difficult for a blind or visually impaired person to recognize this. It is recommended that you add an alert (with the Code window) using the `title` attribute to inform the user that "This link opens in a new browser window."

LESSON 8 Linking within Pages

You can also set links to take the user to a section within a page, not just to a new page. The links discussed previously just take the user to the top of the linked page, not to a particular position on that page. When Web pages are long, it is useful to create **named anchors** or bookmarks in the pages so that you can link directly to those specific positions on the Web page. *FAQs (Frequently Asked Questions)* are great examples of Web pages that use this technique. Often FAQs are set up so that the questions, listed at the page's top, are linked to the answers, which appear below the questions. This approach makes it easier for the user to quickly find a particular question at the page's top and jump down directly to the answer.

Thorneloe University uses named anchors on the pages that list the courses offered by each department. Each course description has a named anchor, enabling the Webmaster to create a link from the course schedules, the degree requirements, or the faculty pages directly to the courses' descriptions.

The course code on the Course Schedule page (middle) links to the course description on the Courses page (left).

On the Course Schedule page (middle) the professors' names (right column) are linked to the professors' CVs on the Faculty page (right).

FIGURE 4.28

Links, whether page links or named anchors, require both a starting and an ending point. The starting point is the anchor tag that uses the **href** attribute such as **<a href="index.html">**. The ending point or destination in this example is a Web page. If the Web page doesn't exist, you have created a dead or broken link. If you are creating links to pages in your site, you must remember to create the destination Web pages. The same principle applies to named anchors — in order to link to a particular position in a Web page, you must create a named anchor at that position.

Named anchors do not produce anything visible on the Web page. There are other HTML elements that also do not produce anything visible on the Web page, such as comments, divisions, and JavaScript. To aid the developer, Dreamweaver displays a shield-like symbol wherever you create an invisible element. An *invisible element* is HTML code that doesn't have a visible representation in a browser. Each invisible element has its own version of the shield symbol. To see the invisible elements, choose Edit>Preferences and choose the Invisible Elements category. The shield symbol for each invisible element is shown; if the element has a check mark, the shield symbol is visible in the Dreamweaver Design view.

In this exercise, you create named anchors and link to them from within the same page. Named anchors are an excellent means of directing the visitor to a particular section in a page. The page may not be long enough to justify breaking the content into different pages — named anchors provide a means of jumping directly to specific content.

Create and Link to Named Anchors

1   **Open products.html from the TO-P4 site.**

You will link the unordered list of products near the top of the page to the product descriptions below.

2   **Click to the left of "Bromeliads", below the "Description" heading.**

3   Click the Named Anchor button in the Common Insert bar.

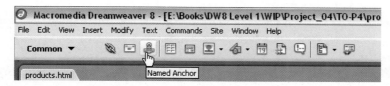

FIGURE 4.29

4   In the Anchor name field, type bromeliads and click OK.

FIGURE 4.30

5   Click to the right of the "Bromeliads" text, and notice the yellow-shield symbol where the named anchor has been inserted.

All invisible elements (the Dreamweaver term for elements or tags with no visible component) have a yellow symbol, indicating their location in the code; the symbol's shape indicates the type of invisible element.

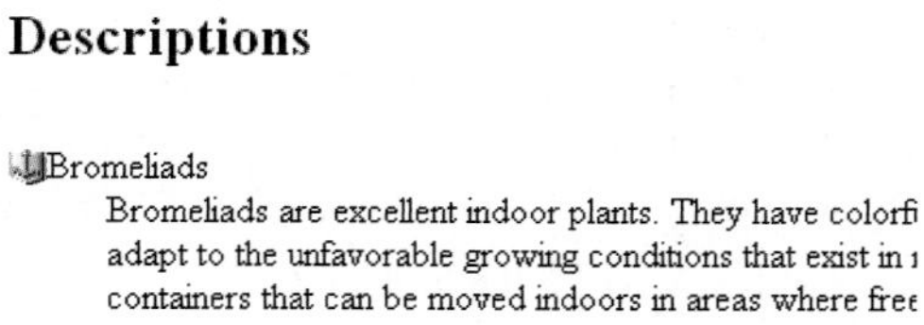

Descriptions

Bromeliads
Bromeliads are excellent indoor plants. They have colorfu
adapt to the unfavorable growing conditions that exist in
containers that can be moved indoors in areas where free

FIGURE 4.31

?   ## If You Have Problems

On Windows systems, the named-anchor invisible-element indicator is visible by default, but it may have been made invisible. On the Macintosh, the shield symbols (including the anchor symbol) are not visible by default.

To make the invisible-element indicators visible, you must first choose View>Visual Aids and select Invisible Elements (to place a check mark next to that option). Next, choose Edit>Preferences, select the Invisible Elements category, and make certain there is a check mark beside Named Anchors. If there is no check mark, click to insert one. Click OK.

---

6   Move to the document's top and select "Bromeliads" just below "Products".

7   Click the Hyperlink button on the Common Insert bar.

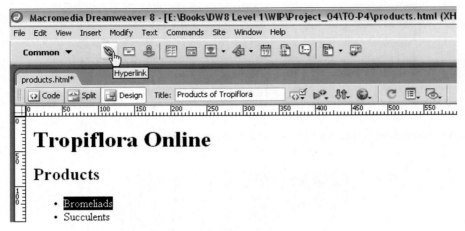

FIGURE 4.32

8   From the Link list in the Hyperlink dialog box, choose #bromeliads and click OK.

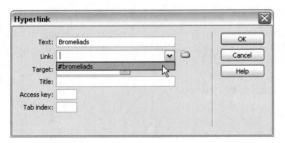

FIGURE 4.33

9   Preview the page in your browser and test the link.

? If You Have Problems

When you click a link to a named anchor, the page should shift to bring the named anchor as close to the top of the browser window as possible. However, if the page is shorter than the browser window, it cannot shift. To enable a demonstration of the named anchors, drag the side of the browser window inward so that the width is quite narrow, and test the links to named anchors. The test should be more effective.

10   Close the browser, return to Dreamweaver, and close products.html.

To Extend Your Knowledge . . .

NAME VS. ID

When HTML 4 was released, the W3C stated that the name attribute will be replaced by the id attribute, which means that `<a name="bookmark">` will now be `<a id="bookmark">`.

In fact, this recommendation has a much larger effect. The **name** attribute is used in only a few tags, such as the `<map>` and `<a>` tags. However, the **id** attribute is a core attribute that may be used in any tag. As a result, the destination `<a name="#bookmark">` could be `<ul id="bookmark">`, `<h1 id="bookmark">`, or `<p id="bookmark">`. The destination does not need to be an anchor tag, just a tag with the correct **id**. Many Web developers create a bookmark as a functionless, empty tag, such as `<a name="bookmark"></a>`. By switching to the **id** attribute instead of the **name** attribute, the developer no longer has to create an empty anchor tag and can simply assign the **id** to a tag that is the link's appropriate destination.

The **id** attribute has other purposes as well. It is used in JavaScript when the code is meant to affect a particular element, such as changing an image during a rollover. The **id** attribute also has uses in CSS and allows a developer to assign a particular style to the tag with that **id**. Now it can also be used as a bookmark.

Unfortunately, Dreamweaver 8 continues to support the named anchor and provides little support, except in the Code window, for the **id** attribute.

LESSON 9 Using Default Pages and Subdomains to Organize a Web Site

As you recall, large Web sites often divide content into many different folders to keep related information together in one folder. You explored content and folder organization in Chapter 2 with the Carver's Online store and Web site. Other methods of content organization include default filenames and subdomains.

Generally, whenever you create a new folder on a Web site, you use it to collect related pages. Creating a home page in each folder allows you to collect and disseminate general information about that particular subject and direct the visitor to more specific information. The home page for each folder should use the default home-page filename according to the Web-server configuration. Generally, index.html and index.htm are the default filenames for HTML pages.

There are two benefits to using default home-page filenames. Using these default names may force you to organize general information about the contents of the folder and provide visitors with better information. Also, using these default names allows you to shorten the URL, both for linking and for providing a link in an e-mail message to a visitor. For example, if you used the default filename for the home page of the Contacts section of your Web site, rather than linking to /contact/index.html, you need only use /contact/, which then prompts the Web server to deliver the default home page of the folder (which is index.html). If you chose to ignore this advice and used contact.html as the home page, the folder URL (/contact/) would not deliver contact.html to the visitor, but would instead display an embarrassing error page. You can and should prevent this by naming the home page of the folder with the default filename.

Very large Web sites also tend to use subdomains to organize content. Laurentian University (www.laurentian.ca) has two affiliated universities that use subdomains as their domains: Thorneloe University's home page is thorneloe.laurentian.ca, and Huntington University's home page is huntington.laurentian.ca. Often, subdomain URLs are shorter and more memorable than folder URLs — compare thorneloe.laurentian.ca with www.laurentian.ca/affiliate/thorneloe.

In this exercise, you explore the structure of the IBM Web site. You look at how this large company has employed default filenames and subdomains to manage its large volume of content.

Explore the Organization of IBM.com

1   **Open your browser and go to http://www.ibm.com.**

Although you did not specify a filename such as index.html, a Web page — the default for this (the root) folder — was delivered to you.

2   **Click the link "change" to the right of United States (at the top right corner); then choose Canada - English and click the Go button.**

Notice that even though no Web page is specified in the Address bar, the default page of the /ca/en folder is delivered to the Web browser by the Web server.

FIGURE 4.34

3   **Click "Products" in the top Navigation bar to the right of "Home".**

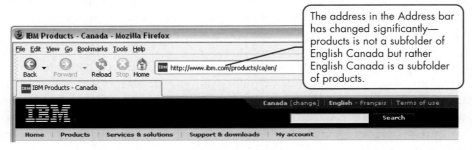

FIGURE 4.35

4   Near the top of the Web page in the main content area, click the "Personal Computing" link.

The domain has changed again because Lenovo corporation now handles sales of IBM personal computing products.

FIGURE 4.36

5   Click the "Desktops" link to explore IBM notebook computers.

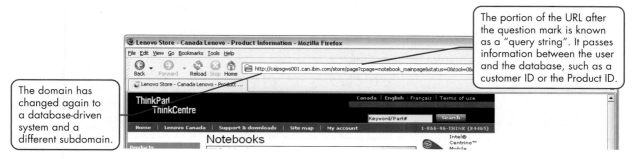

The portion of the URL after the question mark is known as a "query string". It passes information between the user and the database, such as a customer ID or the Product ID.

The domain has changed again to a database-driven system and a different subdomain.

FIGURE 4.37

6   Close your browser.

To Extend Your knowledge . . .

DATABASE CONTENT ORGANIZATION

Some Web sites store their content in databases. Using databases to store and organize content often provides very few clues in the URL as to how the content is organized. For instance, from the URL `http://www.pcmag.com/article2/0,1759,1615757,00.asp`, you have no clue about how the *PC Magazine* stories are grouped or categorized or that the name of this article is "DiskPie Pro: Clean Up Your Hard Drive." However, the *PC Magazine* editors do organize the articles within the database just as you would with folders — Home>Downloads>Utilities>OS Utilities>DiskPie Pro — but they're using a database structure instead of folders.

SUMMARY

In this chapter, you learned about and created different types of links. You learned how to use links to let the viewer move from page to page within a site, to named anchors within a page, and to different sites. You also learned how to create and test e-mail links. You explored the differences between relative and absolute paths, and learned how to create them. You applied links to text and images, and created image maps with hotspots of different shapes. You learned how you can link to a folder if a page uses the default filename, and how to use subdomains to organize content.

KEY TERMS

Alt

Alternate text

Bookmark

Client-side image map

Deep links

DHTML

FAQs (Frequently Asked Questions)

FTP (File Transfer Protocol)

Hotspots

HTTP (HyperText Transfer Protocol)

Image map

Invisible element

Links

Mailto

Named anchors

Navigation bars

Protocol

Server-side image map

Spam/U.C.E. (unsolicited commercial e-mail)

Spammers

URL

CHECKING CONCEPTS AND TERMS

SCREEN ID

Identify the indicated areas from the following list:

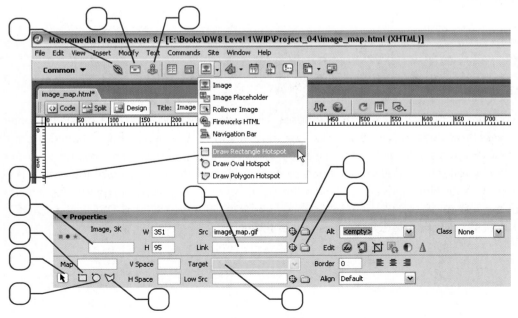

FIGURE 4.38

a. Target of link

b. Browse for File button

c. Oval Hotspot tool

d. Create a link

e. Image map name

f. Images drop-down list

g. Rectangle Hotspot tool

h. Point to File button

i. Pointer Hotspot tool

j. Create an e-mail link

k. Polygon Hotspot tool

l. Create a named anchor

m. Link field

MULTIPLE CHOICE

Circle the letter of the correct answer for each of the following:

1. Links are _____ .

a. the fundamental building blocks of the World Wide Web

b. really called "hyperlinks"

c. for directing the viewer from one page to another location or resource on the Web

d. All of the above

2. The term "protocol" _____ .

a. refers to the specific terms required for cross-platform communications

b. is a resource on the Internet

c. identifies how a browser is to handle the destination of a link

d. is a domain name

3. Which is not true of http?

a. It means that the destination is an e-mail address.

b. It is not required in a relative path.

c. It is the acronym for HyperText Transfer Protocol.

d. It means that the destination is a Web page.

4. An image map in Dreamweaver _____ .

a. must have fewer than 64 colors

b. must be a GIF image

c. has hotspot links

d. All of the above

5. The _____ in the Property inspector can be used to create all types of links.

a. Link field

b. Point to File button

c. Browse for File button

d. All of the above

6. Relative paths _____ .

a. are the same as absolute paths

b. use the location of the current page as a starting point

c. are hotspots

d. use the root folder of the site as a starting point

7. Absolute links are necessary when linking _____ .

a. a page to a named anchor

b. to a target window

c. to a page in another Web site

d. alternate text

8. E-mail links _____ .

a. are Internet addresses

b. are absolute links

c. require the mailto: protocol

d. require hyperlinks

9. Different link regions within a single image
_____ .

   a. are called hotspots

   b. are an image map

   c. do not require alternative text

   d. All of the above

10. Links to sections within a page are called
_____ .

   a. FAQs

   b. target windows

   c. named anchors

   d. image maps

DISCUSSION QUESTIONS

1. Some Web sites use text links and others use image maps. Describe two situations in which using image maps would be more effective than text links. Explain why.

2. If you create a link to an interior page (not their home page) of another Web site, this can cause potential problems for both your visitors using the link and the Web-site owner. What might these problems be? Give an example.

3. The World Wide Web has changed the lives of everyone and every business. What role does hyperlinking play in this change?

SKILL DRILL

Skill Drill exercises reinforce project skills. Each skill that is reinforced is the same as, or nearly the same as, a skill we presented in the chapter. We provide detailed instructions in a step-by-step format. You should do the Skill Drill exercises in order.

1. Explore Other Methods for Creating Links

The browse-for-file method is only one method for establishing a link to a page. There are other methods that you can use to establish links to pages or named anchors. For these methods to work, the Files panel must be expanded so that the filenames are visible.

1. Open about.html from the TO-P4 site.

2. Select Products in the bottom paragraph.

3. Drag the Point to File icon from the Property inspector to default.html in the Files panel, and click products.html to set it as the destination.

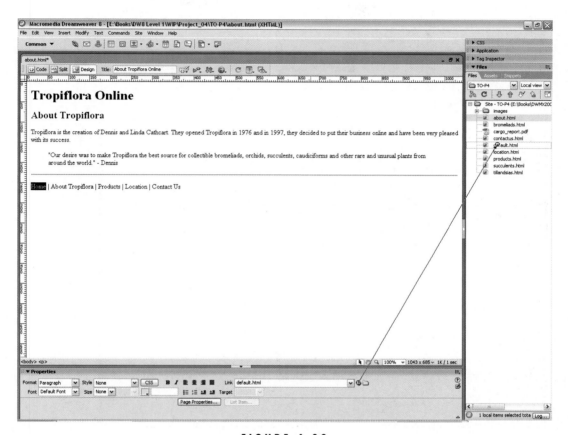

FIGURE 4.39

4. Repeat the procedure to link "Location" to location.html, and "Contact Us" to contactus.html.

5. Preview the page in your browser and test the links.

6. Return to Dreamweaver and close about.html.

7. Open bromeliads.html.

8. Select "Home" at the bottom of the page.

? If You Have Problems

The link method outlined in Step 9 only works on Windows systems. The link methods outlined in Steps 3 and 10 work on both Windows and Macintosh systems. In Step 9, Macintosh users should use the link method outlined in Step 3.

9. Holding the Shift key, drag from the selected text to default.html in the Files panel.

   A line appears between "Home" and the mouse pointer.

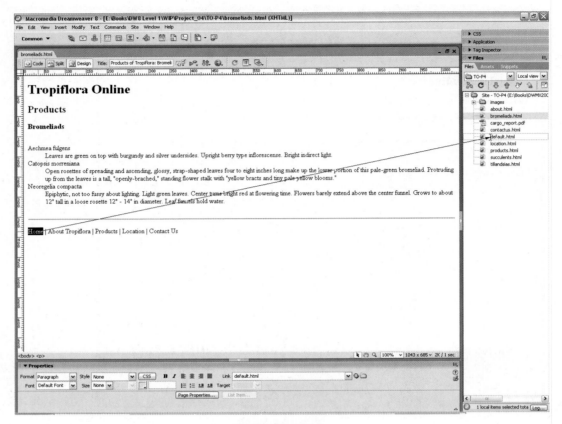

FIGURE 4.40

? **If You Have Problems**

You must hold the Shift key first before using the mouse to drag from the selected text to the filename.

---

10. Select the "About Tropiflora" text. Right/Control-click in the selected text and choose Make Link from the context menu; then select about.html, and click OK/Choose.

    This method works in both Macintosh and Windows systems.

11. Using any of the preceding methods, link "Products" to products.html, "Location" to location.html, and "Contact Us" to contactus.html.

12. Close bromeliads.html, saving the changes.

2. Link Pages Using the Link List

Dreamweaver remembers the links created during a particular session and temporarily stores the links in the Link list. As it is only temporary, the Link list is emptied when you exit Dreamweaver. However, even when Dreamweaver is running, the Link list only contains links that were created during the current session. If a link to default.html was not created during this session, it does not appear in the list.

1. Open succulents.html.

2. Select "Home" from the bottom Navigation-bar paragraph.

3. Click the drop-down arrow to the right of the Link list, and choose default.html from the list.

? If You Have Problems

If you had to close Dreamweaver after the previous Skill Drill, the Link list has emptied. To repopulate the Link list, close succulents.html, open tillandsias.html, and create the links using either of the previous methods. Close, saving tillandsias.html, reopen succulents.html, and continue with Step 2 previously. By creating links using tillandsias.html, you ensure that the Link list is populated with the links needed for succulents.html.

FIGURE 4.41

4. Repeat the procedure for the other items in the Navigation-bar paragraph.

5. Close, saving succulents.html.

6. Open tillandsias.html. Using any method, link the items in the Navigation-bar paragraph to the appropriate files. Close, saving the changes when finished.

3. Link to Named Anchors in Other Pages

In this Skill Drill, you create links to named anchors in pages other than the originating page. You must first create the named anchors, and then create the links.

1. Open bromeliads.html. Move the insertion point to the left of the "Aechmea fulgens" text. Click the Named Anchor button in the Insert bar, type `af` as the name, and click OK. Close, saving the changes to bromeliads.html.

2. Open succulents.html. Create a named anchor called `hz` to the left of the "Hernia zebrina" text. Close, saving the changes.

3. Open tillandsias.html. Create a named anchor called `tl` to the left of the "Tillandsia latifola" text. Close, saving the changes.

4. Open both bromeliads.html and products.html. On Windows systems, choose Window>Tile Vertical to arrange the two pages side by side. On Macintosh systems, manually move and resize the two windows so they are side by side.

5. In products.html, select the "Aechmea fulgens" text below the "Products" heading.

6. Using the Property inspector's Point to File button, drag the pointer to the **af** anchor in the bromeliads.html file.

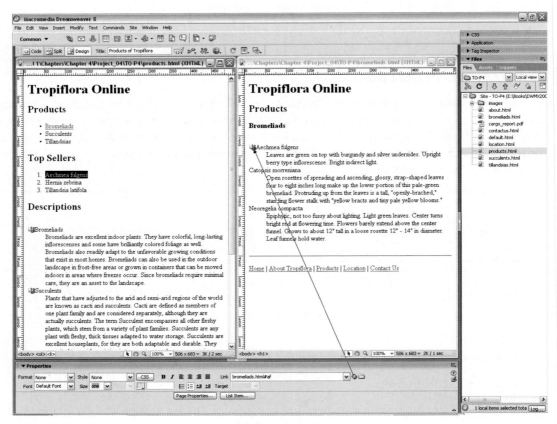

FIGURE 4.42

7. Close bromeliads.html and leave products.html open.

8. Open succulents.html and arrange the two pages side by side.

9. From products.html, select "Hernia zebrina" and link it to the **hz** named anchor in succulents.html.

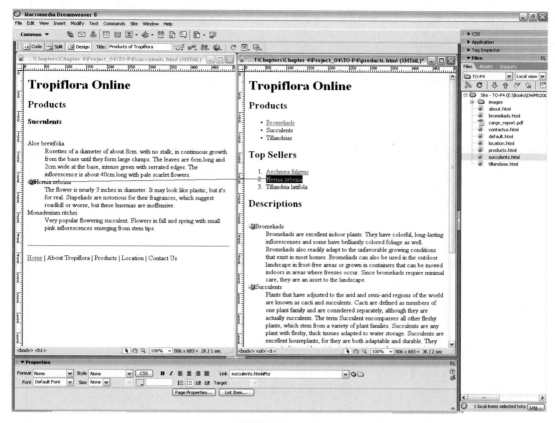

FIGURE 4.43

10. Close, saving the changes to succulents.html. Leave products.html open.

11. Open tillandsias.html and arrange the two pages side by side. In products.html, select "Tillandsia latifola" and link it to the **tl** named anchor in tillandsias.html.

12. Close both documents, saving the changes.

To Extend Your Knowledge . . .

NAMED ANCHORS ON OTHER WEB SITES

In the same way that we can create links to named anchors on our own site, whether on the same page or on other pages, we can also create links to named anchors on pages of other sites. The problem is that we cannot look at a page in the browser and see the named anchors.

One method of finding named anchors on a page is to find any links on the page, often at the top of the page, move your mouse pointer over the link, and note the link's destination. If the link points to the current page and has a # followed by text, you know that you have found a page with a named anchor. Another method is to view the actual code of the page and look for `<a name="something">`. You can then create a link to the page and the named anchor on the page.

Be aware that unlike the pages on your site, you have no control over the content or the structure of others' pages. They may decide to remove the named anchor, rename it, or even remove or rename the page itself, thereby reducing your link to a dead link. Check these links regularly to avoid sending visitors to a dead link.

4. Create an Image-Map Navigation Bar

The single image at the bottom of the Location page was created for use as an image-map Navigation bar. In this exercise, you create an image map using this image and link the different regions to their appropriate Web pages.

1. Open location.html.

2. Scroll to the bottom of the page and click the large image.

   Unlike the individual images in the Contact Us page that were separately linked to the appropriate pages, this single image will serve as a Navigation bar using hotspots that link to the appropriate pages.

3. In the Property inspector's Map field, type `navbar`.

4. Using the Rectangular Hotspot tool, outline a rectangle around the image's Home area, create a link to default.html, and assign Home as the alternative text.

5. Create the remaining hotspots using the name of the area as the Alt text and link them to the appropriate pages in this site.

6. Preview the page in your browser.

7. Return to Dreamweaver and close location.html.

5. Link to a PDF Document

Most links are to other Web pages, but you may need to link to a ***PDF*** document (Portable Document Format, a Web-ready format used when the author wishes to preserve the document's original fonts and layout) or to other types of resources. For the most part, the process is the same, but because a PDF document is not a Web page, an additional attribute is recommended by the W3C. You must edit the link in the Code window to add this attribute.

1. Open products.html.

2. Click after the "Tillandsias" text in the "Products" list.

3. Press Enter/Return once and type `Grower's Supplies (PDF, 69 KB)`.

4. Select "Grower's Supplies (PDF, 69 KB)" and link the text to cargo_report.pdf using any method learned in this chapter.

5. Click the Split button at the top of the Document window.

6. At the end of the opening anchor tag **`<a href="cargo_report.pdf">`**, move the insertion point to the left of the closing angle bracket and type `type="application/pdf"`.

   Dreamweaver's code hints do not include the **type** attribute, although it is a valid attribute for the anchor tag since HTML 4.

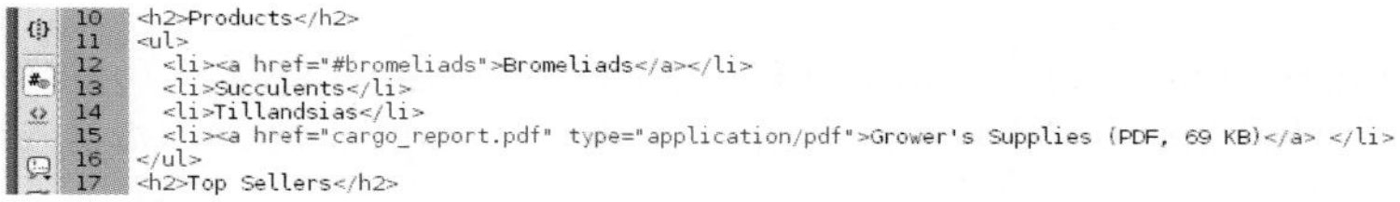

```
10    <h2>Products</h2>
11    <ul>
12      <li><a href="#bromeliads">Bromeliads</a></li>
13      <li>Succulents</li>
14      <li>Tillandsias</li>
15      <li><a href="cargo_report.pdf" type="application/pdf">Grower's Supplies (PDF, 69 KB)</a> </li>
16    </ul>
17    <h2>Top Sellers</h2>
```

FIGURE 4.44

7. Close the Code window by clicking the Design button at the top of the Document window.

8. Preview the page in your browser and click the new link.

   If your system has Acrobat Reader or any other PDF viewer, the PDF document opens in the viewer or reader.

9. Return to Dreamweaver and close products.html.

To Extend Your Knowledge . . .

MIME TYPES

MIME (Multipurpose Internet Mail Extensions) was originally devised for e-mail attachments, so that if you attached a particular type of file to a message, the recipients' e-mail application would know how to handle the attachment, such as by playing the music, showing the video, or opening the PDF document in Acrobat Reader. MIME types also play a role in Web-page links, enabling the visitors' browsers to open the file with the appropriate application. It is not always necessary to add the MIME type to the link, especially for common types of files like PDFs. However, uncommon types of files or filename extensions, such as .pdfx, benefit from the use of the MIME type in the link; without the MIME type, users are asked by their browser which application should be used to open the file.

The MIME type is divided into the major and minor types. Major types include `application`, `audio`, and `video`, among others. In each major type, there are few to many minor types, depending on the major type. For example, the major type `application` has more than 30 minor types whereas audio has only a few. The MIME type format identifies the major type, followed by a forward slash, then the minor type: `application/pdf`, for example. You can find a brief description of MIME types and a breakdown of the major and minor types at http://www.ltsw.se/knbase/internet/mime.htp. The Webopedia is also a good resource for many computer-related terms: MIME types are described at http://www.webopedia.com /TERM/M/MIME.html.

6. Use Link Management in Dreamweaver

Without question, one of Dreamweaver's strongest features is its ability to update and fix links that somehow get broken. The first step in managing links is to identify the current state of your links. The Check Links Sitewide function causes Dreamweaver to check every link on the site. When you issue the command, the program produces a report that categorizes all links on the site, letting you know which need attention. You can choose to look at broken links, external links, or *orphaned files* — files that exist in the site but aren't linked to any of the site's active pages.

If you rename a file in the site folder, Dreamweaver recognizes that other files link to this file and that their links need to change to reflect the filename change. It asks you if you want to update dependent files with the new link directions.

All of these functions are possible if you define a site in Dreamweaver. If the Chapter_04 folder was not set up as a site, it would still be possible to do all of the exercises in this project; if you changed a filename, you would have to manually change the links in all files that link to it. This is why defining a site is so important.

1. Right/Control-click default.html in the Files panel.

2. Choose Check Links>Entire Current Site from the menu.

3. Observe that the Results panel opens below the Property inspector.

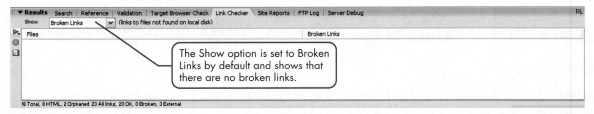

FIGURE 4.45

4. Click the down arrow to choose External Links from the Show list.

    E-mail links and links to external Web pages are both considered external links.

5. Choose Orphaned Files from the Show list.

    There are no pages or files in the TO-P4 folder to which there are no links.

6. Close the Results panel by clicking the panel menu at the far right of the panel and choosing Close Panel Group.

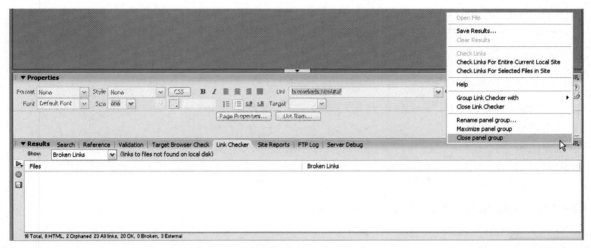

FIGURE 4.46

7. In the Files panel, Right/Control-click default.html and choose Edit>Rename.

8. Type `index.html` and press Enter/Return.

9. Click the Update button to update the links in the displayed files.

   All pages in this Web site are linked to default.html, the Home page. When you renamed the file, the links could have gone dead if Dreamweaver did not manage the Web site.

CHALLENGE

Challenge exercises expand on or are somewhat related to skills we presented in the lessons. Each exercise provides a brief narrative introduction, followed by numbered-step instructions that are not as detailed as those in the Skill Drill section. You should do these Challenge exercises in order.

1. Set Links in a Page to the Others in the Site

In this Challenge, you create the links from the FAQ page to the other pages in the site. You can use any method taught previously in the lessons or Skill Drills — this is a good opportunity to experiment with all of the methods to get comfortable with them.

The pages in this site contain images, JavaScript, and CSS. When you create the links in this page, the text changes color. This is a function of the styles applied to the link text.

1. Set the Chapter_04>DF-P4 folder as a defined site in Dreamweaver. Name it DF-P4 and ensure Access (in both the Remote Info and Testing Server categories) and Server Model are set to None.

2. Open faqs.htm.

The two major groups of links are those down the page's left side and along the bottom in the footer area. For the most part they are identical, except for the link to the design agency that created this Web site. This link is only in the footer area.

3. Using any method taught previously, link "Home" to index.htm, "About" to about.htm, "Formal Wear" to formalwear.htm, and so on in both the left navbar and the footer navbar.

4. In the page's footer, link "redrhino" to http://www.redrhino.co.uk.

5. In the last paragraph above the footer, link "Contact Us" to contact.htm.

6. In the top-right corner of the page is a Contact Us image — link it to contact.htm and add Contact Us as the alt text.

7. Preview the page in your browser and test the links.

8. Return to Dreamweaver and leave the file open for the next Challenge.

2. Create Named Anchors and Links

At the top of the FAQs page are the frequently asked questions. You will link them to the appropriate paragraphs below where the questions are repeated and the answers are given. First you create the named anchors and then the links.

1. In the open file faqs.htm, click in front of the first paragraph that has the answer to the first question. You can place the named anchor in front of the sentence beginning with "How much notice" or in front of the answer immediately below it beginning with "With wedding suits."

2. Create a named anchor simply called a1 (numeral one).

3. Repeat the same procedure for the remaining 11 questions — create a named anchor either in front of the question or at the beginning of the answer.

4. Scroll to the top.

5. Select the first question in the list.

6. Using the Property inspector's Point to File button, point to the first named anchor.

7. Select the second question in the list.

8. In the Property inspector's Link field, type `#a2` (the named anchor for the second answer).

9. Continue to link the questions at the top with the named anchors beside the answers below.

? If You Have Problems

The page is too long to see the last few questions and their answers below in the same screen. To link the questions at the top and the answers at the bottom, there are two possible methods:

1. Select the question and then type the anchor name in the Property inspector's Link field.

2. Select the question, scroll down until the named anchor is visible, and then drag the Point to File icon to the named anchor. The selected text does not need to be visible to create a link from it to the named anchor.

---

10. In the bottom-right corner is an image of the text Top. Click the Top image and link it to #top either by typing `#top` in the Link field or by scrolling up and using the Point to File button to point to the named anchor in the page's top-left corner. This link's purpose is to return the reader quickly to the page's top.

11. Preview the page in your browser and test the links.

12. Return to Dreamweaver and close faqs.htm.

3. Create Links from Appropriately Descriptive Text

You learned earlier that "click here" is not appropriate link text. In this exercise, the home page of Debonair Formalwear has been changed to include many "click here" phrases. Your task is to remove them and create links from appropriate words or phrases in the remaining text.

1. Open index.htm.

2. Under the section entitled "Formal Wear-the last word in Black Tie", click the link text "here" and note the link's destination page.

3. From that paragraph, delete the last sentence that includes the "here" text link.

4. Select an appropriate word or phrase in the remaining sentence, and create a link to the same destination to which "here" was previously linked.

5. Continue to refine the links in the main content of this page (leaving the left and bottom Navigation bars alone).

6. Preview this page in your browser to ensure that the links are working correctly.

7. Return to Dreamweaver and close index.htm.

4. Create a List of Links to Competitive Businesses

Debonair Formalwear competes with other businesses to provide clients in the UK with formalwear. Your task is to search the Internet for five other businesses in the UK that offer formalwear for rent or purchase, and to list them as other competitive businesses.

1. Open competition.htm.

   The first business has been created for you as the first list item. Find five others and record them using the same formatting.

2. Using your browser and your favorite search engine, search for another business in the UK that may compete with Debonair Formalwear.

When you perform your search, use the search term "hire" instead of "rent". Note the URL to the business's Web site, a brief description (a single sentence is fine) indicating the products and/or services of the business, and the phone number of the business.

3. Type the business's name in the next bullet.

4. Select the business's name and link it to the URL of the business's Web site. Set the link to open in a new browser window, and add a `title` attribute to the opening anchor tag that reads "Link opens

in new window." Press Shift-Enter/Return and type (or copy and paste) a descriptive paragraph about the business's services or products. Press Shift-Enter/Return and type (or copy and paste) the business's phone number. Press Enter/Return to create a new bullet.

5. Continue to insert four more businesses in the same manner.

6. Open faqs.htm and create a link from an appropriate word or phrase in the document to competition.htm.

7. Close and save the changes to faqs.htm.

8. Preview competition.htm in your browser.

9. Return to Dreamweaver and close competition.htm.

PORTFOLIO BUILDER

Create a Portal Site

A "portal" site is one that provides related links and information specific to one or more subjects. There are many examples of such sites on the Web. In this assignment, you're going to create one of your own.

1. Pick a subject about which you have a personal interest. It could be anything you like — carpentry, fishing, hiking, skating, skiing, etc.

2. Create a Home page to act as a container for links to related sites.

3. Use Google or another search engine to locate at least 12 sites that provide information that is relevant to the subject.

4. Create links to each of the sites, including space for a small amount of descriptive text.

5. Check the links to make sure they all work as you expected them to.

6. Include an e-mail link so visitors can submit new sites to include in the list.

CHAPTER 5

Inline Images

OBJECTIVES

In this chapter, you learn how to:

- Choose the correct image format

- Insert images into a Web page

- Align images within a paragraph

- Set image borders and spacing

- Crop oversized images

- Resize, resample, sharpen, and adjust images

- Work with image placeholders

Why Would I Do This?

It wasn't so long ago that colors, images, and computing didn't coexist gracefully. Prior to the mid-1980s, most computer systems were character-based and would not display images, let alone multiple colors. Early computer monitors displayed text in either green or amber, and few would call those displays "color monitors." Putting images onto computer screens is a relatively recent advance.

Although the Internet was first created in the late 1960s, it wasn't until the early 1990s that images began to appear on Web pages. The appeal of images in Web pages was significant to the Internet, becoming part of almost everyone's life. If pictures were worth a thousand words, as the saying goes, how many words would Flash animation, videos, or downloadable music be worth? Without the media-rich content we've grown accustomed to, the Web would be a much less popular place.

Although you can build entire Web sites using images alone, it is not recommended. Certainly some sites require an extensive number of images — catalog sites and artists' portfolio sites are just a few such examples. Some individuals, however, make images out of the text to preserve its formatting. When image designers create elaborate printed works, they don't have to worry about whether the text is in a standard or highly modified font. The amount of file space that the resulting brochure may take on the designer's computer does not affect the reader of the printed product. However, if you primarily use images to build your sites, you have to take into account that images weigh more; that is, they take longer to download than does type. For this reason, it is generally recommended that you use HTML and CSS to style your text instead of creating an image from the text.

Spotted in an e-mail: "A picture may be worth a thousand words, but a thousand words take less time to download." Selective use of images, appropriate choice of formats, and application of available image options ensures the fastest possible access speed for your visitors. Image designers with extensive print experience are accustomed to having many color choices and layout options available for print design; they often feel frustrated by the apparent limitation of design options available for Web work. Yet you can achieve great Web design with the right tools and knowledge.

In this chapter, you learn about the different types of image formats so you can make choices about which format is appropriate in each situation. You learn how to insert images on a page; align them to the left or right; place borders around them; and use Dreamweaver's image-editing tools to crop, resize, resample, and sharpen images. Not all Web sites need lots of images, but virtually all Web sites have some. This chapter enables you to work with images, few or many, in your Web pages.

VISUAL SUMMARY

Dreamweaver has many functions with which you can insert and manipulate images. You can insert images from the Files panel, the Assets panel, or the Images drop-down menu on the Common Insert bar (Figure 5.1). From the Common Insert bar, you can select the Images:Image button, which also has a drop-down list of other image-related functions. You can also use the Image Placeholder function, which allows you to reserve space for an image until the final version is available to insert into the Web page.

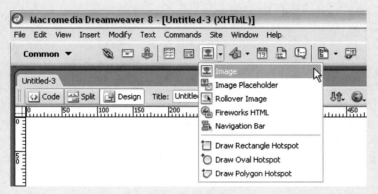

FIGURE 5.1

The Assets panel is part of the Files panel group; expand it by clicking the Assets tab. Assets are resources — such as images, library items, and templates — that you can use in your Web site. Select the type of asset by clicking the appropriate button at the left of the Assets panel. At the top of this panel is a preview window that allows you to see the image before inserting it. Below the preview window is a list of the images available in the folders of the current site.

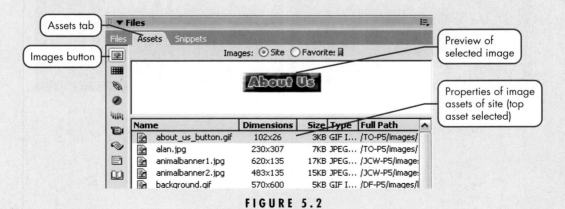

FIGURE 5.2

When you select an image, many properties of the image appear in the Property inspector, such as file size (measured in kilobytes), width, and height. The Property inspector displays other attributes of the image, such as alternate text, alignment, border, and horizontal and vertical spacing. View or modify any of these properties using the Property inspector.

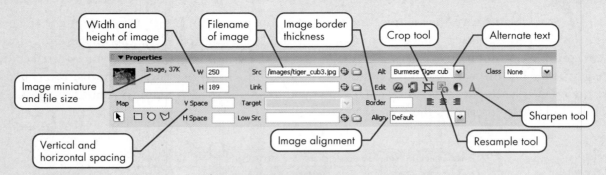

FIGURE 5.3

You can identify a selected image in the Document window because it has three handles. Drag these handles to enlarge or reduce the size of the image. Dreamweaver also offers some basic image-editing tools, such as the Crop, Resample, and Sharpen tools. In Figure 5.4, the image on the right in the Dreamweaver window is ready for cropping — the crop area is outlined with a border, eight handles, and a darkened surrounding area of the image. You can resize the crop area using any of the handles that appear around it.

FIGURE 5.4

LESSON 1 Exploring Image Formats

In this lesson, you learn why different types of image formats are better suited for particular situations by comparing different types of images — photo images and text images. You cannot create images in Dreamweaver, but as a Web designer, you can work with an image designer who prepares the images. Knowing which formats are best suited for Web pages for different purposes will help you either guide the graphic designer or select among the image options. We restrict our comparisons to JPEG, GIF, and PNG images because visitors can view them all using most modern browsers.

There are dozens of image-file formats, but only a few are Web-compatible. Virtually all popular illustration and imaging programs — Macromedia Fireworks, Adobe Illustrator, Macromedia FreeHand, Adobe Photoshop, and others — can convert images to these formats. You need to understand the differences between the various formats and the options available for each, so that you can choose the appropriate format for the situation.

Image formats for the Web fall into two broad categories. ***Bitmap images*** are comprised of individual pixels, each containing a specific color or tone value. This group includes GIF (.gif), JPEG (.jpeg or .jpg), and PNG (.png) image formats.

The GIF format is the most common image format used for Web images. ***GIF*** is an acronym for Graphics Interchange Format. It's best to use this GIF format for relatively simple images with large areas of solid (or ***flat***) color, such as button elements, because the GIF format can only contain 256 colors (also referred to as ***8-bit color*** because $2 \times 2 \times 2 \times 2 \times 2 \times 2 \times 2 \times 2 = 2^8 = 256$). This format has several features and options. You can specify that it contain transparent regions by choosing one color, generally the background, to be transparent. ***Animated GIFs*** are multiple-layered GIFs in which layers display sequentially, simulating movement. You can also set GIFs to ***interlace***, that is, load in a series of steps. Each step makes the image appear sharper until the image reaches its final quality. Interlacing is useful for displaying a large image — impatient visitors who see the progressive display of the image are less likely to move from your Web site before the image has finished loading. GIF images use ***lossless compression***, which means that the file size is smaller without losing any image information.

The ***JPEG*** image format (developed by and named after the Joint Photographic Experts Group) is best for ***high-color images***, or images containing many subtle colors, such as photographs or gradients. The JPEG image format supports up to 16.7 million colors (or 24-bit color). In contrast to GIFs, JPEGs use ***lossy compression*** — the higher the compression, the smaller the file size and the more information is lost. Most digital cameras store their photos in JPEG format with a low compression ratio, allowing some shrinkage of the file size with limited loss of photographic information. Like GIFs, JPEGs have a progressive-loading option.

The ***PNG (Portable Network Graphics)*** format is the least-common format. It is a relative newcomer to the Web images scene, so some of its features are not supported by all browsers. It has many features similar to GIFs (which it was designed to replace), such as transparency, lossless compression, and progressive loading, but in all cases the features are much better implemented. The PNG format does not support animation, although the related format MNG (Multiple-image Network Graphics) is being developed for that purpose. You can save PNGs in either 8-bit (256 colors) or 24-bit (16.7 million colors) format. While it may seem that the 24-bit color mode is suitable to replace JPEGs, the lossy compression routine in JPEGs produces smaller file sizes than 24-bit PNGs.

Vector images are comprised of mathematically described lines and shapes. The use of vector images on the Web is relatively new and includes Flash animation and Scalable Vector Graphics (SVG). CorelDRAW, Adobe Illustrator, and Macromedia FreeHand and Fireworks all primarily create vector images, but often users convert their illustrations to GIF, PNG, or JPEG format for use in a Web page.

Flash objects can be static or animated and can even change in response to user actions, such as responding to the position of the mouse pointer or to keystrokes. The Flash format is compressed, enabling quick downloads. Dreamweaver cannot create complex Flash objects or animations, but it can create static Flash text and some simple Flash-animated buttons. For more information about Flash and to learn how to create elements that you can use in your Dreamweaver sites, refer to *Essentials for Design Flash 8 Level One.*

The ***Scalable Vector Graphics (SVG)*** format is a new vector format that can incorporate vector images, bitmap images, and text. It can be both dynamic and interactive. Although some image-illustration software (such as CorelDRAW and Adobe Illustrator) can save to the SVG format, Internet Explorer, the most popular browser, cannot display these images without a plug-in (the recently released Opera 8 and soon to be released Firefox 1.5, both can display SVG natively, without a plugin). There is much hope that this format will be widely adopted but, given the seven years since the PNG format was recommended by the W3C without yet achieving complete acceptance by the general population and all browsers, the SVG format may be a few years away from widespread adoption. SVG is a text-based format, like HTML, in which code describes the shapes, positions, and colors, as in Figure 5.5 — here, the tenth and eleventh lines in the code describes the red circle with a blue outline (stroke) shown to the left.

```
<?xml version="1.0" standalone="no"?>
<!DOCTYPE svg PUBLIC "-//W3C//DTD SVG 1.1//EN"
    "http://www.w3.org/Graphics/SVG/1.1/DTD/svg11.dtd">
<svg width="12cm" height="4cm" viewBox="0 0 1200 400"
    xmlns="http://www.w3.org/2000/svg" version="1.1">
  <desc>Example circle01 - circle filled with red and stroked with blue</desc>
  <!-- Show outline of canvas using 'rect' element -->
  <rect x="1" y="1" width="1198" height="398"
        fill="none" stroke="blue" stroke-width="2"/>
  <circle cx="600" cy="200" r="100"
        fill="red" stroke="blue" stroke-width="10"  />
</svg>
```

FIGURE 5.5

Until you compare images using these formats, you cannot truly appreciate the differences between them and how one can be better than another in different circumstances. To what degree does JPEG's lossy compression have an effect on the quality of the image? Does the 256-color depth of GIF images limit its use? How do the compression routines of GIF and PNG images compare in terms of final file size? Should you choose index or alpha-transparency? Although you cannot create images in Dreamweaver, knowing about the different image formats will enable you to work with a graphic designer to make the best choices and give good advice.

Explore Different Image Formats for Photographs

In this exercise, you learn that the JPEG format is best for photographs, even when there are few enough colors in the photos for the GIF format. File size rather than image quality becomes the determining factor in the choice of image formats.

1   **Define the Chapter_05>Images folder as a site called Images using the methods outlined in previous chapters. Do not click Done — leave the Site Definition dialog box open for the next step.**

2   **Click the first site in the list and click the Remove button. When asked to confirm the removal, click Yes. Repeat until you have removed all sites from the list (except the Images site you defined in Step 1). Click Done when finished.**

As you create more and more Web sites and site definitions, your list of sites in the Files panel and Site Definition dialog box can become long and cumbersome. By removing the site definitions, it is easier to work with your current Web site projects. Removing a site definition from the site listing does not delete the site from your computer — the folders and files remain as they were, but they are not listed in the sites list. You can re-create the site definition for removed sites at any time to work on them again.

? If You Have Problems

Complex sites may have remote access, testing server, and other advanced settings that require more effort to recreate the site definition. For these more-complex site definitions, record all settings before removing the site definition. The site definitions in this book are very simple and require very little effort to recreate if you wish to do so.

3 Open photos.html in Dreamweaver and preview it in your browser.

4 Compare the photos in cells 1a and 1b.

Both are high-quality images, but the lossy compression routine in the JPEG format makes smaller file size possible.

FIGURE 5.6

5 Compare the photos in cells 2a, 2b, and 2c.

The JPEG format is better for photographs because it supports a wider range of colors and tones — the 8-bit GIF and PNG formats do not smoothly render the blending of greens in the background. If the JPEG compression setting is too high (Figure 5.7, cell 2a), the quality of the image is sacrificed.

FIGURE 5.7

6 **In Figure 5.8, compare the photos in cells 3a, 3b, and 3c.**

A black-and-white photograph (as a digital file) can contain up to 256 shades of gray. The GIF and 8-bit PNG formats support up to 256 colors, allowing the formats to display all of the shades of gray. However, accurate rendering of a black-and-white photograph in these GIF and PNG images comes at a cost in file size — more than double that of the JPEG image.

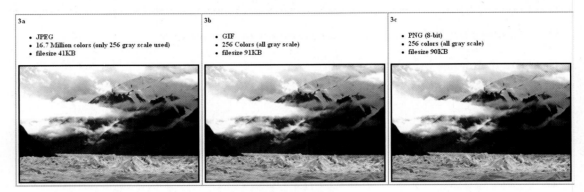

FIGURE 5.8

7 **Return to Dreamweaver and close photos.html.**

To Extend Your Knowledge . . .

FAVICON IMAGES

Favicon is a word created from "favorite" and "icon". It refers to the icon that appears at the left end of the Address bar or at the left end of a bookmark entry in your Favorites list (hence "favorite"). Commonly the icon is similar to the logo of the company or the Web site. A favicon is a 16 × 16 pixel image saved in a special icon format. Not all image applications can create this type of image, but you can create one for free online at http://www.chami.com/html-kit/services/favicon/.

To use the icon so that people visiting your Web site see it in their browser's address bar, you must save the icon as favicon.ico in the root folder of your Web site, not in the images folder or any other folder. You must also add the following code in the <head> section of your Web pages: `<link rel="shortcut icon" href="/favicon.ico" type="image/x-icon" />`. You must code this manually, as Dreamweaver does not have any menu functions to assist you.

Explore Different Image Formats for Simple Images

In this next exercise, you discover that GIF and PNG formats are best suited to simple images. You also observe that splitting an image into complex and simple components reduces the total download time by optimizing the different parts of the images for the appropriate file type.

1   **Open buttons.html and then preview the page in your browser.**

2   **In Figure 5.9, compare the images in cells 1a and 1b.**

The file-size difference is obvious, although, in reality, using the JPEG image only adds 11KB to the total download. However, if every simple image were saved in JPEG format instead of the GIF format, the *weight* of the Web page (the number of bytes used by the Web page between images, HTML, and other resources) would climb unnecessarily.

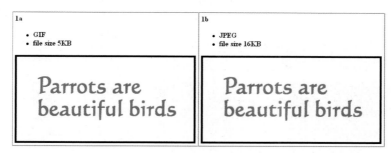

FIGURE 5.9

3   **In Figure 5.10, compare the images in cells 2a and 2b.**

GIF animation can add some interest to a page, but it can also be distracting. These animations have much larger file sizes than static images, even with optimization.

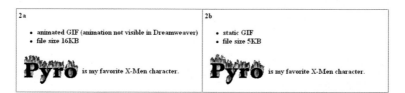

FIGURE 5.10

4   **In Figure 5.11, compare the images in cells 3a and 3b.**

Setting a color to be transparent in a GIF image does not take any additional file space.

FIGURE 5.11

5   **Switch to Dreamweaver without closing your browser.**

6   **In Figure 5.12, compare the images in cells 4a, 4b, and 4c.**

These three cells compare the transparency options of PNG and GIF image formats. Cell 4a contains a PNG with ***alpha-transparency***, a form of transparency that supports a range of transparency from opaque to transparent. At the time of this writing, no version of IE displays a PNG with alpha-transparency, although IE7 will support alpha-transparency. Only PNG images can use alpha-transparency. Both GIF (cell 4b) and PNG (4c) can use ***index transparency***, a form of transparency in which you can set one color, generally the background color, to 100% transparent. Again, the PNG image has a smaller file size than the identical image in GIF format.

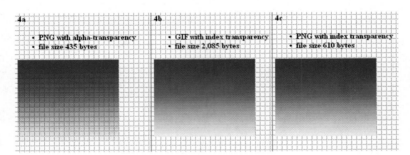

FIGURE 5.12

7   **Return to your browser and compare the images in Figure 5.13, cells 5a and 5b.**

The banner in 5a is a single, large JPEG image. You learned that JPEG is a good format for photos but wastes file space where the image information is simple. The banner in 5b was split into two parts — the left photo of the birds and the right black box with red text.

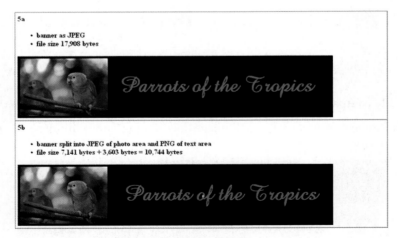

FIGURE 5.13

8   **Return to Dreamweaver and close buttons.html.**

To Extend Your Knowledge . . .

INDEX VS. ALPHA-TRANSPARENCY

As you saw, both GIF images and PNG images can employ transparency. Both formats support index transparency — one specific color, generally the background color, is set to 100% transparency.

Alpha-transparency is not limited to a single color or to 100% transparency. Each pixel in an image has an **RGB (red, green, blue)** code that specifies how much of each color should be used to create the color of the pixel. Images that support alpha-transparency use a color palette that is sometimes referred to as "RGBa," where the "a" represents the alpha channel. The alpha channel, just like the R, G, and B channels (or colors) in an image, has a range of values from 0 to 255; instead of a color, however, the alpha channel specifies the transparency of the pixel — 0 is opaque and 255 is transparent. This means that adjacent pixels of different colors may have different levels of transparency.

LESSON 2   Inserting Images into a Web Page

An *inline image* is an image that you insert into the foreground of the Web page among the other content. (We discuss background images in Chapter 6.) You can use inline images in interesting and novel ways in a Web site. For a business Web site, you might use the corporate logo as a link to the home page. You could use images in navigation bars to dress up parts of a Web page, as you saw in Chapter 4. You could use photos to accompany news stories. In a Web-based photo album, you might link *thumbnails* (miniature photos) to larger versions of the photos for better viewing.

While you can use images effectively and creatively, remember that images cost more in download time than text. The term "cost" may seem odd, given that most *ISPs (Internet Service Providers)* — businesses that provide access to the Internet — offer unlimited access to the Internet for a fixed fee. If your ISP doesn't charge based on usage, how could a large image cost more than a small image? ISPs may not charge based on *bandwidth* (the quantity of megabytes being transferred to and from their Web servers), but Web-hosting providers and high-volume Internet connections do. If your image-heavy designs cost your clients large bandwidth fees, they will not be happy. Before you use an image, evaluate its value, size, format, and quality — controlling all of these will enable you to balance design needs, download speed, and bandwidth costs.

An image uses the `<img />` tag, an empty tag. This tag has two required attributes — the `src` (source) attribute and the `alt` (alternate text) attribute. An `<img />` tag without an image source does not display an image, so this attribute is never omitted. However, many people do not realize that the `alt` attribute is also required according to the W3C specifications. An `<img />` tag without alternate text hinders people who use screen-reader software, character-based browsers, or browsers with images disabled, from being able to use your Web site efficiently.

Once you've determined which images you want to use, you need to know how to place them on pages and how Dreamweaver handles images as components of a defined site. On the Common Insert bar is an Images button that opens the Image dialog box, allowing you to select an image. You can also drag an image from the Files panel into the page. Do not, however, double-click an image in the Files panel — that action tries to open the image in an image-editing application, such as Fireworks.

Insert Images from the Insert Bar

There are several different methods for inserting inline images into your Web page. Inserting images from the Common Insert bar is just one of them. Through this chapter, you learn other methods as well.

1 Define the Chapter_05>TO-P5 folder as a site called TO-P5 using the methods outlined in previous chapters.

2 Open index.html and delete the top "Tropiflora Online" heading.

3 From the Common Insert bar, click the Images:Image button.

The button is called "Images:Image" because it is a drop-down button providing access to several image options. The current function is the Image function for inserting images into the page. The button's tool-tip text and icon change to reflect the last image function used, such as Images:Image Placeholder or Images:Rollover Image.

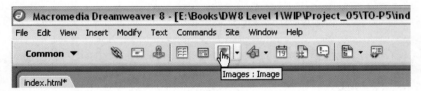

FIGURE 5.14

? ## If You Have Problems

If the Common Insert bar is not visible, use the pop-up menu at the left of the Insert bar and choose Common. If the fifth button from the left does not look like the Images button, click the drop-down list arrow to the right of the fifth button and choose Images from the top of the list. The Images:Image button changes its icon to represent the last image function selected from this list.

---

4 In the Select Image Source dialog box, double-click the images folder.

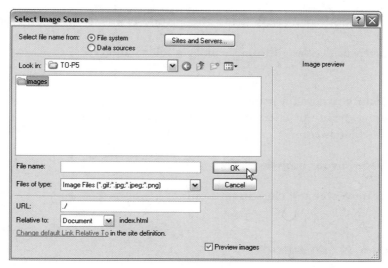

FIGURE 5.15

5   Choose tropiflora_online.jpg and click OK/Choose.

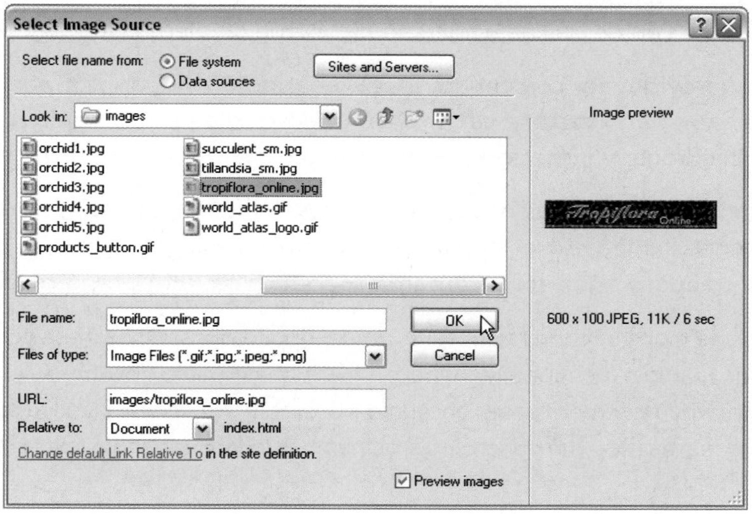

FIGURE 5.16

6   In the Alternate text field of the Image Tag Accessibility Attributes dialog box, type
Tropiflora Online, and click OK.

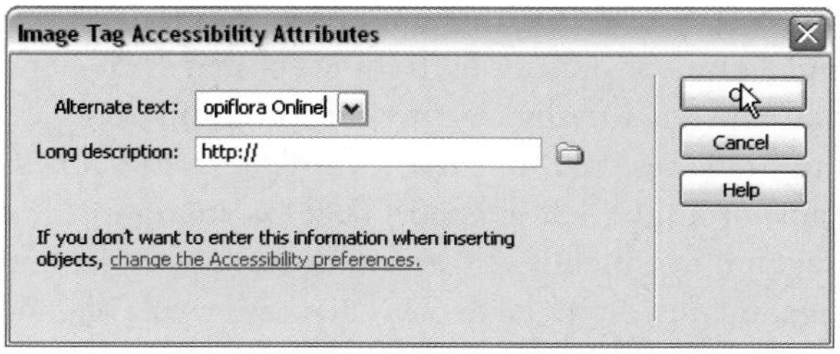

FIGURE 5.17

7   Click in the first empty paragraph below the "Exotic Plants from Around the World" heading.

8   Insert the image world_atlas.gif from the images folder, and type `World Atlas` in the Alternate text field.

9   Click in the empty paragraph below, insert world_atlas_logo.gif, type `Logo of WorldAtlas.Com` in the Alternate text field, and link the image to http://www.worldatlas.com.

10   Preview the page in your browser.

11   Return to Dreamweaver and close index.html.

To Extend Your Knowledge . . .

APPROPRIATE ALTERNATE TEXT FOR IMAGES

All images should have alternate text so users not viewing the images receive the appropriate information about images they encounter. You first categorize the image as decorative, simple, or complex. This categorization helps you determine what amount or type of alternate text is appropriate.

Decorative images provide no content to the Web page. The appropriate alternate text is `alt=""`, which is known as an ***empty alt***. In Dreamweaver, the <empty> option in the Alternate text field (or Alt field of the Property inspector) inserts an empty alt.

Simple images include button images or company logos. When these images are simply images of text, make the alternate text the text in the image. Otherwise, keep this text very brief: "Home" for a home page and the company name for a corporate logo such as "IBM Corporation".

Complex images include maps or charts from spreadsheet applications. Since these images convey a large amount of information, explain them briefly. Although there is no limit to how much text you can put in the alternate-text attribute, when a screen reader encounters alternate text, it reads it all to the user who is forced to listen to it all before moving on. The general rule of thumb is to limit alternate text to a few words at most.

LESSON 3   Aligning Images

You can align images in your Web designs but with somewhat more limited options than you would have in print design. The most common alignment options used for Web images are left and right. However, when you select left or right alignment for an image, the alignment works a bit differently than text alignment. Of course, the image shifts to the left or right, as selected, but the text of the paragraph flows around the image on the opposite side — text flows (wraps) around a left-aligned image on its right side and vice versa. If the image is taller than the height of the paragraph in which it is inserted, the following paragraph also wraps around it until, reaching the bottom of the image, the text flows below it. The other result of choosing left or right alignment is that the top of the image aligns with the top of the characters. Without any alignment chosen, by default the bottom of the image aligns with the bottom of the characters.

There is no center option for alignment of images — you must apply center alignment to the entire paragraph (or other block element) in which the image resides. In addition, any text in the same centered paragraph does not flow around it on either or both sides. Generally, you center an image only if it is the only content in a paragraph.

Align Images

1   **Open products.html.**

2   **In the Descriptions section of the page, click to the left of the named anchor on the left of the Bromeliads text.**

3   **Using the Images:Image button in the Common Insert bar, insert bromeliad_sm.jpg from the images folder, and give the image an empty alt attribute.**

When you insert an image, by default it displays with the bottom of the image aligned with the bottom of the surrounding text.

4   **Align the image to the right by choosing Right from the Align list in the Property inspector.**

FIGURE 5.18

5   **Click to the left of the Succulents text in the next section.**

6   **Insert succulent_sm.jpg, align it to the right, and give it an empty alt attribute.**

7   **Insert tillandsia_sm.jpg in front of the Tillandsia text, align it to the right, and give it an empty alt attribute.**

8   **Close, saving the changes to products.html.**

To Extend Your Knowledge . . .

IMAGE ALIGN VS. PARAGRAPH ALIGN

Just above the Align list are three icons representing left, center, and right alignment. You may wonder why we did not use these options instead of the alignment list. These options apply to the paragraph as a whole, not just to the selected image, so all text shifts to the left, center, or right. The alignment-options list applies to the image only and floats the image within the paragraph. Choosing right alignment of the paragraph pushes all text and images to the right, but the image does not float to the right of the paragraph text.

LESSON 4 Specifying Image Height and Width

Attributes of the `<img />` tag include `height` and `width`. These attributes specify the size of the image in pixels, the individual dots on your computer screen. ("Pixels" is a shortening of "picture elements".) You can modify the width and height of an image using `height` and `width`, but doing so can reduce the quality of the image. Enlarging a 100 × 100 image to 300 × 300 reduces its quality even though the proportions are the same. Compressing a 300 × 300 to 100 × 100 does not affect image quality as much as enlarging it, but if you want the image to display at 100 × 100 pixels, you should properly reduce the image itself so that its true or natural size is 100 × 100. A 300 × 300 image has a much larger file size than a 100 × 100 version of the same image, and it has a longer download time.

You should always specify the height and width of an image. Browsers take more time to *render* (display) a Web page if you haven't specified the image dimensions, because until the image finishes downloading, the browser does not know its size. The content around it shifts back and forth as the image loads, because the browser must keep making room for it. If you specify the dimensions, however, the browser reserves that space for it, and the text content remains fixed. Users can start to read the text content during the image download, which gives the impression of a faster download time. To make this easy for you, Dreamweaver always automatically inserts the image dimensions.

Dreamweaver enables you to resize images by changing their height and width attributes after you've inserted them into the Web page. Using the height and width attributes, however, isn't the appropriate way to resize an image. Resizing an image using the image attributes does not change its file size, just the amount of space in which it displays on the Web page. If the image is not the correct size, use image-editing software to resize it or create the image at the correct size.

To select an image in a Web page in Dreamweaver, click it. Selected images display three handles — one at the right side, one at the bottom-right corner, and one at the bottom side.

Explore Image Height and Width

1. **Open index.html.**

2. **Click the Tropiflora Online image at the top of the page to select it.**

   The Property inspector indicates that this image has a width of 600 and a height of 100. Note also that the Property inspector identifies the image as 11K (kilobytes) in size.

FIGURE 5.19

3   **Drag the right handle of the image to the left until the Property inspector shows that the width is 300 pixels.**

Observe that the 300 in the Width field displays in bold characters, indicating that the current dimension is not the natural size of the image.

FIGURE 5.20

4   **In the Property inspector, delete 100 from the H (Height) field, type 50, and press Enter/Return.**

The image is proportionately smaller than its original size.

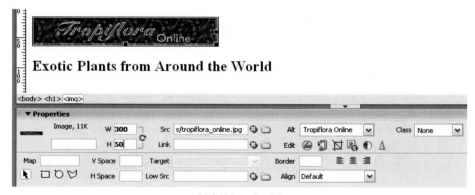

FIGURE 5.21

5   **Note that the image size remains 11K despite the resizing of the image.**

Resizing an image, as we have done, changes the amount of space it takes on a Web page, not its file size.

6   **Click the Reset Size/Reset Image to Original Size button to the right of the Width or Height fields in the Property inspector.**

The Reset Size button (Windows) does not have a tool tip to identify it, although the Reset Image to Original Size button (Macintosh) does. This button appears only when the size of an image (width and height) has been changed from its original size.

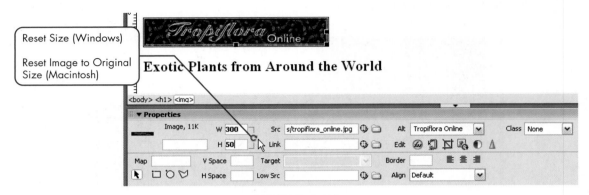

FIGURE 5.22

7   Close index.html. You may choose to save or not to save — the changes you made were returned to the original settings.

To Extend Your Knowledge . . .

SIZE IMAGES FIRST

When you use Dreamweaver to insert images into a Web page, the program adds the dimensions of the image to the `<img />` tag. If you find that the image is too large or too small, you can use the image's handles to resize it, but doing so distorts the image. Furthermore, as you saw, when you resize an image, it does not change the file size of the image, just the amount of space the image occupies on the Web page. Dreamweaver offers limited image-editing tools with which you can modify an image, but many professionals prefer to use image-editing software.

LESSON 5   Setting Image Borders and Spacing

Browsers apply a border around an image at the size specified in the code. However, if you do not specify the border width, browsers treat the borders of linking and nonlinking images differently. If the image is not a link and the border width is not specified, browsers assume a 0-px (zero-pixel) border. If the image is used as a link and the border width is not specified, the browser assumes a 2-px border. Most developers don't like to use borders around images. Dreamweaver has been programmed to understand this, so if an image is used as a link, Dreamweaver automatically sets the border to 0 (zero). Like the alignment attribute, borders are best handled through the **border** property of CSS. One difference between CSS and HTML attributes is that HTML borders affect all four sides of the image equally, whereas the CSS **border** property allows you to specify different measurements, colors, thickness, and styles for each side.

The default color for links, whether image or text links, is blue. If you change the default color, the color of the borders around image links also changes to the new color. Most Web designers find the border color around image links distracting, because the color may not match the image or the surrounding content. Generally, if they want a border around an image, they build the border into the image and set HTML borders to zero.

You can also put space around images by using **hspace** (horizontal space) and **vspace** (vertical space) attributes. If you set **hspace** to 5, a 5-px space appears on both the left and right sides of the image; **vspace** applies to both top and bottom at the same time. The **hspace** and **vspace** attributes are measured in pixels, but you don't have to specify pixels as the unit of measurement because pixels are the only unit allowed. These attributes are useful for keeping some white space around an image so that text does not butt up against them.

Create Image Borders

1 Open products.html.

2 Click the photograph of the bromeliad.

3 In the Property inspector, type 3 in the Border field and press Enter/Return.

FIGURE 5.23

? If You Have Problems

It is difficult to see the border around an image when it is selected. Click away from the image to deselect it so the changes are more apparent.

4 Close, saving the changes to products.html.

5 Open contactus.html.

6   **Click the email.gif image of the two computers.**

The Border width field is set to 0 pixels.

FIGURE 5.24

7   **Apply a 3-pixel border to the image and click away from it.**

The border created around this image is blue because the image is a link.

Email:

sales@tropiflora.com

FIGURE 5.25

8   **Reset the Border width to 0.**

9   **Save the changes, but leave the document open for the next exercise.**

Set Image Spacing

1   **In the open contactus.html document, click the Home image at the bottom of the Web page.**

Note that the images are pushed up against each other without any space between them.

2   **Set the H Space (Horizontal Spacing in the tool tip) to 3 and press Enter/Return.**

Observe that the Home image now has a space between it and the About Us image.

FIGURE 5.26

3   **One by one, click the remaining images in the navigation bar and apply 3-pixel horizontal spacing to each.**

4   **Preview the page in your browser.**

Email:

sales@tropiflora.com

<figure>
Home   About Us   Products   Location   Contact Us
</figure>

FIGURE 5.27

5   **Close your browser, return to Dreamweaver, and close contactus.html.**

LESSON 6   Cropping an Image

Dreamweaver has a few basic functions for editing images, as well as the ability to use the Edit and Optimize functions in Fireworks, a Macromedia application used for image creation and editing. You can perform basic image functions in Dreamweaver, but you would need a more sophisticated application for more complex image creation and editing.

The crop function allows you to specify an area of an image to keep. You select an image in the Document window and click the Crop button — a rectangle outlined with a border, eight handles and a darkened surrounding area of the image. This outline shows the area that will be kept when cropping occurs. You can reposition the crop area by dragging the outline — the mouse-pointer cursor changes to a move cursor (four arrows) to indicate that you can move the crop area. Eight handles around the crop area allow you to select the section of the image you want to keep. In the crop area, the image displays in its full color and brightness; outside the crop area, the image is darkened. The eight handles may not be clearly visible if the surrounding area of the image is dark. If this is the case, move the mouse pointer to the approximate position of the handles — the mouse-pointer cursor changes when it is over the handle. Even with a dark image, the boundary of the crop area is visible.

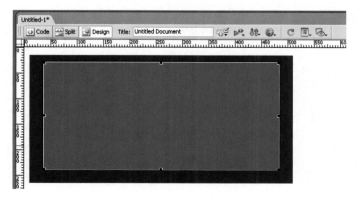

FIGURE 5.28

When you modify an image using the Crop button, you permanently change the image. For this reason, it is very important that you keep a duplicate copy of the original image elsewhere in another folder. If you make a mistake when cropping, make another copy of the original image and place it into the working image folder for your site.

Crop an Image

In this lesson, you reduce the size of some images that are oversized. You use the crop function to crop the unnecessary surrounding image material.

1 **Open staff.html.**

2 **Click the photo of Jeff.**

3 **Click the Crop button in the Property inspector.**

FIGURE 5.29

4 **Read the warning, Leave the Don't Show Me This Message Again option unchecked and click OK.**

FIGURE 5.30

5   Click in the crop area and drag the crop area down to the base of the figure. Ensure that both of Jeff's arms are in the crop area.

Drag the cross-hair mouse cursor down to keep the bottom of the photograph and crop the top

FIGURE 5.31

6   Drag the top handle in the middle of the top dashed line down to just above Jeff's head.

If the sides are too narrow or too wide, use the handles in the middle of the left and right sides to resize the width of the crop area. Drag the handle to enlarge or reduce the crop area.

FIGURE 5.32

7   Double-click in the crop area to activate the crop function.

Note the new dimensions of Jeff's photo so that in Lesson 8 you can crop Alan's photo to similar dimensions.

?   If You Have Problems

If you have cropped an image and the image simply resized to the dimensions of the crop area, you must relaunch Dreamweaver to restore its functionality. Close the page without saving, shut down Dreamweaver, and then restart it. Recopy the image file from the folder in which the original is located to your site's working folder, and repeat the cropping procedure.

8   **Save the changes.**

9   **Repeat the same procedures from Step 2 through Step 8 on the photo of Alan.**

If you run into the cropping issue described in the preceding "If You Have Problems" sidebar while working on this photo, follow the instructions in the sidebar, but just replace the alan.jpg image.

Staff of Tropiflora

F I G U R E   5 . 3 3

? **If You Have Problems**

Dreamweaver's cropping tool is quite basic. It is difficult to crop two or more images to exactly the same size — the images may slightly differ in height by a pixel or two. In the next lesson, you learn to properly resize and resample an image. If you crop these two images to different heights, proceed with the next lesson, then return to this one and resize and resample the images so they are the same height.

---

10   **Preview the page in your browser.**

11   **Return to Dreamweaver and close staff.html.**

LESSON 7   Resizing, Resampling, and Sharpening Images

When an image is not the right size, you can resize it by using the height and width options in the Property inspector or by dragging the image's handles; but this does not alter the image's file size, just the display area. Dreamweaver offers two image-editing tools that are useful when you resize an image: Resample and Sharpen.

Resampling is a two-step process that changes the number of pixels in an image: You resize the image and then resample it to add or discard pixels. After resampling, the original image is modified to the size for the width and height you set.

A side effect of resampling is that the image becomes soft. The outlines are not distinct because Dreamweaver uses ***antialiasing*** (a technique of blending bitmap-based images to reduce the stair-stepping or jagged appearance) to smooth the gradient between adjacent colors. You sharpen to increase the gradations between differing colors. ***Sharpening*** is a method of exaggerating edges in an image to give enhanced definition. Dreamweaver's sharpen function does not offer the same degree of fine control that equivalent tools in other graphic-arts software provide; however, it is certainly convenient and, with care, can produce good results. Cropping does not create any softness because a portion of the image is just cut out, not resized. For this reason, the resampling option is unavailable (grayed out) when you just crop.

Like the Crop button, both Sharpen and Resample irreversibly modify the image. If you are unsatisfied with the results, you must replace the file with the original copy and retry. For this reason, you should always keep copies of the original image files elsewhere on your computer.

When you resize an image, you can resize it proportionately or disproportionately. ***Proportionate resizing*** is modifying the size of an image while keeping the ratio of width to height constant. For example, resizing a 300 × 300 image to 100 × 100 is proportionate resizing, but resizing it to 100 × 120 is disproportionate resizing. In this example, it is very easy for you to proportionately resize the image simply by typing 100 in both the width and height fields. On the other hand, as you might imagine, it would be much more difficult to proportionately resize an 843 × 539 image by calculating the ratio in your head. In Dreamweaver, however, if you hold down the Shift key while dragging a corner handle, the height and width remain proportionate as you resize the image.

Resize and Resample An Image

1   **Open orchids.html.**

2   **Click the first image.**

Note the file size shows as 25K in the Property inspector.

FIGURE 5.34

3   Holding down the Shift key, drag the bottom-right handle up toward the top-left corner of the image until the height (H) in the Property inspector reads 150; release the mouse button before the Shift key.

FIGURE 5.35

4   Click the Resample button in the Property inspector.

FIGURE 5.36

5   Click OK to accept the warning.

6   Observe that the Property inspector shows the image's file size is now 5K and its natural dimensions are 134 pixels wide and 150 high.

You know these are the natural dimensions of the image because the Resize Image button is not visible to the right of the Width/Height fields.

FIGURE 5.37

7   Save the changes to orchids.html, but leave it open for the next exercise.

Sharpen an Image

Resampling softens an image. In this exercise, you sharpen the image to reverse the softening effect of resampling.

1   In the open orchids.html file, click the resized image.

2   In the Property inspector, click the Sharpen button and then click OK to accept the warning.

FIGURE 5.38

3   Move the slider to the first notch and click OK.

You can experiment with other settings to find a setting you like. With the Preview option checked, the image in the Design window shows how the image will appear at each setting.

FIGURE 5.39

4 With the image still selected, set the H Space (horizontal spacing) field in the Property inspector to 2.

FIGURE 5.40

5 Apply the procedures from this and the preceding exercise to the remaining four images until you have reduced them all to 150 pixels high with 2-pixel horizontal spacing.

The proportions of the images are different, so they have different widths but the same height of 150 pixels.

FIGURE 5.41

6 Preview the page in your browser.

7 Return to Dreamweaver and close orchids.html.

To Extend Your Knowledge . . .

MINOR ADJUSTMENTS TO IMAGE SIZE

At times, because of the dimensions of an image, you may not be able to proportionally resize the image to exactly the height or width that you would like. For example, picture an image of 843 × 539 pixels that you want to resize from 843 to 450 pixels high. You may discover that the closest to 450 that you can achieve is 451 or 449. Given that it is only different by one pixel, resize the image to 451 or 449 and then manually type 450 in the height field before resampling. You will not be able to detect the slight distortion that this disproportionate adjustment may create.

LESSON 8   Working with Image Placeholders

As you develop Web pages, some images may not yet be ready to place. Rather than leave the space empty, you can insert an image placeholder that reserves the space for the image and can later be replaced with the final image. Designers often work visually, creating their designs by arranging the elements in relation to one another — size, proportion, alignment, white space, and more. Using image placeholders enables them to create the page design, finalize the text in relation to the images, complete most of the technical work, and leave only minor adjustments for when they replace the placeholders with the final images. A placeholder is also a good reminder that an image is missing. Although simple to use, you may find that reminder invaluable.

Insert and Replace an Image Placeholder

In this exercise, you are waiting for a photograph of David, the Shipping/Receiving clerk, to place on the staff page. You create the image placeholder to remind you of the missing image. A short while later, when the photograph is taken and sent to you, you replace the image placeholder with the photograph.

1   **Open staff.html.**

2   **Click to the right of Alan's photo.**

3   **From the Common Insert bar, choose Image Placeholder from the Images drop-down menu.**

4   **In the Image Placeholder dialog box, type** `photo_of_david` **in the Name field,** `208` **in the Width field,** `238` **in the Height field, and** `Photo of David` **in the Alternate Text field. Click OK.**

The dimensions — 208 pixels wide by 238 pixels high — are based on the dimensions of the cropped images of Jeff and Alan. You may substitute the numbers noted in Lesson 6 if your cropped images have different dimensions.

?   **If You Have Problems**

The Image Placeholder name does not allow spaces or other upper ASCII characters. If you use one or more, a warning dialog box appears, and your text is removed from the Name field. To fake a space, you can use the underscore character (_) but not a hyphen (-).

FIGURE 5.42

5   **Preview the page in your browser.**

The placeholder displays as a missing image, but the alternate text identifies the content of the image.

FIGURE 5.43

6   **Return to Dreamweaver.**

7   **Double-click the image placeholder and choose david.jpg from the images folder.**

When your image designer delivers the final image, you can use it to replace the image placeholder.

8   **Crop the image to dimensions similar to the other two.**

9   **Preview the page in your browser.**

FIGURE 5.44

10   **Return to Dreamweaver and close staff.html.**

SUMMARY

In this chapter, you learned about the different image formats used on the Web and how one format may be better than another for different types of images. You learned how to insert images from the Images button on the Common Insert bar and from the Files panel. You discovered how to set alignments and add borders and space around images using the Property inspector. You cropped images to remove unwanted information and resized images to different sizes. You also discovered how to improve images with resampling and sharpening. You learned to create a placeholder for an image that has not arrived and then to replace the placeholder with the finished image.

CAREERS IN DESIGN

EXPLORING PROFESSIONAL PORTFOLIO SITES

In the early days of digital publishing technology, imaging and layout software was accepted more by image artists and designers than it was by "niche" professionals — people like photographers, illustrators, painters, and (little wonder) typographers. Although the widespread acceptance of what was then known as "desktop" publishing applications did in fact spell the end of certain specializations (like typesetters), other fields like photography were hardly affected at all.

Why is this important to you as a Web site designer? Because photographers in particular weathered the storm of desktop technology and emerged on the other end, evolved but in many ways exactly the same as they were before. Their ability to see the world through a lens comes through in their Web sites.

Spend time researching how professional photographers display their wares on the Web. They provide some of the best examples of portfolio sites you can imagine. Use Google or Yahoo! to look for photographers in your particular region of the country who show their work on the Web. Call a few of them — particularly those whose sites you find compelling — and interview them about how they view their Web presence. What things are important to them from a design standpoint? Who designed their sites and what software was used? You might be surprised to find that most of them were done using Dreamweaver.

KEY TERMS

8-bit color	GIF	PNG (Portable Network Graphics)
Alpha-transparency	High-color images	Proportionate resizing
Animated GIFs	Index transparency	Render
Antialiasing	Inline image	Resampling
Bandwidth	Interlace	RGB (red, green, blue)
Bitmap images	Internet Service Providers (ISPs)	Scalable Vector Graphics (SVG)
Empty alt	JPEG	Sharpening
Favicon	Lossless compression	Thumbnails
Flat	Lossy compression	Vector images

CHECKING CONCEPTS AND TERMS

SCREEN ID

Identify the indicated areas from the following list:

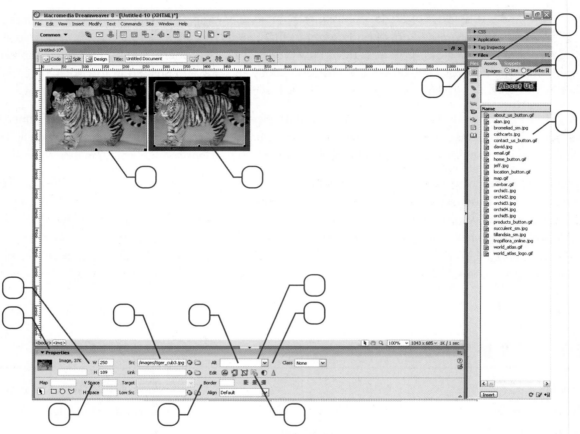

FIGURE 5.45

a. Assets tab

b. Thumbnail and file size of image

c. Alternate text

d. Selected image

e. Images button of the Assets panel

f. Sharpen tool

g. Filename of an image

h. Preview of selected image

i. Crop tool

j. Horizontal/Vertical spacing

k. Image assets of site

l. Resample tool

m. Image in crop mode

n. Width/Height of image

o. Image Border/Alignment

MULTIPLE CHOICE

Circle the letter of the correct answer for each of the following:

1. Images _____.

   a. can be inserted using the Property inspector

   b. use the `<image />` tag with the `source` and `alt` attributes

   c. when selected, display eight handles

   d. All of the above

2. GIF and JPEG image formats _____.

   a. are the storage format of digital cameras

   b. are limited to 256 colors

   c. are bitmapped images

   d. can be animated

3. JPEGs are better than GIFs for _____.

   a. image text buttons

   b. background images

   c. color-photograph images

   d. None of the above

4. The PNG image format _____.

   a. is a relatively new file format

   b. can display animation

   c. is fully supported by all Web browsers

   d. uses the same compression method as a JPEG

5. Dreamweaver has the following image-editing tools:

   a. Sharpen, Crop, and Luminance

   b. Resize, Resample, and Revert

   c. Resample, Sharpen, and Crop

   d. Crop, Contrast, and Image Map

6. One Web-ready vector format is _____.

   a. 24-bit PNG

   b. CorelDRAW (CDR)

   c. SVG

   d. Fireworks

7. In Dreamweaver, image files are also referred to as _____.

   a. GIS files

   b. Assets

   c. Placeholders

   d. Paragraph attributes

8. A Web-page image can be aligned _____.

   a. with the paragraph-alignment tool

   b. using its handles

   c. to the left or right

   d. All of the above

9. Which of the following pairs are related?

   a. RGBa, animation

   b. 16.7 million colors, JPG

   c. Alpha-transparency, GIF

   d. Lossy compression, PNG

10. The _____ attribute does not contribute to the weight of an image file.

   a. width

   b. image format

   c. border thickness

   d. transparency color

DISCUSSION QUESTIONS

1. Without Dreamweaver's image-editing tools, every time you wanted to alter an image, you would have to return to an image-illustration program to make your changes. Which types of changes can you make to your images through Dreamweaver, and which would you have to return to the original program to do? Give an example. What limitations do Dreamweaver's image-editing tools have?

2. You have been hired by the Communications Services Branch as the organization's new Webmaster. The image artist who, to date, has only created printed work has been assigned to help

you. What type of guidance might you provide this image artist when you need images for the Web site?

3. Given the fact that images weigh more than text, what types of considerations would you use to evaluate which images should or should not appear on a Web site or Web page?

SKILL DRILL

Skill Drill exercises reinforce project skills. Each skill that is reinforced is the same as, or nearly the same as, a skill we presented in the chapter. We provide detailed instructions in a step-by-step format. You should work through the exercises in order.

1. Insert Images from the Files and Assets Panels

Dragging an image into a Web page is probably the easiest method of inserting an image. You can drag an image from the Files panel or from the Assets panel. The Files panel shows the files and folders of your Web site. The Assets panel collects and displays assets of a Web site by types, such as images. This can make finding an image much simpler rather than opening a series of folders to locate the image.

1. Open succulents.html from the TO_P5 Site.

2. Click the Assets tab in the Files panel group to expand the Assets panel.

3. Click the Images button at the top of the Assets panel to display the image assets.

4. Drag succulent_sm.jpg to the left of "Succulents" near the top of the page and assign an empty alt to the image.

    The insertion point (black vertical bar) moves with the dragged image to indicate where the image will be inserted. Ensure that the insertion point is to the left of "Succulents".

5. Click the image and choose Right from the Align menu in the Property inspector.

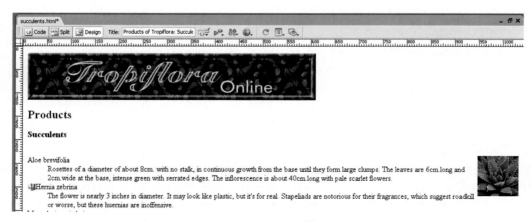

FIGURE 5.46

6. Close, saving succulents.html.

7. Open bromeliads.html. From the Assets panel, drag bromeliad_sm.jpg to the left of "Bromeliads" near the top of the page, assign an empty alt to the image, and align the image to the right. Close, saving the changes.

8. Insert tillandsia_sm.jpg to the left of "Tillandsias" in tillandsias.html, assign an empty alt to the image, and align the image to the right.

9. Close, saving the changes.

2. Adjust Image Brightness and Contrast

You may receive an image that is too bright or dark or in which the contrast is too high or too low. Dreamweaver offers a tool to correct these types of errors. As with the Crop button, this function irreversibly changes the original image. You would be wise to keep a copy of the original image in another folder if you want to be able to retry adjusting the contrast or brightness again.

1. Open about.html.

2. Click to the left of the "About Tropiflora" heading.

3. Insert the image cathcarts.jpg, type `Photo of Dennis and Linda Cathcart with their dog Bucky` in the Alternate text field and set the alignment to left.

4. Click the image.

5. In the Property inspector, click the Brightness and Contrast button (two buttons to the right of the Crop button).

6. Click OK to acknowledge the warning.

7. Set the Brightness slider to 40 and the Contrast slider to 10.

   The slider can be difficult to position at a particular setting; you may prefer to type the values in the fields to the right of each slider.

8. Compare the image before and after the settings by unchecking and checking the Preview check box.

9. Click OK to accept the settings.

10. Set the border to 2 pixels and the horizontal spacing to 5.

11. Preview the page in your browser.

FIGURE 5.47

12. Return to Dreamweaver and close about.html.

To Extend Your Knowledge . . .

IMAGE BORDERS AND VERTICAL/HORIZONTAL SPACING

Dreamweaver 8 displays the combination of image borders and image vertical/horizontal spacing incorrectly. Vertical and horizontal spacing should appear outside the border but in Dreamweaver 8, the spacing appears between the image and the border. Web browsers display image borders and vertical/horizontal spacing correctly. This is not a critical issue but may be confusing to new students of Web design.

3. Choose the Best Image

In this exercise, you replace each image placeholder with the best image. Three or four images are available for each placeholder. Your task is to examine all options for each placeholder and evaluate each image based on quality and file size. For the purpose of this exercise, ignore alternate text until you have made your final selection of the images.

1. Define a site named JCW-P5 from the Chapter_05>JCW-P5 folder using the standard settings.

2. Open wildlife_safari.html. (Skipping the logo_and_animal_banner placeholder, double-click the tiger_cub placeholder.)

3. Choose tiger_cub1.jpg from the images folder. Examine the image for quality and make note of its file size.

4. Press Control/Command-Z to Undo the last action (or choose Edit>Undo).

5. Double-click the tiger_cub placeholder, replace it with tiger_cub2.jpg, and examine the image for quality and file size.

6. Repeat Steps 4 and 5 with tiger_cub3.jpg.

7. Evaluate the three choices and insert the best one. Set the alignment to left and the horizontal spacing to 3.

8. Repeat the process for the burmese_python placeholder, but do not set the alignment or horizontal spacing.

9. Choose the best image for the monitor placeholder, align the image to the left, and set the horizontal spacing to 3.

   Leave the placeholder for the turkey_vulture untouched for now — you deal with that image in the next exercise.

10. Scroll to the top to replace the logo_and_animal_banner placeholder.

    You must insert both a logo and an animal banner, but you may choose either two separate images or a single combined image.

11.   Leave the alignment of the image (or images) that replaces the logo_and_animal_banner placeholder set to Default, but set the horizontal spacing to zero (0).

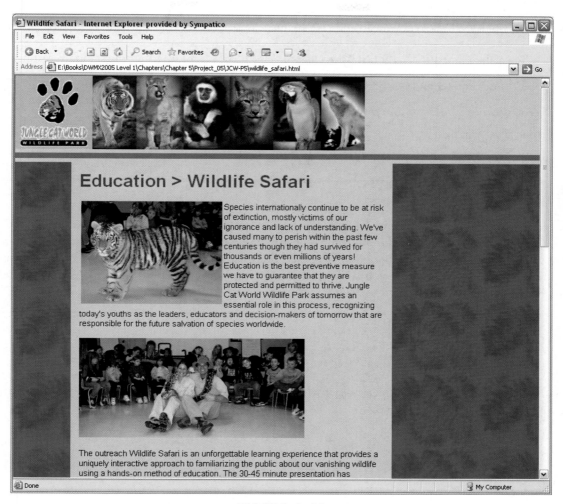

FIGURE 5.48

12.   Apply alternate text descriptions to all of the images.

13.   Close, saving your changes when finished.

4. Save Images from the Internet

Before you start this exercise, you need to be aware that many images on Web pages are copyrighted, so you should not use these images for your own purposes, whether or not you earn any income from their use. However, it is perfectly fine to use an image as inspiration, as long as you do not copy the image directly or incorporate it into another image. You may also use an image if the author/owner of the image gives you permission to do so. Permission may come with a price tag.

There are Web sites that offer images at no cost and with no royalties attached. You may download and use these images at your leisure for personal or professional use. However, in many cases, these images are relatively low quality and may not be suitable for professional Web-site design.

In this exercise, you learn how to download and save an image for later use. (Web-site content used by permission.)

1. Define a site named JCW-P5 from the Chapter_05>JCW-P5 folder using the standard settings.

2. Open your browser and go to http://www.junglecatworld.com/wildlife_safari.html.

3. Scroll down to the last photo on the page, the turkey vulture.

4. Right/Control-click the image and choose Save Picture As. Navigate to your Chapter_05> JCW-P5>images folder, and save the image using its given filename.

? If You Have Problems

Internet Explorer uses the phrase "Save Picture As", Mozilla/Netscape uses "Save Image As", and Opera uses "Save Image" for the same function. If you are using the Safari browser on a Macintosh system, choose Download Image to Disk, and Safari saves the image to your desktop. You can then move the image wherever you wish. In this exercise, you move it to the WIP>Chapter_05>JCW-P5>images folder. If you are using another browser, look for a similar command.

5. Close your browser.

6. Open wildlife_safari.html from the JCW-P5 site in Dreamweaver.

7. Replace the turkey_vulture placeholder with the downloaded image, align the image to the right, and set the horizontal spacing to 3.

8. Close, saving the changes.

CHALLENGE

Challenge exercises expand on or are somewhat related to skills we presented in the lessons. Each exercise provides a brief narrative introduction, followed by numbered-step instructions that are not as detailed as those in the Skill Drills. You should do the Challenge exercises in the order given.

1. Link Thumbnails to Detail Pages

1. Define a site named DR-P5 from the Chapter_05>DR-P5 folder using the standard settings.

2. Open bechstein-details.html and expand the Assets panel.

3. Drag bechstein.jpg into the large open cell below the Comments cell.

4. Make the alternate text `Photo of a Bechstein piano`. Close, saving bechstein-details.html.

5. Open piano-stock.html.

The Thumbnail column is reserved for thumbnail images of the various pianos available for sale. The filenames of the thumbnail images end with _thm.jpg to distinguish them from the full-sized images.

6. Drag bechstein_thm.jpg into the thumbnail table cell of the Bechstein row. Make the alternate text `Photo of a Bechstein piano.`

7. Proportionately resize the image to 80 pixels in height (using the Shift key).

8. Resample and sharpen the image. Using the Preview option, choose the best sharpen setting for the image.

9. Link the image to bechstein-details.html.

10. Select "info »" in the Detail column of the Bechstein table row, and link the text to bechstein-details.html.

11. Continue the process. Insert the detail images into the detail pages, insert the thumbnail images (proportionately resized to 80 pixels high) into the piano-stock page, and provide alternate text for each image.

12. Close, saving any open detail pages, and preview piano-stock.html in your browser. Test the links you created, returning to Dreamweaver to repair any incorrect ones.

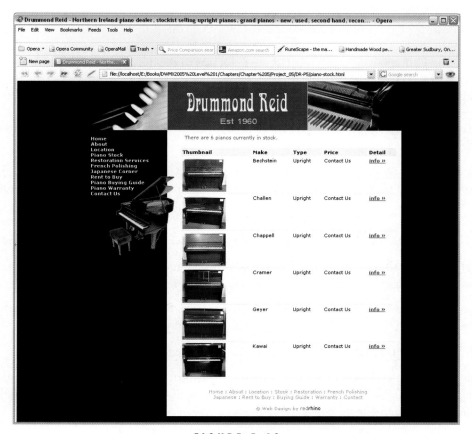

FIGURE 5.49

13. Return to Dreamweaver and close piano-stock.html.

2. Make the Images Accessible

Your task is to create appropriate descriptions of the images in a page. Review the discussions in this chapter on how to categorize images and what types of descriptions would be appropriate for images according to their category. Review the images in this page and apply the correct description to each.

1. Define a site named DF-P5 from the Chapter_05>DF-P5 folder using the standard site-definition settings.

2. Open visitor-stats.html.

3. Switch to the Assets panel and make note of the images for this Web page.

    You can ignore background.gif; it is a background image to the page and does not need a description. Only inline images must be described.

4. One by one, click each image and apply the appropriate description (hint: shim.gif is used twice on this page).

5. Close, saving visitor-stats.html.

3. Create a Photo Album

Your task is to create a photo album from supplied images. In the thumbs folder are duplicate copies of the photos in the photos folder. You must add photos (resizing, resampling, and sharpening as necessary) from the thumbs folder to the filmstrip pages. You must also add photos to the detail pages; when you click a thumbnail, the larger photo of the image appears in the middle frame. You are not expected to create the frame layout, just the thumbnails, the details pages, and the links between them.

1. Define a site named Album from the Chapter_05>Album folder using the standard site-definition settings.

2. Open index.html and preview the page in your browser. Click the thumbnail image of the boat in the bottom frame and observe that a larger copy of the boat photograph appears in the middle frame.

3. Return to Dreamweaver and close index.html.

4. Open boats.html. Insert boat2.jpg from the thumbs folder to the right of the first thumbnail image.

5. Proportionately resize the photo to a height of 80 pixels, and resample the image. You can also sharpen and adjust the brightness and/or contrast, if you feel it is necessary.

6. Repeat the process with the remaining three boat images. Space each image from the others using an H Space setting of 5. Close, saving the changes to boats.html.

7. Open boat1.htm from the Album>details folder. Save the file as boat2.htm.

8. Replace the photo with boat2.jpg from the Album>photos folder. Proportionately resize the photo to a height of 350 pixels, and resample the image. You can also sharpen and adjust the brightness and/or contrast, if necessary. Close, saving the changes.

9. Repeat Steps 7–8 until you have created boat3.htm, boat4.htm, and boat5.htm.

10.   Reopen boats.html from the root folder. One by one, link the thumbnail images to the newly created detail pages. Close, saving the changes to boats.html.

11.   Open index.html and preview the page in your browser.

4. Resize Images to Fit in Pop-Up Windows

You have been asked to create a photo album of the planets of our solar system. In this album, when a visitor clicks a planet, a larger photo appears in a pop-up window. The image map and JavaScript have been prepared for you; your task is to insert the images into their individual pages. The images of the planets are different sizes, so they need cropping and resizing.

1.   Define a site named Planets from the Chapter_05>Planets folder using the standard site-definition settings.

2.   Open index.html and then preview it in your browser. Click Mercury (first planet from the sun) and notice that it opens in a pop-up window. The planet is too large for the window.

3.   Do not close your browser; return to Dreamweaver and open mercury.html.

4.   Crop the image of Mercury to remove any extra black from around the planet. Proportionately resize the remaining image so the height is 300 pixels. Resample the image and apply any of the other image-editing tools, as necessary. Add appropriate alt text. Close, saving the changes.

5.   One by one, open the remaining planet pages, insert the appropriate photo from the images folder, and apply the procedures outlined in Step 4. Close, saving each after completing it.

6.   Switch to your open browser with index.html open. Test the links from all of the planets to verify that each planet is fully visible in the pop-up windows.

7. Close your browser, return to Dreamweaver, and close any open pages.

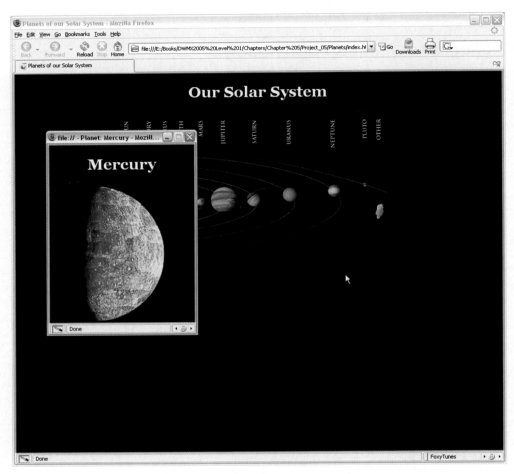

FIGURE 5.50

PORTFOLIO BUILDER

Create an Online Image Gallery

Gallery sites provide access to photographs, illustrations, maps, and other visual objects that are either for sale or available "royalty free," which means that they're in the public domain and can be used without cost. In this assignment, you're going to create a small gallery site containing both thumbnails (small images) and links to larger, high-resolution versions of each image.

1. To see an example of this type of site, visit a commercial image library; a perfect one to look at is gettyimages.com (one of the largest commercial sites of its kind on the Web).

2. Spend some time looking through the company's offerings, noting how images are organized into related categories.

3. Using a search engine such as Google.com, search the Web for "royalty free images".

4. Select five to ten images to use in your gallery site and save them to your hard drive.

5. Build a small site that provides a home page displaying small (thumbnail) images, with links to individual pages containing large versions.

6. Construct the links so the larger version of each image is displayed in a separate window when selected by the viewer.

CHAPTER  6

Backgrounds and Colors

OBJECTIVES

In this chapter, you learn how to:

- Insert tiled, margin, and watermark backgrounds

- Identify suitable background images

- Avoid transparent background images

- Use Web-safe colors and correct notation

- Set text and link colors

- Choose background colors for background images

- Use CSS properties to modify background images

- Selectively apply text and background color

Why Would I Do This?

Once you have established the content you want to appear on your Web pages — either through structured text or images (with appropriate alternate text) — you can next turn to the task of developing a theme for your Web site. You develop this theme through the use of color and background images. You may think that you can only use color for text or the background and that once you choose a background image for your page, you've done all that you can do: this would be true if you limited your options to HTML presentational tags and attributes. In fact, your options are no longer that limited. By using CSS, you have many more options for applying color and background images. With CSS, you can apply color to text and backgrounds to any portion of a Web page, such as paragraphs, links, and headings. In fact, using CSS, you could even apply a different background color and text color to every paragraph, if you wanted. (You still have to provide the good taste and design sense, however.) The same might be said for background images. There are several CSS background options and, unlike HTML backgrounds, CSS enables you to apply backgrounds to almost every HTML tag in a Web page.

In this chapter, you explore the basic principles of using color and background images, as well as the specific methods for applying them. In all cases, you learn to apply colors and background images using CSS. Although you can apply color and background images using HTML, your options are much more limited and less powerful than using CSS. If you are going to be a designer of note, you must learn as much as you can about CSS: CSS provides the means for creating the style of a Web site.

Using Background Images

As noted, by using CSS you can apply backgrounds to any element in a page. Background images are similar to colored, textured, or watermarked paper—they appear behind the body content. Unlike inline or foreground images, which only appear once where they are set to appear, background images, by default, repeat to fill the background, a process known as *tiling*. Although backgrounds on Web pages are the most common use of backgrounds, the principles of background images apply to other elements as well, such as tables, paragraphs, and headings, all of which can have a background image. CSS offers additional options for background images that are not available through HTML.

There are some important caveats and considerations for using background images:

- Text must be visible and readable against the background. It's essential that you test text colors against the background to ensure readability. You should check the color of link text as well, because link text is often set to a different color than running text.

- Background images with transparent regions can cause problems. If you have not specified a background color, a visitor's browser may apply its own background color that shows through the transparent regions. The color showing through may not match your color patterns, so the visitor sees a very different Web page than what you intended. You should edit the image and disable the transparency option.

- Be careful about using complex images as backgrounds. In the past, this was not recommended because complex backgrounds require more processing power to display than simpler images. Web pages with background images can hesitate during scrolling because of the processing power needed to draw the background as it moves — complex images exaggerate this condition. However, given the processing power of current computers, this recommendation is less relevant. On the other hand, if you need to ensure universal access to your site, even for those using older computers, you need to avoid using complex background images. There are still plenty of people in this country, not to mention around the world, using slower connections and equipment.

- Do not use animated GIFs as background images.

- You can use GIF, JPEG, or PNG image formats in the background of your Web page. The same principles used in determining the image format of a foreground image also apply to background images.

- Test your page at different monitor resolutions, especially if you are using either a margin or watermark style of background.

There are three styles of backgrounds that you can use: wallpaper patterns, margin (or strip) tiles, and watermarks. It does not matter which style of background image you choose to use — the method for inserting the background image is the same. The difference between the three styles lies in the development of the image.

Prior to CSS, HTML allowed background images, but their use was severely limited. Only the `<body>`, `<table>`, `<tr>`, and `<td>` tags supported background images, whereas CSS enables the designer to place background images behind most elements of a page. Using HTML, all you could do was place an image in the background. However, using CSS, you may specify the position of the background image, how it is to repeat (or tile), and whether it scrolls with the page or remains fixed in the browser window. Given the versatility and flexibility of CSS, it is extremely important for you, as a designer, to know and understand the background properties of CSS and how they can empower you to create amazing Web-page designs.

Working with the Colors of the Web

You also need to know and understand not only basic color principles but also the capabilities of computer monitors. With print design, you need to understand the capabilities of the printing process because the printer and printing process determine the colors of your printed product. Once you have that information and submit your files, your printed product remains essentially identical — fonts, images, and color selection do not arbitrarily change. With Web design, the final product displays on the computer monitors of all of your site's visitors, and you have no control over the size, color depth, or quality of their computer monitors. You may be able to make some basic assumptions, such as assuming high-technology markets have quality equipment and, equally, assuming that the K-12 educational market may not have high-quality equipment. Based on such assumptions, you can be better prepared to decide how to use colors in your Web designs.

The earliest color monitors from the early 1990s supported just 256 colors. Current monitors commonly support 16.7 million colors and even 4.3 billion colors. The color depth of monitors is described in bits, such as 8-bit, 16-bit, and 24-bit color monitors. Each bit can contain one of two numbers — a zero or a one. One-bit color has only two options, zero or one, or in color terms, black or white. Two-bit color has four options: 00, 01, 10, and 11, which can also be represented as 2^2 or 2×2, which equals 4. For every additional bit, the number of possible colors doubles. Eight-bit color, or 2^8 is $2 \times 2 \times 2 \times 2 \times 2 \times 2 \times 2 \times 2$ or 256 colors; 16-bit color is 2^{16}, or 65,356 colors; 24-bit color is 2^{24}, or 16.7 million colors; and 32-bit color is 2^{32}, or 4.3 billion colors. Twenty-four-bit color is also known as "true color." According to recent browser statistics (http://www.w3schools.com/browsers/browsers_stats.asp), 97% of Internet users use 16-bit color monitors (65,356 colors) or better, and 70% use 24-bit color or better.

Most developers use a system with 24-bit or 32-bit color monitors. If you are one of them, you must remember that you can't always depend on all of your visitors having similarly capable monitors. If a visitor views your images with a monitor displaying fewer colors, the image will be visible but won't seem as attractive as what you created. In many cases, the less-capable monitor uses dithering to simulate colors that it can't display. **Dithering** is a process of creating the illusion of new colors and shades by varying the pattern of pixels. Newspapers, which have only black and white dots, produce various shades of grays by dithering the black and white areas.

Although dithering does enable even low-color monitors to display the images, they do not look very attractive. In response to this problem, many authors recommend limiting the **palette**, the set of available colors, to 256 colors or less. However, the 256 colors on Windows systems, Macintosh systems, and Unix systems are not all the same; some colors from one system dither on another. This issue further reduces the 8-bit palette of 256 colors to 216 nondithering colors, known as "the Web-safe palette."

Dreamweaver displays the Web-safe color palette in two different layouts — color cubes and continuous tones. When the mouse pointer is in the colors of the color palette, it changes to an eyedropper shape to enable you to choose a color. A pop-out menu to the right of the color palette enables you to choose the color layout, the available colors, and whether or not to display only Web-safe colors.

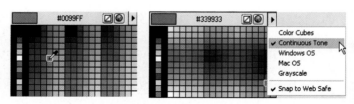

FIGURE 6.1

There are a variety of ways (models) to describe a color; the RGB model is used for Web images. The **RGB model** defines all colors in a palette by mixing different intensities of red, green, and blue light, such as black (0% each of red, green, and blue) and white (100% each of red, green, and blue). There are two common systems for describing colors — by name and by hexadecimal color code. Of course, the simpler method is by name, but there are only 16 color names common to all browsers. Internet Explorer has color names for all 216 Web-safe colors, but other browsers do not recognize all of those names. All browsers, however, recognize the hexadecimal color codes for all 216 Web-safe colors.

Hexadecimal means 16 (*hexa* is 6 and *deci* is 10). In our decimal or 10-digit system, there are 10 unique single-digit numerals, 0–9. Numbers beyond 9 in our decimal system are represented using two digits. To represent the next six single-digit numerals beyond 9 in a hexadecimal system, we use the characters A–F.

Decimal Notation	1	2	3	4	5	6	7	8	9	10	11	12	13	14	15
Hexadecimal Notation	1	2	3	4	5	6	7	8	9	A	B	C	D	E	F

FIGURE 6.2

The hexadecimal color system uses a group of six hexadecimal numbers to describe a color — the first pair is for red, the second for green, and the last for blue. Each primary color has six possible values equating to 0%, 20%, 40%, 60%, 80%, and 100%. If you convert percentages to hexadecimal notations from 0 to F, they would be 0, 3, 6, 9, C, and F. In the hexadecimal system, those numbers are paired to result in 00, 33, 66, 99, CC, and FF. To describe the color of pure red (which has no green or blue component), you would use FF0000. Pure green would be 00FF00; pure blue would be 0000FF; white would be all colors, FFFFFF; and black would be no color, 000000. Yellow is the opposite of blue, so it would be FFFF00. With 6 intensities of red, 6 intensities of green, and 6 intensities of blue, you have 216 colors: multiplying 6 × 6 × 6 = 216, the number of colors in a Web-safe palette. When coding hexadecimal color codes, you must always remember to precede the color code with the hash (#) character.

Visibone.com's Color Laboratory (http://www.visibone.com/colorlab) provides a free, Web-based, color-picking tool that enables you to experiment with color options before applying them to your Web page. Each of the color options displays with its hexadecimal color code, and text of each color is shown in each block of color to demonstrate text color against the chosen backgrounds.

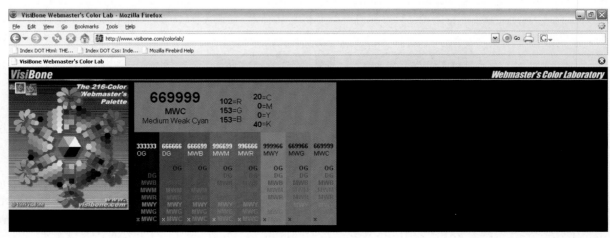

FIGURE 6.3

VISUAL SUMMARY

The Page Properties dialog box has many options for setting a background color and/or a background image. You can open the Page Properties dialog box by clicking the Page Properties button in the Property inspector, choosing Modify>Page Properties from the menu, or by pressing Control-J. The Page Properties dialog box groups related properties into categories.

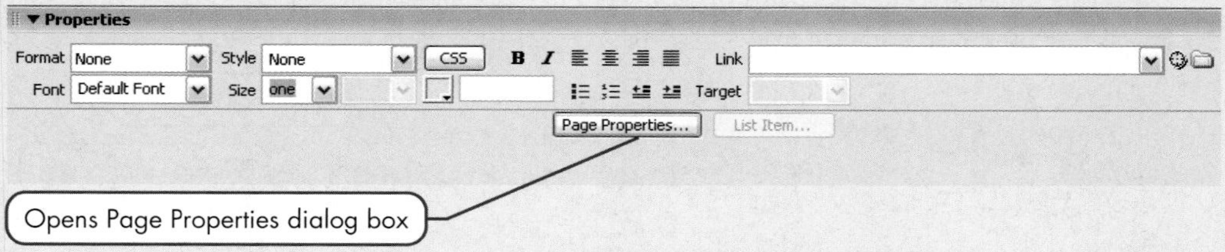

Opens Page Properties dialog box

FIGURE 6.4

The Appearance category allows you to set the default text color, background color, and background image (we discuss the other options in other chapters). The Links category allows you to set the color of unvisited-, visited-, active-, and rollover-link states. The Headings category allows you to set the color of headings, such as Heading 1 and Heading 2.

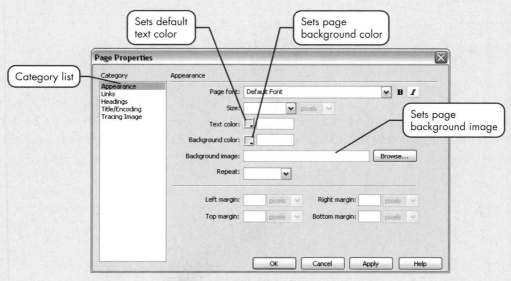

FIGURE 6.5

To specify a color, whether a text or background color, you either type the hexadecimal code of the color into the color field or click the color button. When you click the color button, a color palette appears. You can use the mouse pointer, which changes to an eyedropper, to choose a color from this palette. As the eyedropper moves across the color palette, the color swatch displays the color at the tip of the eyedropper, and the hexadecimal color code displays to the right of the color swatch. The pop-out menu to the right allows you to enable/disable the use of Web-safe colors and to switch between color palettes.

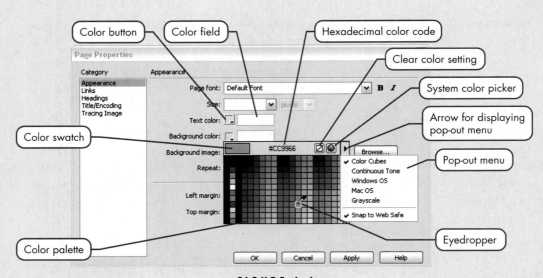

FIGURE 6.6

You modify CSS Styles often in this project. To view and work with existing CSS Styles, you must expand the CSS panel group and (if necessary) click the CSS Styles tab to display the CSS Styles panel. If you Right/Control-click a style rule, a drop-down menu appears, allowing you to edit the style (among other options).

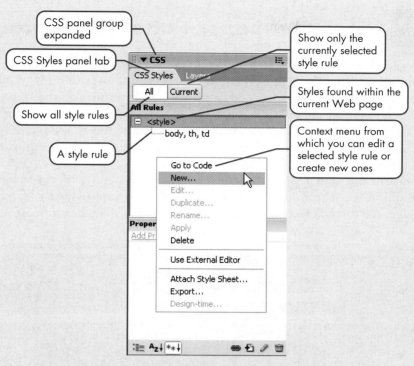

FIGURE 6.7

The CSS Rule Definition dialog box offers the same options as the Page Properties dialog box, plus many more. As you use CSS more and more in your designs, you will probably use the Page Properties dialog box less often and the CSS Rule Definition dialog box more frequently. This dialog box also has several categories, including the Background category, which you will use often.

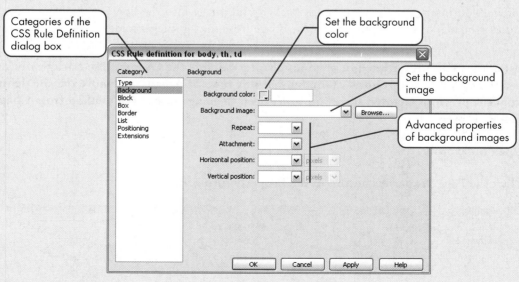

FIGURE 6.8

LESSON 1   Using Wallpaper-Pattern Backgrounds

Wallpaper patterns are tiled images that repeat across and down a page. Properly designed, wallpaper patterns are seamless — there are no clear distinctions between one tile and the adjacent tiles. Unlike the other two background styles (margin and watermark), it doesn't matter how large or small the Web page is — the tiled background image repeats horizontally and vertically until it fills the background of the page. The images used in wallpaper patterns are rectangular or square, commonly no larger than 300 × 300 pixels. Although wallpaper patterns were often used in Web designs in the past, they have gone out of style unless the pattern is very subtle.

It is always best to experiment with a variety of colors to test the readability and appearance of the text color against the background image. The BackgroundCity.com Web site (http://www.backgroundcity.com) offers free background images and displays text using different colors against your chosen background image.

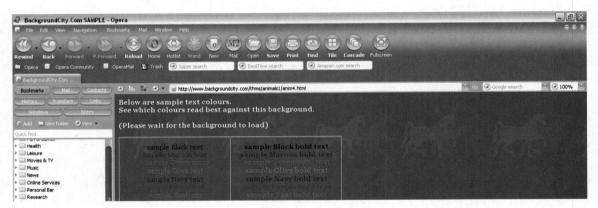

FIGURE 6.9

Insert a Wallpaper-Pattern Background Image

In this exercise, you insert a wallpaper-pattern background image into the body of the page using the Page Properties dialog box. To do so, simply choose the image from the bg-images folder.

1   Using the methods outlined in previous chapters, define the Chapter_06>Backgrounds folder as a site called "Backgrounds". (You may, at this time, also want to remove the site definitions from the previous chapter, since you won't need them again. Use the method from Chapter 5, Lesson 1, Step 2.)

2   Open index.html.

3   Click the Page Properties button in the Property inspector.

FIGURE 6.10

4   In the Appearance category of the Page Properties dialog box, click the Browse button (to the right of the Background Image field).

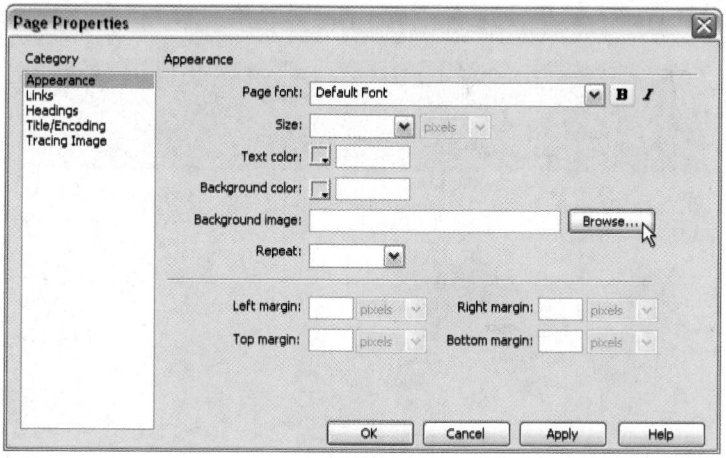

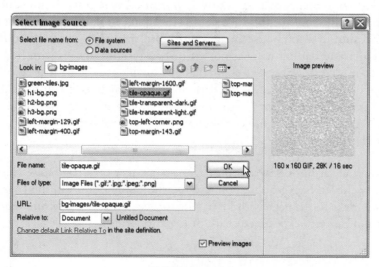

FIGURE 6.11

5   Open the bg-images folder, click tile-opaque.gif, and then click OK/Choose.

The Image Preview window displays the image and, below it, various properties of the image. This image is just 160 pixels wide by 160 pixels in height, so it tiles both vertically and horizontally to fill the Web page.

FIGURE 6.12

6   In the Page Properties dialog box, click OK.

The background of the page is tiled with the background image.

FIGURE 6.13

7   Close the document, saving the changes.

LESSON 2   Avoiding Unsuitable Background Images

It is best to choose background images that are relatively *flat in color depth* (do not contain too many colors). If you don't, you may find it difficult to choose a color for text that can stand out sufficiently against all of those background colors. You should also choose images with *low contrast*, where the difference in brightness between the brightest color and darkest color is not great. Background images with high contrast can make it difficult for you to choose a contrasting text color that is readable — a light text color may be hard to read against the light portion of the background, and a dark text color may be difficult to read against the dark portion of the background image. Whether you create or simply choose an image for the background, ensure that the tiling matches properly. This is not unlike hanging patterned wallpaper — the pattern must start at the same place it ended on the adjacent strip.

In this exercise, you examine various background images against text on a page to see just how difficult it is to read text against a poorly chosen background. You also use the Apply button in the Page Properties dialog box to apply the changes you make to the page without having to close the dialog box and reopen it each time. With this button, it is faster and easier to experiment with different options.

Explore Unsuitable Background Images

1   Open poor-backgrounds.html.

2   Examine the background and overlaying text in the left cell.

The background of the left table cell is a moderately dark and busy background pattern; only the white text can be read, and only if the text is large.

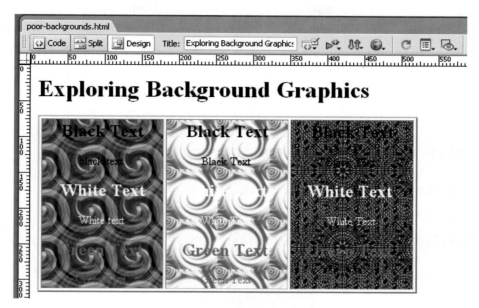

FIGURE 6.14

3   **Examine the background and overlaying text in the center cell.**

The background of the center table cell is a lighter but still busy background pattern; because of the high contrast between the white and the darker areas, even the black text is difficult to read.

4   **Examine the background and overlaying text in the right cell.**

Although the right cell contains a somewhat busy pattern and there is high contrast between the light areas and the dark areas, the individual areas of colors are quite small, making the white text more visible than against the other two background patterns. The pattern would be quite distracting, however, if used throughout the entire page.

5   **Close poor-backgrounds.html.**

LESSON 3   Exploring Problems with Transparent Background Images

You should avoid choosing or creating background images with transparent areas, because the background color shows through the transparent area. This is not an issue if the background color is the same as the transparent color (before it was chosen as the transparent color), but if the background color is different from what the designer intended, a halo appears around the image.

Most browsers display Web pages against a default white background if no other background color or image is specified. Some browsers, however, use a gray background. You should be aware that users can specify their own background image or color. In some cases, those who do simply prefer their own background color. In other cases, they may be visually impaired (for example, having color blindness), and therefore may specify particular text and background color combinations that they can read more easily than the original design. For all of these reasons, you should avoid using background images with transparent areas. Either choose images without such regions, or remove the transparency option using an image-editing application.

In this lesson, you explore the effects of choosing a background image with transparent regions for use against an unsuitable background color. You also learn that you can specify both a background color and background image.

Explore Problems with Transparent Background Images

1   **Open transparent-backgrounds.html and preview the page in your browser.**

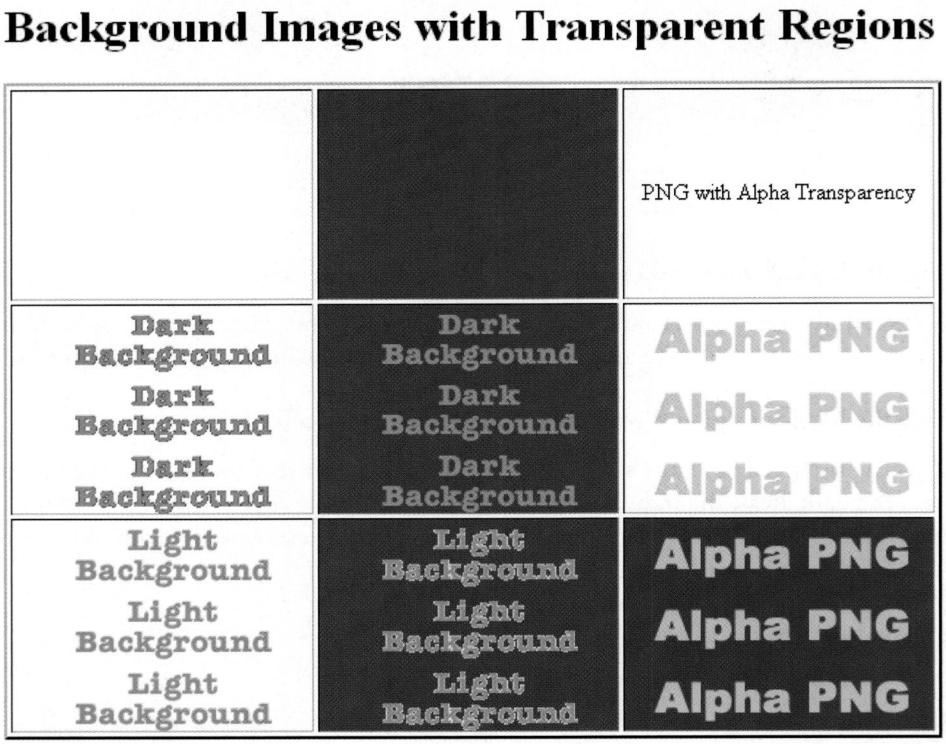

Background Images with Transparent Regions

FIGURE 6.15

? If You Have Problems

Preview this image using any of Firefox, Mozilla, Safari, or Opera browsers; otherwise, the appearance of the right column will be different from what is shown in Figure 6.15. If you do not have access to any of those browsers, refer to this figure for Step 5 of this exercise.

2   **Examine the top-left and top-middle cells.**

These cells display the background color used in their respective columns.

3   **In the middle row, examine the left and middle columns. Look closely at the background image (a GIF image with index transparency) and the background color.**

The middle row in both the left and middle columns uses the same background image. This background image was created against a dark green background, just as you see in the middle cell. The letters in the left cell, however, have a dark halo where the medium green of the text gradually blends with the dark green used as the original background. The gradient is apparent as a halo when the image is placed against a white background.

4   **In the bottom row, examine the left and middle columns. Look at the two background colors and the background image (also a GIF image with index transparency).**

The bottom row in both the left and middle columns displays a background image that was originally created against a white background and was later made transparent. The gradient or halo shows against the dark background of the middle cell.

5   **Examine the right column in which the same PNG background image is used in both the middle and bottom cells.**

As you had learned in Chapter 5, the PNG image format supports alpha-transparency. When alpha-transparency is employed, the gradient from one color to another color (from the yellow text color to the white background color in this example) is rendered as a gradient of transparency that allows the white background color to increasingly show through the yellow at the edges of the text. Therefore, this image may be placed against any color, and, because of the gradient of transparency, no ugly halo will appear. Be aware, however, that IE currently does not support alpha-transparency: Pixels with 100% transparency will be transparent, and all other pixels will be opaque, thereby creating the halo effect that alpha-transparency had been used to try to avoid.

6   **Close your browser, return to Dreamweaver, and close transparent-backgrounds.html.**

To Extend Your Knowledge . . .

THE HALO AROUND TRANSPARENT GIFS

When different colors are adjacent to each other in an image, image-editing applications create a gradient of colors in the transitional area. When the background color is made the transparent color, the gradient still exists, but the transparent region allows whatever color is in the background to show through. The halo is the remaining gradient of colors in the transition zone. For example, consider an image consisting of green text placed on a yellow background with the yellow identified as the transparent color. If the image is placed on a blue background, the blue shows through where the yellow color was. However, consider the regions in the image where the color is in transition from green to yellow. This gradient still exists, creating a gradient from green to almost yellow, and then blue where the background shows through. The image seems to have a yellow halo.

You may recognize that we're discussing index transparency. When we use alpha-transparency (PNG images) instead, this problem does not exist. The transition of colors between the image and the background would not be created as a transition of colors but, instead, as a transition in transparency. The closer the pixels are to the image, the more opaque they are, showing the image color more intensely; the closer the pixels are to the background, the more transparent they are, showing more and more of the background through the image. Therefore, it does not matter what the background color is, because the gradient of transparency creates the gradient by blending the image and background colors.

There are some JavaScript methods that may be used to enable the proper display of PNGs with alpha-transparency in IE 5.5 and later; one method may be found at http://webfx.eae.net/dhtml/pngbe-havior/pngbehavior.html. There are several alternative methods, but all are somewhat complicated to apply. The next version of IE, IE7, will support alpha-transparency, but existing versions will be unaffected; secondly, IE7 will be available only for Windows XP and later.

LESSON 4 Using Margin Background Images

The tiled images in Lesson 2 demonstrate that when an image is smaller than the background area of a Web page, the image tiles or repeats across and down the page until it fills the background. Tiling occurs by default, no matter which type of background you choose — tile, margin, or watermark. The difference between the three is both in the design of the image and in the CSS background options that you set. For example, an image designed for tiling tends to be small and is also designed to hide the visible seam between images. Its small size and invisible seams make it suitable to repeat both horizontally and vertically. A margin image tends to be larger, generally the full width of a browser window, and therefore repeats only down the browser window. A watermark image tends to be an image that does not lend itself to tiling or repeating at all — a photograph, for instance, would be appropriate for this type of background.

Margin or Strip-Tile Backgrounds

The margin or strip-tile background is generally used to create a border down the left side of the page, where a navigation bar is typically positioned. It is currently the most common style of background. Margin-style images are generally much wider than they are high. As long as the width of the image is wider than the width of the browser window, it won't repeat across the browser window, just down. The height of the repeating pattern determines the height of the image — it can be as little as a few pixels high and as large as 50 pixels high. If the left border is a small buttercup flower, the image is short, but if the repeating image is an ivy vine or tall pine tree, the image is tall.

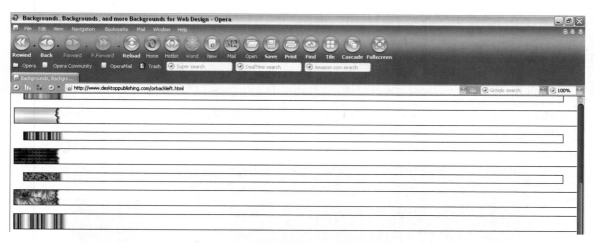

FIGURE 6.16

The width of the image is very important. If the image is 640 px wide, then the left border appears once on a 640 × 480 monitor, twice on a 800 × 600 monitor, and three times on a 1600 × 1200 monitor, as it repeats across the Web page. Given the nature of the compression routine in GIFs and PNGs, increasing the width of the body area of a margin-style image doesn't add much to its file size. For instance, using the image in the following figure, the 640-px-wide version took 2394 bytes of storage space, whereas increasing the white area of the image to create a 1600-px-wide version increased the file size by only 279 bytes.

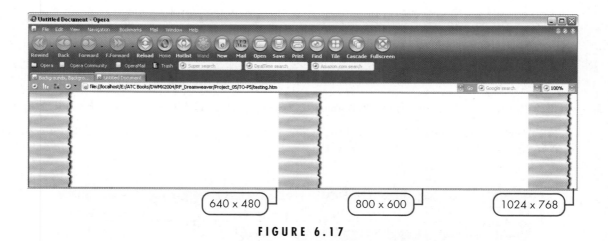

FIGURE 6.17

Although the most common form of this style of background creates a border down the left side of the Web page, it is possible to create a border along the top. The challenge with top borders is to make the image tall enough for all Web pages — you don't want the top border repeating partway down the page. A better solution is to use CSS to specify that the background image repeat across the width of the browser only, not down the height.

In this exercise, you explore different widths and heights of margin images. You learn firsthand that too narrow an image repeats across a Web page and too short an image repeats down a Web page. You also learn to use the CSS `background-repeat` property to specify in which direction the repeating occurs — across or down.

Use Appropriately Sized Margin Images

1   **Open index.html, then open the Page Properties dialog box.**

2   **Click the Browse button, choose left-margin-400.gif, click OK/Choose, and then click Apply.**

This background image is too narrow for the width of the Web page and repeats horizontally, giving the page a very unprofessional appearance.

FIGURE 6.18

?   **If You Have Problems**

If you cannot see the repeating pattern across your Document window, either expand the width of the Document window (or the Dreamweaver application) or use the Zoom tool (magnifying glass icon) on the Status bar of the Document window and select a smaller percentage.

---

3   **Click the Browse button, choose left-margin-1600.gif, click OK/Choose, and then click Apply.**

This image, which is virtually identical to the one used in the previous step, differs in that it was created 1600 px wide, which is too wide to repeat.

FIGURE 6.19

4 Click the Browse button, choose top-margin-300.gif, click OK/Choose, and then click Apply.

This margin image was designed to work as a top border, but it is too short and repeats both vertically and horizontally.

FIGURE 6.20

5 Click the Browse button, choose top-margin-2000.gif, click OK/Choose, and then click OK again.

This image is 2000 px high. For the relatively short pages in Tropiflora Online, this height would be sufficient. In other circumstances, it might not be sufficiently tall.

6 Save the changes to index.html, leaving it open for the next lesson.

To Extend Your Knowledge . . .

CREATING BACKGROUND IMAGES

So far, you have explored different types of background images — some that work and some that do not. Dreamweaver's image-editing tools cannot help to create a background image; to do so, you need to use a graphics program, such as Photoshop, Fireworks, or CorelDRAW. Even modifying a background image is beyond the tools found in Dreamweaver.

When you create an image for tiling, ensure that the color depth and contrast are fairly flat. Many graphics programs come with patterns that you can use as backgrounds. There are also many Web sites, such as BackgroundCity.com, which are collections of free patterns and other images. In addition, there are many tutorials posted on the Internet on how to create patterns with graphics software. At http://classic.gimp.org/tut-patt1.html, for example, you'll find a tutorial on how to create patterns using the Linux graphics application called "GIMP" (which also is available for Windows and Macintosh). The tutorial can be adapted to other Windows or Macintosh graphics applications. (The tutorial on creating easy patterns was made for version 1.2 of GIMP, but GIMP 2.3 has now been released. With some modification, you can adapt this tutorial to GIMP 2.3.)

Left-margin patterns should not be so narrow that they repeat across a page. It is uncommon to find a computer monitor that has a higher resolution than 1600 pixels wide. However, some designers create images that are 1610 pixels wide, just to give them an extra degree of insurance that the image is larger than the monitor width. Top-margin patterns should not repeat down a page, but that is a much greater challenge when pages are very long. Other methods are much easier to use, such as putting the top pattern in the top cell of a table or using CSS to specify that the pattern only repeat across the page, not down it.

LESSON 5   Using Watermark Background Images

The difference between the first two styles of backgrounds — tiled and margin — and the third type — watermark backgrounds — is not so much how you insert the background or how you construct it, but how it is applied. Tiled background images are designed to create a consistent pattern in the background of the page. Margin images are designed to create a margin pattern that appears along just one side of the body of the page, and generally they repeat in just one direction. Watermark images are intended to appear just once on a page with no repetition in either direction. Generally, watermark background images are not generic patterns but are specific to the site, such as a photograph of the designer or a faint image of the company logo.

Watermark Backgrounds

A watermark-style background image is typically made large. Generally, this style of background is restricted from repeating. You can make this restriction either by creating a large image or by setting the CSS **background-repeat** property to **no-repeat**. The problem with creating a large image is that it can appear too large in a small monitor or too small in a large monitor. Done properly, however, this background style can create some stunning Web-page effects.

In the background of the home page of Czech Web designer Petr Stanicek (aka Pixy), a flattened image (flattened both in contrast and color depth) of his photo shows in the background. This page uses multiple CSS techniques to push the image to the bottom-right corner of the page as well as to keep it from moving when the scrollbar is moved. He has added a humorous notation to the background image: in pale gray to the right of the top of his head, he has added <head> and just below his chin, he has added <body> — only people with HTML experience are likely to understand his joke.

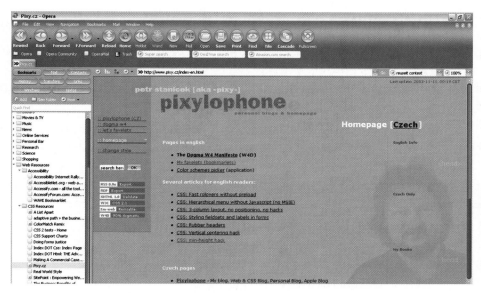

FIGURE 6.21

In the following redesign of Jakob Nielsen's Useit.com Web site, the photograph in the background is neither low in contrast nor low in color depth. However, to prevent readability issues with text over the complex background, the width of the content is restricted so it does not reach to the right side and overlap the background image.

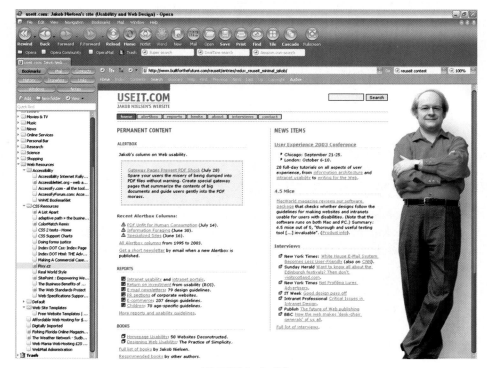

FIGURE 6.22

Insert a Watermark Image

1   In the open document index.html, open the Page Properties dialog box.

2   Click the Browse button, choose bromeliad-watermark.jpg, click OK/Choose, and then click Apply.

This image of a bromeliad is lightened to reduce contrast and color depth. It is large but not quite large enough, you may see it start to repeat on the bottom-right side.

FIGURE 6.23

3   Close index.html, saving the changes.

To Extend Your Knowledge . . .

NO ALTERNATE TEXT FOR BACKGROUND IMAGES

Background images do not need and cannot have alternate text. There is no alt attribute available for background images. This fact may be useful to you when you create a Web site. If you can set a decorative image as a background image, you do not need to specify even an empty alt.

LESSON 6   Applying Both Background Image and Color

Current browsers, by default, display Web pages against a white background. Older browsers tended to display Web pages against a light-gray background. For the most part, text colors displayed against either of these backgrounds are quite readable. However, some Web-page designers add very dark background images against their pages. This is fine except for visitors who have disabled images in their browser. If you use a dark background image behind your page, you use light text colors to make your text readable. However, if a visitor disables the display of images, the background does not display, and the light text is placed against a white or light gray background and is not readable. You should, therefore, add a background color in addition to a background image if your background image is significantly different from white or light gray. Adding this color ensures that your text is visible and legible against the background.

In this exercise, you learn to apply a background color in addition to a background image. You also see why it is beneficial to specify both.

Apply Both Background Color and Image

1   **Define a site named "Telescopes" from the Chapter_06>Telescopes folder.**

2   **Open index.html.**

The document appears empty because the text is colored white. You must apply a dark background.

3   **Open the Page Properties dialog box.**

4   **Click the Background Color button to open the color palettes.**

The square button to the right of Background Color opens the color palettes. This button appears in many places in Dreamweaver and opens the same color palette dialog box each time.

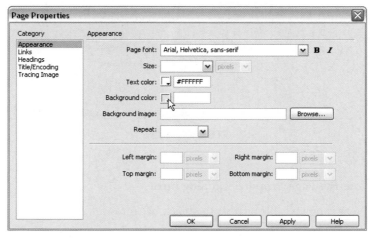

FIGURE 6.24

5   **Move the mouse pointer around the color palette.**

Notice that the color-swatch window (top-left corner of the palette window) displays the color closest to the mouse pointer, and the top of the palette window displays the hexadecimal code of the highlighted color. Notice, also, that the mouse pointer takes the shape of an eyedropper, a tool found in many graphics applications and commonly used for choosing a color.

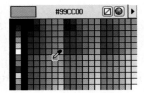

FIGURE 6.25

6   **Click the black square at the top left of the palette.**

Black has a hexadecimal code of #000000 — you can use this code to ensure that you have found a black square.

7   **Click Apply.**

Notice that the Background Color button has a black center and the hexadecimal code for black is in the text field to its right.

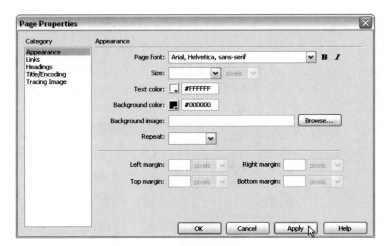

FIGURE 6.26

8   **Click OK to close the Page Properties dialog box.**

Notice that the text is now visible against the black background color.

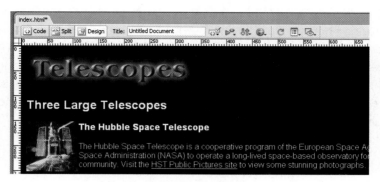

FIGURE 6.27

Although the background color works, it is rather boring. Next, you add a background image.

9   **Open the Page Properties dialog box, click the Browse button, and navigate to the Telescopes>images folder. Choose stars.jpg, click OK/Choose, and then click OK/Choose again.**

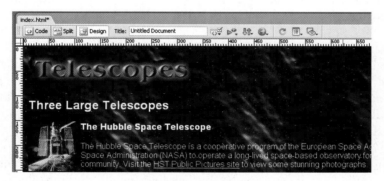

FIGURE 6.28

10   **Save the changes to index.html, leaving it open for the next lesson.**

To Extend Your Knowledge . . .

BACKGROUNDS CAN REPLACE GRAPHIC BUTTONS

Many navigation bars use graphic buttons as links to provide interesting style to the navigation bar. In most cases, the buttons are identical, but the text is different because they represent links to different sections of the Web site. Graphic buttons are an annoyance to create: spelling mistakes, design changes, and additional links all require the designer to modify or create new, custom graphic buttons. Because the only thing that changes from button to button is the text, many CSS-aware designers instead create a background image to place behind each link, thereby creating the appearance of a button. This has the added benefit of employing just one background image that is used multiple times. A change in the design requires a change to only one graphic. Spelling mistake? No problem — just fix the error in the text. A new link to add? Just type the text, create the link, and apply the same background image. Whenever there is a common background to a series of elements, whether they be links, paragraphs, or headings, consider creating a background image and placing it behind each of the elements rather than creating graphic buttons or graphic text.

LESSON 7   Setting Default Text Colors

You have learned to apply a background image and also a background color. In this lesson, you learn to set text colors. You can set one color that applies to all text, whether it is a paragraph or a heading. However, you can set a different color for each text format, such as different colors for paragraphs and for each heading level. All of these options are available through the Page Properties dialog box. You can also apply colors to link text — link text is traditionally blue, but you can change that.

In this lesson, you learn to work with the ***System Color Picker***. The name of this dialog box is somewhat confusing — it is titled the Color/Colors dialog box, but in the help documentation, it is also referred to as the "System Color Picker." To open the System Color Picker, click the Color Wheel button at the top of the color palette. In the Color dialog box, the rainbow of colors is called the ***Color Matrix*** (Windows) and ***Color Wheel*** (Macintosh). There are some differences between the Windows Color dialog box and the Macintosh Colors dialog box, but these differences are cosmetic, not functional.

Drag your mouse pointer in the Color Matrix/Wheel to select a color: the crosshair/point control identifies the position of the color. In Windows, if you slide the crosshair horizontally, the Hue value below the Color Matrix changes. On a Macintosh, positions around the Color Wheel circle represent the hue; if you move the point control around the outside of the Color Wheel, you change the hue. In Windows, if you slide the crosshair vertically, the saturation value changes. On a Macintosh, the saturation value changes when you move the point control to and from the center of the circle. On both systems, the slider on the right changes the luminosity. In Windows, the HSL and RGB values for the current color display below the Color Matrix. In Macintosh, to obtain the RGB or HSB values, you click the Color Slider button and select either RGB or HSB (among others) from the pop-up list.

The Color/Colors dialog boxes allow you to select colors outside of the Web-safe color palette, but only if the Snap to Web-safe option in the Color Picker is disabled. The Color/Colors dialog box also allows you to see and record the RGB values of your selected color. This is useful if you want to use the `rgb()` method of specifying your color using CSS, such as `rgb(255, 0, 0)` for red.

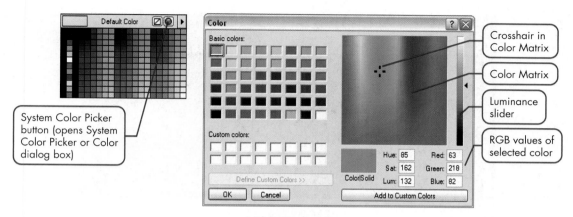

FIGURE 6.29

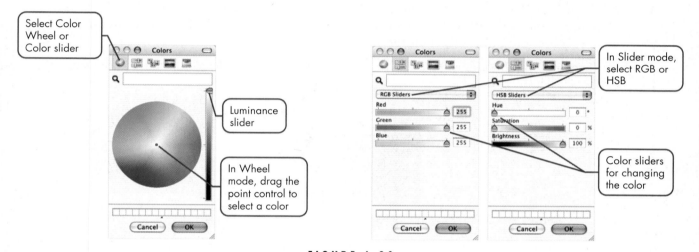

FIGURE 6.30

Set Default Text Colors

1 **In the open document index.html, open the Page Properties dialog box.**

The white text, heading, and link colors are not the default colors for text in a Web page or Dreamweaver. Text is normally black and links are normally blue. In order to demonstrate the need to set the background color in case the background image was not downloaded in the previous exercise, the default text colors are purposely set to white.

2 **Click the Text Color button, choose yellow with the eyedropper, and click Apply.**

Both heading and paragraph text become yellow. Link text stays white because it is controlled by a separate option.

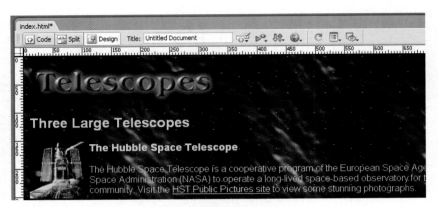

FIGURE 6.31

3 | Click the Text Color button to open the color palette, and then click the Color Wheel button. (The text at the top of the color palette window says "System Color Picker" when your mouse pointer is over the Color Wheel button.)

The System Color Picker is a tool that allows you to choose or specify a color from the entire range of colors available on your system.

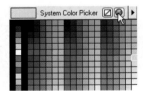

FIGURE 6.32

4 | In the Color dialog box, hold down the (left) mouse button and drag the mouse pointer around the Color Matrix/Wheel.

Watch the Red, Green, and Blue values change.

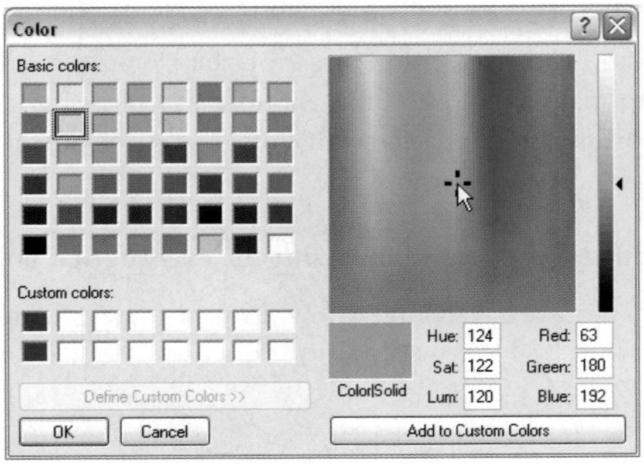

FIGURE 6.33

5   Drag the crosshair/point control to the most intense lime-green. In Windows, move the crosshair to the top of the Color Matrix. On a Macintosh, move the point control to the edge of the Color Wheel.

The crosshair/point control indicates the position of the color in the palette.

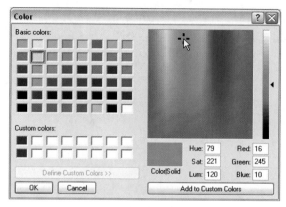

FIGURE 6.34

6   In Windows, drag the crosshair left and right to explore different hues; drag it up and down to explore different saturation levels. On a Macintosh, drag the point control around the Color Wheel to explore different hues, and drag to the center and back to the edge to explore different saturation levels.

7   Drag the slider up and down to explore different luminosities (both Windows and Macintosh); then stop at a luminosity that produces a light-blue color, and click OK.

Notice that although there were no hexadecimal color codes in the System Color Picker dialog box, Dreamweaver converts the RGB values to hexadecimal codes for you and places the code in the Text Color field.

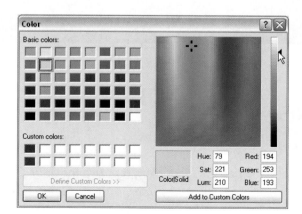

FIGURE 6.35

8 | Click OK to apply the default text color to the document.

The System Color Picker is another method for choosing a color.

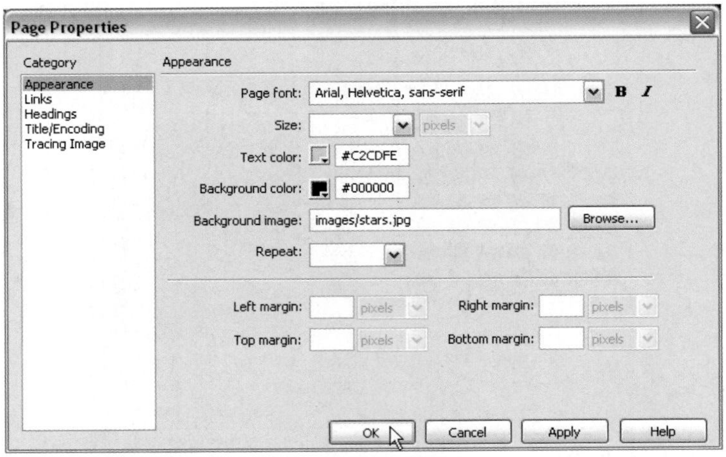

Page Properties

Category | Appearance

Appearance
Links
Headings
Title/Encoding
Tracing Image

Page font: Arial, Helvetica, sans-serif ▾ **B** *I*

Size: ▾ pixels ▾

Text color: ☐ #C2CDFE

Background color: ■ #000000

Background image: images/stars.jpg   Browse...

Repeat: ▾

Left margin: ___ pixels ▾   Right margin: ___ pixels ▾

Top margin: ___ pixels ▾   Bottom margin: ___ pixels ▾

OK   Cancel   Apply   Help

FIGURE 6.36

9 | Save the changes to index.html, leaving it open for the next lesson.

FIGURE 6.37

To Extend Your Knowledge . . .

HEXADECIMAL AND RGB

There are different palettes and methods of identifying a particular color. So far, we have identified two methods — using color names such as blue and yellow, and specifying hexadecimal color codes.

CSS allows an alternate form of hexadecimal color codes for colors that use the triplet pair of color codes. Web-safe colors use the triplet pairs of color codes, such as 003366. CSS allows a short form, in which 036 is equivalent to 003366. You can use 147 in place of 114477, despite the fact that it is not a Web-safe color — the triplet-pair pattern holds.

In the previous exercise, you saw that Dreamweaver converted the colors from the System Color Picker, which uses numerical codes for RGB, to hexadecimal color codes. Without Dreamweaver, conversion from numerical values to hexadecimal values is very difficult without using a calculator or conversion program. CSS allows a numerical format for RGB values — for example, `rgb(134, 87, 179)`. This form is very simple to use because it allows you to simply type the three numbers from the System Color Picker into the format without having to convert it to hexadecimal.

LESSON 8   Setting Link Colors

As you know, you can establish links from either text or images. Links were traditionally three colors, but with CSS and Dreamweaver, a fourth color option is available. Unvisited links (or just links) can use one color (traditionally blue), visited links can use a second color (traditionally purple), and active links can use a third (traditionally red). Active link colors are not often used — this color appears only briefly when you click the link. The fourth and newest link property is the CSS `:hover` property, which allows you to apply a color that appears when the mouse pointer rolls over a link.

Dreamweaver refers to the `:hover` property as the "rollover property", which can be confusing. This property, by whichever name, changes the color of a link when the mouse pointer rolls over the link. You set up this `:hover` (rollover) property through the Page Properties dialog box.

As you know, Dreamweaver is not a browser. It does not respond to user-triggered events, such as the `:hover` or `:active` properties of CSS. Therefore, you must test the active, visited, and rollover link colors in a browser. (The unvisited link color does not respond to any user actions, so it appears the same in Dreamweaver as it does in a browser.)

Set Link Colors

1 In the open document index.html, open the Page Properties dialog box.

2 Switch to the Links category in the dialog box.

The Link Color was previously set to white so the text would show up against the dark background of the stars. Normally, link text is blue, and the Link Color field would be blank.

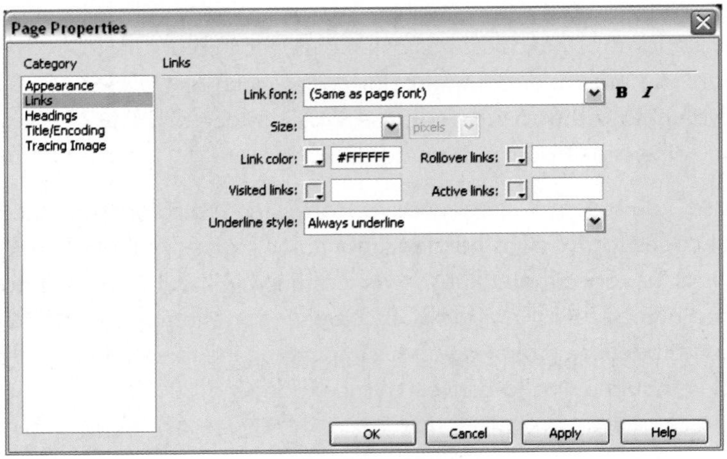

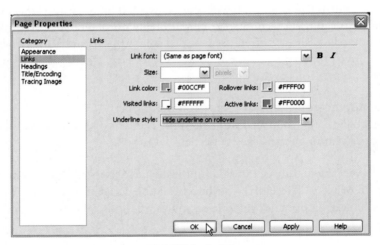

FIGURE 6.38

3 Change the Link Color to a light blue. Set the color of Visited Links to white, Rollover Links to yellow, and Active Links to red. Set the Underline Style to Hide Underline on Rollover.

FIGURE 6.39

4 Click OK when finished.

5 Preview the page in your browser.

6 Move your mouse pointer over a link and watch as the rollover color changes to yellow and the underline disappears.

7 Click a link and observe the flash of red when you click a link.

8   Click the back button in your browser to return to this page, and note that the visited link has changed to white.

FIGURE 6.40

9   Return to Dreamweaver.

10   Close index.html.

To Extend Your Knowledge . . .

CSS PSEUDO-CLASSES

The Page Properties dialog box allows you to change the text color of four link states: link (unvisited), visited, active, and hover (rollover). These states are properly known as "CSS pseudo-classes" and their forms are: `:link, :visited, :active,` and `:hover`. When you set a link color, Dreamweaver creates `a:link`, which means the anchor tag (`a`) has been defined with properties of a link state.

There are a few more pseudo-classes than the four discussed so far, but these are the most popular and have the widest support. Support for these pseudo-classes goes back as far as Internet Explorer 3. Other pseudo-classes include `:focus`, which is useful in a form — you can use it to change the background color of the text box when the user is entering text.

You can only use the link and visited pseudo-classes with the anchor tag — these pseudo-classes only make sense to a link. You can use the active and hover pseudo-class with other tags. The CSS documentation allows you to use the active pseudo-class with other tags, but browser support is virtually nonexistent. The hover pseudo-class can be used with any element as well and is supported by most current browsers (except Internet Explorer).

CAREERS IN DESIGN

USING BACKGROUNDS EFFECTIVELY

Nothing in the world can ruin a perfectly good Web site faster or more effectively than an annoying and distracting background image. Tiled, sliced, diced, or repeated, many textures and images used for backgrounds on amateur sites are so horrid that visiting them proves to be agonizing.

Professional sites stand out from amateur sites — both in layouts, the use of background images, and even (in some cases) color combinations. The amateur site designer is often a technophile with little or no sense of fashion. We're not only talking about wearing white socks with sandals, mind you — fashion sense makes itself known in many ways. Some are subtle, others not so subtle.

Use Google or Yahoo! to search for bad Web designs. You will be astounded at the number of hits you receive, as much as you'll be amazed by how bad sites can look. A good place to start your search for the shocking (in a bad but not-so bad-way) is http://www.ratz.com/featuresbad.html — which provides an outline of what not to do when designing a site.

SUMMARY

In this chapter, you learned different methods of using background images — as tiled backgrounds, as strip or margin backgrounds, and as watermark backgrounds. You saw that highly contrasting and highly colored background images may make it difficult to choose a foreground text color that can be read against them. You discovered that transparent images show an unwanted halo if the background color of the page is incorrect. You learned that you should add a background color similar to that of the background image in case a visitor views your pages with graphics disabled. You learned about RGB and hexadecimal color notations, and about the Web-safe color palette. You learned how to apply colors to text, headings, and the four link states. You also learned how to choose a color from the Web-safe color palette and from the System Color Picker.

KEY TERMS

Color matrix	Hexa	RGB model
Color wheel	Hexadecimal	System Color Picker
Deci	Low contrast	Tiling
Dithering	Palette	Wallpaper patterns
Flat in color depth		

CHECKING CONCEPTS AND TERMS

SCREEN ID

Identify the indicated areas from the following list:

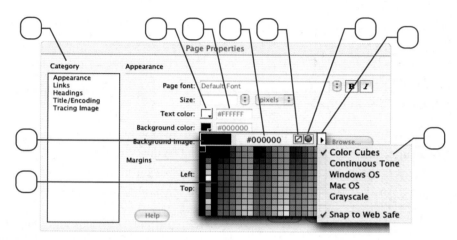

FIGURE 6.41

a. Category list

b. Color button

c. Color field

d. Color swatch

e. Reset color

f. Hexadecimal color code

g. System Color Picker

h. Pop-out menu

i. Color palette

j. Arrow to display pop-out menu

MULTIPLE CHOICE

Circle the letter of the correct answer for each of the following:

1. Which of the following is recommended when choosing a background image for a Web page?

  a. Use animated GIFs as backgrounds.

  b. Use many colors in the background image.

  c. Use transparent regions in background images.

  d. Make overlaying text visible and readable.

2. A reason to avoid complex background images is that they _____ .

  a. can slow down scrolling as the image moves

  b. can prevent universal access to your page

  c. require more computer processing power

  d. All the above

3. Which is not one of the three styles of background images?

  a. wallpaper

  b. watermark

  c. textured

  d. margin tile

4. Color depth of monitors is described _____ .

  a. as true color

  b. as $2 \times 2 \times 2 \times 2 \times 2 \times 2 \times 2 \times 2$ or 256 colors

  c. in bits, such as 8-bit, 16-bit, and 24-bit color

  d. as dithering

5. Hexadecimal _____ .

  a. means 16

  b. is used for the Web color system

  c. includes numerals 0-9 and characters A-F

  d. All of the above

6. How many colors are considered Web-safe?

  a. 256

  b. 16.7 million

  c. 216

  d. 64

7. All browsers recognize _____ .

  a. hexadecimal

  b. color names

  c. HSB/HSL

  d. Pantone

8. Background color and background images are applied to the Web page using the _____ .

  a. Property inspector

  b. Assets panel

  c. Preferences dialog box

  d. Page Properties dialog box

9. In the Page Properties dialog box, you cannot set _____ .

  a. text color

  b. syntax coloring

  c. background image

  d. All of the above

10. If you apply a background image to a Web page, you should set the background color to _____ .

  a. black or #000000

  b. white or #FFFFFF

  c. a color that contrasts with the text color

  d. it doesn't matter — the color will never show

DISCUSSION QUESTIONS

1. You can find many images and graphics on the Web, from private Web sites (belonging to individuals, companies, or organizations) to free image/graphic/photo sites and to sites that charge a fee for their images. You may also have images belonging to your employer or client, and you may have access to a digital camera. Imagine that you are creating and implementing a theme and color scheme for a Web site you are designing. What would you consider the pros and cons of each of these sources of images? List at least one pro and one con for each source.

2. What different choices for colors and background images might you make if you were designing Web sites for a sports retail store, a business school, and a personal wedding? Justify your answers.

3. How can you establish the tone or mood of a Web site through the selection of background and foreground images? Give an example, stating the tone you want to create, the business or organization you are imagining designing a Web site for, and the types of choices you would make to sustain that mood with background and foreground images.

SKILL DRILL

Skill Drill exercises reinforce project skills. Each skill that is reinforced is the same as, or nearly the same as, a skill we presented in the chapter. We provide detailed instructions in a step-by-step format. You should work through the exercises in order.

1. Choose a Color from an Image

The reach of the eyedropper color picker extends beyond the Color Picker window. You can use it to choose a color from any component in the Dreamweaver application window. If you have a graphic with a color you would like to match, as long as you can see the graphic in the Document window, you can use the color picker to pick up a color from the graphic.

In this exercise you learn to use the eyedropper to obtain a color from a graphic, and then make the chosen color the background color.

1. Open index.html from the Telescopes site and open the Page Properties dialog box.

2. Drag to select the contents of the Background Image field (images/stars.jpg) and press Delete to remove it.

3. Click Apply to confirm that the starry background is removed.

4. Click the Background Color button.

5. Click the pop-out arrow at the top right of the Color Picker window.

6. If there is a check mark next to Snap to Web Safe, skip to Step 7. If there is no check mark next to Snap to Web Safe, click Snap to Web Safe.

    In the previous exercises, we did not need to worry about whether Snap to Web Safe was enabled or not because the colors in the color palette are all Web-safe. Colors outside of the color palette, however, may not be Web-safe.

7. Move the mouse pointer (eyedropper) over the Telescopes graphic near the top of the Document window. Watch the swatch window and hexadecimal codes change as the mouse pointer moves across the graphic.

    You can see that the hexadecimal codes are always paired triplets, such as 330066 or 003300. The Snap to Web Safe option converts the color at the tip of the eyedropper to the closest Web-safe color.

The eyedropper can select a color from anywhere within the Document window, including images in the Web page.

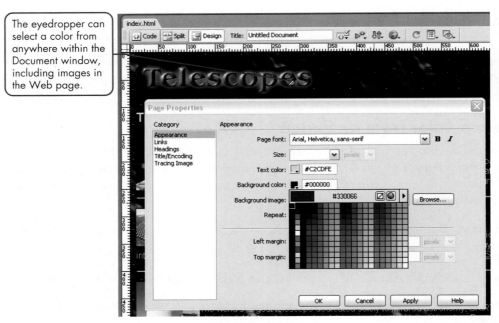

FIGURE 6.42

8. Return the mouse pointer to the color palette and disable the Snap to Web Safe option.

9. Hover the eyedropper over the same graphic.

   Notice that the hexadecimal codes are no longer paired triplets. With the Snap to Web Safe option disabled, the hexadecimal codes display the true colors at the point of the eyedropper.

10. Click a color from the Telescopes graphic. Click OK in the Page Properties dialog box to accept and apply the color.

11. Save the changes to index.html, leaving it open for the next exercise.

2. Set Heading Colors

So far, you have learned to apply a color to text, which sets the same color for all text in the page. However, different text elements on a page can have their own text colors, such as the different heading levels. You can apply these text colors through the Page Properties dialog box. In addition to font size, you can use colors to distinguish between heading levels.

1. In the open document index.html (from the Telescope site), open the Page Properties dialog box.

2. Choose Headings from the Category list.

3. On the right side of the Heading-1 row, click the color button and choose red from the color palette.

4. Choose yellow as the color for Heading 2 and light green for Heading 3.

5. Click OK to see the effects of the color selections.

The Heading-1 red color is not visible in Dreamweaver because the graphic of the Telescopes text is the Heading-1 content. If the graphic did not download, the alt text Telescopes would appear in red (as shown in the Figure 6.43 of the Firefox browser, in which the graphics are turned off using Chris Pederick's Web Developer extension, available from http://chrispederick.com/work/firefox/webdeveloper/). The white and light blue text is link text. The alt text of the photos is also white and light blue because it represents links. The link to the Hubble Space Telescope Web site is white because the photo is a link to the home page; it has been visited, so it takes on the visited-link color (white) you defined in Lesson 8.

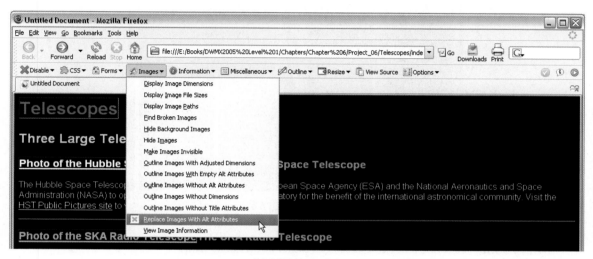

FIGURE 6.43

6.   Close, saving the changes to index.html.

3. Set the Background Repeat Options

CSS has a number of useful background properties. With CSS, you can specify the direction you want your background image to repeat. You can also specify that it not repeat at all. Another background property allows you to position a background image on the page.

You can set your background images to repeat vertically or horizontally, or to not repeat at all. The vertical and horizontal repeat options allow you to use a small image and specify that it only repeat in one direction, creating a left margin (vertical repeat) or a top margin (horizontal repeat). CSS uses the values **repeat-x** and **repeat-y** to achieve these effects: x refers to the x-axis, which runs horizontally across the bottom of a chart, and y refers to the y-axis, which runs vertically up the side of the chart.

The background position options allow you to specify where in the background of the page you want your background image to appear. The pairing of background position and background repeat (set not to repeat) is a very useful combination of CSS properties, especially with a watermark style of background image.

1.   Open index.html from the Backgrounds site.

2.   Expand the CSS panel group. If the CSS Styles tab is not selected, click it. If All is not selected, click All.

3. Right/Control-click body and choose Edit from the pop-up menu. Choose the Background category. Browse to choose left-margin-129.gif from the bg-images folder, click OK/Choose, and then click OK to insert the background image into the page.

    The background image is 129 pixels wide and 153 pixels high. By default, it repeats both vertically and horizontally. This image is suited to a vertical (y-axis) repeat.

FIGURE 6.44

4. Right/Control-click body in the CSS Styles panel and choose Edit.

5. In the Background category, choose **repeat-y** from the Repeat field and click OK.

    Although the image is only 129 pixels wide, it does not repeat across the background, just down the page.

6. Right/Control-click body in the CSS Styles panel and choose Edit.

7. In the Background category, browse to choose top-margin-143.gif as the Background Image, set the Repeat option to **repeat-x**, and click OK.

    This image is 143 pixels high, but because of the **repeat-x** setting in CSS, it only repeats across the page, not down it.

8. Right/Control-click body in the CSS Styles panel and choose Edit.

9. In the Background category, browse to choose bromeliad-watermark-small.jpg as the Background Image, set Repeat to **no-repeat**, and click OK.

    Although partly obscured by other content on this page, this image appears just once in the background of the page. You can use CSS to position a background such as this in the center of the page.

10. Right/Control-click body in the CSS Styles panel and choose Edit.

11. In the Background category, choose **center** from both the Horizontal Position and Vertical Position drop-down lists, and click OK.

The single background image is positioned in the center of the page, both vertically and horizontally.

FIGURE 6.45

12.   Close index.html, saving the changes.

To Extend Your Knowledge . . .

PAGE PROPERTIES = CSS

Dreamweaver 8 implements CSS very well and uses CSS for most functions that change a style. The options you apply using the Page Properties dialog box are written into the code using CSS, which is why you can easily switch between the Page Properties dialog box and the CSS Styles panel — many of the options and features are similar. However, the Page Properties dialog box is more limiting than the CSS Styles panel. As you gain experience, you will find it easier to use the CSS Styles panel to apply a background image and modify some of its properties rather than doing some work in the Page Properties dialog box and the rest in the CSS Styles panel.

4. Apply Background Colors to Other Elements

Prior to CSS, you could only apply background images and colors to the Web page itself, using the body element and a few other tags. With the advent of CSS, any element can have a background — a color, an image, or both.

One significant advantage of CSS over HTML methods of styling is that when you apply a property to a particular tag, such as the Heading 2 (`<h2>`) tag, all such `<h2>` tags on the page take on that property. This ability of CSS allows you to easily create a consistent look and feel for the same element throughout the entire page. (We discuss many other advantages of CSS over HTML styles in *Essentials for Design: Dreamweaver 8, Level 2*.)

1. Open elements.html from the Backgrounds site.

2. If the CSS Styles panel is not expanded, open it from the CSS panel group.

3. Right/Control-click h1 in the CSS Styles panel, and choose Edit from the menu.

4. Choose the Background category, type `#005D8C` in the Background Color field, and click OK.

   Notice that a dark-blue background appears behind the Heading 1 block. You would normally have to lighten the color of the Heading 1 text so it could be read against the dark background. In this case, however, you will modify the background (in the next Skill Drill), restoring the contrast.

5. Right/Control-click h2 in the CSS Styles panel and choose Edit.

6. Choose the Background category, type `#00A4F1` in the Background Color field, and click OK.

   The medium-blue background appears behind both Heading 2 blocks on the page.

7. Right/Control-click **a:hover** in the CSS Styles panel and choose Edit.

   The **a:hover** code refers to a rollover property. It had been preset to change the text color to white when the mouse pointer rolls over the link. You added a change in background color to the :**hover** pseudo-class.

8. From the Background category, set the Background Color to `#005D8C`, and click OK.

9. Preview the page in your browser and move your mouse pointer over the link text.

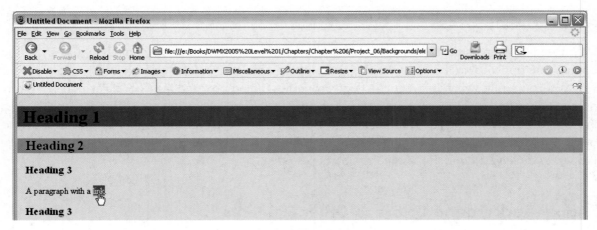

FIGURE 6.46

10. Return to Dreamweaver, leaving elements.html open for the next exercise.

To Extend Your Knowledge . . .

TAGS AND ELEMENTS

In Chapter 2, you learned that HTML consists of tags, such as the paragraph tag <p>. A tag is an element surrounded by angle brackets. Therefore, p is the paragraph element and a is the anchor element. In CSS, when you want to apply a background to the body, only the element portion of the tag is used, which is why the CSS Styles panel does not display any angle brackets, just the element.

5. Explore Design Options with Background Images

You can apply all of the background properties you have learned equally well to any element on the page or to the page itself. You can specify `background-repeat`, `background-position`, `background-image`, and `background-color` just as you did for the background of the full page.

1. In the open document elements.html, Right/Control-click h1 in the CSS Styles panel and choose Edit.

2. From the Background category, click the Browse button beside the Background Image field, choose h1-bg.png from the bg-images folder, click OK/Choose, and then click OK.

    The background image for the h1 element, as you see at the bottom of the page, is smaller (shorter and narrower) than the h1 block and repeats both vertically and horizontally.

3. Edit the h1 style again, set Background Repeat to `repeat-y`, and click OK.

4. Edit the h2 style, choose h2-bg.png from the bg-images folder as the Background Image, click OK/Choose, and click OK.

    The image contains a gradient from the middle white out to the top and bottom blue regions. The white part (middle) of the gradient is at the bottom of the h2 element, not across the middle of it.

5. Edit the h2 style again, set the Vertical Position of the Background Image to `center`, and click OK.

    Now the middle of the image is across the middle of the h2 element. The background color for the h2 element is covered by the background image and could have been removed.

6. Edit the h3 style and set the Background Image to h3-bg.png.

    Like the h1 background image, the h3 background image repeats across the width of the h3 element.

7. Edit the h3 style and set the Repeat option of the background image to `no-repeat`.

    The background image appears behind the Heading 3 text. However, this type of image can also be used as a form of underlining.

8. Edit the h3 style again and choose the Box category.

9. Uncheck Same for All in the Padding group. In the Bottom field in the Padding group, type `23` and set the units to pixels.

    Increasing the padding around an element creates a larger area for background colors or images. Increasing the bottom padding allows you to push the background image down below the Heading 3 text, but you must still set two more options.

10. Switch to the Background category, set the Horizontal Position to **left**, set the Vertical Position to **bottom**, and then click OK.

   The background image now appears as a fancy underline below the Heading 3 text.

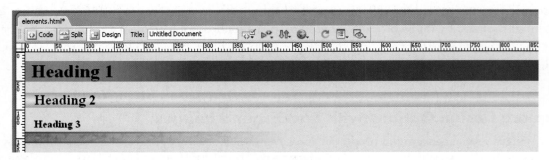

FIGURE 6.47

11. Close, saving elements.html.

To Extend Your Knowledge . . .

PADDING VS. MARGIN

In the Box category of the CSS Styles dialog box, both padding and margin options are available (although we only discussed padding). Margin also expands the space taken by the element, but unlike padding, backgrounds (colors or images) cannot extend into the margin area.

6. Prevent a Background Image from Scrolling

In the Useit.com Web page, shown in Figure 6.22, the photo of Jakob Nielsen does not scroll up or down, even though the content to its left does. They achieved this by preventing the background from scrolling and specifying the position of the background image. If you use these techniques, you can then choose to use a low-contrast image, such as shown in the home page of Czech Web designer Petr Stanicek, (Figure 6.21), and allow your text to flow over it; or you can choose to use a high-contrast image, such as the photo of Jakob Nielsen, and prevent the text from flowing over it.

1. Open products.html from the Backgrounds site.

2. Using the Page Properties dialog box, insert bromeliad-solid-small.jpg from the bg-images folder as a background image.

   The background image repeats both horizontally and vertically. It is also high-contrast, so the text on top of it is difficult to read.

3. Right/Control-click body in the CSS Styles panel and choose Edit. From the Background category, set the Repeat option to **no-repeat**, the Horizontal Position to **right**, and the Vertical Position to **top**. Click OK.

4. Preview the page in your browser and scroll the page up and down.

   Observe that the background image scrolls up and down, just as the content does.

? If You Have Problems

If your browser window is too large, all of the page content is already visible, so scrolling is neither necessary nor possible. Resize the browser window to be narrower and shorter so you can scroll.

---

5. Reduce the width of the browser window so it is as wide as the Tropiflora Online logo graphic.

   The top of the plant is hidden behind the logo graphic. It should be pushed down below the logo.

6. Return to Dreamweaver.

7. Edit the style of the body element again. In the Background category, set Attachment to Fixed. Change the Horizontal Position to **100%** (choose % from the drop-down list) and the Vertical Position to **115** pixels, and click OK.

8. Preview the page in your browser, scrolling up and down.

   Observe that the background is now fixed and does not scroll. Dreamweaver cannot display the attachment-fixed behavior — you must preview the page in a browser to see this effect. Also notice that the position of the image has shifted down below the logo graphic.

9. Return to Dreamweaver.

   To create an effect similar to that of the redesign of the Useit.com Web page, in which the content does not flow over the background image, you must set the padding on the right side of the body to the width of the background image.

10. Edit the body styles again and switch to the Box category. In the Padding group of options, uncheck the Same for All option, type **250** in the Right field, set the units to pixels, and click OK.

    The width of the background image is 250 pixels. Setting the right padding of the body to 250 pixels keeps the content away from the right side.

11. Preview the page in your browser and scroll again.

    The content does not overlap the background image, and the text is always readable.

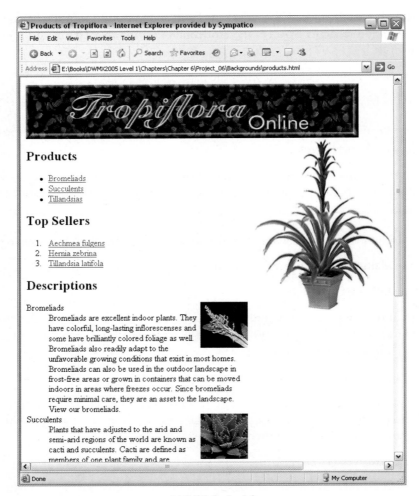

FIGURE 6.48

12.   Return to Dreamweaver and close products.html.

CHALLENGE

Challenge exercises expand on, or are somewhat related to, skills we presented in the lessons. Each exercise provides a brief introduction, followed by numbered-step instructions that are not as detailed as those in the Skill Drill exercises. You should work through them in order.

1. Add Decorative Corners around a Block of Content

You have learned that with proper application of CSS, you can place backgrounds, whether a color or an image, behind any element. However, you can use just one background image per tag — there is only one body tag, so you can only place one background image in the body tag. You can create a new background for each paragraph, but to do so you must identify each paragraph with a unique ID; you then use the ID to identify which background image to apply to the paragraph. Many designers use the `<div>` tag (the div element refers to division, such as a division or section of a document). The `<div>` tag by itself does nothing — it was devised as a container and, as such, you can use it to deliver styles.

In this Challenge, you surround a block of text with two `<div>` tags. You uniquely identify the two `<div>` tags with different IDs and apply different backgrounds to each. This process could be extended to create four corners by creating four divs. Brian Williams wrote an article, entitled "Onion Skinned Drop Shadows," on a similar technique (http://alistapart.com/articles/onionskin/).

1. Open shakespeare.html from the Backgrounds site.

2. Select all content in the page.

3. Switch the Insert bar to the Layout mode by clicking the Menu button at the right side of the Insert bar.

4. Click the second button, Insert Div Tag. Type `top-left` in the ID field, ensure that Insert is set to Wrap Around Selection, and click OK.

5. With the block still selected (if not, select it), insert another div. Type `bottom-right` as the ID for the second div, ensure that Insert is set to Wrap Around Selection, and click OK.

6. Open the CSS Styles panel and edit the style rule div#top-left.

    When you add an **id** to a tag, you must use the # symbol when referring to it in styles. In this case, the div#top-left style rule, although empty, was created for you.

7. Insert top-left-corner.png from the bg-images folder as the Background Image, set Repeat to **no-repeat**, and click Apply.

    The background image appears directly behind the content, making the text difficult to read.

8. Switch to the Box category, uncheck Same for All in the Padding Group, apply 40 pixels to both top and left, and click OK.

    The content is now pushed down and to the right, away from the background image.

9. Edit the div#bottom-right style. Insert bottom-right-corner.png from the bg-images folder as the Background Image, set Repeat to **no-repeat**, set Horizontal Position to **right**, set Vertical Position to **bottom**, and click Apply.

    By default, divs extend the full width of the available space. This means the divs spread out to the right edge of the browser window. To fix this, we need to specify a width for the div.

10. Click the Box category, set the width to 325 pixels, and click OK.

    Just as we saw with the top-left corner image, this image also interferes with reading the text that overlays it.

11. Switch to the Box category, uncheck Same for All in the Padding Group, apply 40 pixels to both bottom and right padding, and click OK.

12. Close, saving the changes.

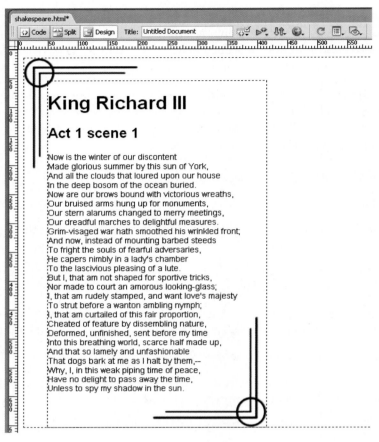

FIGURE 6.49

2. Place Decorative Images in the Background

As you recall, the **alt** (alternate text) attribute is mandatory for all inline (foreground) images on a Web page. You should assign a decorative image an empty alt attribute, which adds no content to the Web page. Background images do not need alternate text; in fact, they cannot have alternate text because they cannot be assigned the **alt** attribute. It is useful, therefore, to move foreground decorative images into the background.

The page you are modifying uses a table-based layout, as do many others you have worked with in this book. More and more designers take issue with table-based layout for several reasons (as we discuss in Chapter 8). With proper application of CSS, you can replace parts of the table with much simpler code.

1. Define a new site called DF-P6 using the Chapter_06>DF-P6 folder.

2. Open faqs.htm.

3. At the top of the page is an image of a bow tie that has been split between two cells — the top portion without text and the bottom containing the text "Debonair". Click bowtie-top.gif and delete it.

4. Right/Control-click the selected `<td>` tag in the Tag selector, choose Set ID from the menu, and select bowtie-top from the list.

5. In the CSS Styles panel, in the <style> group, Right/Control-click td#bowtie-top and choose Edit. In the Background category, set bowtie-top.gif from the images folder as the Background Image, set Repeat to **no-repeat**, and click OK.

6. Click in the left navigation bar and look at the Tag selector.

    Notice that there are two `<table>` tags. The navigation bar is enclosed in a small table that is enclosed in a cell in the left column.

7. Click the photo of the wrist below the navigation-bar links, and then click the front of the waistcoat, to the right of the navigations-bar links.

    The navigation bar is surrounded by two sliced images. You can re-create this appearance with much less code, eliminating the need for alt text.

8. Click any of the links in the navigation bar, click the <ul#menu> tag in the Tag selector, and cut the unordered list out and paste it into the clipboard.

9. Click the second `<table>` tag in the Tag selector (the one that contained the navigation bar) and press Delete/Backspace to remove the table. Paste the unordered list back into the page without the table structure around it.

10. Edit ul#menu in the CSS Styles panel from the <style>group, set menu-bg.jpg from the images folder as the Background Image, and click Apply. Switch to the Box category, set the height to 281 pixels, and click OK.

11. Click in the main table cell containing the frequently asked questions, Right/Control-click the `<td>` tag in the Tag selector, and add `id="body"` to the tag.

12. Edit td#body in the CSS Styles panel, set background.gif as the Background Image, set Repeat to **no-repeat**, Horizontal Position to **center**, Vertical Position to **top**, and click OK.

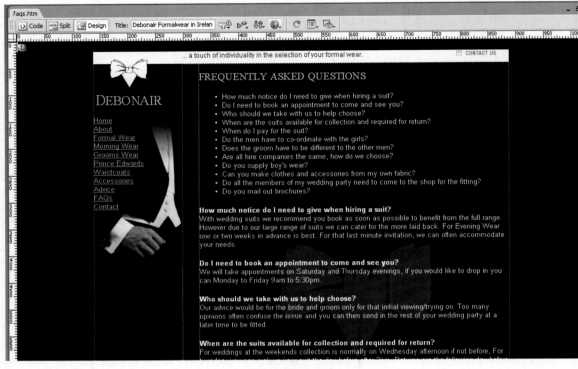

FIGURE 6.50

13.   Close, saving faqs.htm.

PORTFOLIO BUILDER

Create Alternative Color Schemes

In this assignment, you're going to create a "comprehensive" layout to use for a client presentation. The prospective client is a furniture manufacturer, and they've indicated that their first choice for a design would be one that used a wood texture for the background of the site. You have some concerns about using such a background, because as you know, background images can easily clutter a site and distract from the content. You need to create three different page formats for the presentation.

To determine complementary colors, try visiting the visibone.com site and looking through their color chips.

1. Search the Web for wood textures. There are a number of sites where you can download samples for use in a presentation.

2. Create one design that uses the wood texture for the total background.

3. Create a second design that uses the texture only for a top or side navigation bar and a light complementary color for the balance of the site.

4. Create a third site that uses the texture only for buttons and navigational elements.

5. If you have access to a color printer, output the three designs so they can be presented in a physical form.

CHAPTER 7

Frames

OBJECTIVES

In this chapter, you learn how to:

- Identify effective ways to use frames

- Use the properties of framesets and frames

- Create a framed-layout with new pages

- Create a framed-layout using existing pages

- Apply frameset options

- Use targets to create links between frames

- Set page properties in framed pages

- Accommodate browsers that do not support frames

Why Would I Do This?

Frames are a method of splitting the browser window into separate sections. Each section or *frame* that you create is a separate HTML page. The *frameset page* is the master document that specifies the number of frames on a page, the size and placement of each frame, and the Web page contained in each individual frame. The frameset itself does not display in the browser — it remains behind the scenes. Only the pages within the frames appear in the browser. Frames enable you to keep some sections of the content continuously visible and available when other parts change after the user clicks a link or scrolls up or down.

Once very popular, frames are now seldom used. One leading cause of their decline is a history of poorly designed pages, produced by novice designers, with horrible-looking results. The W3C has eliminated frames from the HTML standard beginning with XHTML 1.1.

Regardless of their history and whether the HTML standards keep or drop frames, some sites continue to use them. You need to understand what they are and how to work with them so you are prepared if you are required to work on such sites.

Pros and Cons of Using Frames

Designed and implemented correctly, frames present a number of advantages. In a framed layout, the content of some frames remains static while you scroll the content in others. This can ensure that, for example, the navigation bar in the left frame and the company logo in the top frame are always visible and available. Similarly, you might use frames for a photo album, in which one scrolling frame displays thumbnail images and another fixed frame displays a single large photo.

Another advantage is that individual frames can load separately, decreasing the download size and time. In a site where the navigation bar and the company logo remain fixed in their own frames, only the body-content frame changes when the user selects different links. Without the need to download the navigation bar or logo each time users click a link, downloads are smaller and faster. Frames can also reduce site maintenance and save time. If you need to change the navigation bar, for example, you only have to alter the navigation page, not every page on the site.

There are also many disadvantages of using frames as a layout method. Not all browsers support frames, so you could lose an important customer who cannot access them. Frames are difficult to navigate for those who depend on assistive technologies (such as screen-reading software), partly because the navigation components are typically separated from the content and partly because it is more difficult to make them accessible.

Bookmarking a framed page is difficult for browsers. You can set a bookmark, but the browser may only bookmark the frameset page. If you bookmark a specific page within a frame, when you return to the page, it loses the other framed content around it, creating confusion by the lack of a navigation bar or other means to explore the rest of the site. Search engines suffer from the same problem. If you search for a page that was designed to be part of framed content, you probably won't get the other pages (frames) that surround it.

Printing a frameset page was difficult in the past: older browsers either printed the frameset page, which is essentially empty, or printed only the selected frame. Current browsers have overcome this limitation, and they all support various printing options — all frames together as on the screen, only the selected page, or all pages separately.

Much of the ongoing debate about frames focuses on improperly set up pages. For instance, you can provide the same content to both frames-capable and frames-incapable browsers. All too often, however, developers don't employ the techniques to do so. When they don't, users of frames-incapable browsers just see a notice stating that the site was built using frames so they should upgrade their browser. Similarly, ignorance of the weaknesses and pitfalls of framed design leads to many problems.

By completing this chapter, you learn what you need to know to produce quality-framed layouts. You can use frames appropriately and avoid the pitfalls of poor design and implementation.

VISUAL SUMMARY

The tools and functions in this chapter are for the design, assembly, and control of frames. The frames are the individual rectangles that have names. One of the most useful tools for working with frames is the Frames panel, which shows you the layout and names of the frames. You can also use it to select frames and framesets. To select a frame, you click the named rectangle. Framesets bind together frames and are indicated by raised lines in the Frames panel. In the following example, nav and main are enclosed in a frameset. You select framesets by clicking the raised line that outlines the frameset. Figure 7.1 shows the nav/main frameset is selected — it has a black raised line. As you see, you can nest framesets within other frames: the nav/main frameset is enclosed in the lower frame of the frameset for which header is the upper frame. Knowing how to use the Frames panel allows you to easily work with frames and framesets.

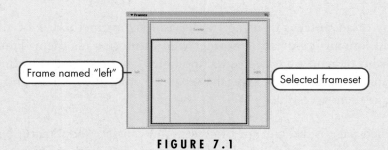

FIGURE 7.1

The Property inspector has two possible modes when you work with framed layouts: one mode displays frame properties and the other displays frameset properties. Figure 7.2 shows the Property inspector with a frameset selected. You can set borders to display or not and determine the width and color of the borders. Using the RowCol Selection area, you see how many columns (or rows) there are in the current frameset. This figure displays the properties of the nav/main frameset from Figure 7.1. The darkened rectangle identifies which frame in the frameset is selected. You can select the specific row or column by clicking the appropriate rectangle in the RowCol Selection area. The size of the selected row or column also displays and can be modified.

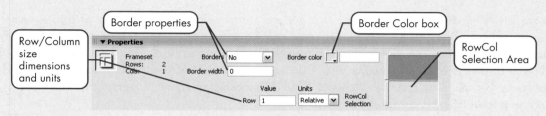

FIGURE 7.2

When you select a frame in the Frames panel, the Property inspector displays the properties of the individual frame. You can change the name of the frame in the Property inspector. From the Scroll options, you may select from Auto (which means scroll bars appear only when needed), No (never display scroll bars), or Yes (always display scroll bars). The Web page that appears in the selected frame is shown in the Src (source) field — you can type the name of the page or choose it using either the point-to-file or browse-for-file options. The No Resize option, when unchecked, allows the user to grab the frame border (if visible) and resize the frame. In addition to frameset borders, individual frames may also have borders, which you can set using the Property inspector.

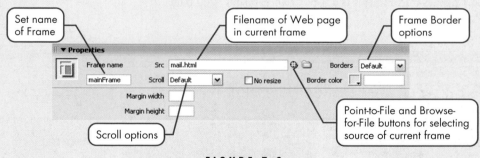

FIGURE 7.3

LESSON 1   Exploring Frames-Based Web Sites

In this lesson, you explore how two Web sites use frames-based layouts in their design. In both examples, these companies use frames to display part of their site in one frame and another site in the other frame. By displaying both sites in a single browser window, they can show the visitor the external Web site while maintaining the bond to their own Web site.

About.com is a *Web directory*, a Web site that collects information about a variety of topics such as Web design, arts and entertainment, homework help, and travel, just to name a few. In addition to the information they provide in their pages, the editors also link to other Web sites that offer additional information. Links to external pages display in a frames-based layout — the top frame contains About.com information, and the larger, lower frame contains the external Web site. This relationship of frames suggests that the content of the frames is also related (there is continuity of thought).

The Google.com images gallery also uses a frames-based layout. When you choose an image to view at full size, Google.com uses a frames-based layout showing the thumbnail image in the top frame and the Web site it came from in the bottom frame. The top frame has two purposes: to remind you which image you chose so that you can find it in the Web page in the lower frame, and to remind you that you came from Google.com.

Examine Frames-Based Web Sites

1   **Open your browser and go to http://webdesign.about.com/cs/framesproscons/.**

2   **Scroll down about two-thirds of the page, and click the link "Search Engines and Frames".**

Search Engines and Frames is a link to an external Web page.

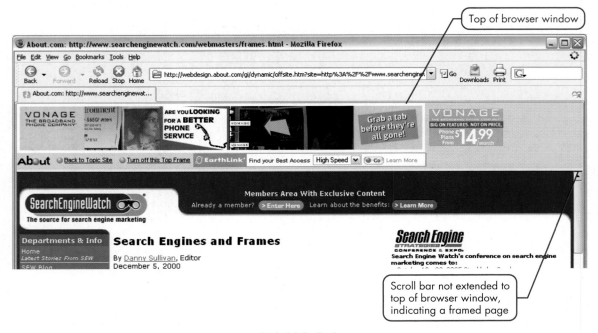

FIGURE 7.4

3 **In the top frame (below the About.com logo), click the "Turn off this Top Frame" link.**

The top frame disappears — the link takes you to the Web page you were previously viewing and allows you to view it without frames. Enclosing another Web site's pages in one of your frames is called *trapping*, which is normally a design flaw. In this case, it is intentional and its purpose is to suggest that About.com is providing you access to more information, but information that they did not create.

FIGURE 7.5

4 **Go to http://www.google.com and click the Images link.**

Google picks up your location and delivers a more local URL, if there is one.

5 **In the search field, type** `house` **and either press Enter/Return or click Google Search.**

You see an image gallery of houses. The gallery of images changes often: you may see different images than shown here.

FIGURE 7.6

6 **Click any image of a house.**

Notice the right scroll bar does not extend to the top of the browser window. This is a framed page showing Google information at the top with the photo, and the Web page from which the photo came in the bottom frame.

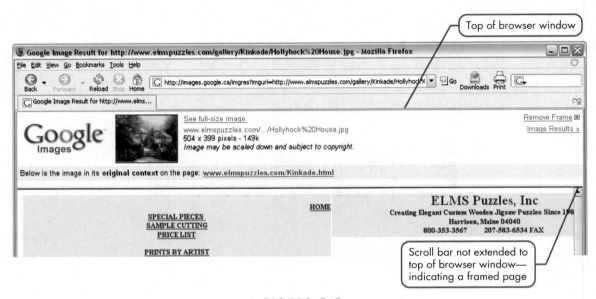

FIGURE 7.7

7   **At the top-right corner of the top frame, click the Remove Frame link.**

Much like "Turn off this Top Frame" in About.com, this link displays the lower page without frames.

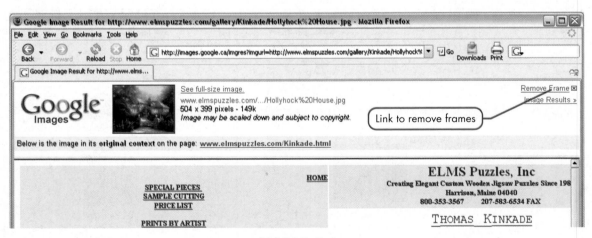

FIGURE 7.8

8   **Close your browser.**

To Extend Your Knowledge . . .

DISCUSSIONS OF PROS AND CONS

Whether or not to use frames as a layout method is a hotly contested issue. A number of Web pages are dedicated to this debate. Read a review of when frames make sense at http://gooddocuments.com/Techniques/whenframes.htm. For the other side, read Jakob Nielsen's article "Why Frames Suck (Most of the Time)" at http://useit.com/alertbox/9612.html. One key argument, both pro and con, is over usability—whether frames make the content more or less user-friendly.

LESSON 2 Exploring the Properties of a Framed Layout

In this lesson, you work with the framed-layout home page of the Web site of a fictitious school. You explore how the site was constructed, which Web pages are used in the different frames, and some of the properties of framesets and frames.

The frames-based layouts for About.com and Google.com, as you saw in the last exercise, are basic—just two frames forming two rows. Most frames-based sites use more complex layouts, dividing the page into both rows and columns. Commonly, the header, footer, and navigation-bar portions of a Web page are set up as three frames that surround the main content in the fourth and central frame.

The Frames panel is normally closed in Dreamweaver because most Web sites do not use frames. Keeping the Frames panel open routinely takes workspace away from the more commonly used panels. However, when you work with frames-based sites, leaving the Frames panel open is very beneficial. It allows you, for example, to view the layout of the frames.

Using the Frames panel, you can also select a frame or frameset and then, through the Property inspector, modify the properties of that selected frame or frameset. The frame name that appears in the Property inspector also appears in the frame in the Frames panel. You select a frame by clicking its rectangle in the Frames panel, and select a frameset by clicking the thick border surrounding a frameset. When you select a frame or frameset in the Frame panel, a dotted line appears around the frameset in the Document window.

With a frame selected in the Frames panel, the Property inspector displays the name of the Web page that appears in that frame, the scroll (scroll bar) options, border thickness, border-color options, and the name of the frame. With a frameset selected in the Frames panel, the Property inspector displays the border options and, most importantly, the dimensions of the different frames in the selected frameset. Although you can use the Property inspector to modify most of the frame and frameset properties, you cannot add or delete frames using the Property inspector—you must use other tools.

The HTML code of frames-based pages involves two primary tags—the **<frameset>** tag and the **<frame />** tag. The **<frameset>** tag uses the **cols** or **rows** attributes to identify whether the frameset is to be divided into columns or rows. The dimensions of the frames are specified in the **cols** and **rows** attributes, which also identify how many columns or rows appear in the frameset. The **<frame />** tag identifies the Web page that appears in the current frame. Both the **<frameset>** and **<frame />** tags have other attributes, such as **border, scroll, name,** and **noresize**.

Framesets can be nested in other framesets. In the following figure, the outer frameset is divided into two columns, and the right frame is divided into two rows.

```
<frameset rows="*" cols="191,*" frameborder="no" border="0" framespacing="0">
    <frame src="leftnav.html" name="left" scrolling="No" noresize="noresize" id="left" />
    <frameset rows="135,*" cols="*" framespacing="0" frameborder="no" border="0">
        <frame src="top.html" name="top" scrolling="No" noresize="noresize" id="top" />
        <frame src="main.html" name="main" id="main" />
    </frameset>
</frameset>
```

FIGURE 7.9

Examine a Framed Layout in Dreamweaver

In this exercise, you examine the properties of both frames and framesets. You learn how to navigate around a frames-based layout in Dreamweaver, how to open the Frames panel, and how to select frames and framesets.

1 Define the folder Chapter_07>GMMS as a new site called GMMS. (You may want to remove the site definitions from the previous chapter, as you won't need them again. Use the method from Chapter 5, Lesson 1, Step 2.)

2 Open index.html and scroll down using the scroll bar on the right side of the screen.

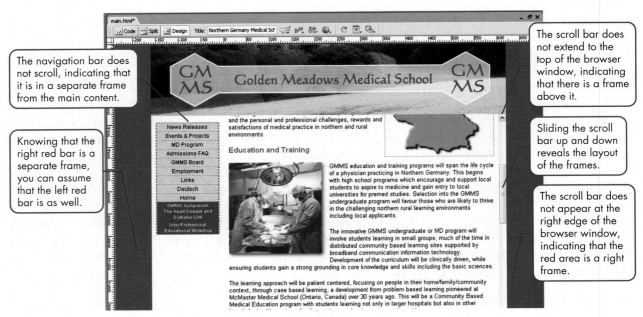

FIGURE 7.10

3 Choose Window>Frames.

The Frames panel appears below the Files panel group. The Frames panel contains a number of rectangles, each representing a frame and enabling you to select individual frames and framesets.

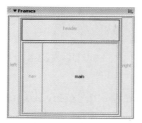

FIGURE 7.11

4 In the Frames panel, click the Main box (frame) and look at the Document window.

There is a dotted line around the main content region of the page that scrolls using the scroll bar. You can use the Frames panel to select individual frames.

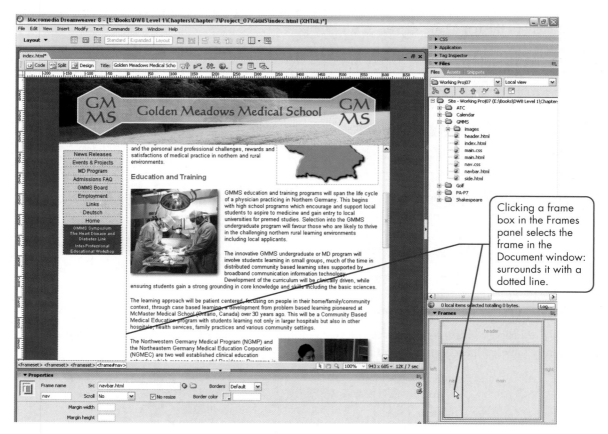

Clicking a frame box in the Frames panel selects the frame in the Document window: surrounds it with a dotted line.

FIGURE 7.12

5 Click the nav frame in the Frames panel and look at the Property inspector.

The Property inspector indicates the frame is named nav, which you also see in the Frames panel. This nav frame contains the navbar.html Web page.

FIGURE 7.13

6 **Click the header frame and look at the Property inspector.**

The header frame has the frame name header and contains the header.html Web page.

7 **Click first in the left frame and then the right while examining the Property inspector.**

Although the two frames have different names, they both contain the side.html Web page.

8 **In the Frames panel, click the nav frame.**

9 **In the Tag selector at the bottom of the Document window, click the `<frameset>` tag immediately to the left of the `<frame#nav>` tag.**

As discussed previously, the `<frameset>` tag contains the frames and defines the orientation (row, column), number, and sizes of the frames. Notice that the box surrounding the nav and main frames is black, indicating the frameset that encloses both of those frames is selected.

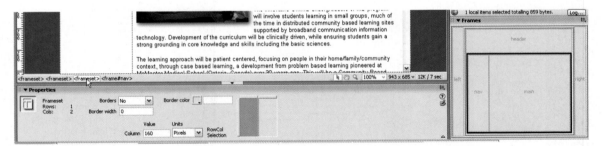

FIGURE 7.14

10 **Look at the Property inspector.**

In the Property inspector, you see the two columns in the RowCol Selection area; note that the currently selected left column is 160 pixels wide.

FIGURE 7.15

11   **Click the middle `<frameset>` tag in the Tag selector.**

The box or frameset of the middle column is selected. From the Property inspector, you see that this frameset is divided into two rows: the top frame contains the header frame and the bottom frame contains the nav/main frameset.

FIGURE 7.16

12   **In the Tag selector, click the left `<frameset>` tag.**

The outermost box in the Frames panel is selected. In the Property inspector, you see that this frameset is divided into three columns, the middle one containing the header frameset.

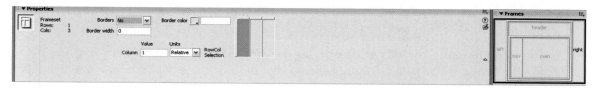

FIGURE 7.17

13   **Keep index.html open for the next exercise.**

Work with Web Pages in Frames

In the last exercise, you learned some of the properties of frames and framesets. In this exercise, you learn to work with the individual Web pages in the frames. You also discover that when you make a change to the content of just one frame, only that Web page needs saving.

When you make changes to the Web page in a frame, you must save that page. When you make changes to the frameset, you must save the frameset page, in this case index.html. Prior to this chapter, it was always clear that changes had been made to a page. When you work with frames, however, it isn't always clear, because the telltale asterisk beside the filename at the top of the Document window may not always be visible. Dreamweaver keeps track of which files in a frameset have been modified, so that if you modify one and then close the frameset, Dreamweaver asks you if you want to save the changes to the modified page. It also identifies which page was modified.

1   In the open document index.html, look at the filename tab at the top of the Document window and note that it shows index.html.

With the `<frameset>` tag selected in the Tag selector, the frameset page, index.html, is selected.

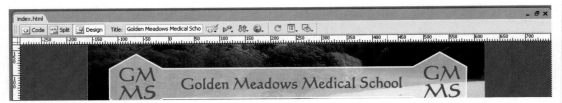

FIGURE 7.18

2   Click the header frame in the Document window (without using the Frames panel) and note that the tab now reads header.html.

FIGURE 7.19

3   Click the left frame in the Document window — the tab now reads side.html.

When you select a frame from the Document window, you can edit the contents of the Web page in that frame.

4   Type `Hello!` in the left frame and observe that the filename tab now contains an asterisk, indicating that the Web page has changed since it was last saved.

FIGURE 7.20

5   Click the nav frame in the Document window and observe that the filename tab has no asterisk beside navbar.html. This Web page has not been modified.

6   Close index.html, but do not save the changes to side.html.

FIGURE 7.21

LESSON 3   Creating a Frameset with New Pages

Dreamweaver comes with a number of predefined frameset layouts. One of these may be exactly what you need or close to what you need. You do not need to assume that these are the only possible layouts with framesets in Dreamweaver — you can use any as a starting point and modify or add to it.

In frameset layouts, Dreamweaver uses *fixed* to mean that the identified frame has a specified dimension measured in pixels. For example, Fixed Left means that the left frame is fixed at a particular measurement and the right frame is allowed to fill the rest of the browser-window width. Fixed Top, Fixed Bottom has three frames: the top and bottom frames are fixed in height, and the middle frame fills the remaining space.

There are two methods of creating a frameset. You can choose the Frameset category from the Start page, or you can create a standard blank HTML page and choose a frameset using either the Layout Insert bar or Insert>HTML>Frames. You can then make some modifications using the Frames panel or the Property inspector, such as changing the width of a frame. You cannot, however, add or delete a frame or nest a frameset from the Property inspector or the Frames panel.

In this lesson, you choose a frameset from the many options provided with Dreamweaver. You modify the default frameset, save the changes, and prepare the individual pages in the frames.

Choose the Frames Layout

1   Create a new site definition named PA-P7 (PhotoAlbum, Project 7) using the Chapter_07>PA-P7 folder.

2   Choose File>New.

3   From the categories on the left, choose Framesets.

In the Framesets category, you see a series of predefined framesets; the top one is initially selected and visible in the Preview window.

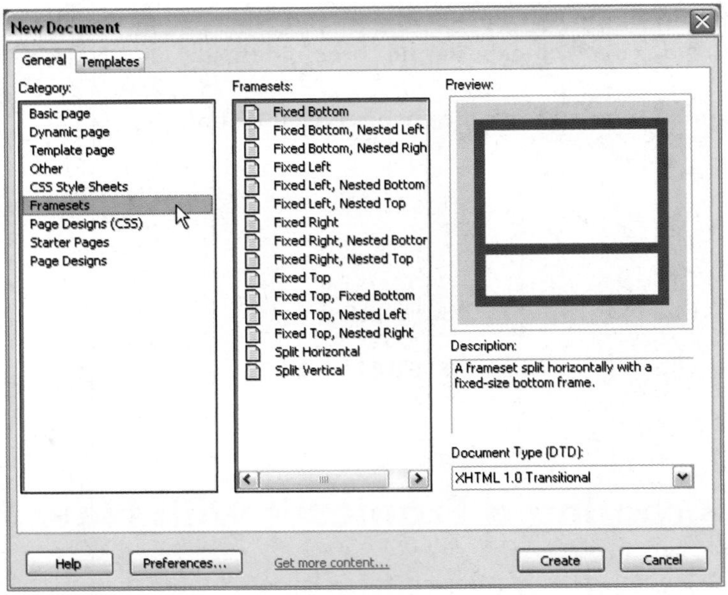

FIGURE 7.22

4 **Explore the different predefined framesets by clicking them and viewing their formats in the Preview window.**

All but the bottom two options use the word "Fixed" in the description, such as Fixed Bottom. In this example, the bottom frame has a defined width, and the top frame fills the remainder of the browser window.

5 **Choose Fixed Top, Fixed Bottom and click Create.**

6 **Accept the default frame titles and click OK.**

FIGURE 7.23

7 Examine the new frameset page.

In the Document window, the divisions between the top, middle, and bottom frames are visible as light-gray lines.

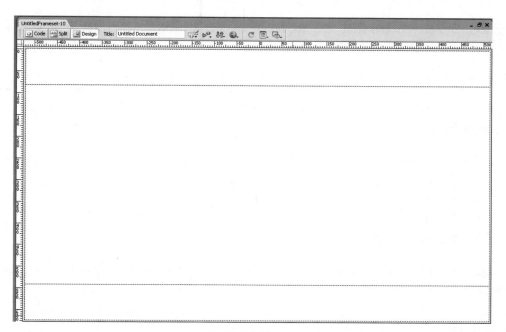

FIGURE 7.24

To Extend Your Knowledge . . .

FRAME TITLES, DOCUMENT TITLES, AND FRAME NAMES

The frame title is an attribute of the `<frame />` tag that assists users requiring screen-reading software. It identifies to these users the purpose or contents of the frame such as navigation bar or main content. Unlike other applications of the title attribute, such as within the `<a>` or `<abbr>` tags where the title attribute text appears as a tool-tip, current browsers do not display the title attribute of the `<frame />` tag. This attribute appears within the code of the frameset page.

Document titles are applied to every page using the Document title field at the top of the Document window. Every page in a framed layout — the frameset page and every frame page — should have a document title. The purpose of the Document title remains the same whether or not you use a framed layout: to identify the purpose or contents of the page. Unlike the `title` attribute of the `<frame />` tag, the document title appears in the title bar of the browser and as the document name in search-engine results and your browser's bookmarks list. The document title of the frameset page is especially important because, for a frames-based Web site, it identifies the name of the site or business in search-engine results or bookmarks: A Document title that is empty or useless, such as Untitled Document, will significantly reduce the Web site's search-engine ranking. Document titles should also be applied to every page within the framed site. Although it is uncommon to see frame pages outside of their frame-sets, search engines commonly separate frame pages from their frameset; without a Document title, the purpose of the page is unclear, and a reduced search-engine ranking will result.

Frame names, similar to frame titles, are not visible within the browser. However, frame names enable links in one frame to open a page into another frame using the target attribute.

All three attributes should be used properly for the accessibility and usability of your framed site.

Rename the Frames

The predefined frame templates come with generic names. It is helpful to name the frames with names that are more appropriate for your use.

1 If the Frames panel is not open, choose Window>Frames.

2 Click topFrame in the Frames panel.

3 In the Property inspector, delete topFrame from the Frame Name field, type `top_nav`, and press Enter/Return or Tab.

You must press Enter/Return or Tab after typing the new frame name. The new name does not register properly if you don't.

FIGURE 7.25

4 Click mainFrame in the Frames panel; in the Property inspector, change the Frame Name to photo_large.

5 Change the Frame Name of bottomFrame to photo_thumbs.

You have given the three frames new names, which may be more meaningful to you when you work with the frames.

Resize the Frames

The frame dimensions must be resized to match the size of your content.

1 Click the top_nav frame in the Frames panel, and then move your mouse pointer over the divider between the top_nav frame and the middle photo_large frame.

The mouse pointer changes to a double-pointed arrow, indicating that the divider may be moved up or down. If the divider separates two columns, the arrows point left and right instead of up and down.

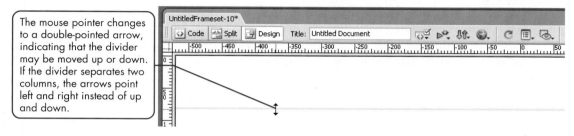

FIGURE 7.26

2 Drag the divider down until the Row Value (height) is 120 pixels (or as close as you can get).

This technique is not easy to perform because the Row Value field in the Property inspector does not change as you drag the divider — you must release the mouse button to see the measurement. This technique makes more sense when you don't know the numerical value of the height but must visually adjust the height to fit a graphic or content in the frame.

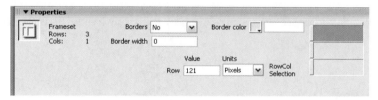

FIGURE 7.27

3 Select the bottom frame using the RowCol Selection area in the Property inspector.

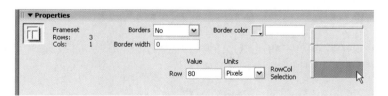

FIGURE 7.28

4 Change the Row size to 120 pixels by typing in the Value field, and press Enter/Return to apply the change.

Typing the Row Value (or Column Value) is a much easier way of applying a specific dimension to the frame, but if you don't know the dimension, it is better to drag the divider until the dimensions match the content in the frames. If, in Step 2, you couldn't drag the top row height to exactly 120 pixels, you can now click the top frame in the RowCol Selection area and set the height to 120 pixels.

To Extend Your Knowledge . . .

UNITS OF MEASUREMENT FOR FRAMES

You can use any of three units of measurement to specify the dimensions of frames: pixels, percentages, and relative units. Pixels allow you to specify the exact dimensions (height or width) of a particular frame. The Dreamweaver predefined frame layouts that have Fixed in the description use a pixel measurement for the fixed frames. In the Fixed Left frame layout, for example, the left frame has a fixed measurement in pixels.

When a particular frame does not need to be a specific dimension, percentages may suffice, such as two frames that are each 50%. The advantage of using percentages is that the frames then expand or shrink with different sizes of browser windows. Percentages are based on the available space in the current frameset. In a framed layout that uses just one frameset, the dimensions of the frameset equal the dimensions of the browser window.

Although percentages are relative units, Dreamweaver uses the term "relative units" differently. Generally, when you design a frameset, you give all but one of the frames a specific measurement; the remaining frame uses the rest of the space. For example, in Dreamweaver's Fixed Left layout, the left frame is 80 pixels wide and the right frame uses whatever space remains. In the frameset code, the <frameset> tag appears as <frameset cols="80, *">, where the first column (left frame) is 80 pixels wide (the lack of a unit is interpreted as pixels), and the right frame uses the remaining browser-window width.

Add Content to the Frames

In this exercise, you add content directly to the individual frame pages. Many designers find it easier to create the basic pages for the individual frames first, and then assemble them in a frameset, but the choice is yours.

1   **Click the top_nav frame and type** `This frame contains links to different photo albums.`

2   **Click the photo_large frame and type** `This frame contains the large photos from the photo album.`

3   **Click the photo_thumbs frame and type** `This frame contains the thumbnail images of the photos in the photo album.`

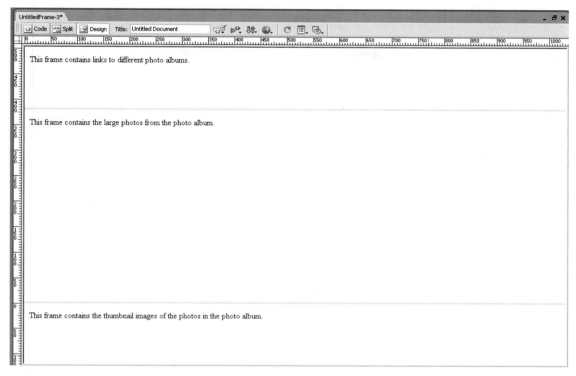

FIGURE 7.29

Save the Frameset and Frames

When you create a nonframed Web page, you save just one file. When you save a framed layout, you must save the frameset page and all of the individual frames.

Some additional save options appear when you work with a framed layout, including Save Frameset, Save Frame, and Save All. Save Frameset saves just the frameset page but not any of the pages that exist within the individual frames. Save Frame saves just the page in the currently selected frame (that page is identified in the filename tab at the top of the Document window). In this lesson, there are three frame files — one for each of the three frames. Again, you could save each of the frame pages separately, but unless you save the frameset, too, you won't have saved every open file. Save All saves all open pages — the frameset and the frame pages.

1 Click any of the frames in the Frames panel.

2 Choose File>Save Frameset, type `frameset.html`, and click Save.

You have saved the frameset page, but you have not saved any of the individual pages within the frames.

3 Choose File>Save All.

Notice the hatched line around the bottom frame. This line identifies which frame is currently being saved. In this case, it is the bottom frame (photo_thumbs).

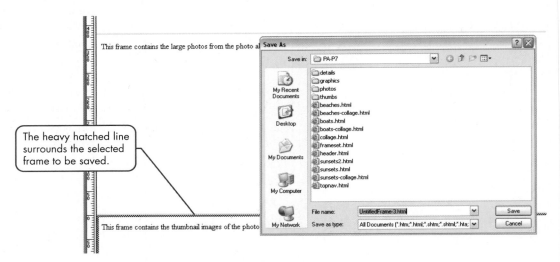

The heavy hatched line surrounds the selected frame to be saved.

FIGURE 7.30

4 Type `bottom.html` and click Save (or press Enter/Return).

The hatched line now surrounds the middle frame (photo_large).

5 Save the photo_large frame's page as **middle.html**.

6 Save the page in the top_nav frame as **top.html**.

7 Click the text in the top_nav frame and set the format to Heading 1.

FIGURE 7.31

8 Close the frameset, saving the changes to top.html.

To Extend Your Knowledge . . .

INITIAL STATES OF FRAMESETS

When you create a new frameset, you save the layout of the frameset and the filenames of the Web pages in the frames. Saving the frameset defines the initial state of the frames in the frameset. When you save the frameset, if you have page-4.html in the frame named body_frame, then when you open the frameset, it will open with page-4.html in the body_frame frame.

How you intend to use the frameset plays a role in deciding the filename you use to save the frameset page. If you are building a Web site using a frame-based layout, the frameset page must use the default filename such as index.html. If the framed layout is only to be used as a component of a Web site, you may use whatever filename you prefer.

LESSON 4   Creating a Frameset with Existing Pages

When you create a frameset using existing pages, the process you use is very similar to what you did in the previous lesson, with minor modifications. You bring the already-created pages into the frameset in place of the default blank pages. You can size the frames in the frameset using visual methods, but that is only one option. If you know that the Web page in the top frame requires 100 pixels in height, you could instead just type that measurement into the Property inspector.

In this exercise, unlike the preceding one, you do not create the pages that appear in the frames. You simply specify which existing pages are to appear in the frames. You won't be prompted to save the individual frames because they already exist. However, by selecting these pages and specifying that they be used in the frames of the frameset, you are modifying the properties of the frameset page so you must save it.

In this lesson, you also learn another method for creating a frameset page. You create a blank HTML page and then, using the Frames button on the Layout Insert bar, modify the blank HTML page into a frameset page.

Choose and Prepare the Frameset

1   Create a new Basic HTML page by choosing File>New, choosing Basic Page from the Category list, choosing HTML from the Basic Page list, and clicking Create.

2   Switch to the Layout Insert bar.

3   The Frames drop-down list is the second button on the right. Click the drop-down list and choose Top and Bottom Frames.

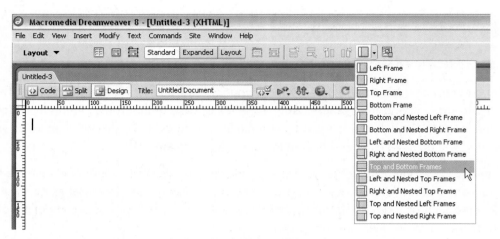

FIGURE 7.32

4 Type `Thumbnail photos` in the Title field for the bottomFrame frame.

FIGURE 7.33

5 Select topFrame from the Frame list and type `Navigation bar` in the Title field. Select mainFrame and type `Large Photos` in the Title field. Click OK.

6 Type `Photo Galleries of Boats, Sunsets and Beaches` in the Document title field of the Document toolbar.

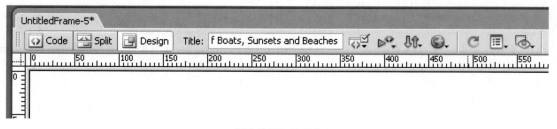

FIGURE 7.34

7 Click topFrame in the Frames panel; in the Property inspector, change the Frame Name to `top_nav`.

8 Click mainFrame in the Frames panel, and change the Frame Name to `photo_large` in the Property inspector.

9 Choose bottomFrame in the Frames panel, and change the Frame Name to `photo_thumbs`.

10 Choose File>Save Frameset, type `index.html`, and click Save.

You have prepared and saved the frameset. The next step is to insert existing pages into the frames.

Insert Existing Web Pages into Frames

In the Property inspector with a frame selected, the Src (source) field identifies the path and the filename of the page that appears within it. To insert a Web page into a particular frame, select the frame from the Frames panel, and then type the path and filename into the Src field; alternatively, you can use the point-to-file or browse-for-file function. These functions behave exactly the same as they do when you link to a file.

1 Select the top_nav frame in the Frames panel.

2 In the Property inspector, click the Browse for File icon, choose topnav.html, and click OK/Choose.

? **If You Have Problems**

Remember that absolute paths are not properly interpreted when you preview your pages on your computer. This applies to the paths to images, links, and pages in a frameset. If you preview a frameset in your browser and nothing appears, return to Dreamweaver and check the Src of the pages. If the path to the page begins with "/", use the browse-for-file method to reset the Src to the page (or pages), and ensure that the Relative To option is set to Document and not to Site.

3 Drag the divider between the top and middle frames downward until you can clearly see the three links in top_nav.

4 Select the photo_large frame in the Frames panel.

5 Using the Point to File icon, choose collage.html.

6 Select the photo_thumbs frame in the Frames panel.

7 Using either the browse-for-file or point-to-file method, and choose boats.html as the Src for this frame.

8   Set the height of the photo_thumbs frame to 120 pixels.

FIGURE 7.35

9   Choose File>Save All.

LESSON 5 Using Frameset Options

There are a few commonly used frameset options, most of which are preset in the frameset templates supplied with Dreamweaver. The default settings are not always appropriate, however, so you learn to change them in this lesson.

Scroll bars have three settings: Yes, No, and Default. Default is equivalent to auto in HTML. Auto scrolling means that scroll bars appear only when necessary. For example, if the content of a frame is too wide but not too tall for the frame dimensions, then just the horizontal scroll bar appears. The Scroll setting of Yes sets both scroll bars as visible all of the time, and No sets both scroll bars as never visible. The No setting is a problem if the content of the frame is too large — it is impossible for the visitor to scroll to see the rest of the content. A Yes setting displays both scroll bars, whether or not one or both are needed. Displaying scroll bars requires approximately 15 pixels. This space is taken from the frame space, changing a frame height of 100 pixels to 85 pixels of usable space. You must be careful when you decide how to use scroll bars.

Frames can have borders, which can be useful when you want to clearly distinguish between frames. You can set these borders to different sizes and colors. You can also disable borders if you want to create a seamless layout.

Frames have an option to allow the visitor to resize the frames. If you want to use this option, you must also take into account the border and scrolling settings. The option to resize is available to the visitor only if the border has width — a visitor can only resize by dragging the border, which is impossible if the border is set to 0 pixels wide. For your frames to be resizable, you should set the scrolling options to Yes or Auto so that the content remains available in the resized frames.

Explore Frameset Options

1 **Preview index.html in your browser.**

2 **Resize the browser window so it is narrower than the collage graphic in the middle frame.**

A horizontal scroll bar appears at the bottom of the middle frame, allowing you to scroll back and forth to see the whole collage image in the middle frame.

FIGURE 7.36

3 Resize the browser window's height until a vertical scroll bar appears to the right of the middle frame.

FIGURE 7.37

4 Return to Dreamweaver but keep your browser window open in its reduced size.

Set and Test the Scroll Options

1 Click the photo_large frame in the Frames panel.

Note that the Scroll option in the Property inspector is set to Default. This setting is perfectly fine — the scroll bars will appear when needed.

2 Click the photo_thumbs frame in the Frames panel.

The Scroll setting is set to No. This is a problem because, as you saw, the browser window was narrower than the group of five thumbnails. Had there been many more thumbnails, some would not be accessible, perhaps not even if the browser window was fully maximized.

3   Set the Scroll setting to Auto.

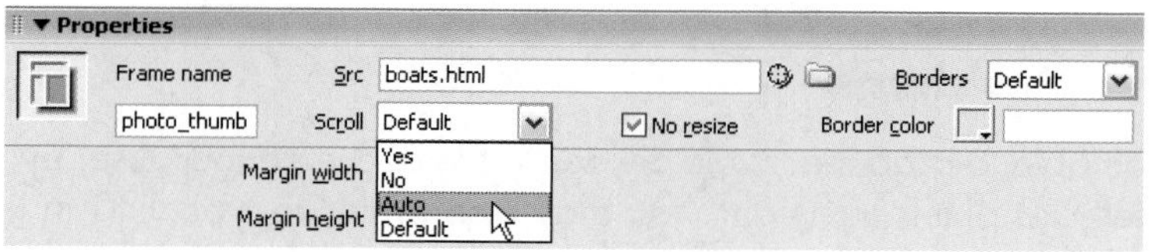

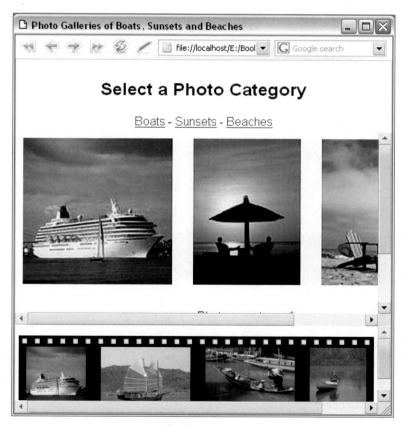

FIGURE 7.38

4   Preview the page in your browser.

Leave the browser in its small state. Notice that the photo_thumbs frame has both vertical and horizontal scroll bars. The total width of the thumbnails is wider than the browser window, and the height of the thumbnails is taller than this frame's height.

FIGURE 7.39

5   Return to Dreamweaver and set the Scroll setting for the photo_thumbs frame to Yes.

Setting the Scroll setting to Yes enables you to see how much space the scroll bars take up and allows you to work around them. This is just a temporary setting that you will change in a later step.

6 Increase the height of the photo_thumbs frame until you can see the bottom of the filmstrip background above the horizontal scroll bar (approximately 140 pixels).

? If You Have Problems

You may not be able to grab the frame divider in the document because, by default, the frame border width is set to 0 pixels in height. You may also prefer to type 140 in the Row/Column Value field, but to do so you must select the frameset. Click one of the frames in the Frames panel to select the frameset page, click the `<frameset>` tag in the Tag selector, and then select the row or column you want to modify using the RowCol Selection area in the Property inspector.

---

7 Select the photo_thumbs frame in the Frames panel; set Scroll to Auto in the Property inspector.

8 Preview the page in your browser.

9 Increase and decrease the width of your browser.

Only the horizontal scroll bar appears in the photo_thumbs frame when you decrease the browser window size. The new height of the photo_thumbs frame is sufficient to allow the full height of the thumbnail images to be visible all of the time, whether or not the scroll bar displays.

FIGURE 7.40

10   Return to Dreamweaver, but keep both the browser and these files open for the next exercise.

Explore Frameset Border Settings

The situation surrounding frameset and frame borders is confusing. Frameset and frame borders have never been part of any HTML standard, yet Dreamweaver offers borders as options for framesets and frames. Internet Explorer is the only current browser that displays frame borders. Netscape and Internet Explorer disagree on the values used to enable and disable frameset borders. Adding to this confusion, Dreamweaver displays borders when working with frames, which would seem to imply that borders are enabled by default; in fact, they are not. In Dreamweaver's defense, borders in the Design view do make it much easier to see the divisions between the frames and easier to use for resizing frames. Despite this confusion, most frames-based layouts are designed to be seamless, which means that borders would be disabled. If your design requires one frame to be distinguished from another, you could use different backgrounds or you could use a page border to separate the frames.

Additionally, if you want to give visitors to your Web site the option of resizing frames, the border must be visible so they can grab and move it with the mouse pointer. Therefore, knowing how to put borders around framed pages enables you to create borders as dividers or as a resizable frameset.

1   In Dreamweaver, click one of the dividers between two frames.

?   **If You Have Problems**

If you cannot select the dividers between the frames, click in the Frames panel, and then click the `<frameset>` tag in the Tag selector.

---

2   In the Property inspector, change the Borders option to Yes, set the Border Width to 5, and choose black using the Border Color box.

FIGURE 7.41

3   Choose File>Save.

4 **Preview the page in your browser.**

The borders clearly delineate the frames.

FIGURE 7.42

Set the Frame-Resize Option

Web-site designers who have used frames for layout rarely allow frames to be resized. Generally, designers are interested in ensuring that the design they spent so much time and effort creating remains as they designed it. Allowing resizing disturbs the design.

1 **In Dreamweaver, select top_nav in the Frames panel.**

You must enable or disable the resize option on a frame-by-frame basis.

2 **In the Property inspector, uncheck No Resize.**

This is equivalent to enabling Resize.

3 **Save the change and preview the page in your browser.**

4 **Hover your mouse pointer over the border that divides the top and middle frames.**

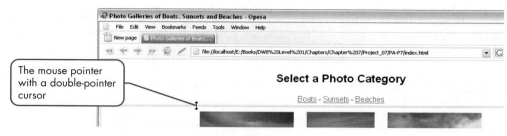

The mouse pointer with a double-pointer cursor

FIGURE 7.43

5 **Hover your mouse pointer over the border that divides the middle and bottom frames.**

The mouse pointer does not change to a double-pointer cursor — this division is not moveable.

6 **Grab the top divider and drag it up so the Boats — Sunsets — Beaches paragraph is hidden.**

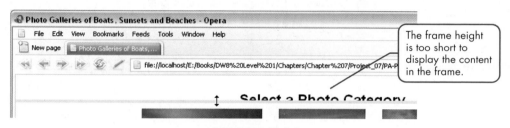

The frame height is too short to display the content in the frame.

FIGURE 7.44

7 **Return to Dreamweaver.**

8 **Set the top_nav Scroll option to Auto, save the change, and preview the page in your browser.**

As you move the frame border up to hide the bottom paragraph, the scroll bars appear and disappear when you have resized the frame enough to see the content.

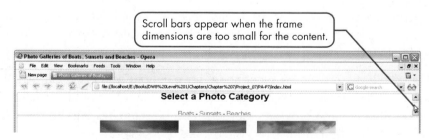

Scroll bars appear when the frame dimensions are too small for the content.

FIGURE 7.45

9 **Return to Dreamweaver.**

10 Click the top_nav frame in the Frames panel and set Scroll to No in the Property inspector. Click the <frameset> tag in the Tag selector, and set the Border Width to 0 in the Property inspector. Preview the page in your browser.

11 Move your mouse pointer between the top of the collage graphic and the text in the top frame, and try to find the frame border.

If you want to use resizable frames, you must ensure that you set Borders to Yes and the width to greater than 0 pixels.

FIGURE 7.46

12 Return to Dreamweaver but keep your browser and the files open for the next lesson.

To Extend Your Knowledge . . .

FRAME BORDERS, BORDER WIDTHS, RESIZING, AND BROWSERS

Browsers interpret Borders and Border Width settings differently with respect to the no-resizing option. Internet Explorer shows a border color if Borders is set to Yes, even when the Border Width is set to 0 pixels. However, you cannot grab the border for resizing if the Border Width is set to 0 pixels.

If Borders is set to No and the Border Width to 1 pixel or more, the border is not visible, but you can find it with the mouse pointer and resize the frame. In other words, the ability to resize a frame in Internet Explorer is a function of the border thickness, and the ability to see the border is a function of the Borders Yes/No option.

The Opera and Mozilla browsers, on the other hand, have a more sensible approach. If Borders is set to No or the Border Width is set to 0, the border is neither visible nor findable with the mouse pointer. In order to resize a frame in these browsers, Borders must be set to Yes and Border Width to at least 1 pixel — in other words, the border must be visible to be resizable.

LESSON 6 Linking between Frames

In a nonframed layout, there is only one frame — the browser window. Therefore, there are only two places a destination page can appear: the current browser window or a new browser window. In a frames-based Web site, there are many more targets that you can use.

`Target` is an attribute of the `<a>` tag. The `_blank` target option opens a link in a new browser window. This option works just as well in frames-based layouts as in nonframed layouts. The `_self` target option opens the destination page in the current window or frame — this is the default behavior of links.

A frameset page generally fills the whole browser window (you explore exceptions to this rule in later exercises) and divides the window into as many frames as specified in the `<frameset>` tag. The frameset page is considered the top element in a framed layout. You can use the `_top` attribute target to replace the frameset page with the destination page — this is sometimes referred to as *breaking out of frames*.

The `_parent` target may be difficult to visualize without experience with nested framesets. In a frameset layout, a frame page is a child of the frameset, and the frameset is the parent of the frame page. You can create a link from a child page to completely replace the frameset page: you must use the `_parent` target to achieve this. If the browser window has only one frameset, then `_parent` and `_top` achieve the same results. However, if a frameset is nested in the frame of another frameset, then a link from a "grandchild" page with the `_parent` target would replace the inner nested frameset (parent) but not the outer frameset (grandparent) — that requires the `_top` target.

The last target option of the anchor tag is the frame names. These targets change according to the names you gave the frames when you designed the frameset. To display a photo in the photo_large frame, the target must be photo_large. This is why it is essential to name the frames, and name them appropriately. Although Dreamweaver creates frame names for you, they aren't always meaningful.

Either of the `_blank` or `_top` options of the target attribute can be used to prevent trapping — displaying an external Web page or Web site in a frame of your site rather than in the entire browser window. Trapping is generally frowned upon because you are not respecting the right of the external Web site to utilize the full browser window; trapping also hides the Web page's URL, thereby implying that you are taking credit for someone else's content.

Target Links to Frames

In this exercise, you create links from the top_nav frame to open the thumbnail pages in the photo_thumbs frame by setting the target of each link to photo_thumbs.

1	**Preview the PA-P7>index.html page in your browser, and click the Beaches link in the top_nav frame.**

The beaches.html page appears in the top_nav frame because, by default, destination pages open in the same frame as the linking pages.

2	**Keep your browser open and return to Dreamweaver.**

3 Select the Beaches link in the topnav.html page, and then choose photo_thumbs from the Target list in the Property inspector.

Dreamweaver automatically populates the Target list with the names of the frames.

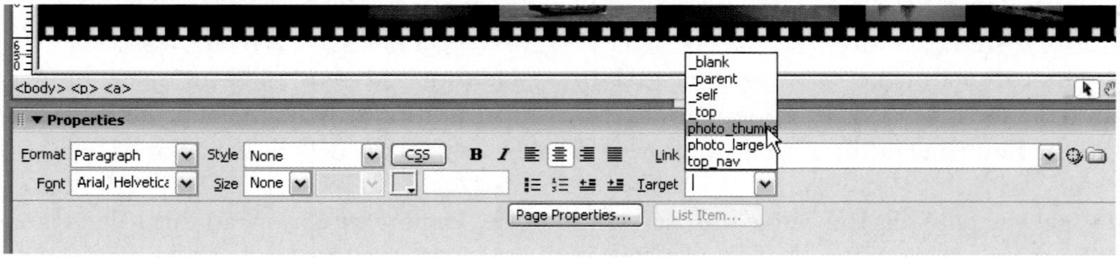

FIGURE 7.47

4 Save the changes and test the link again in your browser.

This time, the beaches.html file appears in the photo_thumbs frame, as it should.

5 Return to Dreamweaver and set the target of the Boats and Sunsets links in the topnav.html page to photo_thumbs.

6 Save the changes and test the links in your browser.

Link Thumbnail Images to Large Photos

In this exercise, you create links from thumbnail images of boats to the pages with the large images of these boats. You set the target in each case to the photo_large frame, so the linked pages appear in the photo_large frame.

You learned that you can choose frame names from the Target list in addition to the four predefined targets. When you work with a frames-based layout, the Target list displays the names of the frames so you can simply choose the target frame from the list. However, if you do not have the frameset page open in the Document window, the Target list does not show the frame names. You can type the frame names, of course, but you risk making a mistake. It is best to work with frame pages nested in the frameset page, so the Target list displays the frame names.

1 Link the first boat thumbnail image to boat1.html in the details folder.

If you plan to use the point-to-file method, you must expand the details folder to see the Web pages in the folder.

2 Select photo_large from the list of targets in the Property inspector.

FIGURE 7.48

3   **Repeat this process for the four other thumbnail images.**

The filenames of the thumbnail images are in ascending numerical order, from left to right, and match the boat pages in the details folder.

4   **Save the changes and test the links in your browser.**

Link Thumbnail Images from Outside the Frameset

In this exercise, you learn that the Target list is not populated with frame names if the page in the Document window is not a frameset page. You learn to type a frame name in the Target field and to name the frames with names that you can remember. You also learn the trick of temporarily replacing the source in the frameset so it is easier to set the targets of the links.

1   **Open beaches.html from the root folder of the PA-P7 site.**

Do not open beaches.html into the frameset. Instead, double-click the filename in the Files panel or choose File>Open to open the page.

FIGURE 7.49

2   **Link the first beach thumbnail to beach1.html in the details folder.**

3   **Click the Target drop-down list.**

Notice that the frame names do not appear in the Target list. This list only displays frame names if the open page is viewed in a frameset.

FIGURE 7.50

4 **In the Target field, type** `photo_large`.

If the frame name does not appear in the Target list, you must type the frame name into the Target field. One benefit of naming the frames yourself is that if you have to apply a frame name manually, it may be easier to remember your chosen frame name rather than Dreamweaver's default names.

5 **Close, saving the changes to beaches.html.**

6 **In index.html, click the photo_thumbs frame in the Frames panel. Using the Property inspector, change the Src (source) of the photo_thumbs frame to beaches.html.**

The beaches.html page will now appear in the photo_thumbs frame; when you link it, the Target field will display the frame names of the open frameset.

7 **Link the four remaining beach thumbnail images to the appropriate beach files in numerical sequence (beach2.jpg to beach2.html through beach5.jpg to beach5.html — the html files are in the details folder).**

The Target drop-down list shows the frame names because the Document window contains a frameset, from which Dreamweaver can extract the frame names.

8 **Save the changes to beaches.html.**

9 **Click the photo_thumbs frame in the Frames panel.**

10 **From the Property inspector, change the Src back to boats.html.**

Remember, the Web pages that appear in the frameset are the pages that appear when you open the frameset. You inserted beaches.html into the photo_thumbs frame to ensure that the Target list would be populated, making it easier to choose a target.

11 **Preview the frameset in your browser and test the links from the beaches.html page.**

Use the <base /> Tag to Set the Common Target

The <base /> tag is helpful for framed Web sites because you can use it to specify the default target for every link in the page. This saves you a great deal of time and effort by eliminating the need to specify the `target` attribute for each link. However, if a link requires a different target than the one specified in the <base /> tag, you must set the target for that link.

The <base /> tag is not available from any of the menus: you can create it either in the Code view or using the Tag chooser. The `target` attribute of the <base /> tag is not automatically populated with frame names of the current frameset — you must type them in manually.

1 **Click the photo_thumbs frame in the Frames panel.**

2 **Using the Property inspector, set the Src to sunsets.html.**

3 **Click to the left of the sunset thumbnail images so the insertion point is in the page but none of the images are selected.**

4 Click the Tag Chooser at the right end of the Common Insert bar.

5 In the Tag Chooser dialog box, click the plus symbol/arrow to the left of HTML tags, click Page Composition, and then double-click base in the right panel.

6 Click the Target drop-down list.

Notice that the Target list does not display the frame names. You must type the frame name in the Target field.

7 Type photo_large in the Target field, click OK to set the base target, and then click Close to close the Tag Chooser dialog box.

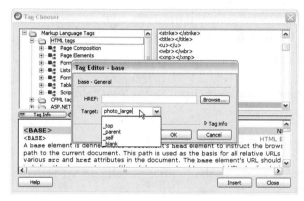

FIGURE 7.51

8 Click the Design button to close the Code window.

9 Link the five sunset thumbnail images to the sunset pages in the details folder in numerical order, but do not set their targets.

10 Save the changes and preview the frameset in your browser.

11 Test the links from the thumbnail images.

The larger images appear in the photo_large frame because of the base target setting.

12 Return to Dreamweaver but do not close your browser.

Set the _self Target

When you use the **<base />** tag to set the default target of links in the page to a particular target, you must remember to set the **target** attribute for links whose targets are different. By default, links open in the same frame or browser window as the page with the link, which is the same as specifying **target="_self"**. It is normally unnecessary to set the **_self** target, but when you use the **<base />** tag to set a different default target, you may need the **_self** target to override the **<base />** target.

| 1 | Link the Next graphic to sunsets2.html in the root folder of the PA-P7 site. Set the Target of the Next graphic to _self. |

| 2 | Preview the page in your browser and test the Next link. |

Unlike the rest of the links in the sunsets.html page, the Next link opens sunsets2.html in the photo_thumbs frame.

| 3 | Return to Dreamweaver. |

| 4 | Click the photo_thumbs frame in the Frames panel, and set Src to sunsets2.html. |

| 5 | Using the Tag chooser, insert a <base /> tag, and set the base target to photo_large. |

| 6 | Link the thumbnail images to sunsets6.html through sunsets10.html in numerical order: the html files are in the details folder. |

Do not set the targets — they will use the base target.

| 7 | Link the Previous graphic to sunsets.html in the root folder of this site, and set the target to _self. |

| 8 | Save the changes to sunsets2.html. |

| 9 | Click the photo_thumbs frame in the Frames panel, and set Src to boats.html. |

| 10 | Choose File>Save All to save the changes to the frameset. |

| 11 | Preview the frameset in your browser, and test the links from the sunsets2.html thumbnail images and the Previous graphic. |

| 12 | Return to Dreamweaver and keep the frameset open for the next lesson. |

To Extend Your Knowledge . . .

OPEN MULTIPLE FRAMES FROM ONE LINK

One question commonly asked about framesets is whether or not you can change the contents of two frames at the same time with just one link. Yes, you can, and there are two ways to do so. One method is to build a nested frameset within a frame. In this process, you use the _parent target to replace the frameset with another frameset, thus creating the appearance of changing more than one frame with one link.

The other method is to use JavaScript. This process is more flexible, enabling you to change different frames that don't need to be part of a nested frameset. However, the technique does depend on JavaScript, so users of JavaScript-incapable or JavaScript-disabled browsers may not be able to use your Web site as you intended.

LESSON 7   Setting Page Properties of Framed Pages

The pages in a frameset are independent of one another, so you must set the colors and backgrounds for each individually. You cannot set a style, CSS or otherwise, for the frameset and apply it to all pages that appear in the frameset. There are no frameset styles options, because the purpose of the frameset is just to divide the browser window into frames, set the dimensions of those frames, and specify the pages that are to appear in the frames.

You can, however, use a common style for the pages that appear in the frames, just as you can set a common style for pages in a nonframed site. Often in framed sites, though, some frames are treated or styled differently because of their position in the frameset. The frame containing the company's branding and the frame containing the navigation bar might each be styled differently than the rest. At times you may want to create a seamless frameset. At other times you may want to clearly delineate the frames, either with frame borders or with different styles in each frame.

Set the Page Properties from the Frameset

In this exercise, you set the background properties of two pages that are nested in the frames of the frameset.

1   **In the open frameset, click to the right of the Select a Photo Category text in topnav.html (in the top_nav frame), and then click the Page Properties button in the Property inspector.**

2   **From the Appearance category, click the Background Color button, choose the lightest gray (#CCCCCC) from the color palette, and click OK to accept the choice.**

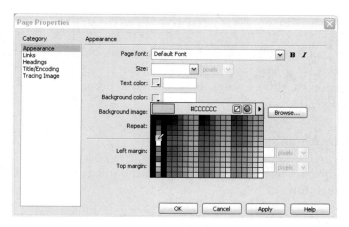

FIGURE 7.52

3   **Click to the left of the boat thumbnail images in the bottom frame.**

4   **Click the Page Properties button in the Property inspector, set the Background image to bg-water.jpg from the graphics folder, and then click OK when finished.**

5   **Choose File>Save All to save the changes to both the topnav.html and boats.html pages.**

6 Preview the frameset in your browser, and note the backgrounds of the pages in the two frames.

FIGURE 7.53

7 Return to Dreamweaver and leave the frameset open for the next exercise.

Set Page Backgrounds from Outside the Frameset

In the previous exercise, you set the backgrounds of two pages while working with them in the frameset. Page properties are not part of frameset properties, so you can set them whether you are editing the page from within or from outside the frameset. In this exercise, you set the page properties of two pages while working with them from outside the frameset.

1 Double-click beaches.html in the Files panel.

2 Click the Page Properties button, set the Background image to bg-sand.gif from the graphics folder, and then click OK.

3 Close, saving the changes to beaches.html.

4 Open sunsets.html from the Files panel, click the Page Properties button, set the background image to sunset-gradient.gif from the graphics folder, and then click OK.

5 Close, saving the changes.

6   Open sunsets2.html from the Files panel and apply the sunset-gradient.gif image as the background image of this page.

7   Close, saving the changes.

8   From index.html in the Document window, preview the frameset in your browser.

9   Click the Beaches link in the top frame and note the background of beaches.html in the photo_thumbs frame at the bottom.

10   Click the Sunsets link in the top frame and note the sunset-gradient background of the sunsets.html page.

FIGURE 7.54

11   Click the Next link in the sunsets.html page and note the background image in the sunsets2.html page.

12   Return to Dreamweaver and keep index.html open for the next lesson.

LESSON 8   Creating NoFrames Content

Not all browsers support frames, and as a result, some visitors cannot see the content in your frames-based Web site. When a frames-incapable browser opens a frameset page, it cannot interpret the frameset and leaves the visitor looking at a blank page. The **`<noframes>`** tag, created to remedy this problem, allows you to provide some information for these visitors. In most cases, Web-site designers simply provide text that states, "This Web site has been built using frames and your browser does not support frames." However, the alternatives are (1) to suggest that the visitors upgrade their browsers (which may not be possible or appealing for some visitors), or (2) to provide the content in a nonframed layout, such as tables. Developing both framed and nonframed layouts typically means double the work. In this exercise, you learn how to add basic noframes content.

Create Basic Noframes Content

1   With index.html open in the Document window, choose Modify>Frameset>Edit NoFrames Content.

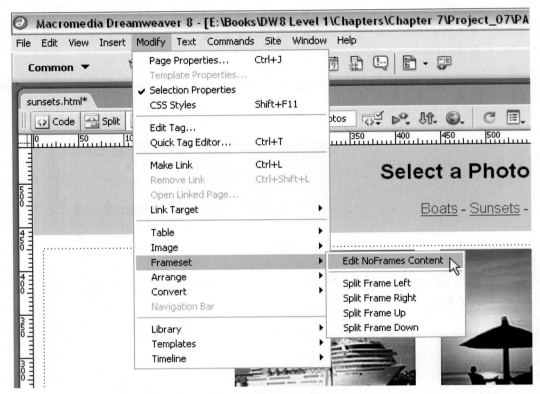

FIGURE 7.55

2   Set the Format in the Property inspector to Heading 1. Type We apologize... and press Enter/Return. Type This Web site has been built using frames and your browser does not support frames.

3   Choose Modify>Frameset>Edit NoFrames Content to return to the frameset view of the layout.

4   Choose File>Save All. Preview the page in your browser.

The Web page appears the same as before because your browser supports frames and does not need to display the noframes content.

5   Return to Dreamweaver.

6 Click any frame in the Frames panel, and then click the Code button at the top of the Document window.

The <body> tag does not appear after the closing </head> tag in a frameset page.

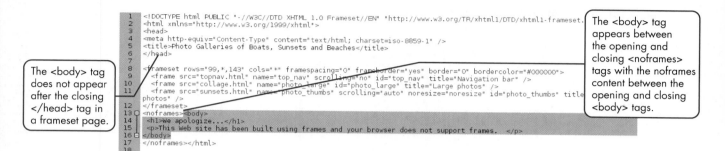

```
1   <!DOCTYPE html PUBLIC "-//W3C//DTD XHTML 1.0 Frameset//EN" "http://www.w3.org/TR/xhtml1/DTD/xhtml1-frameset.
2   <html xmlns="http://www.w3.org/1999/xhtml">
3   <head>
4   <meta http-equiv="Content-Type" content="text/html; charset=iso-8859-1" />
5   <title>Photo Galleries of Boats, Sunsets and Beaches</title>
6   </head>
7
8   <frameset rows="99,*,143" cols="*" framespacing="0" frameborder="yes" border="0" bordercolor="#000000">
9     <frame src="topnav.html" name="top_nav" scrolling="no" id="top_nav" title="Navigation bar" />
10    <frame src="collage.html" name="photo_large" id="photo_large" title="Large photos" />
11    <frame src="sunsets.html" name="photo_thumbs" scrolling="auto" noresize="noresize" id="photo_thumbs" title
      photos" />
12  </frameset>
13  <noframes><body>
14    <h1>We apologize...</h1>
15    <p>This Web site has been built using frames and your browser does not support frames. </p>
16  </body>
17  </noframes></html>
18
```

The <body> tag appears between the opening and closing <noframes> tags with the noframes content between the opening and closing <body> tags.

FIGURE 7.56

7 Click the Design button to return to the Design view.

To Extend Your Knowledge . . .

VIEWING NOFRAMES CONTENT IN OPERA

Of the current graphical browsers, only the Opera browser presently allows you to disable frames and view noframes content. To do so in Opera 7, choose File>Preferences, choose the Page Style category, uncheck Enable Frames, and click OK. (In Opera 8, choose Tools>Preferences, click the Advanced tab, select the Content category, uncheck Enable Frames, and click OK.) Reload the page and view the noframes content. Enable frames by repeating the same steps and placing a check next to the Enable Frames option. Reload the page to see the framed content.

S U M M A R Y

In this chapter, you learned how to create a frames-based layout. You explored choosing a frameset layout from the many that are available in Dreamweaver and modifying the dimensions of the frames. You learned about various options available for frames such as borders, resizing, and scroll bars, and discovered how these options interact with one another. You created a framed layout from existing pages and learned about the different target attributes that are available for linking. You also learned how to create noframes content so that both frames-capable and frames-incapable browsers can access the same content.

K E Y   T E R M S

Breaking out of frames   Frame   Trapping

Fixed   Frameset page   Web directory

CHECKING CONCEPTS AND TERMS

SCREEN ID

Identify the indicated areas from the following list:

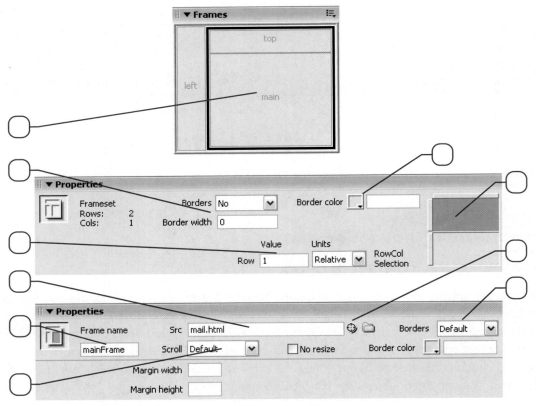

FIGURE 7.57

a. Frame border option

b. Border properties

c. Frame name

d. Point-to-file and browse-for-file source link

e. Selected frame

f. Border Color box

g. Scroll options

h. RowCol Selection area

i. Filename of frame source

j. Row/Column size dimensions and units

MULTIPLE CHOICE

Circle the letter of the correct answer for each of the following:

1. A frame in a frameset _____ .

   a. can be another frameset

   b. cannot be viewed outside of the frameset

   c. contains a standard Web page

   d. All of the above

2. The common tools used to assemble framesets are the _____ .

a. Code view, Frameset panel, and Property inspector

b. Property inspector, RowCol Selection area, and Frames panel

c. Page Properties dialog box, Property inspector, and Design view

d. Document window, Property inspector, and Frames panel

3. A frameset page _____ .

a. is not visible in a browser

b. binds together the frames

c. can be nested in another frameset

d. All of the above

4. A frames-based layout _____ .

a. enables you to design Web pages that are split into sections

b. requires less code for less download time

c. is the easiest layout method for beginners

d. is always seamless

5. Which of the following is not true of frames and framesets?

a. They are difficult to use with assistive technology.

b. Frames are supported by all browsers.

c. Individual pages in a framed site weigh less than those of a nonframed site.

d. Frames can reduce maintenance time for a Web site.

6. The main controversy over the use of frames concerns _____ .

a. download time

b. incompatibility with tables

c. universal usability

d. trapped external pages

7. To add content to a frame in a frameset, you can _____ .

a. import graphics and text files

b. type and format text

c. link the frame to a source HTML document

d. All of the above

8. A fixed frame _____ .

a. cannot be edited

b. can only be a navbar

c. is the link target

d. has a specific width or height

9. When the target of a link is set to _top, the link opens the destination page _____ .

a. above the current frame of the frameset

b. in a new browser window

c. in the current browser window, filling it

d. only in the frame named _top

10. Scroll bars are required _____ .

a. for all frames

b. if the content is larger than the frame

c. to resize frame dimensions

d. All of the above

DISCUSSION QUESTIONS

1. Frames-based layouts have a bad reputation because many amateur designers have made a mess of them. Your employer would like you to design their Web site, and you believe that a frames-based layout would be appropriate for the needs of the site. You argue your case enough for your employer to say, "I don't really like frames, but convince me that you won't make the same mistakes as the amateur designers did before you." Name as many features of frames-based layouts as you can, identify how these features may be misused, resulting in amateurish layouts, and state what options you would use to prevent your design from being reduced to similar amateurish quality.

2. Frames allow the designer to maintain some material on the screen while other material scrolls or changes. For example, an FAQ might place the questions in one frame and the answers in another. Identify two types of information presentation, whether visual or text-based, that should take advantage of these capabilities. Give at least one example of each type and explain how it would benefit from this type of layout.

SKILL DRILL

Skill Drills reinforce project skills. Each skill that is reinforced is the same as, or nearly the same as, a skill presented in the lessons. We provide detailed instructions in a step-by-step format. You should complete the exercises in order.

1. Link to External Sites

As you recall, there are two target attributes that you are recommended to use to link to an external site: the **_blank** attribute and the **_top** attribute. Both methods prevent trapping but in slightly different ways. The **_blank** target opens a new blank page, whereas the **_top** target opens the destination page in the current browser window, replacing the current frameset.

1. Open index.html from the PA-P7 site.

2. Click the PhotoSpin graphic in the middle frame and set it as a link to http://www.photospin.com. Save the change.

3. Preview the frameset in your browser and click on the PhotoSpin graphic to link to PhotoSpin.com.

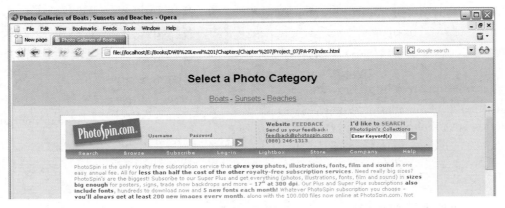

FIGURE 7.58

4. Return to Dreamweaver. Choose the PhotoSpin logo graphic, set the target to **_blank**, and retest the link in your browser.

This time, the link opens the PhotoSpin.com Web site in a new browser window.

5. Close the new browser window and return to Dreamweaver.

6. Choose the PhotoSpin logo graphic, set the target to **_top**, and retest the link in your browser.

   This time, the PhotoSpin.com Web site appears in the same browser window, replacing the frameset that was there before.

7. Click the Back button in your browser.

   You return to the frameset page with the Back button in your browser if you use the **_top** target, whereas you must close the new browser window to return to the frameset page if you use the **_blank** target.

8. Return to Dreamweaver and close index.html.

2. Embed a Frameset in a Frame

Commonly, a link opens a single page, whether the source page is in a frameset or not. However, it is possible to create a link to open a frameset.

In this Skill Drill, you redesign the photo-album frameset layout to better display the photos in the three collections — boats, beaches, and sunset photos. Previously, the frameset contained three frames: the top frame with links to the collections; the middle frame, which held the photo collages; and the bottom frame with the thumbnails of the series of photos. You now reduce the outer frameset to two frames: the same top frame and only one larger frame below it. The bottom frame will contain a nested frameset, in which one frame contains the thumbnails and one frame contains the collage for each collection of images.

In the previous exercises, the links from the top frame replace only the thumbnails in the bottom frame; in this exercise, the links from the top frame will open nested framesets into the lower frame of the outer frameset.

1. Choose File>New, select Framesets from the Category list, choose Fixed Bottom from the Framesets category, and then click Create. Accept the default titles and click OK.

2. Click the divider between the two frames. In the Property inspector, click the bottom row of the RowCol Selection area, set the row height to 140 pixels, and press Enter/Return.

3. Select mainFrame in the Frames panel; in the Property inspector, rename the frame photo_large, and press Enter/Return. Select bottomFrame in the Frames panel; in the Property inspector, rename the frame photo_thumbs, and press Enter/Return.

4. Set the source of the photo_thumbs frame as boats.html, and set Scroll to Auto. Select the photo_large frame in the Frames panel, and set the source to boats-collage.html.

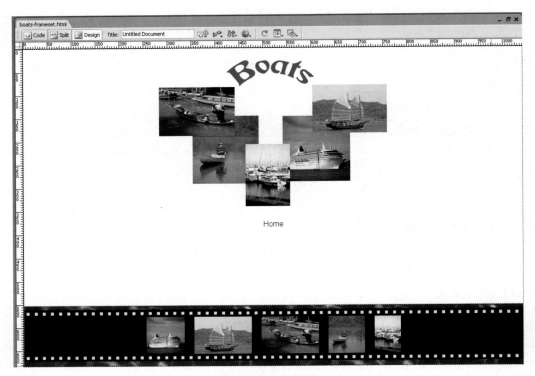

FIGURE 7.59

5. Close, saving the frameset as boats-frameset.html.

6. Repeat Steps 1 through 5, creating sunsets-frameset.html and beaches-frameset.html, in which sunsets-collage.html and beaches-collage.html appear in the photo_large frame at the top and sunsets.html and beaches.html appear in the photo_thumbs frame below.

7. Create a new frameset using the Fixed Top design. Rename mainFrame to nested_frame. Rename topFrame to top_nav and set its height to 100 pixels.

8. Set topnav.html to be the source of top_nav frame and collage.html to be the source of nested_frame.

9. Choose File>Save Frameset and save the frameset as alternate.html. Keep it open for the next Skill Drill exercise.

3. Link Nested Framesets

In this Skill Drill, you create links from Boats, Sunsets, and Beaches in the topnav.html file to the appropriate framesets. Doing this loads two pages into one frame at the same time by loading the appropriate frameset into the nested_frame frame.

You also learn the role of the **_parent** target. The **_parent** of a framed page is the frameset page that defines the current frame. In this Skill Drill and the previous one, the beaches, boats, and sunsets framesets are the parents of the photo_thumbs and photo_large for each of these photo collections. A link with the **_parent** target replaces the nested framesets, but not the outer frameset (for which you would use the **_top** target).

1. In alternate.html, select the Boats text from topnav.html, change the link to boats-frameset.html, and set the target to nested_frame. Repeat this process for the Sunsets and Beaches links, setting the links to the appropriate frameset page and the target to nested_frame.

2. Save the changes and preview the frameset in your browser.

3. Click each of the links in top_nav frame, and notice how the appropriate frameset loads into the nested_frame frame.

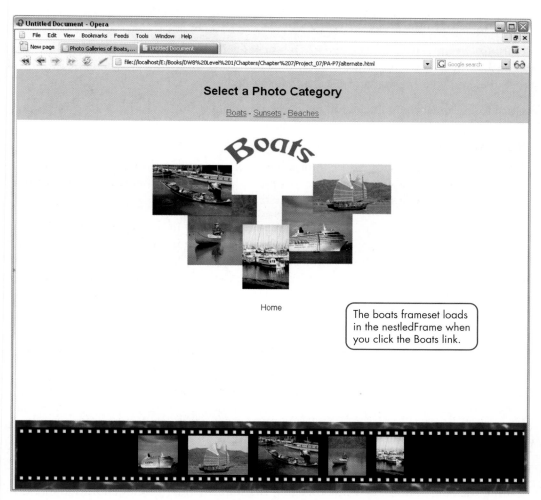

FIGURE 7.60

4. Click some of the thumbnail images. Observe that they load their large photos into the middle frame in the same way as you saw in Lesson 6.

5. Return to Dreamweaver and open boats-collage.html. Select Home below the collage graphic and link it to collage.html. Close, saving the change.

6. Preview the frameset in your browser again, click the Boats link in the top_nav frame, and then click the Home link.

   The collage.html page opens in the photo_large frame and does not replace the boats-frameset.html frameset page.

7. Return to Dreamweaver and reopen boats-collage.html. Change the target of the Home link to **_parent** and then close, saving the changes. Preview the frameset in your browser and retest the link.

   This time, collage.html replaces the boats-frameset.html page and fills the nested_frame frame.

8. Return to Dreamweaver. One by one, open beaches-collage.html and sunsets-collage.html. Link Home in both cases to collage.html with a target of **_parent**, and save and close each file. Preview the frameset in your browser and test the Home links.

9. Return to Dreamweaver and close all open files.

4. Create a Complex Frameset

In this Skill Drill exercise, you re-create the complex framed-layout used in the GMMS Web site you examined in the second lesson of this chapter. Remember in Lesson 2, you learned that the structure of this frameset consists of one frameset file with multiple framesets nested in it.

In this exercise, you nest framesets within framesets in a single design. In the previous exercise, you nested the framesets dynamically — the nesting resulted from links. Now you build the nested framesets into the single frameset page. You learn two methods of creating nested framesets. One method is to insert a frameset in a frame. The other method is to create new frames by dragging the outer borders in combination with either the Control/Command or the Alt/Option key.

1. Switch to the GMMS site in the Files panel.

2. Choose File>New, select Framesets from the Category list, choose Fixed Left from the Framesets category, and then click Create. Click OK to accept the default frame titles.

   For the outer frameset, you need to create a three-column design with relative left and right columns. This default layout is close, but not an exact match because it has only two columns, and the left column is fixed where it should be relative. None of the Dreamweaver predefined frameset layouts exactly match the layout you need, so you must modify this one.

3. Holding down the Alt/Option key, drag the vertical divider toward the right.

   Holding the Alt/Option key while dragging the frame divider creates another frame divider (and frame) with the same orientation. In this case it creates another column; it would create a new row if the divider were horizontal.

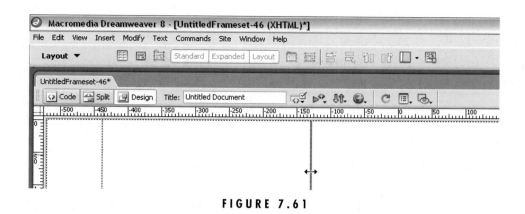

FIGURE 7.61

4. In the Property inspector, select the left column with the RowCol Selection area, and set the Width to 1 Relative.

It is easier to set Relative first and then type 1 in the Width field.

5. Set the other two frames as follows: Select the right column and set its Width to 1 Relative. Select the middle column and set the Width to 780 pixels.

6. Click the middle frame (no name) in the Frames panel, then return to the Document window and drag (no Alt/Option key) the top of the middle frame downward.

   This technique works only if you are dragging from the edge of the Document window. It does not work if you want to create an inner frame, like the navigation frame.

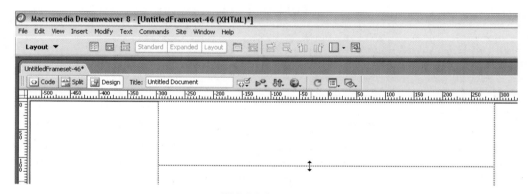

FIGURE 7.62

7. From the Property inspector, set the height of the top row to 160 pixels.

8. Click the bottom row of the middle column in the Frames panel. Switch to the Layout Insert bar, and choose Left Frame from the Frames drop-down list. Accept the default frame titles.

   Because you preselected the bottom-middle frame before you chose a frame layout from the Layout Insert bar, the layout was created within the selected frame.

9. Click the newly created column divider and set the width of the left column to 160 pixels.

10. Using the Frames panel to select frames and the Property inspector to name the frames, name the frames left, header, navbar, main, and right. Press Enter/Return after typing each frame name to force Dreamweaver to register the name.

11. Set the source of the left and right frames to side.html and the Scroll option to No. Set the header frame source to header.html and Scroll to No. Set the navbar frame source to navbar.html and Scroll to No. Set the main frame source to main.html and Scroll to Auto.

12. Save the frameset as alternate.html and preview it in your browser.

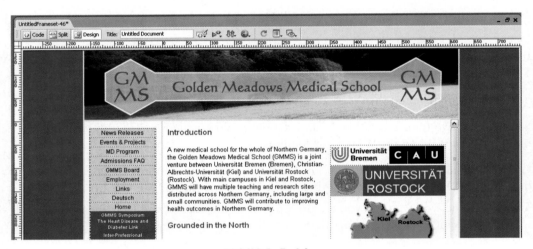

FIGURE 7.63

13. Return to Dreamweaver and close alternate.html.

CHALLENGE

Challenge exercises expand on or are somewhat related to skills we presented in the lessons. Each exercise provides a brief introduction, followed by numbered-step instructions that are not as detailed as those in the Skill Drill exercises. You should work through the Challenge exercises in order.

1. Create a Seamless Framed Layout

In this Challenge exercise, you modify the background images in three frame pages so the frameset looks seamless. You adjust background images — the Web pages have very little content.

It is not necessarily poor design to clearly differentiate between frames, but the page you are working on presently creates the impression that the designer did not think through this design. The problem is that the height of the top frame is 150 pixels and the width of the left frame is also 150 pixels, but the background graphic is 110 pixels in height and width. As a result, the background graphic is partially through its second repetition when it encounters the main frame, creating a disjointed appearance.

There are several possible fixes for this situation. You could resize the graphic either down to 75 × 75 pixels or up to 150 × 150 pixels. This would work in this particular situation because the dimensions of the left and top frames are both 150 pixels; if the two frames were different dimensions, however, proportionate resizing would not solve the problem and disproportionate resizing would distort the graphic. Another possible solution would be to resize the frames to either 110 or 220 pixels. However, 110 pixels would cut off content in the frames and 220 pixels would take up a lot of unnecessary screen real estate. The third method is to change the vertical and horizontal positioning of the background image so the repetitions of the background images match up with each other.

1. Define a site called Golf-P7 from the Chapter_07>Golf folder.

2. Open index.html and note the disjointed breaks between the backgrounds in the top, left, and main frames.

3. Click to the right of the golf logo graphic in the top frame.

4. Right/Control-click the **body** element in the CSS Styles panel and choose Edit. Choose the Background category, set Horizontal position to 40 pixels, set Vertical position to 40 pixels, and click OK.

    Notice how the division between the main and top frames is no longer visible. (The choice of 40 pixels was made because that is the difference between the graphic's height of 110 pixels and the frame's height of 150 pixels.)

5. Click in the left navigation-bar frame.

6. Right/Control-click **body** in the CSS Styles panel and choose Edit. Choose the Background category, set Horizontal position to 40 pixels, set Vertical position to 0 pixels, and click OK.

    The division between the navigation-bar frame and the main frame disappears, and the layout looks seamless until you move the scroll bar in the main frame. You must set both horizontal and vertical positioning because if just one is set, the browser assumes that the other should be treated as center, not 0 pixels.

7. Click the main frame.

8. Right/Control-click body in the CSS Styles panel and choose Edit. Choose the Background category, set Attachment to Fixed, and click OK.

9. Preview the frameset in your browser, choosing Yes to save the changes as prompted.

This time, when you scroll the main frame up and down, the background does not move and always looks seamless. Dreamweaver does not display the **attachment: fixed** CSS property — you must view this property in a browser.

FIGURE 7.64

10.   Return to Dreamweaver and close index.html.

2. Splitting a Nonframed Page into Frames

There may be times when you need to create a framed layout from pages that do not use frames. Many Web designers use Adobe Photoshop or Illustrator or CorelDRAW to design the look and layout of Web pages. Although these programs can create Web pages that use HTML tables for layout, they cannot create a framed page from the design. This Challenge exercise shows you how to take a table-based layout and convert it into a frames-based layout.

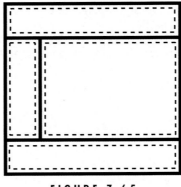

FIGURE 7.65

The inner dashed lines in Figure 7.65 indicate the inner or nested tables. The solid lines indicate the cells of the outer table. In this exercise, you create a similar layout, but instead of a table with four cells binding together the four inner tables, you use four frames to bind together four pages. Each of these pages has one of the four tables copied from the inner tables of the original layout.

1. Define a new site called ATC-P7 from the Chapter_07>ATC folder.

2. Open authors.html from the ATC folder.

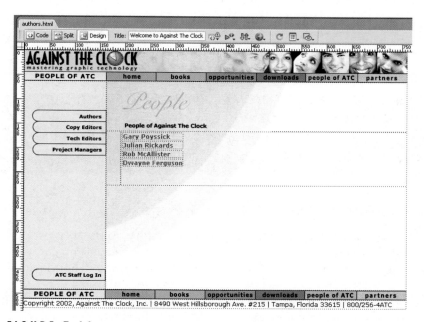

FIGURE 7.66 *(Copyright Against The Clock, Inc. Used by permission of Against the Clock, Inc.)*

3. Click the top Against The Clock logo graphic, click the **<table>** tag closest to the right end of the Tag selector, and copy the table into the clipboard. Open header.html, paste the copied table, and close, saving the changes.

4. Click the light-blue navigation-bar region of authors.html below People of ATC, click the **<table>** tag closest to the right end of the Tag selector, and copy it into the clipboard. Open navbar.html, paste the copied table, and close, saving the changes.

5. Click the People of ATC graphic at the bottom of the authors.html page, click the second **<table>** tag in the Tag selector, and copy the table into the clipboard. Open footer.html, paste the copied table, and close, saving the changes.

6. Click the large People graphic in the central area of the page, select the second **<table>** tag in the Tag selector, and copy the table to the clipboard. Open main.html, paste the copied table and close, saving the changes.

7. Close authors.html.

8. Create a new frameset page from the Fixed Top, Fixed Bottom layout. Click the mainFrame and insert a Left Frame from the Layout Insert bar. Counter-clockwise from the top, insert header.html, navbar.html, footer.html, and main.html into the four frames. Adjust the frame dimensions as necessary.

9. Set the link from the Authors graphic in the navbar.html page to main.html with a target of mainFrame.

10. Save all changes and then save the frameset as index.html.

11. Preview the frameset in your browser and test the links to the four author pages.

12. Return to Dreamweaver and close index.html.

PORTFOLIO BUILDER

Create a Frame-Based Product Display Page

An effective use of frames can be seen when a potential shopper wants to view a product — a sweater, purse, or car, for example — in several different colors. For this assignment, you're going to use a frame-based layout to present color choices in one frame and product shots in another.

1. Visit retail sites and locate images and presentations that show products in several different colors. A sweater manufacturer, outdoor supplier, or fashion retailer would all fit the bill.

2. For purposes of this exercise only, copy a few sample images into your WIP folder to use for the layout. Remember, the images belong to someone else! You're just using them for purposes of applying what you've learned about frames.

3. Create a frame-based layout that contains at least two frames — one for text indicating a product color, and a larger frame to display the product shots. You can use predefined framesets for the assignment. You'll need to create the individual pages that will appear in the target frame as well.

4. Create the appropriate links and targets so that clicking on the name of a color displays the correct image in the large frame.

5. Test your work and make sure everything works.

CHAPTER 8

Tables

OBJECTIVES

In this chapter, you learn how to:

- Identify the uses and properties of tables

- Create tables

- Insert rows and columns

- Merge adjacent cells

- Add background colors and alignment to cells

- Create a layout table using the Table dialog box

- Create a layout table in Layout mode

- Create an accessible data table

Why Would I Do This?

Tables are important components of Web-page design. They are commonly used to lay out a Web page and to present tabular data. If you have used word-processing software, you may have worked with tables. However, there are many more options for constructing tables in HTML than in word-processing software. In this chapter, you learn about these options and when and how to apply them.

Basic tables consist of rows and columns; where they intersect, are cells. The names of some of these components are different in HTML than in other software. There are no columns — at least, not in the code — and cells are called "table data." The outermost HTML tags of tables are the opening and closing `<table>` tags that define the beginning and end of a table. Tables are divided into rows, which use the opening and closing `<tr>` tags. Within each row are cells or table data that are defined by opening and closing `<td>` (table-data) tags. Therefore, a basic 2 × 2 table would use the following code:

```
<table>
<tr><td>Row 1, Cell 1</td><td>Row 1, Cell 2</td></tr>
<tr><td>Row 2, Cell 1</td><td>Row 2, Cell 2</td></tr>
</table>
```

As you can see, it takes a lot of code to create a simple four-cell table. As you explore more options for tables, the code expands tremendously. One of the benefits of using WYSIWYG software like Dreamweaver is the ease with which you can create tables. You choose or specify the number of rows and columns, and Dreamweaver creates the code (and the table); you only have to add content to the cells.

HTML tables have many features, some of which are displayed in Figure 8.1. Tables can have captions, table-header cells, and *spanned (merged) cells*. Above the table (Figure 8.1) is a caption created using the `<caption>` tag. The `<caption>` tag only exists in tables and is generally put immediately after the opening `<table>` tag. The caption can appear at the top, left, bottom, or right of the table, but the default is top. You can style caption text with a different font, bold weight, text color, or any other CSS properties.

The top row of the table, immediately below the caption, consists of table-header cells that use the `<th>` tag. These cells display bold, centered text. This special tag identifies cells that describe the cell data in their row or column. In Figure 8.1, the table-header cells are at the top of the columns; in other situations, they might run down the left row or both. By default, table-header cells are bold and aligned to the center of the cell, but you can modify their appearance using CSS.

The Florida, California, 2,500,000, and 5,500,000 cells are spanned cells. In other software they might be called "joined" or "merged" cells, but the HTML attributes responsible for these cells are `colspan` and `rowspan` — hence the origin of the term "spanned cells." (Be aware that Dreamweaver refers to the process of combining cells as "merging cells.") The `colspan` attribute added to the `<td>` tag merges cells belonging to different columns, such as the 2,500,000 cell. In this case, the cell spans two columns, so the tag is `<td colspan="2">`. The Florida and California cells use the `rowspan` attribute in the form `<td rowspan="2">`. The 5,500,000 cell uses both `colspan` and `rowspan`: `<td rowspan="2" colspan="2">`.

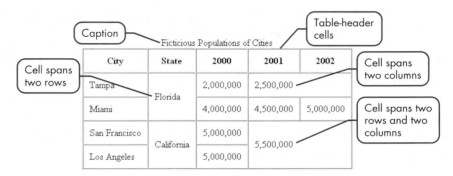

FIGURE 8.1

Dreamweaver provides two methods for working with tables. The Table dialog box allows you to specify the dimensions and some properties of a table. The other technique is the layout method, in which you draw cells and Dreamweaver generates the properties of the cells as you create and modify them. This is a more free-form approach and, as the term suggests, is very helpful for designing the layout of a page.

The Pros and Cons of Table Use

The original purpose for the `<table>` tag and its related tags was to provide a means for presenting tabular data. Knowing this, the origin of the table-data (`<td>`) tag (instead of a <tc> tag for table cell) becomes clear. The `<th>` tag has logical significance — it specifies the relationships between table data and table headings. Table-header cells at the tops of columns indicate that the data below belong to that category. The contrasting default styles of the `<th>` and `<td>` cell contents — bold and centered versus normal and left aligned — help sighted visitors to clearly differentiate one from the other and suggest their relationship.

The other, more popular, use of tables is for laying out the components of a Web page. For example, putting the page header in a top cell, the navigation menu in a left cell, the page footer in the bottom cell, and the content sandwiched between them. Without the use of tables or frames, layout might be quite basic, relying on not much more than left, center, and right alignment. When Web designers realized how they could use tables for layout, they were able to create sophisticated designs. By using spanned cells, they merged some rows and/or columns while keeping other cells separate and individual. Furthermore, many graphic-design programs, such as Adobe Photoshop and Macromedia Fireworks, enabled the designer to create a design, slice it into a complex arrangement of table cells, and then have the software create a table from the results. This process allowed graphic designers to concentrate on design while the software created the complex table layout for them.

Although using tables made possible the creation of complex designs, unanticipated problems arose. As you saw earlier, creating even simple tables requires a large amount of code. Depending on the amount of slicing a designer specified in the design software, the quantity of code could balloon into thousands and thousands of bytes. One analysis that illustrates the extent of the problem is the *content-to-code ratio*, which measures the amount of text on a Web page compared with the amount of code. A number of commercial Web sites that use tables for layout were tested for this ratio at http://www.holovaty.com/tools/getcontentsize/ and commonly contained just 5–10% content versus 90–95% code. By contrast, table-free layouts commonly contained 45–50% content. Complex table code can significantly increase the download time of a Web page.

Another drawback to using tables for layout is that, by design, table content does not display until the whole table has downloaded, thereby creating an apparent delay in the download. This delay is not the fault of the browser manufacturers, but part of the specifications by the W3C.

The final drawback of using tables for layout pertains to screen-reader software. Whenever such software encounters a table, it reads aloud the dimensions of the table, such as: "A table consisting of five columns and twelve rows." When the table displays tabular data, this reading of the table is beneficial because it tells the user how much information the table contains. However, when the table is just used for layout, this information may seem merely annoying.

Table-based layouts are becoming less popular for all of these reasons. However, the table-free methods, which use advanced properties of CSS to position content, are not always well supported. Tables have been well supported by browsers for a long time, but advanced CSS properties have only gained significant ground over the last one to two years and still have a way to go. Therefore, despite the promise of table-free layouts, some forms of complex layouts must still use tables.

You need to understand the properties of tables for laying out tabular data, whether or not you adopt CSS-based layout. Many table features, tags, and attributes also make tabular data accessible and usable by users of screen-reading software. As more and more governments, businesses, and individuals require Web accessibility, knowing how to use these features will better prepare you for designing accessible Web sites.

VISUAL SUMMARY

When you create tables, you commonly use the Table dialog box. You can activate this dialog box from the Common or Layout Insert bar, or by choosing Insert>Table. Using this dialog box, you can set the number of rows and columns, the width of the table, the width of the table border, and the cell-padding and cell-spacing properties. If you use a table for your page layout, you do not need the headers and accessibility features. However, if you create a table to present tabular data, you should choose a Header option and fill in the Caption and Summary fields.

The Table button, found in the Common and Layout insert bars, activates the Table dialog box.

Cell padding is the space between the cell's contents and the cell border. Cell spacing is the spacing between adjacent cell borders.

Set table headers if your table presents tabular data, but not if your table is just for page layout.

The table summary provides a complete recap of the table for screen-reader software. It is not visible on screen.

These fields specify the number of rows and columns.

You can specify the table width in pixels or percent, or leave these fields blank.

The table caption allows you to briefly describe the table contents similar to a heading.

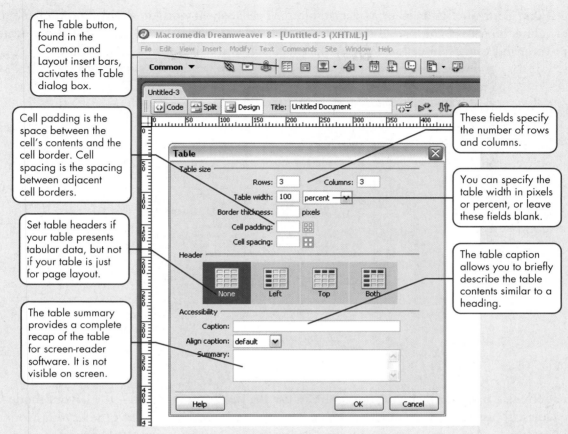

FIGURE 8.2

You can apply numerous properties of table cells through the Property inspector. The top half of the Property inspector displays standard text properties that you can apply to text within a cell. The bottom half of the Property inspector displays properties of table cells, table rows, or the table as a whole, depending on what is selected.

Use these fields to set a cell's width and height.

In this field, you set a background color for a cell.

Set the color of the cell border in this field.

Set a background image behind the cell using the point-to-file or browse-for-file functions.

The Tag selector allows you to select the table, the table row, or the table cell.

This icon identifies whether a cell, a row, or a table is selected.

These option lists set the horizontal and vertical alignment of a cell's contents.

With this check box, you can convert a table-data cell to a table-header cell.

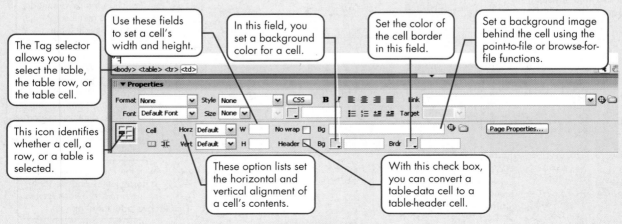

FIGURE 8.3

If you Right/Control-click a cell or a selected block of cells as you work on a table, a contextual menu appears. This menu provides access to many useful functions, such as Merge Cells (only available when two or more adjacent cells are selected), Split Cells, and Insert Rows or Columns.

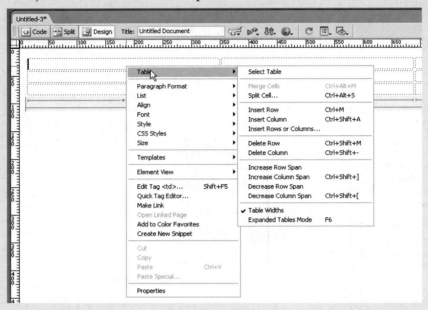

FIGURE 8.4

As an alternative to the Table dialog box, you can use the free-form method — the Layout mode — to create tables. To use the Layout mode, switch to the Layout Insert bar and click the Layout Mode button. Using the Layout Table button, you drag to create a table; then, using the Layout Table Cell button, you drag to create table cells. The dimensional rulers at the bottom of each column allow you to modify the column or table width.

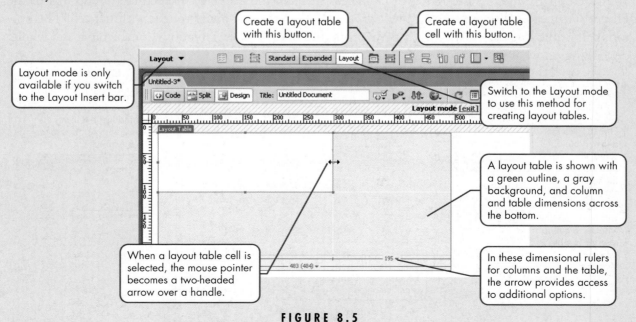

FIGURE 8.5

LESSON 1   Exploring the Applications and Properties of Tables

As you learned earlier, you can use tables to present tabular data. When you do, you should use header cells to identify the information in the column or row. Header cells use the **<th>** tag, which is identified in the Tag selector and the Property inspector. Commonly, tables of tabular data have visible borders to make clear which data fit in which column.

Layout tables, unlike data tables, generally do not use visible borders but do commonly use spanned cells. Sometimes layout tables are nested — tables within the cells of other tables. Nested tables, however, can be difficult to manage, especially if you work directly with the code. Even so, it is sometimes easier to build a nested table than to work with many **colspan** and **rowspan** attributes, especially, if you are hand-coding the layout.

In this lesson, you explore different uses of tables and some of their properties. You examine the code in the Tag selector and the properties in the Property inspector.

Explore the Properties and Features of a Basic Data Table

1   **Define the Chapter_08>Tables folder as a site called Tables. (You may also want to remove the site definitions from the previous chapter, as you won't need them again.)**

If the Frames panel is open from last chapter, you may close it.

2   **Open basic-data.html.**

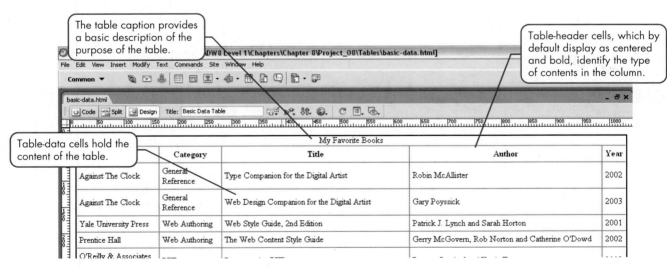

FIGURE 8.6 *(Copyright Against The Clock, Inc. Used by permission of Against the Clock, Inc.)*

3 Click the Publisher text in the top-left cell, and look at both the Tag selector and the Property inspector.

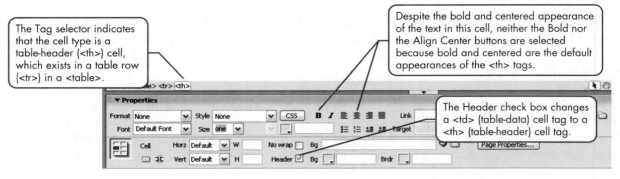

The Tag selector indicates that the cell type is a table-header (<th>) cell, which exists in a table row (<tr>) in a <table>.

Despite the bold and centered appearance of the text in this cell, neither the Bold nor the Align Center buttons are selected because bold and centered are the default appearances of the <th> tags.

The Header check box changes a <td> (table-data) cell tag to a <th> (table-header) cell tag.

FIGURE 8.7

4 With the insertion point still in the Publisher text, click the Align Left button in the Property inspector and examine the Tag selector.

Notice that a **<div>** tag appears after the **<th>** tag in the Tag selector.

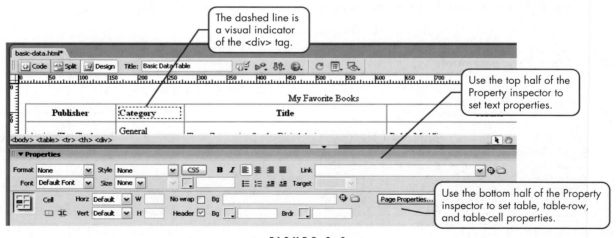

The dashed line is a visual indicator of the <div> tag.

Use the top half of the Property inspector to set text properties.

Use the bottom half of the Property inspector to set table, table-row, and table-cell properties.

FIGURE 8.8

❓ If You Have Problems

If you do not see the bottom half of the Property inspector, click the down-pointing arrow in the bottom-right corner of the Property inspector to expand it.

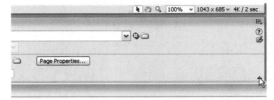

FIGURE 8.9

5   **Undo the left alignment, then choose Left from the Horz list.**

The contents of the cell are aligned to the left, and the Tag selector shows that no additional tags were created to apply the alignment property. This method applies alignment to the **<th>** tag directly as an **align="left"** attribute.

FIGURE 8.10

6   **Control/Command-click the Category, Title, Author, and Year header cells, and then choose Left from the Horz list. Drag across the top row to select the headers cells, and then choose Left from the Horz list.**

❓ If You Have Problems

(Windows) If the third Control-click does not select the third cell but deselects the two previously selected cells, you have encountered an undocumented feature of Dreamweaver 8. The workaround is to release the Control key between Control-clicks. In doing this, you may continue to use Control-click to select many cells.

Control/Command-clicking allows you to select cells as a group. You selected cells in the same row, but you could select multiple cells in a column or random cells throughout a table. Once you have selected the cells, you can apply any of the cell properties from the Property inspector.

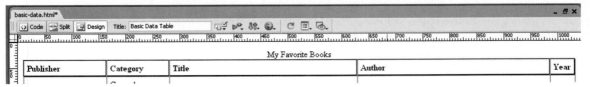

FIGURE 8.11

7 Click the caption text (My Favorite Books) above the table, and note the Tag selector and Property inspector.

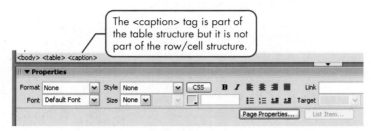

FIGURE 8.12

8 Close basic-data.html, saving the changes.

To Extend Your Knowledge...

ALIGNING CAPTION TEXT

You can align the <caption> tag for tables to the left, right, top, or bottom of the table. Unfortunately, these alignment options are not available through the Design view, only through the Code view. To apply any of these alignment options, click the caption text and click either the Code or Split button at the top of the Document window. Move the insertion point into the <caption> tag to the left of the closing angle bracket, and press the Spacebar once. Press "a" to choose align, press Enter/Return, press the first letter of your alignment option, and press Enter/Return. Click the Design button at the top of the Document window to close the Code window.

In Dreamweaver and most browsers, top, left, and right alignment appear to be equivalent of top-center, top-left, and top-right alignment, respectively. Although Dreamweaver offers a center option, it is not a valid HTML option and would probably be equivalent to top. The bottom alignment option for captions centers the text along the bottom of the table.

Technically, Dreamweaver does not display the right and left caption alignments properly, but it has a lot of company in this respect. Captions aligned to the left should appear to the left of the table, not above it. Right alignment should place the caption text to the right of the table, not above it. Only the Mozilla-based browsers (such as Mozilla, Firefox, and Camino) properly display right and left alignment of captions. However, the alignment option has been deprecated from HTML 4 and XHTML 1.0 and has been removed from the standard in XHTML 1.1. It has been replaced by the caption-side property in CSS with the same values: left, right, top, and bottom. Again, however, only the Mozilla-based browsers currently display the caption-side property properly.

Explore a Layout Table

In this exercise, you explore a Web page that uses tables for layout purposes. When using tables for layout, you do not use the `<th>` tag because the cells do not contain data. Layout tables routinely do not have borders because, as with frames, you typically want the layout to be seamless. Often, pages laid out with tables involve nested tables. Sometimes this occurs because the graphics application the designer used sliced the design into tables; when the designer assembles it, the coding uses nested tables.

In this exercise, you explore a page layout created using a series of nested tables. You explore the tables to see how different options were used to create the layout effects.

1   **Open tropiflora.html from the Tables site.**

Notice that the page content appears centered in the Document window.

FIGURE 8.13

2 Click the "Exotic Plants from Around the World" text, and then click the `<td>` tag (to the immediate left of the `<h2>` tag) in the Tag selector.

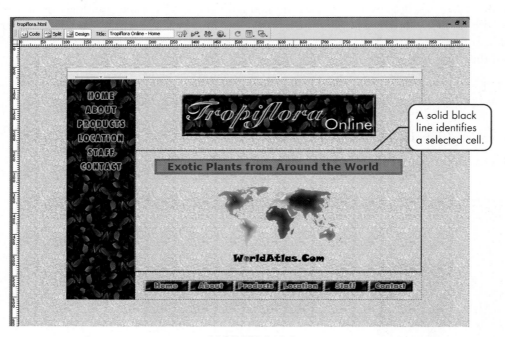

FIGURE 8.14

3 Click the `<table>` tag (two tags to the left of the selected `<td>` tag).

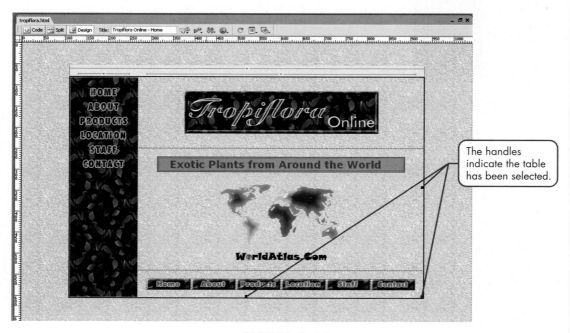

FIGURE 8.15

4 In the Tag selector, click the `<table>` tag to the immediate right of the `<body>` tag.

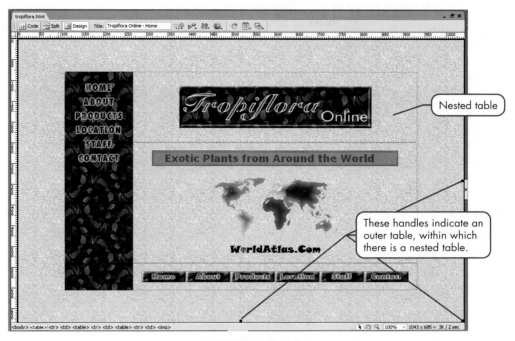

FIGURE 8.16

5 In the Property inspector, look at the W (width), H (height), Rows, and Cols (columns) fields.

Both the width and height are set to 100% so the selected table fills the Document window. With just one row and one column, this table is a single-celled table whose purpose is to center the content. Within this single-celled table is a nested table.

FIGURE 8.17

6 Click the Home graphic at the top of the left navigation bar and look at the Tag selector.

The Tag selector indicates that this graphic is contained by the third nested table, as you can see from the three `<table>` tags.

FIGURE 8.18

7 In the Tag selector, click the `<table>` tag to the immediate right of the `<td#navbar>` tag, and note the table properties in the Property inspector.

This nested table is one column wide and six rows tall and contains the six graphics that will be set as links to other pages in this site.

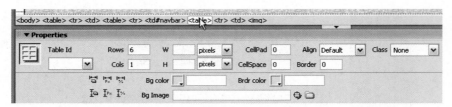

FIGURE 8.19

8 In the Tag selector, click the `<td#navbar>` tag, and look at the properties of this cell in the Property inspector.

The vertical alignment is set to Top. By default, vertical alignment is middle, but that alignment would float the navigation-bar table halfway down this cell. Setting the vertical alignment to Top forces the nested navigation-bar table to the top of the td#navbar cell.

FIGURE 8.20

9 Click the Home graphic in the footer cell of the central table, and note the Tag selector.

Note that the six graphics, which would normally be set as links to the pages of this site, are arranged in a six-column, one-row table.

FIGURE 8.21

10 Click the `<td>` tag closest to the `<body>` tag, and look at its properties in the Property inspector.

The horizontal alignment of this cell is Center and its vertical alignment is Middle, so the contents of this single-celled table are centered both horizontally and vertically.

FIGURE 8.22

11   **Close tropiflora.html.**

LESSON 2   Creating Tables

As you know, you can create tables in two ways with Dreamweaver: using the Table dialog box or the layout method. In this lesson, you use the Table dialog box. You encounter a few properties of tables and make decisions about how to set them.

You can specify Table Width in percentage or in pixels. Percentage is based on the container in which you place the table. If, for example, you are creating a table nested in another table cell, the percentage is measured relative to the containing cell, not the browser window. If, however, you specify the width in pixels, you could have a visitor whose browser window is narrower than the table width, forcing this visitor to scroll horizontally to read the content. Because most computer monitors are set to display 800 pixels or wider, you should generally be safe with table widths of 780 pixels or less. However, regardless of which units of measurement you use, if you have a 2000-pixel-wide graphic in the table, it won't matter whether the table is set to 100% or 780 pixels — the size of the graphic will force the table width to expand to whatever size is necessary to contain the graphic. The other option is to set no table width at all and allow the content to determine the width of the table. If a table has no specified dimensions, it expands enough to accommodate the width of the content up to 100% of the available space, and, where possible, text wraps to additional lines.

Another option in the Table dialog box is Border Thickness. Any value greater than 0 displays a border that you can color as you prefer. If you set the border to 0, no border displays. You can also leave the Border Thickness field blank, which allows browsers to default to their own settings, or you can use CSS to create borders instead. By default, if no border thickness is set, browsers do not display borders.

The Border Width setting is somewhat confusing because the width applies only to the border around the table. When you give a table border any value, cell borders also appear but, no matter what table Border Width setting you use, cell borders are always just 1 pixel thick. Given this lack of flexibility, you may prefer to leave the Border Thickness setting blank and instead set the borders using CSS.

Cell padding and cell spacing are two other settings that are often confused — their names are similar and, at times, they produce a similar result. ***Cell padding*** creates space around the contents in the cell, whereas ***cell spacing*** creates space between the cells. The difference is clear when borders are present. If you set Cell Padding to 15 pixels (both measurements are in pixels) and Cell Spacing to 0 pixels, the borders around each cell press against each other, but these cell borders are 15 pixels from the contents of the cell (see the left table in Figure 8.23). If you set Cell Padding to 0 pixels and Cell Spacing to 15 pixels, there is no space between the content of the cells and the cell borders, but the cell borders are 15 pixels apart from each other and from the edge of the table (see the right table in Figure 8.23). In both tables in Figure 8.23, the cells have a yellow background and the table has a blue background. The table background, if set, appears through the space created by cell spacing. You cannot set the table and cell backgrounds from the Table dialog box, but you can set them later using the Property inspector or CSS.

FIGURE 8.23

You can use the Table dialog box to create a caption and set its alignment. The Caption and Summary fields are grouped in the Accessibility section of this dialog box. (It is debatable whether or not the caption should be considered an accessibility feature because it benefits all users, not just those for whom accessibility initiatives were developed.) Unlike the **summary** attribute, the caption is visible and readable by everyone. You can use this option as a heading or as a simple description of the purpose of the table.

The final option is the Summary, which is an accessibility feature. Unlike the caption, summary text is not visible, but screen readers can read it. The caption text is reserved for short descriptions; the **summary** attribute is for descriptions that might be longer. The purpose of the **summary** attribute is to review the contents of the table, thereby reducing the need for the user of screen-reader software to listen to all of the data. Sighted users can quickly scan the table and determine trends and relationships. Screen-reader users benefit from the summary description for the same information. Consider, for example, the following browser-statistics table:

complex-data.html*								

	Internet Explorer		Opera 7	Mozilla	Netscape		
	IE 6	IE 5			NN 3	NN 4	NN 7
January	71.3%	12.8%	2.1%	8.2%	0.4%	0.5%	1.5%
February	71.5%	11.5%	2.2%	9.0%	0.4%	0.4%	1.5%
March	72.1%	10.7%	2.1%	9.6%	0.4%	0.4%	1.4%
April	72.4%	10.4%	2.1%	10.1%	0.3%	0.3%	1.4%

FIGURE 8.24

The summary attribute for this table might be written as:

```
summary="Internet Explorer 6 accounted for approximately 72% of the vis-
its increasing by 1% from January to April. Internet Explorer 5 account-
ed for approximately 11% and decreased by 1% during the same period.
```

Opera 7 remained steady at approximately 2% whereas Mozilla increased from 8 to 10%. Netscape 3 and 4 remained steady at about 0.4% each and Netscape 7 changed little from its 1.5%."

Create a Table

In this exercise, you create a table that will form the basis of a television schedule. Although this schedule could be considered a data table, for the purposes of this lesson, you use the table solely for layout.

1 **Create a new HTML page with the document Title of** `Television Schedule`**. Save it (but do not close it) as tv-schedule.html.**

2 **Type** `Television Schedule` **at the top of the page, format it as Heading 1, and press Enter/Return at the end of the line.**

3 **In the Common Insert bar, click the Table button (between the Named Anchor and Insert Div Tag buttons).**

If the Insert bar is set to another mode, switch it to Common and click the Table button.

FIGURE 8.25

4 **In the Table dialog box, set Rows to** `4`**, Columns to** `7`**, Table Width to** `100`**%, Border Thickness to** `1`**, Cell Padding to** `0`**, Cell Spacing to** `2`**, and Header to None. Click OK.**

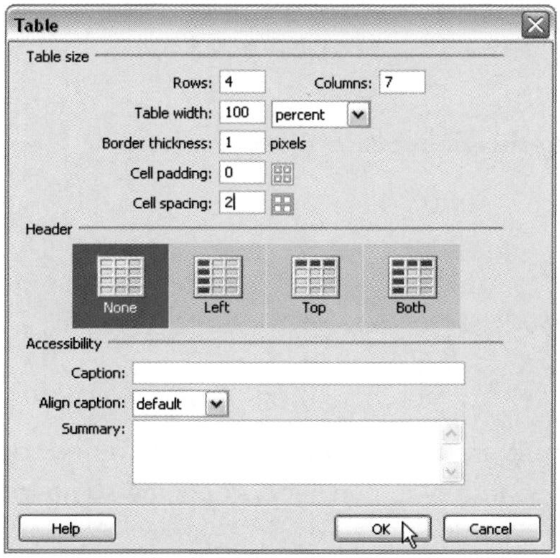

FIGURE 8.26

5   In the top-left cell, type `Station`; in the next cell to the right of it, type `1:00 p.m.` Then type `1:30 p.m.` and so on to `3:30 p.m.` in the last cell of the top row.

6   In the cells below the Station cell, type `CTV`, `CBC`, and `TVO`.

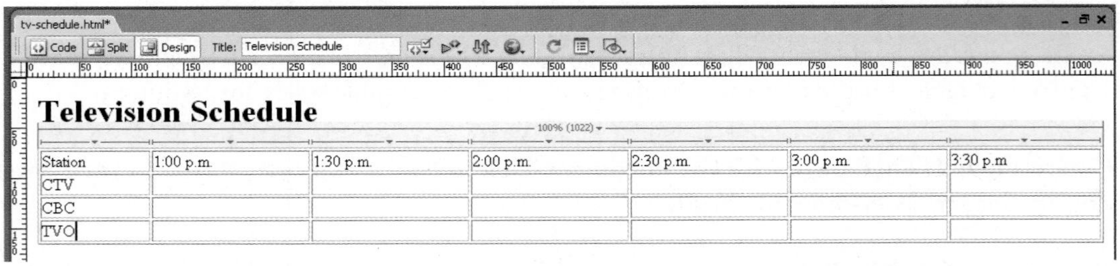

FIGURE 8.27

7   In the CTV row, type `Vicki Gabereau` at **1:00 p.m.**, `Rosie O'Donnell` at **2:00 p.m.**, and `General Hospital` at **3:00 p.m.**

8   In the CBC row, type `Road to Avonlea` at **1:00 p.m.**, `Canadian Gardener` at **2:00 p.m.**, `Pit Pony` at **2:30 p.m.**, and `Nothing Too Good for a Cowboy` at **3:00 p.m.**

9   In the TVO row, type `More to Life` at **1:00 p.m.**, `Studio 2` at **2:00 p.m.**, `Your Health` at **3:00 p.m.**, and `Arthur` at **3:30 p.m.**

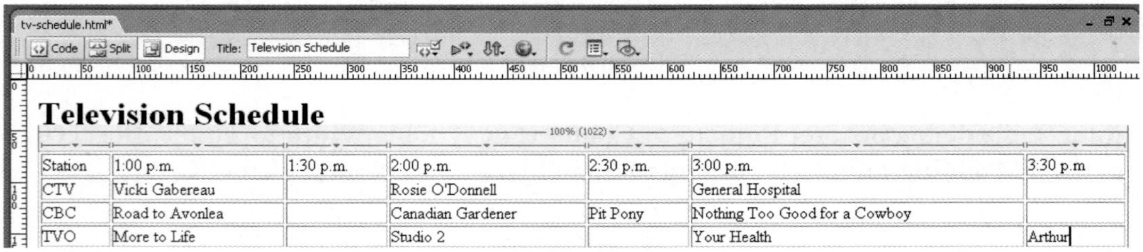

FIGURE 8.28

11   Save the changes, leaving this file open for the next lesson.

To Extend Your Knowledge . . .

CSS BORDERS

CSS borders have three different groups of properties: `border-width`, `border-style`, and `border-color`. In addition to that, you can set borders the same for all, or set the top, right, left, and bottom borders differently.

LESSON 3   Inserting New Rows and Columns

Inserting a new row at the bottom of a table is very simple — move the insertion point to the last cell in the table and press the Tab key, and a new row appears. However, if you want to add a new row in the middle of a table, the Tab key won't work. You must use either a contextual menu or the Menu bar. To insert a new column, you can use either the Menu-bar option or the Column Width menu that appears above or below the table.

Insert New Rows and Columns

In this exercise, you insert new rows at the bottom of the table, a new row in the middle of the table, and a column to the left of the table.

1   **From the bottom-right cell of the table, press the Tab key.**

Notice that a new row appears.

2   **Type WN in the cell under the TVO cell and type `The Weather Network` at 1:00 p.m. Press Tab until a new row appears. Complete the rest of the table as shown in Figure 8.29.**

Station	1:00 p.m.	1:30 p.m.	2:00 p.m.	2:30 p.m.	3:00 p.m.	3:30 p.m
CTV	Vicki Gabereau		Rosie O'Donnell		General Hospital	
CBC	Road to Avonlea		Canadian Gardener	Pit Pony	Nothing Too Good for a Cowboy	
TVO	More to Life		Studio 2		Your Health	Arthur
WN	The Weather Network					
YTV	Oswald	Little Bear	Babar	Rupert	Sailor Moon	Monster Rancher
ABC	All My Children		One Life to Live		General Hospital	

FIGURE 8.29

3   **Right/Control-click the TVO cell and choose Table>Insert Rows or Columns. In the Insert Rows or Columns dialog box, choose Rows, set the Number of Rows to 1, set Where to Above the Selection, and click OK.**

You may notice that Insert Row and Insert Column appeared in the contextual menu. Those options are less flexible — they only allow you to insert one at a time, and rows are always above and columns are always to the left (before).

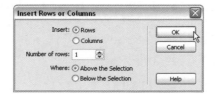

FIGURE 8.30

4   In the new empty row, type `TLC` under the CBC cell, `While You Were Out` under 1:00 p.m., `Date Patrol` under 2:00 p.m., and `Spymaster` under 3:00 p.m.

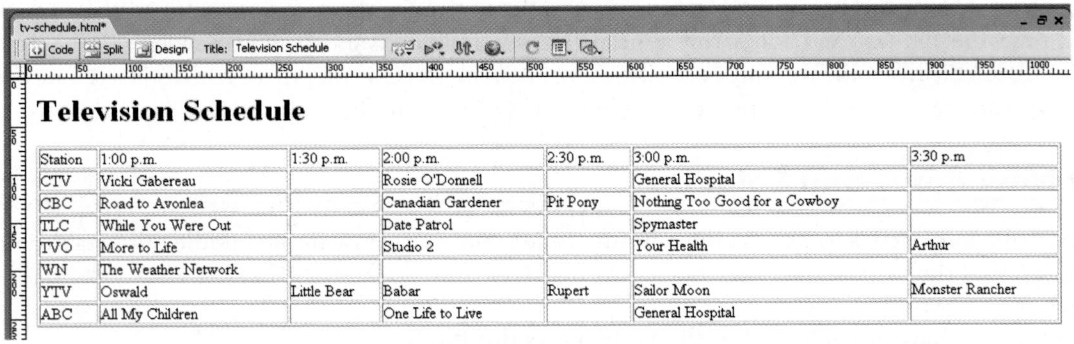

FIGURE 8.31

5   Above the Station cell, click the Column Width menu triangle, and choose Insert Column Left.

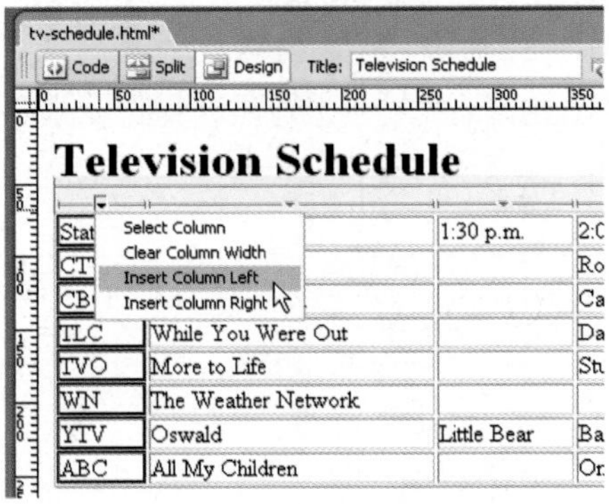

FIGURE 8.32

6   In the top cell of the new column, type `Source`. In the cell below, type `Cable`; in the cell to the left of WN, type `Satellite`.

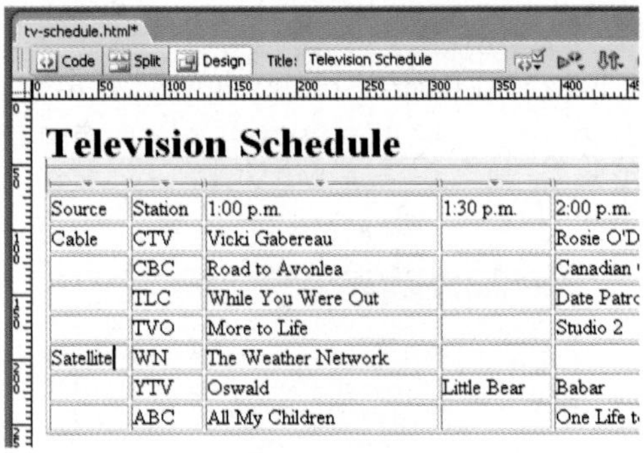

FIGURE 8.33

7   Save the changes, leaving the page open for the next lesson.

LESSON 4 Merging Cells

Merging cells is as simple as choosing a group of adjacent cells and activating the merge function. Dreamweaver automatically adds the **colspan** or **rowspan** attributes as needed. Many die-hard hand-coders agree that table assembly, especially merging cells, is one feature of visual Web-design software that they could benefit by using.

In this exercise, many of the television programs are one hour long, so there is an empty cell to the right of the cell containing the name of the program. You must merge the empty cell with the cell to its left. To do so, select the two cells (in either order) and choose Table>Merge Cells from the contextual menu or Modify>Table>Merge Cells from the Dreamweaver menu. Similarly, you must merge the Cable and Satellite cells with the empty cells below them.

Merge Cells

1 In the first column, drag to select the Cable cell and the three empty cells below it.

2 Right/Control-click in the selected cells and choose Table>Merge Cells.

3 Select the Satellite cell and the two empty cells below it, and merge them by choosing Modify>Table>Merge Cells.

4 Select the Vicki Gabereau cell (CTV, 1:00 p.m.) and the empty cell to the right and press Control-Alt-M/Command-Option-M to merge the two cells.

5 Continue to merge cells where empty cells exist to the right of filled cells. Merge all six cells in the row for The Weather Network.

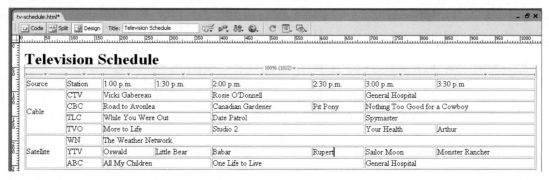

FIGURE 8.34

6 Save the changes, leaving the file open for the next lesson.

LESSON 5 Dressing Up Tables

In this lesson, you learn to apply background colors, horizontal alignment, column widths, and border colors to a table. You can use HTML presentational tags and attributes or CSS to apply style or presentation to a table. *HTML presentational tags* are tags whose sole purpose is to add appearance without affecting structure. The best-known presentational tag is the `<font>` tag, which allows you to change the color, typeface, and size of text. As you learned earlier, all of these options are also available through CSS. *HTML presentational attributes* apply appearances, such as colors and borders. Unlike CSS, HTML presentational attributes are coded in the tags themselves; CSS appears in the `<head>` section of the HTML document. In this lesson, you learn to specify appearances using both HTML and CSS methods, and compare the results.

You can change either or both of the background and border colors in the Property inspector. Dreamweaver provides a Format Table function that allows you to apply predefined color schemes and to apply (and customize) any of the schemes. You apply these appearances with HTML tags and attributes through the Format Table function or the Property inspector.

There are several methods you can use to select cells to apply an appearance to the table, to a row, or to an individual cell. You can click the `<table>`, `<tr>`, or `<td>` tags in the Tag selector. You can use Control/Command-click with or without the Shift key to select multiple cells. You can move the mouse pointer to the top of a column until it becomes a down-pointing arrow, at which point clicking selects the column or, if you drag to either the left or right, you select adjacent columns. To select *discontiguous* (nonadjacent) columns, Control/Command-click one column, which selects it; then move the mouse pointer to the top of another column and, when it changes to the down-pointing arrow cursor, Control/Command-click to select that column as well.

In this lesson, you also learn to adjust the column widths using the green dimensional rulers that appear either below or above the table. You can use these rulers to adjust the width of the entire table or of individual columns. When you change the width of columns, the changes are applied to the cells in the selected columns. As you learned earlier, you build tables using the `<table>`, `<tr>` (table row), and `<td>` and `<th>` (table-cell) tags. The `<col>` and `<colgroup>` tags are rarely used because they have weak browser support, are not available through Dreamweaver's Design interface, and do not define the structure of the table. They just provide a means for applying some common attributes to columns of cells, such as column widths.

Select, Customize, and Apply a Predefined Color Scheme

In this exercise, you change the appearance of the table of television programs using HTML styles. You use the Format Table function to create the basic style and then modify cells with different appearances.

1   **Save the open tv-schedule.html file as tv-schedule-HTML.html.**

The file tv-schedule-1.html is the same as tv-schedule.html. You apply HTML presentation styles to tv-schedule.html. In a following exercise, you apply the same appearances to tv-schedule.html using CSS, and then compare the results.

2   **Click the table and choose Commands>Format Table.**

This function offers a number of predefined table styles that you can apply to your selected table. Explore these predefined styles in the top-left list. Notice also that you can set two row colors to alternate. You can also style the top row with colors, alignment, and text styles, and the left column with alignment and text styles.

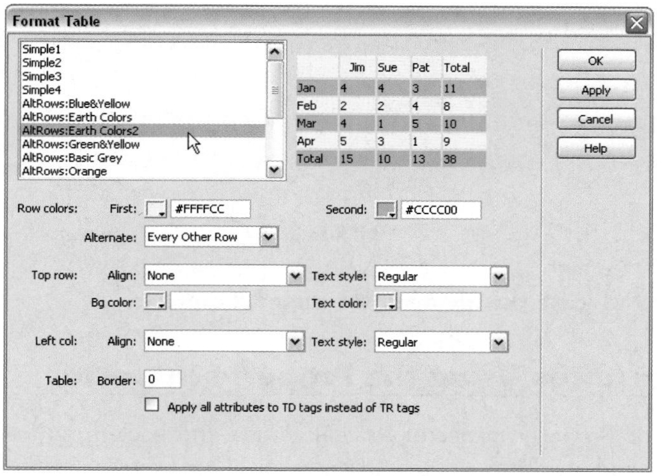

FIGURE 8.35

3 | **Choose AltRows:Earth Colors2 from the list and click the Apply button.**

When you click Apply, the table in the Document window behind the dialog box takes on the selected color scheme.

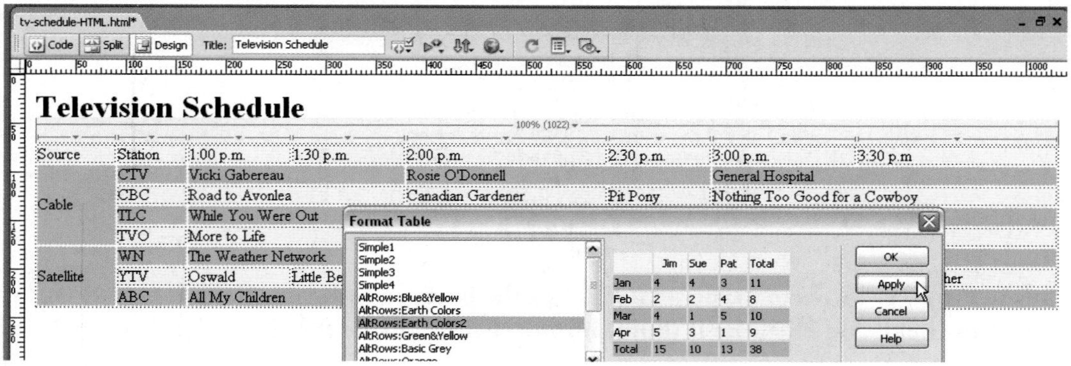

FIGURE 8.36

4 | **In the Format Table dialog box, set the Top Row Text Style to Bold. Set the Bg Color to #802A00 (zeros, not the letter "O") by typing this hexadecimal color code into the text field to the right of the color box. Set the Text Color to #CCCCCC. Click OK.**

Remember to type the # character for both colors.

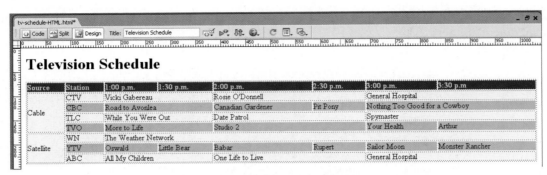

FIGURE 8.37

5 Save the changes and leave the file open for the next exercise.

Modify Cell Appearances Using the Property Inspector

In this exercise, you use the Property inspector to change text and background colors of selected cells with HTML presentational tags and attributes. The bold tag is an HTML presentational tag. The cell background color is an HTML presentational attribute.

1 Control/Command-click the Cable cell, and then Shift-click the ABC cell.

There are no table borders because the table borders were set by default to 0 in the Format Table dialog box.

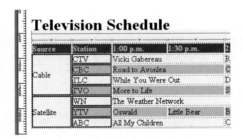

FIGURE 8.38

2 In the Property inspector, type #808000 in the background-color field, type #CCCCCC in the text color field, and click the B (bold) button. Click outside the selected cells when finished.

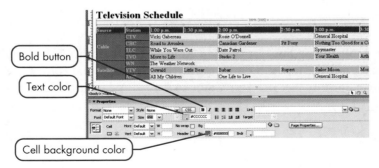

FIGURE 8.39

3 Control/Command-click to select the Road to Avonlea cell, then change the background color to #CC4400 and the text color to #FFFFFF (or choose white using the color box). Set the text to bold. Apply the same color scheme to the Oswald and Rupert cells.

Although you already created the color scheme, you cannot, without going into the code, copy and paste the style properties from one cell to another because you applied the styles with HTML presentation tags and attributes.

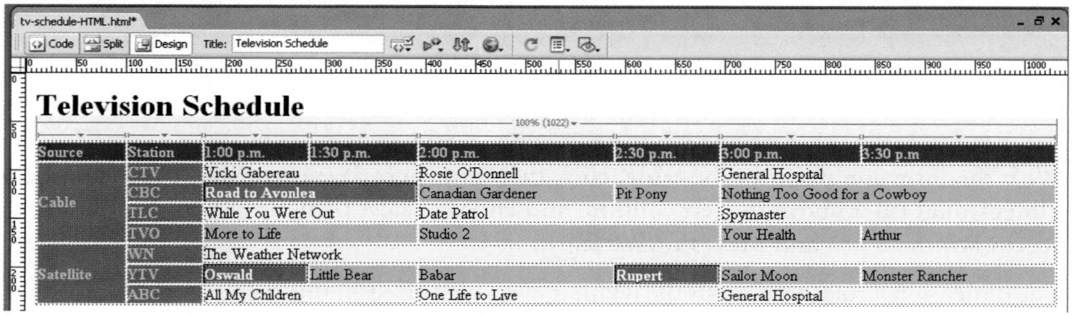

FIGURE 8.40

4 Control/Command-click to select all three cells highlighted with the favorite color scheme, and reverse the colors so that the text color is #CC4400 and the background color is #FFFFFF.

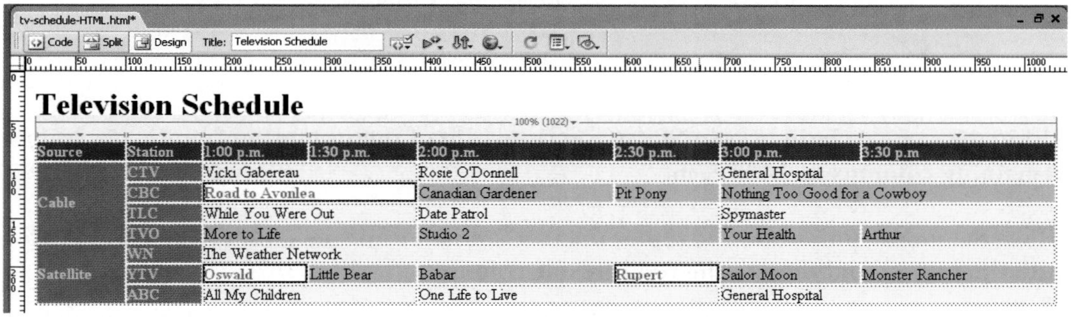

FIGURE 8.41

5 With the insertion point in any cell, click the `<table>` tag in the Tag selector and, in the Property inspector, set the Bg Color (background color) to black (#000000).

Remember: if you type the hexadecimal color code in the background-color field, you must press Enter/Return or Tab to set the color. Note that when cell spacing is set to a value greater than 0, the background color of the table shows through the spacing, giving the appearance of borders.

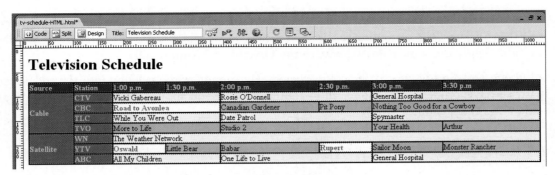

FIGURE 8.42

6 With the insertion point in the table, click the down-pointing arrow in the middle of the dimensional ruler above the left column, and choose Select Column. In the Property inspector, set the width to 8% and press Enter/Return.

The dimensional ruler shows that the width is 8% — 79 pixels in this example. The pixel value changes if the width of the Document window changes, but it is always 8% of the table width.

FIGURE 8.43

7 Using the same technique as in Step 6, set the width of the second column to 8% and the remaining columns to 14% each.

8 Move the mouse pointer to the top of the first column until the pointer changes to a down-pointing arrow, and drag to the right by one column.

The down-pointing arrow is a tool for selecting a column. You can drag to the left or right while the mouse pointer is still a down-pointing arrow to select additional adjacent columns.

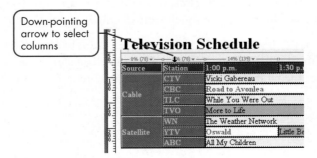

FIGURE 8.44

9   **Choose Center from the Horz (horizontal alignment) list to center the contents of the selected cells.**

If you want to apply a common alignment to all contents of a cell, use the horizontal-alignment attribute of table cells rather than text alignment — it creates less code. However, when you are using a table for layout, you may prefer to center some paragraphs or other blocks and align others differently. In that situation, you apply the text-alignment properties, either with HTML presentation methods or the preferable CSS methods.

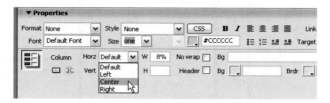

FIGURE 8.45

10   **Close, saving the changes tv-schedule-HTML.html.**

LESSON 6   Using the Table Dialog Box to Create a Layout Table

Most Web sites use tables for layout, and, for the most part, the table structures are quite basic. Commonly, there is a header, a footer, a navigation bar on the left, and a main content area.

Table-based layouts tend not to use borders, which destroys the seamless appearance of the layout. Instead, these layouts tend to use larger cells, because they hold more content, and, therefore, also use vertical or horizontal alignment. Table-based layouts commonly use spanned (merged) cells to extend the footer or header cells across the width of the table.

Create a Table-Based Layout Using the Table Dialog Box

In this exercise, you create a table-based layout. As in all design, it is useful to begin with a clear picture of what you want to create. At least at the beginning, you should create this image on paper. (When you become more familiar with design and layout options, you may be able to think it out by visualizing without drawing.) Before you begin any layout, you should draw it concretely, assigning the components to their own boxes or cells. To determine how many rows and columns you need, extend all lines to the edges of the table (as we did with the dotted line in Figure 8.46). For now, imagine that you drew the layout in Figure 8.46 as your plan for the layout table that you create in this exercise.

1 **Examine the provided layout. Note the number of rows and columns and the information each contains.**

Notice that the planned layout contains two rows: the header row and the navigation/main-content row. It also contains two columns: the navigation bar and the main content. Although the header row does not have separate visible columns, it is constructed by merging the two cells in the top row. The dotted line just shows how the header row would be divided.

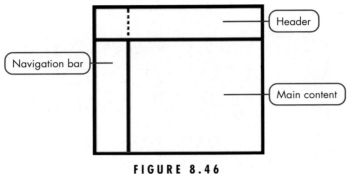

FIGURE 8.46

2 **Open hotrodcars.html from the Tables site.**

3 **Click the Table button and create a 2 × 2 table with a table-width setting of 100%, no borders, 3 cell padding, and 0 cell spacing. Click OK.**

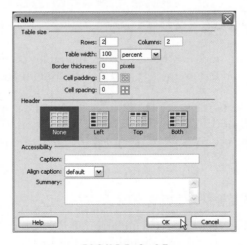

FIGURE 8.47

4 **Drag to select the top two cells, Right/Control-click, and choose Table>Merge Cells.**

5 **Click the top cell and insert the hot-rods-logo.png graphic from the images folder and type** `Hot Rods` **in the Alternate text field.**

6 **Click the right cell of the second row, insert the 1929_phantom.jpg image and type** `Photo of a 1929 Phantom` **in the Alternate text field.**

7 Click the left cell of the second row, insert 1929_phantom_on.png with the Alternate text `1929 Phantom`. Click to the right of the inserted image, press Enter/Return and insert chevy_sedan_off.png with the Alternate text `Chevy Sedan`. Repeat the process and insert ford_coupe_off.png (`Ford Coupe`), ford_modela_off.png (`Ford Model A`), and ford_Victoria_off.png (`Ford Victoria`).

Notice that the top graphic and photo of the 1929 Phantom are both left-aligned in the cells. Notice also that the small graphics on the left are centered vertically. These alignments are the defaults for horizontal and vertical alignment.

FIGURE 8.48

8 Save the changes, leaving the file open for the next exercise.

Change Cell Alignments

In this layout, the graphic buttons on the left look fine with the current content. If, however, the right cell had more content than just the photo of the car — perhaps the statistics on the car, the owner, and more — the left graphics would still center vertically in the cell. In a long page, these centered graphics could appear below the bottom of the browser window. In this exercise, you change the default layouts of the cells to prevent this.

1 Click the top cell to the right of the Hot Rods graphic.

2 In the Property inspector, change the horizontal alignment to Center.

FIGURE 8.49

3 Click the left cell and change the vertical alignment to Top.

4 Close, saving the changes.

To Extend Your Knowledge . . .

AVOID LAYOUT TABLES

As you know, tables were not designed for layout. Their complex and flexible structure and options made it possible for designers to create exciting designs. Layout tables, however, come at a high cost.

Pages do not display until the browser receives all of the table's code and contents. Nested tables add more code to download and display. When a browser displays nested tables, it also evaluates the layout once per table, so if the outer table contains five nested tables, the browser must run six passes through the code before it displays the page. If you can reduce your reliance on nested tables and work with just one table, you can produce far less code and faster-displaying pages.

Screen-reader software announces the number of rows and columns for each table, so nested tables are particularly irritating for users of such software. When table borders are hidden, sighted people do not see the tables or experience similar frustrations. Again, at least try to avoid using nested tables.

You can explore these and other points about layout tables at http://www.hotdesign.com/seybold/. However, because you may run into layout tables when you work on other people's sites, you should know how to work with them.

LESSON 7   Creating Tables in Layout Mode

Simple tables, whether data tables or layout tables, are relatively easy to construct, so determining how many columns and rows to use is also fairly easy. For data tables, you know the number of columns and rows just from the amount of data you have. However, some layouts place graphics of different height and width beside each other. Without measuring each graphic and working your calculator to compute column and row spans, you can't easily create a table for these types of complex layouts. For this reason, Dreamweaver provides the Layout view, in which you can create cells just by dragging the borders wider or narrower. This method of creating a layout is very flexible and supports free-form design.

There are two ways you can use the Layout view to create tables. You can create a layout table and then add layout cells to it, or you can create the layout cells and allow Dreamweaver to create the table around it. Both methods have their advantages and disadvantages, so the choice is really a matter of your preference. In this exercise, you create the layout table first, and then draw the layout cells within it.

Prepare to Use Layout Mode

1   **Open bromeliads.html from the Tables site.**

2   **Switch the Insert bar to the Layout Insert bar, and click the Layout mode button.**

The Layout mode is the mode in which you create the layout table. When you complete the table, switch back to Standard mode for routine editing and design work.

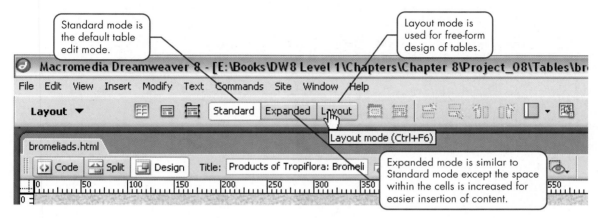

FIGURE 8.50

3   **Read the information in the dialog box, then click OK (do not click the Don't Show Me This Message Again option).**

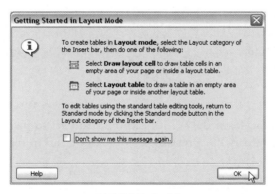

FIGURE 8.51

? If You Have Problems

(Windows only) Whether or not you have checked the Don't Show Me This Message Again option, this dialog box appears only the first time you switch to the Layout mode. If you want to access this dialog box, you must close and relaunch Dreamweaver. When you switch to Layout mode, this Getting Started in Layout Mode dialog box appears.

Create and Fill a Layout Table and Its Cells

You have now prepared a page and switched into Layout mode. In this exercise, you create the layout table and layout cells, and then insert different graphics into each new cell.

1 Click the Layout Table button (to the immediate right of the Layout button) and draw a rectangle in the Document window.

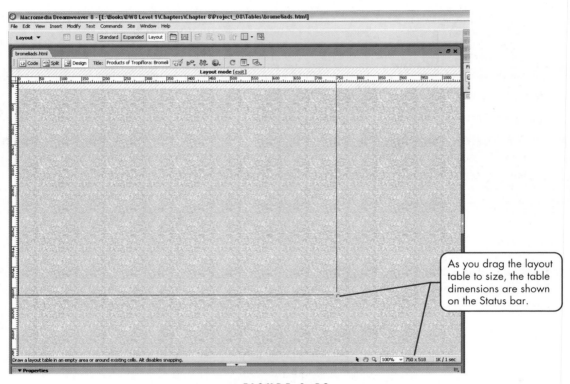

> As you drag the layout table to size, the table dimensions are shown on the Status bar.

FIGURE 8.52

2 In the Property inspector, leave the Width radio button set to Fixed, but change the dimensions to Width: 760 and Height: 420. Press Enter/Return or Tab to register the change.

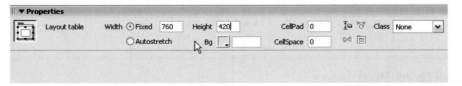

FIGURE 8.53

3 Click the Draw Layout Cell button (to the right of the Layout Table button) and drag to create a short cell across the full width of the table.

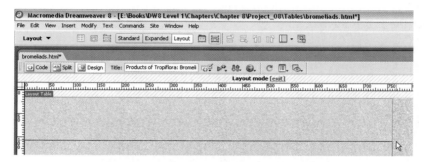

FIGURE 8.54

4 Create another cell across the bottom of the table by clicking the Draw Layout Cell button and dragging across the width of the table. Create three vertical cells in the center area — make the left and right cells relatively narrow and the middle cell wide.

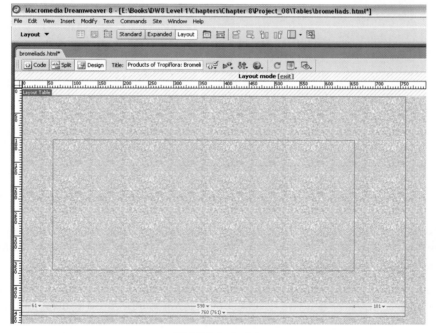

FIGURE 8.55

5 Click the top cell. From the Property inspector, set the format to Heading 1, drag Tropiflora_online.jpg from the images folder into the cell and type `Tropiflora Online` in the alternate text field.

6   Double-click to open bromeliads-navbar.html. Select all of the content, copy it, and then close bromeliads-navbar.html. Click the left cell and paste the copied content.

7   With the insertion point still in the left cell, Right/Control-click the `<td>` tag in the Tag selector and set the `id` to navbar.

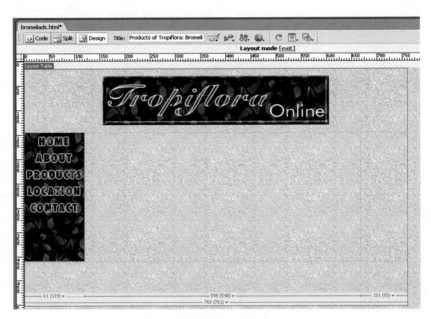

FIGURE 8.56

8   Using the same procedures as in Step 6, copy the content from bromeliads-content.html into the middle cell, the content from bromeliads-special.html into the right cell, and the content from bromeliads-footer.html into the bottom cell.

9   Switch to Standard mode by clicking the Standard button (Standard Layout in the tool tip).

10   At the bottom of the left (navbar) cell, click the down-pointing arrow and choose Clear Column Width. Repeat this step for the other two cells in the middle row, but do not touch the one for the entire table that reads 760.

When you draw a table and cells in Layout mode, the process of drawing defines the width (and height) of cells in pixels. When you select Clear Column Width, the width attributes of the cells in the column are removed from the `<td>` tags. You should realize, however, that this option does not change the table width, just the selected column(s). Without specified column widths, the three columns adjust their width to their content. The graphics in the left and right cells determine those cells' minimum widths. In the middle cell, the text wraps if it cannot fit on one line.

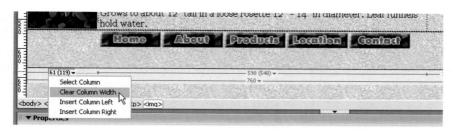

FIGURE 8.57

11   Click the down-pointing arrow below the table dimension (760), and choose Clear All Heights.

FIGURE 8.58

12   Preview the page in your browser, then return to Dreamweaver and close bromeliads.html.

LESSON 8   Creating Basic Accessible Data Tables

You learned earlier that tables were primarily designed for tabular data. However, even if you use a table to present tabular data, you have not ensured that your data is accessible to those who use screen readers. There are a few tags and attributes that you should use to create accessible tables — the `<caption>` tag, the table-header cell tag (`<th>`), and the **summary, scope, id**, and **headers** attributes. Not all of these tags and attributes are required for all data tables. All data tables should use `<th>` cell tag, the `<caption>` tag, and, optionally, the **summary** attribute. Data tables of intermediate complexity also need the **scope** attribute. Complex data tables require the **id** and **header** attributes instead of the **scope** attribute.

The issue with tables and accessibility is not whether or not screen-reader software can read your data, but whether the user of that screen reader can work with your data. For example, if a coworker asked you when the next staff meeting is, you would look through the table of appointments for the week and see "staff meeting"; you would then look up to see that it was in the Tuesday column and then look across to see that it was in the 10:00 a.m. row. You see the relationship between the position of a table-data cell and the header cells at the top of the column and at the beginning of the row. Understanding and using this relationship is the difference between reading the table contents and interpreting or using the table contents. Users of screen-reader software can pause their software in a particular cell and direct it to read aloud the header cells that apply to it. Without proper coding, however, this relationship does not exist, and they cannot use the table as well as sighted individuals.

You should use the `<th>` tags when you create a data table. You apply these tags to the header cells for the columns and/or the rows. If the table has just one *logical header level* (a simple data table), which means that only rows or columns require headers, all you need to do to satisfy accessibility criteria is format the header cells as table-header cells. If the table has two logical header levels (a data table of intermediate complexity), which means that both rows and columns have header cells, then in addition to table-header tags, you need to add the `scope` attribute to each header cell. The `scope` attribute identifies the direction in which the header cells apply — column or row. If the table has three or more logical header levels, then either rows or columns (or both) have multiple levels of headers. The `scope` attribute no longer suffices, and you must use the `id` and `headers` attributes.

You may be concerned about how to insert the table-header tags and apply the `scope` attributes for simple and moderately difficult accessible tables, but Dreamweaver makes it easy. You must consider accessibility, however, before you start creating your data table or you lose the benefits of Dreamweaver's accessibility features, and then must either re-create the table or hand-code the modifications.

Create an Accessible Data Table

1   **Create a new HTML page, and in the document Title field type** Growth Charts of Boys and Girls.

2   **Click the Table button in the Insert bar.**

       Whether the Insert bar is set to Layout or Common, the Table button is available — the first button on the Layout Insert bar or the fourth button on the Common Insert bar.

?   **If You Have Problems**

If the Table button is disabled (if necessary) switch to the Layout Insert bar and click the Standard or Expanded button. If the Layout button is selected, you cannot activate the Table dialog box: you must create a table using the Table and Cell layout functions, not the Table dialog box.

3   **Click the Table button and create a table that is 3 rows by 3 columns and has no width setting. Set the border to** 1, **the cell padding to** 3, **and the cell spacing to** 0.

4   **Choose the Top header option.**

       In the Caption field, type Growth Charts of Boys and Girls.

       In the Summary field, type Although girls are slightly shorter than boys at age 5, at ages 8 and 11 they are taller than boys. By age 14, girls have attained their adult height. Boys tend to be shorter than girls at ages 8 and 11. Between 11 and 14 they experience a growth spurt, which increases their height over girls. At age 17 their growth rate tapers off.

       Click OK when finished.

As you can see, the summary is used to digest the data so screen-reader users do not have to remember the data, cell by cell, to draw their own conclusions.

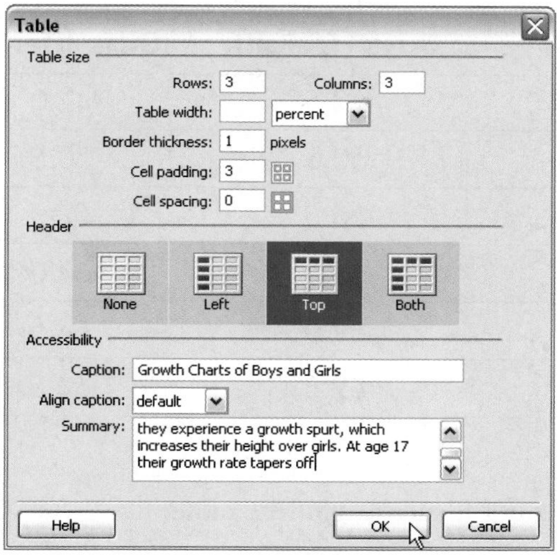

FIGURE 8.59

5 In the Layout Insert bar, click the Expanded layout button, then click OK to close the Getting Started in Expanded Mode dialog box.

Getting Started in Expanded Tables Mode

Expanded Tables mode makes it easier to select inside and around tables.

This mode does not display tables the way a browser does. Before moving or resizing table elements, return to Standard mode by clicking the Standard mode button in the Layout category of the Insert bar.

☐ Don't show me this message again.

Help   OK

FIGURE 8.60

6 Type `Age`, `Boys' Height`, and `Girls' Height` in the top three cells. Complete the table with the following data, pressing Tab to move from cell to cell.

Age	Boys' Height	Girls' Height
5	42.5	42.0
8	50.0	50.5
11	56.5	57.0
14	65.5	64.0
17	69.0	64.5
20	69.5	64.5

7 Examine the appearance and formatting of the table.

Notice that text in the top row is bold and centered whereas the text in the data cells is normal weight and left aligned. The **<th>** tag, by default, displays text as bold and centered.

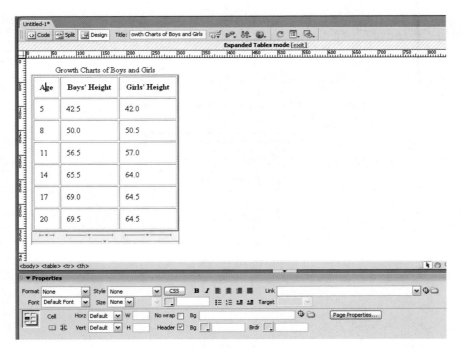

FIGURE 8.61

8   **Click the Split button and examine the `<th>` tags.**

The `<th>` tags use the `scope="col"` attribute, which states that the header cells are related to the data cells in the column below them. This is a simple table and does not necessarily need the `scope` attribute, but it is good form to use it anyway.

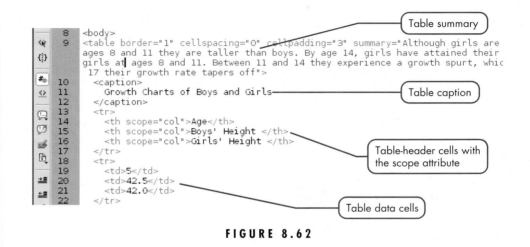

```
8   <body>
9   <table border="1" cellspacing="0" cellpadding="3" summary="Although girls are
    ages 8 and 11 they are taller than boys. By age 14, girls have attained their
    girls at ages 8 and 11. Between 11 and 14 they experience a growth spurt, whic
    17 their growth rate tapers off">
10    <caption>
11      Growth Charts of Boys and Girls
12    </caption>
13    <tr>
14      <th scope="col">Age</th>
15      <th scope="col">Boys' Height </th>
16      <th scope="col">Girls' Height </th>
17    </tr>
18    <tr>
19      <td>5</td>
20      <td>42.5</td>
21      <td>42.0</td>
22    </tr>
```

Table summary

Table caption

Table-header cells with the scope attribute

Table data cells

FIGURE 8.62

9   **Click the Design button to close the Code view.**

10   **Close this page, saving it as accessible1.html in the Tables site.**

S U M M A R Y

In this chapter, you learned to create and modify tables. You learned that you can use tables to present data and to lay out pages. You discovered how to create data tables that make the information they contain accessible and usable by everyone. You learned to create layout tables using both the Standard mode and the Layout mode, and you explored the flexibility of the Layout mode. You also learned how to modify the structure of a table by adding rows and columns, merging cells, and changing alignment and background colors.

K E Y   T E R M S

Cell padding	Discontiguous	Logical header level
Cell spacing	HTML presentational attributes	Spanned (merged) cells
Content-to-code ratio	HTML presentational tags	

CHECKING CONCEPTS AND TERMS

SCREEN ID

Identify the indicated areas from the following list:

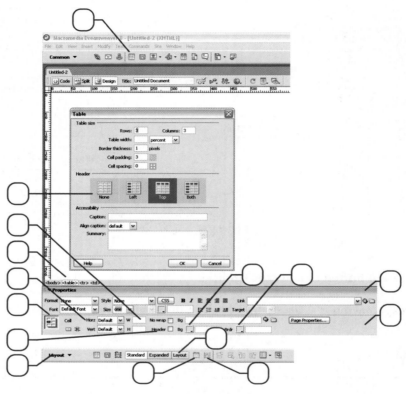

FIGURE 8.63

a. Table button

b. Text properties

c. Layout button

d. Layout Table button

e. Table dialog box

f. Cell icon

g. <table> tag

h. Draw Layout Cell button

i. Table properties

j. Horizontal/Vertical alignment

k. Border Color

l. Layout Insert bar indicator

m. Cell width/height

n. Cell background color box

o. Header cell option

MULTIPLE CHOICE

Circle the letter of the correct answer for each of the following:

1. Two tools you can use to create tables are the _____.
   a. Property inspector and Table dialog box
   b. Table dialog box and Tables panel
   c. Layout mode and Table dialog box
   d. All of the above

2. To use the free-form method of creating a table, you would use the _____.
   a. Table dialog box
   b. Layout mode
   c. Design mode
   d. Code view

3. Tables consist of _____.
   a. cells and borders
   b. columns and rows
   c. table data
   d. All of the above

4. The most popular use of a table in a Web page is _____.
   a. to generate frames
   b. to present tabular data
   c. to lay out components of a Web page
   d. to delimit text blocks

5. One problem with using tables is _____.
   a. they are not compatible with frames
   b. they require a large amount of HTML code
   c. tables must remain flush left in the Document window
   d. they must have a fixed size

6. Cell padding _____.
   a. is the same as cell spacing
   b. creates margin space inside a cell
   c. creates white space between cell borders
   d. can be applied differently to each cell in a table

7. Which would you find in the Tag selector?
   a. `<table><body><tr><td>`
   b. `<table><row><th>`
   c. `<table><tr><td>`
   d. `<table><caption><tr><td>`

8. Merging cells _____.
   a. uses the colspan and rowspan attributes
   b. combines adjacent cells
   c. allows tables to conform to design layout
   d. All of the above

9. Cells of a table _____.
   a. can have a background color or image
   b. can display framesets
   c. must have a fixed size
   d. None of the above

10. The Format Table function _____.
    a. can merge and split table cells
    b. offers predefined table styles
    c. is used to create new tables
    d. is identical to the Table dialog box

DISCUSSION QUESTIONS

1. Tables are the primary layout method for Web design. Both tables and frames offer methods for managing and displaying content in Web pages. What are the advantages of using tables over frames? What are the disadvantages? Provide an example of each and explain how it supports your argument.

2. You should consider accessibility before building a table. Explain why this statement is true and what types of considerations you must weigh before creating a table.

SKILL DRILL

Skill Drill exercises reinforce project skills. Each skill that is reinforced is the same as, or nearly the same as, a skill presented in the lessons. We provide detailed instructions in a step-by-step format. You can work through one or more exercises in any order.

1. Import Tabular Data into a Table

In this Skill Drill, you import data from a Microsoft Excel file into Dreamweaver. (You don't need Excel to complete this Skill Drill — the text has already been exported.) Dreamweaver can import text files saved from Excel or Access in the Comma Separated Value (*.csv) format and convert them to data tables. This process is not automated — you can't just update the text file and expect Dreamweaver to import the data automatically. However, it is useful for inserting tabular information without having to retype it.

1. Create a new HTML file.

2. In the document Title field, type `Weather Forecast`.

3. In the Document window, type `Weather Forecast`, format it as Heading 1, and press Enter/Return.

4. Choose File>Import>Tabular Data.

5. From the Import Tabular Data dialog box, click the browse button and choose weather.csv from the Chapter_08>Tables folder.

6. Set the Delimiter to Comma, Table Width to Fit to Data, set the Cell Padding to `3`, Cell Spacing to `0`, Format Top Row to No Formatting, and Border to `0`. Click OK.

7. Close the file, saving it as weather.html.

2. Make a Moderately Complex Table Accessible

In this Skill Drill, you modify an existing data table to make it accessible. It is much easier to make data accessible if you consider accessibility as you create the table and, conversely, more difficult and time-consuming to do so after creating the table. If accessibility is a requirement in your workplace, be sure to make it part of your original design specifications. In this exercise, you have information in an inaccessible table that requires the table-header cell tags with the **scope** attribute and a caption.

1. Open weather.html from the Tables site.

2. Add the **<caption>** tag and its contents by clicking the top-left cell of the table, clicking the Split button, moving the insertion point to the end of the opening **<table>** tag (to the right of the closing angle bracket), and pressing Enter/Return.

3. Type **<c** and press Enter/Return to accept **<caption>**. Type the closing angle bracket and then type `High Temperatures for the Week of May 16 to 20, 2004`. Type **</** to close the **<caption>** tag.

4. In the Design window, choose the cells from 16 to 20 in the top row, and check the Header box in the Property inspector. Select the cells from New York to Anchorage and make them header cells as well.

5. Click the 16 cell. In the Code window, click between **<th** and **>** in the opening **<th>** tag, press the Spacebar once, type **s**, press Enter/Return to accept **scope**, and type **col**.

6. Select the code you inserted (including the first space), copy the code, move the insertion point after **<th** in the opening **<th>** tag for the 17 cell, and paste. Paste the copied code into the opening **<th>** tags for the 18, 19, and 20 cells as well.

7. In the Design window, click the New York cell. In the Code window, insert **scope="row"** into the **<th>** tag for New York (don't forget the space before the **scope** attribute).

8. Copy the code you inserted in Step 7, click Los Angeles in the Design window, and paste the scope code into the **<th>** tag for the Los Angeles cell. Repeat the process for the Chicago, Houston, and Anchorage cells.

9. Close and save weather.html.

3. Create a Three-Column Layout Using Layout Tables

In this exercise, you create a multicolumn, table-based layout. Figure 8.64 illustrates the basic layout that you build in this exercise. In this Skill Drill, you use supplied styles. These styles assume that each cell in the layout table has specific ids, which you create.

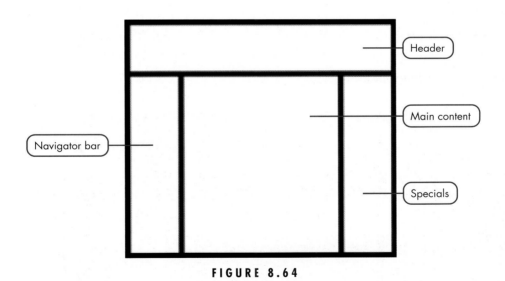

FIGURE 8.64

1. Create a new site definition called Carvers from the Project_08>Carver folder. Open index.html from the new Carvers site.

2. Click the Table button on the Common Insert bar and create a 2-row, 3-column table with a 100% width setting, 0-pixel border, 3-pixel cell padding, 0-pixel cell spacing, and no headers.

3. Drag to select the three cells in the top row, Right/Control-click the selected cells, and choose Table>Merge Cells.

4. From the images folder, insert carvers-logo.gif into the top row, and assign it Carver's Online as the alt text.

5. In the middle cell of the bottom row, type `Quality Products for Discriminating Customers`, format the block as Heading 2, and press Enter/Return. From the images folder, insert the family.jpg photo into the new paragraph, and assign it an empty alt. Press Enter/Return again and type `Shop at Carver's Online`.

6. Open leftnav.html, select all of the content (a table with graphics in each cell), copy the table, and close leftnav.html. In index.html, click the left cell of the bottom row and paste the copied table.

7. Using the same procedures as in Step 6, copy the table from specials.html into the right cell of this layout table.

8. Click the `<table>` tag to the immediate right of the `<body>` tag in the Tag selector. In the Property inspector, delete 100 from the Table Width field and press Enter/Return.

   This removes the table's width setting and allows the table to expand or contract based on its content.

9. Click the top cell and, from the Property inspector, set the cell's horizontal alignment to Center. Set the middle cell of the bottom row to centered-horizontal alignment and top-vertical alignment. Set both the left and right cells in the second row to top-vertical alignment.

10. To create the `id` for the first cell, click the top cell, Right/Control-click the `<td>` tag in the Tag selector, choose Set ID, and choose header from the list. Repeat this process to apply the correct ids to the other cells.

    Be careful with the specials cell. Apply the specials `id` to the `<td>` tag closest to the `<body>` tag—otherwise a cell in the nested table will be assigned that `id`, not the cell from the outer layout table.

11. Preview the page in your browser.

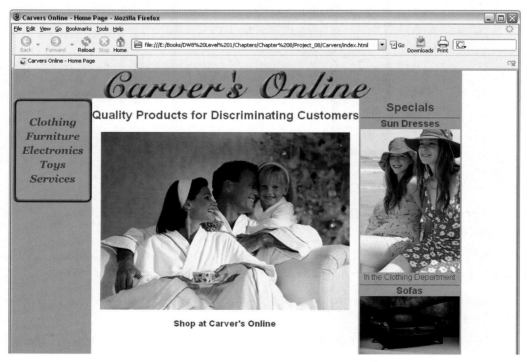

FIGURE 8.65

12.   Close your browser, return to Dreamweaver, and close index.html.

4. Reassemble a Sliced Graphic in a Layout-Mode Table

In this Skill Drill exercise, you place slices of a design into a layout table using the Layout mode. This type of table would be very difficult to create using the Standard mode because the spanning would be difficult to calculate. This is an ideal situation in which to use the Layout mode to create the layout table.

1.   Define a new site called Oranges from the Chapter_08>Oranges folder.

2.   Create a new HTML page, type `Orange Growers of Florida` in the Document Title field, and save the file as index.html.

3.   Switch the Insert bar to the Layout Insert bar, click the Layout button, and draw a layout table about half the width and half the height of the Document window. Click the Draw Layout Cell button, and in the top-left corner of this layout table, draw a cell that is about half the width and about one-third the height of the table.

4.   From the Files panel, drag orange-gro.gif from the images folder into the empty cell and assign it an empty alt.

5.   Click the Draw Layout Cell button again, and draw a cell to the right of the inserted graphic, but make it only about one-half the height of the other graphic. Insert wers-of-florida.gif into the new cell and assign it Orange Growers of Florida as the alt text. Draw a cell below the last one and insert home.gif with the alt text of Home.

6.   Draw eight more layout cells — four in the left column and four in the right column. In the right cells, from top to bottom, insert products.gif, services.gif, regions.gif, and contact_us.gif using Products, Services, Regions, and Contact Us as the alt text, respectively. In the left cells, from top to bottom, insert left-products.gif, left-services.gif, left-regions.gif, and left-contact_us.gif with empty alts for all.

7.   Move the mouse pointer so a red line surrounds the top-left (Orange Grow) graphic, and click the red line to display the cell handles. Drag the top handle up as much as possible, drag the right handle as far to the left as possible, and then drag the bottom handle up as much as possible. Repeat this for all cells in the left column and then from top to bottom in the right column to reduce the dimensions of each cell to the dimensions of the graphics they contain.

8.   Using the Draw Layout Cell button, create cells to the right of Home, Products, Services, Regions, and Contact Us, but not in any space that may exist below the last two graphics.

9. Move your mouse pointer to the bottom-right edge of the table and click the green line to make the table handles appear. Drag the bottom-right handle up and to the left to reduce the width and height of the table to the minimum.

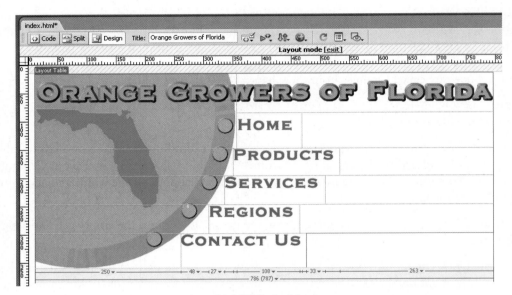

FIGURE 8.66

10. Click the Standard button to switch to Standard mode. Close, saving the changes to index.html.

5. Nest a Table in a Table Cell

Tables expand in width if their content is wider than the table. If you create a 2-column table that is 400 pixels wide and insert a 300-pixel-wide graphic in each of the two columns, the table does not remain 400 pixels wide but expands to fit both graphics. It becomes a 600-pixel-wide table — wider if the settings for border thickness, cell padding, or cell spacing are greater than 0. However, text wraps, so a large amount of text in a 200-pixel-wide cell does not force the cell to be wider, just taller.

If you place a series of graphics side by side in a paragraph, and if their total width is greater than the cell, one or more of the graphics is forced to a new line. However, if you place the graphics in their own cells in a table that is nested in the cell of another table, the outer table cell may be forced wider. Graphics can't be split and wrapped, nor can a table row. For this reason, many Web designers nest tables inside one another — the inner-table structure is rigid and forces the outer container to be wider if necessary.

In this exercise, you create a table nested in a cell of another table. You see why Web-site designers nest tables, despite the extra code that it creates.

1. Open index.html from the Carvers site and, if necessary, switch to Standard mode.

2. Click any of the cells in the bottom row, Right/Control-click, choose Tables>Insert Rows or Columns, and insert one row below the selection.

3. Click the middle cell of the new bottom row, Right/Control-click the `<td>` tag in the Tag selector, and set the `id` to `footer`.

4. Open bottomnav-paragraph.html from the Files panel.

There are seven graphics in a row with no spaces between them — the five graphics with text and the two end graphics.

5. Select all of the content, copy it, and close bottomnav-paragraph.html. With the insertion point in the footer cell, paste the copied content.

    Some of the graphics split from the others because the cell is too narrow for them all to fit on one line.

6. Undo the insertion of the graphics.

7. With the insertion point in the footer cell, create a new table with `1` row, `7` columns, `100`% table width, `0` border thickness, `0` cell padding, `0` cell spacing, and no headers, caption, or summary.

8. Insert bottomnav_r1_c1.gif into the first cell with an empty alt. Insert bottomnav_r1_c2.gif into the second cell (apply the appropriate alt text). Continue to insert the graphics into the cells in order of the "c" number applying the appropriate alt text except the last one, which should be an empty alt.

    As you near the end of the step, notice that the middle row becomes wider. Table rows cannot wrap or they would wrap to another row. Therefore, if a table row is wider than its container, the table forces the container to widen. In this case, the middle column is forced wider.

9. Close, saving the changes.

6. Align Tables for Layout

Aligning tables has two significant effects. The obvious effect is to place the table to the left, right, or center of its container. Of course, alignment only applies if the table is less than 100% of the width of the container.

The other effect is that you can place two or more tables beside each other, thereby creating another way to use tables for layout. The drawback to this method is that if the browser window is too narrow, the two tables do not stay beside each other — the right one shifts below the left one rather than remaining beside it. The advantage to this application of table alignment is that it can reduce the number of nested tables, thus the amount of code. Secondly, if each table is a separate entity, the browser can more quickly display the separate tables, rather than waiting for one large one with multiple nested tables. In this exercise, you create a layout using separate tables rather than an outer layout table containing nested tables.

1. Create a new site called GMMS-08 from the Chapter_08>GMMS-08 folder.

2. Open index.html.

3. Create a 1 × 1 table that is `780` pixels wide, with `0` border width, `0` cell padding, and `0` cell spacing. From the images folder, insert gmms.png into the empty cell with the alternate text `Golden Meadows Medical School`.

4. Click to the right of the table. Open navbar.html, select all, copy, and close the file. Paste to insert the table.

    Depending on its width, your browser window may be able to fit both the 780-pixel-wide logo table and the 140-pixel-wide navigation-bar table side by side. However, by default, the navigation-bar table always repositions below the logo-graphic table.

5. Open main.html. Click the small nested table with the university logos and map. Click the `<table#map>` tag to the right of the `<body>` tag in the Tag selector. In the Property inspector, set the table alignment to Right.

The smaller nested table floats to the right; the text below it shifts up and flows to the left of the table.

6. Select and copy all of the content of the page. Close, saving the changes to this page.

7. In index.html, click to the right of the navigation-bar table and paste to insert the table from main.html.

8. Click the navigation-bar table, click the `<table#navbar>` tag in the Tag selector, and set the alignment to left.

   With the navigation-bar table aligned to the left, the main table can float up to its right.

9. Close, saving the changes.

CHALLENGE

Challenge exercises expand on, or are somewhat related to, skills presented in the lessons. Each exercise provides a brief introduction, followed by numbered-step instructions that are not as detailed as those in the Skill Drill exercises. You should work through these exercises in order.

1. Create a Complex Accessible Table

Complex accessible tables have three or more logical levels of headers. The **scope** attribute does not suffice to relate a data cell to its header cells. You must use another pair of attributes: **id** and **headers**. You used the **id** attribute earlier with CSS. The ids do not have to be words but can be brief or codelike; for instance, in a chart of months, you could put ja in place of january. However, the headers must match the ids.

When a screen reader speaks the headers of the selected data cell, it does not read the contents of the headers attributes. It matches the headers in the headers attributes with the ids of the header cells and speaks the contents of the table-header cells. In this Challenge exercise, you create an accessible browser-statistics chart. You explore some of the challenges of creating complex tables, which may cause you to redesign any that are supplied for sites on which you work. Dreamweaver does not provide any means of creating and matching ids and headers in the Design window. You must create it all in the Code window.

1. Open complex-data.html from the Tables site. 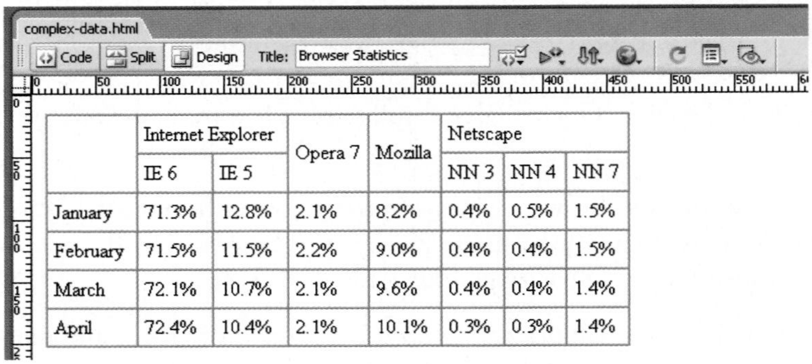

	Internet Explorer		Opera 7	Mozilla	Netscape		
	IE 6	IE 5			NN 3	NN 4	NN 7
January	71.3%	12.8%	2.1%	8.2%	0.4%	0.5%	1.5%
February	71.5%	11.5%	2.2%	9.0%	0.4%	0.4%	1.5%
March	72.1%	10.7%	2.1%	9.6%	0.4%	0.4%	1.4%
April	72.4%	10.4%	2.1%	10.1%	0.3%	0.3%	1.4%

FIGURE 8.67

2.   Select the top two rows and make them header cells by clicking the Header check box in the Property inspector. Select the left column and make the cells header cells.

3.   Click the Split button, then click the Internet Explorer cell in the Design window.

4.   In the Code window, place the insertion point between the **rowspan="2"** and the **>**, press the Spacebar, and type `id="ie"`. Using the same basic technique, assign o7, moz, nn, ie6, ie5, nn3, nn4, and nn7 as the ids for the respective cells across the top. Assign j, f, m, and a as the ids of the month cells down the left.

5.   Click the 71.3% cell in the Design window; in the Code window, place the insertion point between the **d** and **>**, press the Spacebar, and type `headers="ie ie6 j"` to relate the cell to Internet Explorer, IE6, and January. One by one, assign the **headers** attribute to all of the table-data cells, relating the data cell to the ids in the header cells above and to the left.

6.   Close, saving the changes.

2. Minimize Reliance on Tables for Layout

There are current techniques that replace tables for layout, but not all browsers support these features. In Chapter 2, you learned the importance of planning your Web sites. If your plans target people who are likely to use current browsers, then you may employ the latest techniques and features in your designs. Other sites, however, attract users with a wider range of browser versions. Contrary to the chart of browser statistics in the previous exercise (which represents a current, high-technology Web site), the Ontario government Web sites, for example, find that 11 – 12% of their visitors use Netscape 4 browsers. You may have to modify some of your techniques so that your client does not lose customers or visitors who use older browsers.

In this Challenge exercise, you learn to apply a mixture of tables and CSS, including some commonly supported CSS properties. This mixture enables you to reduce the code and speed up delivery of your Web pages. (You also better prepare the site for later removal of all tables.) To do this, you eliminate all nested tables and replace them with structures that are lighter in code. You then re-create the appearance. In this exercise, you replace one nested table, but by further applying the same technique, you could eliminate all nested tables. The result here is similar to the look of the original nested table, but with a savings of 4,904 bytes.

1.   Open index.html from the Carvers site.

2.   Click the Clothing graphic in the left cell, click the **<table>** tag to the right of **<td#navbar>** in the Tag selector, and press Delete.

3.   Click the Unordered List button in the Property inspector, and create a five-item list consisting of Clothing, Furniture, Electronics, Toys, and Services.

4.   Right/Control-click in the CSS Styles panel and choose New. Choose the Selector Type of Advanced, type **td#navbar ul** in the Selector field, and click OK.

5.   Choose the List category, set Type to None, and click Apply.

6.   In the Box category in the Margin group, leave the Same for All option checked, and type 0 (zero) in the Top field. In the Padding group, leave the Same for All option checked, type 0 (zero) in the Top field, and choose pixels. Click Apply.

7.   In the Type category, choose Times New Roman, Times, serif from the Font list; x-large from the Size list; Bold from the Weight list; and Italic from the Style list. Set the Color to #993300. Click Apply.

8. In the Block category, set Text Align to Center and click Apply.

9. In the Background category, choose ul-bg.gif from the images folder and click Apply.

10. Return to the Box category. Set Width to 158 pixels and Height to 177 pixels. Remove the check from Same for All in the Padding Group, and set Top to 37 pixels. Click Apply.

11. Close, saving the changes.

3. Use CSS for Table Styles

In Lesson 5, you learned to apply presentational HTML tags and attributes to create a style or look for the television-program table. In this Challenge exercise, you create the same appearance using CSS instead. Just as you saw in the previous Challenge exercise, using CSS results in a reduction in code and thus in a faster downloading time. It also allows you to more effectively apply and control the look of the table and cells. Compared with the results of Lesson 5, this exercise results in an HTML page that is 54% smaller — 2,577 bytes vs. 5,616 bytes. Even with the CSS file of 598 bytes, the total (3,175 bytes) is still 43% less than the HTML page created in Lesson 5.

Another comparison between presentational HTML and CSS is the ease with which you can apply CSS. In Lesson 5, you learned that to change the text and background colors of all favorite cells, you must select them and then make the changes. If you missed one, it would not take on the color change. With CSS, the process is much easier: just assign a class to a cell and the CSS styles apply to them. Want to change the style? Just change it in the CSS Styles dialog box and the change applies to any instance in which the CSS class was applied.

1. Open tv-schedule.html from the Tables site.

2. Right/Control-click the CSS Styles panel and choose Attach Style Sheet. Click the Browser button, choose tv.css, click OK/Choose, and then click OK again.

3. Move the mouse pointer to the left of the top row until it changes to a right-pointing cursor and the cells in the row are outlined in red — click to select the row. In the Tag selector, Right/Control-click the **<tr>** tag and set the Class to top-row.

4. Click in the CTV cell, Right/Control-click the **<tr>** tag in the Tag selector, and set Class to row1. Repeat this for the TLC, WN, and ABC rows. Using the same procedure, apply the class **<row2>** to the CBC, TVO, and YTV **<tr>** tags.

5. Control/Command-click the Cable cell, and then Shift-click the ABC cell. If necessary, click the plus symbol to the left of tv.css in the CSS Styles panel to display the list of styles. Right/Control-click td.stations in the CSS Styles panel, and choose Apply from the contextual menu.

6. Click the Vicki Gabereau cell, Shift-click the General Hospital cell (bottom-right corner), Right/Control-click td.programs in the CSS Styles panel, and choose Apply.

7. Control/Command-click each of the Road to Avonlea, Oswald, and Rupert cells; Right/Control-click td.favorites in the CSS Styles panel; and choose Apply.

8. Create a new CSS Style to change the background of the table to black by Right/Control-clicking in the CSS Styles panel, choosing New, setting the Selector Type to Tag, typing or choosing table in the Tag list, and clicking OK. In the Background category, set the background-color to black and click OK.

9. Right/Control-click td.favorite in the CSS Styles panel and choose Edit. In the Background category, set the background color to #CC4400. In the Type category, set the color to #FFFFFF. Click OK.

10. Close, saving the changes.

PORTFOLIO BUILDER

CREATE A GALLERY OF ZOO ANIMALS

A local zoo has hired your company to create a photo gallery of animal attractions. Your assignment is to create a table-based site that offers small thumbnail images of each animal with a link to a larger image. The larger, high-resolution images should open in their own windows, leaving the primary table-based page intact.

1. Do some research on zoo sites to see how other designers approached the problem. Pick one that you like and use it as the basis for your design.

2. Create a page with a table, reserving cells for navigation elements and cells to hold the thumbnail images.

3. Split the page into three categories: one for primates, one for reptiles, and one for birds. Add or remove cells as necessary, and use nested tables where required.

4. Find images to use for populating the site. Since this is only an exercise and the site isn't destined for commercial use, you might consider right-clicking images you see on other sites and saving them into the folder containing the assignment pages.

5. Once it's completed, check to make sure everything works as intended.

6. Compare your design to the others you found during your research. Note what's good and bad about your site compared to the others.

INTEGRATING PROJECT

This integrating project reflects a real-world Web site job, drawing on the skills you learned throughout this book. The files you need to complete this project are in the RF_Dreamweaver_L1>IP folder.

Independence Hummer Web Site

The management of Independence Hummer, a car dealership, has hired you to recreate their existing Web site. While this site actually exists (IndependenceHummer.com, graphics and photos used by permission), for the purposes of this project, imagine you are on the Web team creating the site. The client has supplied the information and the images and has approved the design concepts. The team has planned the basic strategy for creating the site and has assembled the components. The final site will feature a frames-based layout that includes tables within the individual pages, as well as text and graphic links.

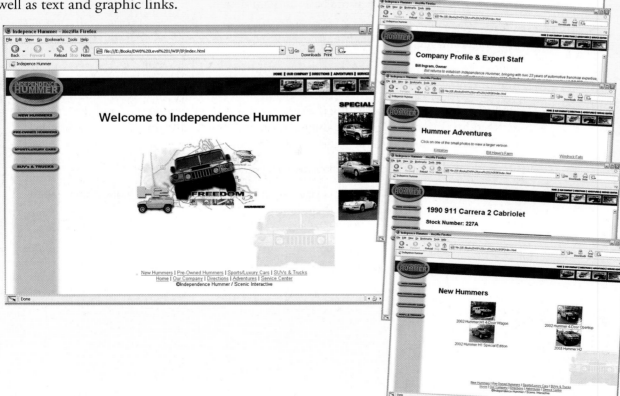

PART 1   Creating the Frames and the Home Page

In this section, you create the pages that appear in the frames that surround the main-content area of the frameset. You create the home page, which later becomes a nested frameset, and then create the main frameset that binds together all of the frames.

Create the Left Page

1   Create a site definition called "Independence Hummer" using the WIP>IP folder.

2   Create a new basic HTML page, title it "Left Navigation", and save it as "left.html" (but do not close the file).

3   Create a 5-row, 1-column table. Set the width to 159 pixels, border to 0, Cell Padding to 0, Cell Spacing to 0, and Header to None. Click OK.

Whenever you use a layout table in this integrating project, apply the same border, cell padding, cell spacing, and header settings as used in Step 3.

4   From top to bottom, insert the following images from the IP>images folder. (All images in this section of the integrating project are from the IP>images folder.)

> logomain.jpg
>
> menu_newhummers.jpg
>
> menu_preownedhummers.jpg
>
> menu_sportsluxury.jpg
>
> menu_suvstrucks.jpg

Insert one image per table cell. Assign appropriate alternate text for each image. (Not knowing the text content on some of the images until you can see them, you may set the alt text from the Property inspector after inserting the image.) Set the vertical spacing of the bottom four images to 10 pixels.

5   Create a new CSS style for this document for the **body** Tag selector for This Document Only. In the Box category, set all margins to 0 pixels. In the Background category, set the Background Image to bgmenu.jpg, set Repeat to **repeat-y**, and click OK.

All CSS styles in this project use the Define in This Document Only option.

6   Close left.html, saving the changes.

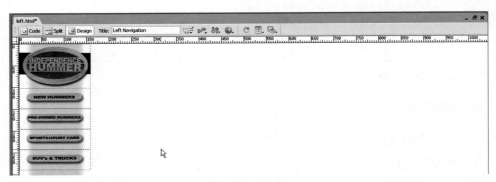

FIGURE IP.1

Create the Top Page

1   Create a new HTML page, title it "Top Navigation", and save it as "top.html" (but don't close the file).

2   Create a 2-row, 1-column layout table with a width of 100%.

3   Insert the following graphics into the top cell in this order, and assign appropriate alternate text for each graphic:

    top_home.jpg

    top_ourcompany.jpg

    top_directions.jpg

    top_adventures.jpg

    top_service.jpg

    top_privacy.jpg

4   In the bottom cell, insert top_pics.jpg. Assign it an empty alt.

5   Create a new CSS style for the **body** Tag selector for This Document Only. In the Box category, set all margins to 0 pixels. In the Background category, set the Background Image to bgtop.jpg and set the Repeat option to **repeat-x**. Click OK.

6   Create another new CSS style for the **td** Tag selector. In the Block category, set the Text Align to **right**. Click OK.

7   Close the file, saving your changes.

FIGURE IP.2

Create the Bottom Page

1 Create a new HTML page, title it "Bottom Navigation", and save it as "bottom.html" (but do not close the file).

2 Type `New Hummers | Pre-Owned Hummers | Sports/Luxury Cars | SUVs & Trucks`, and press Enter/Return.

Create the " | " (pipe) character by pressing the Shift key and typing the " \ " character.

3 Type `Home | Our Company | Directions | Adventures | Service Center`, and press Enter/Return. Insert the Copyright character from the Text Insert bar Character list, and then type `Independence Hummer / Scenic Interactive`.

Scenic Interactive is the name of the Web-design agency that originally built this Web site. You may substitute your name in place of Scenic Interactive.

4 Create a new CSS style for this document for the **p** Tag selector for This Document Only. In the Type category, choose Arial, Helvetica, sans-serif from the Font list and set the Size to **small**. In the Block category, set Text Align to **center**. In the Box category, set all margins to 0 pixels, and then click OK.

5 Close the file, saving your changes.

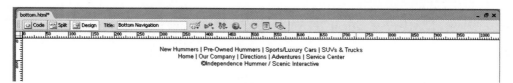

FIGURE IP.3

Create the Main Page

The home page will be a nested frameset containing the main page and a specials page. You create the main page first, then develop the specials page, and then create the frameset page.

1 Create a new HTML page, title it "Main Page", and save it as "main.html".

2 Type `Welcome to Independence Hummer` and set the Format to Heading 1.

3 Press Enter/Return, insert main_body.jpg, and assign the image an empty alt.

4 Create a new CSS style for this document for the **body** Tag selector for This Document Only. In the Type category, choose Arial, Helvetica, sans-serif from the Font list. In the Background category, choose bgbody.jpg as the Background Image, set Repeat to **no-repeat**, Horizontal Position to **right**, Vertical Position to **bottom**, and Attachment to **fixed**, and then click OK.

5 Create a new CSS style for this document for the **h1** Tag selector for This Document Only. In the Block category, set Text Align to **center** and click OK.

6 Create a new CSS style for this document for the **p** Tag selector for This Document Only. In the Block category, set Text Align to **center** and click OK.

7   Close the file, saving your changes.

FIGURE IP.4

Create the Specials Page

1   Create a new HTML page, title it "Current Specials", and save it as "specials.html".

2   Create a 4-row, 1-column layout table. Set the width to 130 pixels.

3   In the top cell, insert specials.jpg and add the appropriate alt text.

4   In the remaining cells, insert the following images from the IP>vehicles>images folder:

Filename	Alt text
suv_0201sm.jpg	2000 Toyota 4Runner
sl_0229sm.jpg	1998 Mercedes CLK 320
sl_0227asm.jpg	1990 Porsche 911 Carrera

5   Apply 10 pixels of horizontal spacing and 10 pixels of vertical spacing to each of the three car photos.

6   Create a new CSS Style for this document for the **body** Tag selector in This Document Only. In the Box category, set all margins to 0 pixels and click OK.

7   Close the file, saving your changes.

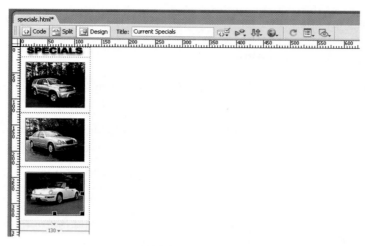

FIGURE IP.5

Create the Home-Page Frameset

1 Create a new Frameset from the Fixed Right predefined layout and set the mainFrame title to Main and the rightFrame title to Specials.

2 Type `Home Frameset` in the Document title, and save the frameset page as "home.html".

3 Using the RowCol Selection area in the Property inspector, click the right frame, and set the column width to 130 pixels.

4 Press Shift-F2 to open the Frames panel.

5 Click the right frame in the Frames panel, and in the Property inspector, name the frame "specials". Set specials.html as the source of the frame.

6 Click the left frame in the Frames panel, and in the Property inspector, name the frame "main". Set main.html as the source of the frame.

FIGURE IP.6

7 Close home.html, saving your changes.

Create the Primary Frameset

1 Create a new frameset page using Fixed Left as the template and set the mainFrame title to Main Frameset and the leftFrame title to Left Navigation.

2 Type `Independence Hummer` in the Document title field, and save the frameset as "index.html".

3 Rename the left frame "leftnav", resize it to 159 pixels wide, and set its source to left.html.

4 Select the larger frame in the Frames panel.

5 From the Frames button on the Layout Insert bar, choose Top and Bottom Frames and set the topFrame title to Top Navigation and the bottomFrame title to Bottom Navigation.

6 Rename the top frame "top", resize it to 88 pixels high, and set the source to top.html.

7 Rename the bottom frame "bottom", resize it to 75 pixels high, and set the source to bottom.html.

8 Rename the middle frame "main" and set the source to home.html.

9 Save the changes to index.html and leave it open for the next exercise.

FIGURE IP.7

Evaluate the Frameset Scroll Options

1 Preview index.html in your browser.

2 Resize your browser both in width and height. Observe the scroll bars and determine whether or not they are necessary.

When you create custom frame layouts in Dreamweaver, the scroll bars may not be set correctly. You must ensure that when viewed in a small browser window, all of the content may be accessible. If the scroll bar setting is Auto, the scroll bars can appear when not needed; if they are set to No, scroll bars are prevented from appearing when they are needed.

F I G U R E   I P . 8

3 Return to Dreamweaver.

4 If you need to modify the Scroll option for any of the frames, click the frame in the Frames panel and change the Scroll option in the Property inspector.

5 If you made changes to the Scroll option for any of the frames, preview index.html in your browser and review your changes.

6 Return to Dreamweaver and close index.html.

PART 2   Creating Vehicle-Category Pages

In this section, you create one page for each of the four categories of vehicles: New Hummers, Pre-Owned Hummers, Sport/Luxury Cars, and SUVs/Trucks. You create a template page, and then use that template to build pages with information for each vehicle. You do not work with the frameset in the next few exercises, so you can close the Frames panel if you wish.

Create the Category Template

1   Create a new HTML page, title it `Category Template`, and save it as "category-template.html" in the IP>vehicles folder.

2   Type `Vehicle Category` at the top of the page, and set the Format as Heading 1.

3   Create a 2 × 2 cell layout table with a width of 100%.

4   Click the top-right cell, and create a 110 × 110 pixel image placeholder with the name "vehicle_photo"; assign any color and assign "photo" as the alt text.

5   Click to the right of the image placeholder, press Enter/Return, and type `Vehicle Description`.

6   Copy the text and image placeholder, and paste them into the three empty cells.

7   Create a new CSS style for the **body** Tag selector for This Document Only. In the Type category, set the Font to Arial, Helvetica, sans-serif. In the Background category, choose IP>images>bgbody.jpg as the Background Image, set Repeat to **no-repeat**, Horizontal Position to **right**, Vertical Position to **bottom**, and Attachment to **fixed**. In the Box category, set all margins to 40 pixels and click OK.

8   Create a new CSS style for the **p** Tag selector for This Document Only. In the Block category, set the Text Align to **center**. In the Box category, uncheck Same for All for the margins, and set both Top and Bottom margins to 0 pixels. Click OK.

9   Close the file, saving your changes.

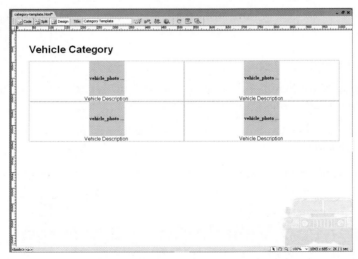

FIGURE IP.9

Build Category Pages from the Template

1   Open category-template.html and save it as "new-hummers.html" in the IP>vehicles folder.

2   Change both the document title and Heading 1 text to "New Hummers".

3 Replace the four image placeholders with the images identified in the following table. In all cases, the image filenames end with sm.jpg (thumbnail images), and the images are in the IP>vehicles>images folder. Replace the Vehicle Description text with the text provided below.

Placeholder	Image	Description
1	nh_0107sm.jpg	2002 Hummer H1 4-Door Wagon
2	nh_0203sm.jpg	2002 Hummer 4-Door Opentop
3	nh_0271sm.jpg	2002 Hummer H1 Special Edition
4	nh_h2h2sm.jpg	2003 Hummer H2

4 Close new-hummers.html, saving your changes.

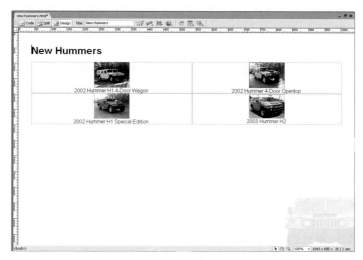

FIGURE IP.10

5 Open category-template.html and save it as "preowned-hummers.html".

6 Change both the document title and Heading 1 text to "Pre-Owned Hummers".

7 Applying the same procedures as you used in Step 3, use the following information to complete the page. When you finish, close the page, saving your changes.

Placeholder	Image	Description
1	poh_0104sm.jpg	1993 Hummer H1 4-Door Opentop
2	poh_0145sm.jpg	2001 Hummer H1 4-Door Opentop
3	poh_0206sm.jpg	2000 Hummer H1 4-Door Wagon
4	poh_0218sm.jpg	1995 Hummer H1 4-Door Opentop

8   Create "sports-luxury.html" from the category-template.html page. Change the document title and Heading 1 to "Sports and Luxury Vehicles". Use the following information to complete the page. When you finish, close the page, saving your changes.

Placeholder	Image	Description
1	sl_0140sm.jpg	1994 Red Lotus Esprit G4
2	sl_0227asm.jpg	1990 Porsche 911 Carrera 2
3	sl_0229sm.jpg	1998 Mercedes CLK 320
4	sl_0247sm.jpg	1997 Mercedes-Benz E320

9   Create "suvs-trucks.html" from the category-template.html page. Change the document title and Heading 1 to "SUVs and Trucks". Use the following information to complete the page. When you finish, close the page, saving your changes.

Placeholder	Image	Description
1	suv_0201sm.jpg	2000 Toyota 4Runner Limited
2	suv_0219sm.jpg	1999 Lexus LX470
3	suv_0246sm.jpg	1993 Land Rover Defender 90
4	suv_0313sm.jpg	1999 Land Rover 4.6 HSE

PART 3   Building Vehicle-Detail Pages

In this section, you apply the same methodology you used to create the category pages. You create a template for an individual vehicle page, and then use that template to create the specific pages. Given that there are 16 vehicles in the site (4 per category), 12 of the vehicle-detail pages were created for you. Your task is to create the detail pages for the New Hummers category.

Create the Vehicle-Detail Template Page

1   Create a new HTML page, title it "Detail Vehicle Template", and save the page as "detail-template.html" in the IP>vehicles folder.

2   Type `Vehicle Name` and set the Format as Heading 1. Press Enter/Return, and type `Stock Number: 1234`; set the Format as Heading 2, and press Enter/Return.

3 Create a 1-row, 3-column layout table with a width of 100%. Select all three cells, set the vertical alignment to **top**, and set the width to 33%. Click the middle cell and set the horizontal alignment to **center**.

4 In the left cell, type **Specifications**, set the Format as Heading 3, and press Enter/Return. Create a definition list (click "dl" in the Text Insert bar) and type **Exterior Color**. Press Enter/Return and type **xxx**.

5 Continue to create the definition list, making the following blocks of text the definition terms —"Interior Color:", "Make:", "Model:", "Year:", and "Price:"— use "xxx" as the definition description.

6 In the right cell, type **Features**, set the Format as Heading 3, and press Enter/Return. Create an unordered list and type **engine**.

7 In the middle cell, insert a 250 × 250 image placeholder with the name "vehicle_photo" and the alt text "photo".

8 Create a new CSS style for the **body** Tag selector for This Document Only. From the Type category, set the Font to Arial, Helvetica, sans-serif. In the Background category, choose IP>images>bgbody.jpg as the Background Image, set Repeat to **no-repeat**, Horizontal Position to **right**, Vertical Position to **bottom**, and Attachment to **fixed**. In the Box category, set all margins to 40 pixels and click OK.

9 Create a new CSS style for the **dt** Tag selector. In the Type category, set the Weight to Bold and click OK.

10 Create a new CSS style for the **dd** Tag selector. In the Type category, set the Style to Italic and click OK.

11 Create a new CSS style for the **ul** Tag selector. In the Type category, set the Style to Italic and click OK.

12 Close the file, saving your changes.

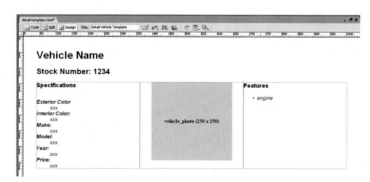

FIGURE IP.11

Build Details Pages from the Template

1 Create a new folder called "newhummers" below the IP>vehicles folder.

It should appear with the other category folders.

2 Open detail-template.html and save it as "nh_0107.html" in the IP>vehicles>newhummers folder.

If prompted to Update links, click No: there are none yet.

3 Change both the document title and Heading 1 text to "2002 Hummer H1 4-Door Wagon", and change the stock number to "107".

4 Replace the image placeholder with nh_0107lg.jpg from the IP>vehicles>images folder, and assign it an empty alt.

5 Replacing the "xxx" in each case, change the Exterior Color to "White", Interior Color to "Tan", Make to "Hummer", Model to "H1 4-Door Wagon", Year to "2002", and Price to "$111,302".

6 Under Features, create an unordered list with the following list items: "V8 6.5L Turbo Diesel", "Automatic", "4-Wheel Drive", "Luxury Package", "All Power Options".

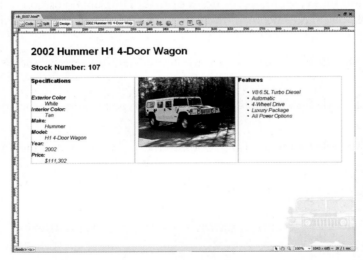

FIGURE IP.12

7 Close the file, saving your changes.

8 Repeat Steps 2–7 using the following information to create the three remaining vehicle-detail pages.

Filename	**nh_0203.html**	**nh_0271.html**	**nh_h2h2.html**
Document Title	2002 Hummer 4-Door Opentop	2002 Hummer H1 Special Edition	2003 Hummer H2
Stock #	203	271	H2h2
Image	nh_0203lg.jpg	nh_0271lg.jpg	nh_h2h2lg.jpg
Specifications	Pewter, Tan, Hummer, H1 4-Door Opentop, 2002, $104,049	Bronze Metallic, Tan Hummer, H1 10th Anniversary Edition, 2002, $116,560	Pewter, Gray, Hummer, H2, 2003, $56,500
Features	V8 6.5L Turbo Diesel, Automatic, ABS, Air Conditioning, Full-Time 4WD, Brush Guard, Towing Package, Heated Mirrors, Heated Windshield, Keyless Entry, Monsoon Stereo with CD, Aluminum Wheels	Anniversary Special Edition (#4 of 65), First One Released to the Public for Sale after Arnold Schwarzennegger, First H1 to Offer Factory Leather, Heated Seats, Wood-Grain Panels	V8 5.0 liter, Automatic, 4Wheel Drive, Adventure Package, Towing Package, Alloy Wheels, Roof Rack

PART 4   Creating Common Pages

Common pages are those pages to which every page links, such as the Privacy Policy, Directions, and Service Center pages. Your task is to create and format these pages for the Independence Hummer Web site. For this section, the text is in the IP>common folder, and the images are in the IP>common>images folder. The text is in MS Word format, ready for you to import and format. Save all pages you create in this section in the IP>common folder.

Create the Service-Center Page

1 Create a new HTML page, title it "Service Center", and save it as "service.html".

2 Windows users: Import service.doc into this empty page.

Macintosh users: Open service.txt, select and copy all of the text, close service.txt, and paste into the empty page.

3 Select the top line and format it as Heading 1.

4 Format the address line using the **<address>** tag (Common Insert bar, Tag Chooser button).

5 In the address block, insert line breaks in front of Charlotte, Phone, and Fax.

6 Create a new CSS style for the **body** Tag selector in This Document Only. Set the font to Arial, Helvetica, sans-serif. Set the Background Image to IP>images>bgbody.jpg, set Repeat to **no-repeat**, Horizontal Position to **right**, Vertical Position to **bottom**, and Attachment to **fixed**.

7 Close the file, saving your changes.

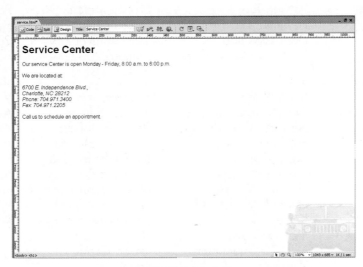

FIGURE IP.13

Create the Directions Page

1 Create a new HTML page, title it "Directions to Independence Hummer", and save it as "directions.html" (but do not close the page).

2 Windows users: Import directions.doc into this empty page.

Macintosh users: Open directions.txt, select and copy all of the text, close directions.txt, and paste into the empty page.

3 Format the top line as Heading 1.

4 Format the address with the **<address>** tag as you did in Step 3 of the previous exercise. Insert a line break in front of Charlotte, Phone, and Fax.

5 Insert ih_map.gif, using "Map" as the alt text, at the beginning of the first paragraph of directions, and align the image to the left.

6 Create a new CSS style for the **body** Tag selector in This document only. Set the font to Arial, Helvetica, sans-serif. Set the Background Image to IP>images>bgbody.jpg, Repeat to **no-repeat**, Horizontal Position to **right**, Vertical Position to **bottom**, and Attachment to **fixed**.

7 Close the file, saving your changes.

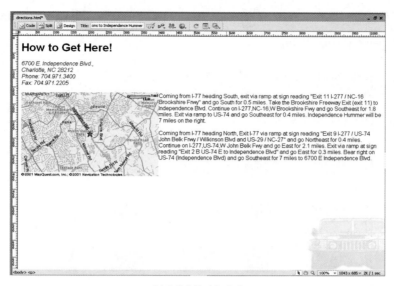

FIGURE IP.14

Create the Adventures Page

1 Create a new HTML page, title it "Hummer Adventures", and save it as "adventures.html".

2 Type `Hummer Adventures` and format it as Heading 1. Press Enter/Return. Type `Click on one of the small photos to view a larger version.` and press Enter/Return.

3 Create a 1-row, 3-column layout table with a width of 100%. Select all three cells and set the horizontal alignment to **center**. In the left cell, type `Kinzalow`; in the center cell, type `Bill Hawe's Farm`; and in the right cell, type `Windrock Falls`.

4 Below the table, type `Kinzalow` and format it as Heading 2. Insert an named anchor named "kinzalow" in front of the text you just typed.

5 Create a 1-row, 5-column layout table with a width of 100%. Select all five cells, and set the horizontal alignment to **center** and width to 20%. Insert into the table cells the small Kinzalow photos from the images folder (they all begin with kinzalow and end in sm.jpg) and apply "Kinzalow Photo 1", changing the number each time, as the alt text. Proportionately resize and resample the images so they are 100 pixels wide.

6 Repeat Steps 4 and 5 twice, using "Bill Hawe's Farm" and "Windrock Falls" as the Heading 2 text and "billhawes" and "windrock" as the named anchor names. After each of the two headings, create a 1-row, 5-column table and insert the appropriate sm.jpg photos (using "Bill Hawe's Farm Photo 1" and "Windrock Falls Photo 1" as the patterns for the alt texts), resizing and resampling all images.

7 Create links from each small photo to the larger version of the photo (same filename except it ends with lg.jpg).

You won't be creating Web pages for each photo, just links to the photos.

8 Create a new CSS style for the **body** Tag selector in This Document Only. Set the font to Arial, Helvetica, sans-serif. Set the Background Image to IP>images>bgbody.jpg, set Repeat to **no-repeat**, Horizontal Position to **right**, Vertical Position to **bottom**, and Attachment to **fixed**.

9 Close the file, saving your changes.

FIGURE IP.15

Create the Privacy Page

1 Create a new HTML page, title it "Privacy Policy of Independence Hummer", and save it as "privacy.html". Import privacy.doc (Windows) or privacy.txt (Macintosh) into this empty page.

2 Format the top line as Heading 1.

3 You may use either of two methods to format the rest of the page. Either format each short block of text as Heading 2 or create a definition list in which the short blocks of text are the definition terms and the paragraphs below are definition descriptions.

Either is appropriate document structure for this text.

4 Create a new CSS style for the **body** Tag selector. Set the font to Arial, Helvetica, sans-serif. Set the Background Image to IP>images>bgbody.jpg, set Repeat to **no-repeat**, Horizontal Position to **right**, Vertical Position to **bottom**, and Attachment to **fixed**.

5 If you chose to use a definition list, create the following two styles (otherwise skip to Step 6). Create a new CSS style for the **dt** Tag selector. In the Type category, set the Weight to Bold and click OK. Create a new CSS style for the **dd** Tag selector. In the Type category, set the Style to Italic and click OK.

6 Close the file, saving your changes.

Create the Company Page

In this exercise, the staff names, title, photos, and descriptions are provided. You may lay out the staff directory page as you see fit. You might use a table, paragraphs, or a list if you feel that is appropriate. You could use a nested frameset, as you did in Chapter 7. You could create JavaScript pop-up pages using the JavaScript code you learned in Challenge 4 of Chapter 5. You might align the photos to the left, right, or alternating, and could even resize and/or crop them if you find them too large.

1 Create a new HTML page, title it "Independence Hummer Staff Directory", and save it as "company.html" (do not close the page).

2 Type `Company Profile & Expert Staff` and format it as Heading 1.

3 Create a new CSS style for the **body** Tag selector. Set the font to Arial, Helvetica, sans-serif. Set the Background Image to IP>images>bgbody.jpg, set Repeat to **no-repeat**, Horizontal Position to **right**, Vertical Position to **bottom**, and Attachment to **fixed**.

4 Create a new HTML page and import company.doc (Windows) or company.txt (Macintosh) into the empty page. Examine the information, consider various layout options, choose one you would like to use, and create it.

Remember, if you use one method for creating multiple pages, give each page a document title and a Heading 1 block that identifies the purpose of the page. You may want to repeat Step 3 for each page to keep the styles the same for all pages. You may also want to create a template page first and then build the specific pages from the template.

5 When you are finished, close, saving the page (or pages).

PART 5   Linking the Pages

In this final exercise, you create the links that enable your visitors to navigate the pages on your Independence Hummer Web site. You first create the links from the initial frameset pages and then create the links from the vehicle-category pages. As often as you feel is necessary, preview in your browser and test the links to ensure that they open the correct pages in the correct frames.

Create Links from the Initial Frameset Pages

1 Open index.html.

2 Create links from the bottom four graphics in the left frame to open the appropriate category pages in the main frame.

(Remember to use the **<base />** tag to assign a target when most or all links in a page use the same target.)

3 Create links from the text graphics in the top frame to the appropriate pages (in the IP>common folder), so they open in the main frame.

4 Create links from the text in the bottom frame to the appropriate pages, so they open in the main frame.

5 Link the three special vehicle images to their specific pages. Choose a target that opens the destination pages in the main frame and replaces the home.html frameset page.

6 Close, saving your changes to all pages.

Create Links from the Category Pages

1 Open new-hummers.html from the IP>vehicles folder, and link the photos to the appropriate vehicle-detail pages. Evaluate whether or not you need to specify a target; if so, determine which target and whether or not you need to use the **<base />** tag. Close the file, saving your changes.

2 Open index.html and preview it in your browser. Click a link to open the New Hummers category page. Test the links from the category page to ensure these links are targeted correctly.

3 Repeat Steps 1 and 2 with the three remaining category pages.

4 Test any links you created in the staff directory page. When you are finished, close the file, saving your changes.

TASK GUIDE

Task	Windows	Macintosh

Managing Files

Task	Windows	Macintosh
New document	Control-N	Command-N
Open an HTML file	Control-O	Command-O
Open in frame	Control-Shift-O	Command-Shift-O
Close	Control-W	Command-W
Save	Control-S	Command-S
Save as	Control-Shift-S	Command-Shift-S
Exit/Quit	Control-Q	Command-Q

Opening and Closing Panels

Task	Windows	Macintosh
Insert bar	Control-F2	Command-F2
Properties	Control-F3	Command-F3
CSS Styles	Shift-F11	Shift-F11
Tag Inspector	F9	F9
Reference	Shift-F1	Shift-F1
Files	F8	F8
Assets	F11	F11
Show/Hide panels	F4	F4

Viewing Page Elements

Task	Windows	Macintosh
Page Properties	Control-J	Command-J

Inserting Objects

Task	Windows	Macintosh
Any object (image, Shockwave movie, etc.)	Drag file from the Explorer or Site panel to the Document window	Drag file from the Finder or Site panel to the Document window
Image	Control-Alt-I	Command-Option-I
Table	Control-Alt-T	Command-Option-T
Named Anchor	Control-Alt-A	Command-Option-A

Task	Macintosh	Windows

General Editing

Task	Macintosh	Windows
Undo	Control-Z	Command-Z
Redo	Control-Y	Command-Y
Cut	Control-X	Command-X
Copy	Control-C	Command-C
Paste	Control-V	Command-V
Clear	Delete	Delete
Bold	Control-B	Command-B
Italic	Control-I	Command-I
Select All	Control-A	Command-A
Move to page up	Page Up	Page Up
Move to page down	Page Down	Page Down
Select to page up	Shift-Page Up	Shift-Page Up
Select to page down	Shift-Page Down	Shift-Page Down
Select line up/down	Shift-Up/Down	Shift-Up/Down
Move to start of line	Home	Home
Move to end of line	End	End
Select to start of line	Shift-Home	Shift-Home
Select to end of line	Shift-End	Shift-End
Go to previous/next paragraph	Control-Up/Down	Command-Up/Down
Go to next/previous word	Control-Right/Left	Command-Right/Left
Delete word left	Control-Backspace	Command-Backspace
Delete word right	Control-Delete	Command-Delete
Select character left/right	Shift-Left/Right	Shift-Left/Right
Find and Replace	Control-F	Command-F
Find next/find again	F3	Command-G
Preferences	Control-U	Command-U

Task	Macintosh	Windows

Code Editing

Print code	Control-P	Command-P
Open Quick Tag Editor	Control-T	Command-T
Tag Chooser	Control-E	Command-E
Go to line	Control-G	Control-,
Move to top of code	Control-Home	Command-Home
Move to end of code	Control-End	Command-End
Select to top of code	Control-Shift-Home	Command-Shift-Home
Select to end of code	Control-Shift-End	Command-Shift-End

Text Editing

Create a new paragraph	Enter	Return
Insert a line break 	Shift-Enter	Shift-Return
Insert a nonbreaking space	Control-Shift-Spacebar	Command-Shift-Spacebar
Move text or object to another place in the page	Drag selected item	Drag selected item
Copy text or object to another place in the page	Control-drag selected item	Option-drag selected item
Check spelling	Shift-F7	Shift-F7

Working in Tables

Move to the next cell	Tab	Tab
Move to the previous cell	Shift-Tab	Shift-Tab
Insert a row (before current)	Control-M	Command-M
Add a row at end of table	Tab in the last cell	Tab in the last cell

Working with Images

Change image source	Double-click image	Double-click image
Edit image in external editor	Control-double-click image	Command-Double-click image

Task	Macintosh	Windows
Working with Frames		
Select a frame	Alt-click in frame	Shift-Option-click in frame
Select next frame or frameset	Alt-Right Arrow	Command-Right Arrow
Select previous frame or frameset	Alt-Left Arrow	Command-Left Arrow
Select parent frameset	Alt-Up Arrow	Command-Up Arrow
Select first child frame or frameset	Alt-Down Arrow	Command-Down Arrow
Add a new frame to frameset	Alt-drag border of selected frame	Option-drag border of selected frame
Add a new frame to frameset (push method)	Alt-Control-drag border of selected frame	Command-Option-drag border of selected frame
Managing Hyperlinks		
Drag and drop to create a hyperlink from a document	Select the object, then Shift-drag the selection to a file in the Site panel	Select the object, then Shift-drag the selection to a file in the Site panel
Drag and drop to create a hyperlink using the Property inspector	Select the object, then drag the Point-to-File icon in Property inspector to a file in the Site panel	Select the object, then drag the Point-to-File icon in Property inspector to a file in the Site panel
Open the linked-to document in Dreamweaver	Control-double-click link	Command-double-click link
Previewing and Debugging in Browsers		
Preview in primary browser	F12	F12
Preview in secondary browser	Shift-F12	Shift-F12
Getting Help		
Using Dreamweaver Help Topics	F1	F1
Using ColdFusion Help Topics	Control-F1	Command-F1
Reference	Shift-F1	Shift-F1

GLOSSARY

_blank A predefined target that opens the destination of the link in a new blank browser window.

_parent A predefined frame target that replaces the parent frameset of the current frame with the page identified by the link.

_self A predefined target that opens the destination of the link in the current window or frame. Not commonly used because _self is the default target of a link but if the <base /> tag defines a different base target, the _self target will override the base target and open the page in the same frame as the linking page.

_top A predefined target that opens the destination link in the current browser window, replacing all framesets.

above the fold The area of a Web page that a user can view without scrolling either vertically or horizontally.

absolute path The location of a file or Web page beginning with the root. Includes all necessary information to find the file or page. In the case of a Web page, called "absolute URL." See *relative path*.

accessibility Web design techniques that enable everyone to use a Web site.

alt text Alternate Text. Text that can be used in lieu of an image.

animated GIF A type of sequential file format where multiple bitmap images are displayed one after another.

antialiasing A graphics software feature that eliminates or softens the jaggedness of low-resolution curved edges.

ASP Active Server Pages. A specification for a dynamically created Web page that contains either Visual Basic or JavaScript code. When a browser requests an ASP page, the Web server generates a page with HTML code. Available only on Windows servers.

asset An image, sound, video, or other file that may be in use in a Web page.

assistive device Hardware enabling a disabled viewer to use a Web site.

attribute Attributes augment the element in which they appear; they also provide additional information about the element. Attributes appear as name-value pairs in the element's start-tag.

background A static object or color that lies behind all other objects.

bandwidth The transmission capacity, usually measured in bits per second of a network connection.

bit (binary digit) A computer's smallest unit of information. Bits can have only two values: 0 or 1.

bit depth A measure of how many colors can be contained in an image. 8-bit color is 256 colors (2 × 2 × 2 × 2 × 2 × 2 × 2 × 2), 16-bit color is 32,768 colors (2 × 2 × 2 × 2 × 2 × 2 × 2 × 2 × 2 × 2 × 2 × 2 × 2 × 2 × 2), and so on.

bitmap image An image constructed from individual dots or pixels set to a gridlike mosaic. The file must contain information about the color and position of each pixel, so the disk space needed for bitmap images can be very large.

browser Software program that allows you to surf the Web. The most popular browser is Microsoft Internet Explorer. The very first browsers, such as Lynx, only allowed users to see text. Also called "Web browser."

browser compatibility A term that compares the way a Web page functions on different browsers. Incompatibilities often exist due to the way a browser interprets the HTML. The differences may be very slight or significant.

bullet A marker preceding text, usually a solid dot; generally indicates the text is part of a list.

button An element a user can click to cause an effect, such as the submission of form data.

byte A unit of measure equal to 8 bits (decimal 256) of digital information, sufficient to represent one text character. The standard unit measure of file size.

Cascading Style Sheets (CSS) A Web language used to create the appearance of a Web page and a Web site. Often, CSS is stored in an external file for all pages on the site to use.

cell A unit of information within a table.

cell padding The whitespace between table cell contents and the table cell borders.

cell spacing The whitespace between table cell borders.

CFML ColdFusion Markup Language. A proprietary markup language owned by Macromedia that is mixed within HTML. ColdFusion may perform functions and interact with databases. It only runs on a Cold Fusion Server.

client A computer system or application that requests a service of another computer system on the network. See *server*.

client-side Scripting or other actions that take place within the browser, as opposed to on the server.

clip art Collections of predrawn and digitized graphics.

code hint A pop-up menu presenting code options for HTML tags, attributes, and options; CSS; and some programming languages. Code hints are only available when working with the code directly.

color picker A function within a graphics application that assists in selecting or setting a color.

column A series of table cells arranged vertically.

compression A technique used to reduce file size by analyzing occurrences of similar data. Compressed files occupy less space, and their use improves digital transmission speeds. Lossy compression results in greatest file compression ratios while sacrificing some image quality and/or resolution. Lossless compression achieves lower compression ratios but with no loss of image data.

copyright Ownership of a work. Permits the owner of material to prevent its use without express permission or acknowledgment of the originator. Copyright may be sold, transferred, or given up contractually.

dead link A link whose destination has been changed or removed. Also called "broken links."

deprecated The status of a tag or attribute that can still be used but that will eventually be removed, and so should be avoided if possible.

DHTML Dynamic HTML. JavaScript programs that dynamically change cascading style sheet properties, allowing parts of your Web page to be hidden, shown, or animated.

digital camera A camera that stores images directly into an electronic file format for transfer to a computer.

disabilities Challenges that hinder some people from using computers in general, including Web pages. Included are blindness, low vision (requiring magnification), color blindness, motility (shakiness or loss of function), and some mental challenges such as dyslexia. The goal of the WAI is to provide guidelines for Web designers to enable their sites to accommodate disabilities in their design.

dithering A technique in which a color is represented using dots of two different colors displayed or printed very close together. Dithering is often used to compress digital images and in special screening algorithms.

DNS Domain Name Server or Domain Name System. Maps IP numbers to a more easily remembered name. When you type http://www.somedomain.com into a browser, the DNS searches for a matching IP address (228.28.202.95).

document root The main directory for a Web site.

document title Text that appears in the Title bar of the user's browser when the page is viewed.

domain name A unique name that is used to identify a Web site, FTP site, and/or e-mail server. A domain name always points to one specific server, even though the server may host many domain names.

domain name registrar A company who may sell domain names. Some provide hosting and other related services as well.

download Transfer of data from a server to your computer's hard disk.

DTD Document Type Definition. A separate document that contains formal definitions of all of the data elements in a particular type of HTML, SGML, or XML document. By consulting the DTD for a document, a program called a "parser" can work with the markup codes that the document contains.

ECMA European Computer Manufacturers Association.

ECMAScript An official, standardized version of JavaScript maintained by ECMA.

editable text A text element that the user can modify by entering or deleting keystrokes.

e-mail address An electronic mail address. E-mail addresses are in the form of user@domain.com (for example, chris@webguest.net).

empty tag A tag that has no closing element tag.

FAQs Frequently Asked Questions. A document that contains the most common questions and answers on a particular subject or product.

file compression The process of reducing the number of bytes in a file, file compression is usually used when transferring files between computers.

flat color Color that lacks contrast or tonal variation. Also called "flat tint."

flowchart A sketch that shows the relationships of each page to the other pages in the site.

font The complete collection of all the characters (numbers, uppercase and lowercase letters, and in some cases, small caps and symbols) of a given typeface in a specific style; for example, Helvetica Bold.

frame A section of the browser window displaying a content document that is independent of all other areas within the browser window. This window-within-a-window can be referenced by links in other frames.

frameset The document defining the layout on a framed page and breaking it into one or more frames.

Frameset DTD A version of (X)HTML that includes tags that involve frames.

frame trapping Improper use of a frames-based layout in which an external Web site's page is displayed within the frame of another site and not allowed full access to the whole browser window.

freeware Software available at no cost. Freeware does not necessarily mean copyright-free.

FTP File Transfer Protocol. Internet method to transfer files through the Internet from one computer to another. FTP is used to download files from another computer and to upload files from your computer to a remote computer.

GIF Graphics Interchange Format. A popular format for online clip art and drawn graphics. Graphics in this format are acceptable at low resolution. See *JPEG*.

graceful degradation A technique that ensures content remains usable, even if all features are not available. Graceful degradation is the goal when designing pages using standards that may not be supported in older browsers.

gradient A gradual transition from one color to another. The shape of the gradient and the proportion of the two colors can be varied. Also known as "blends," "gradations," "graduated fills," and "vignettes."

handles Black squares (commonly eight) at the corners and sides of a selected image enabling the user to resize the graphic.

home page Entry page to a Web site.

hotspot A region in an image that has been marked up as a link. A hotspot may be a rectangle, circle, or polygon.

HREF Hyperlink Reference. HTML code that specifies a URL as the linked resource.

HSB Color model used to define color in terms of Hue, Saturation, and Brightness.

HSV/HSL A color model based on three coordinates: Hue, Saturation, and Value/Luminance.

HTML   Hypertext Markup Language. A tagging language used to define the structure of content in a Web page document.

HTTP   Hypertext Transfer Protocol. The method used by browsers and Web servers to communicate, such as to request and deliver content, respectively.

hue   The wavelength of light of a color in its purest state (without adding white or black).

hyperlink   An HTML tag that directs the computer to a different anchor or URL. A hyperlink can be a word, phrase, sentence, graphic, or icon. A hyperlink can also cause an action, such as opening or downloading a file.

image map   A graphic containing hotspots, or areas of an image that are defined as links. When a viewer clicks the part of the image that is a hotspot, they are actually clicking on a link.

information architecture   The structure and organization of the data on a Web site.

inline graphic   A graphic that is inserted within a body of text; inline graphics move with the body of text in which they are placed.

interlacing   A characteristic of GIF and PNG files, in which the file is displayed in progressively greater detail as it is downloaded.

Internet   A global system of interconnected computers.

InterNIC   Internet Network Information Center. The entity that keeps track of the domain names. Recently the right to register domain names has been widely granted to private companies, so the cost and services associated with obtaining a new domain can vary.

intranet   A small network dedicated to information and resources about and for the corporation or organization that maintains it, enabling a company to share resources with employees without confidential information being made available across the Internet.

ISP   Internet Service Provider. An organization that provides access to the Internet for such things as electronic mail, bulletin boards, chat rooms, or use of the World Wide Web.

JavaScript   A scripting language, primarily client-side, designed by Netscape that can be embedded into HTML documents to respond to user actions as the programmer had intended.

JPEG   A compression algorithm that reduces the file size of bitmapped images, named for the Joint Photographic Experts Group, which created the standard. JPEG is "lossy" compression; image quality is reduced in direct proportion to the amount of compression.

JScript   Microsoft's proprietary implementation of JavaScript.

JSP   Java Servlet Pages. Web pages created using the Java programming language run on a Web server.

KB   Kilobyte. 1,024 bytes, the nearest binary equivalent to decimal 1,000 bytes.

layout   The arrangement of text and graphics on a page.

left alignment   Text having a straight left edge and a ragged (uneven) right edge.

linking   The act of placing a reference to one file (sound, graphic, or video) into another file. When the referenced file is modified, the placed reference is automatically (or manually, depending on the application) updated.

Linux   UNIX-like operating system that is available for little or no cost and offers developers free access to the uncompiled code.

list   A series of items.

lossless   Refers to data compression techniques in which no data is lost.

lossy   A data compression method characterized by the loss of some data.

Lynx   A text-only browser.

mailto: A protocol used to tell the browser to create a new e-mail message.

MIME type   An indication of the kind of data being sent to the browser. Used by the browser to know what to do with the data.

Mosaic   The first Web browser (developed by NSCA) with the ability to display graphics. The Mosaic browser caused a major breakthrough in the way people could access the resources of the World Wide Web.

Mozilla   The organization created when Netscape Corporation decided to open-source the code of their Netscape browser. Mozilla.org has released the powerful and sophisticated Mozilla, Firefox, and Camino browsers. Netscape version 6+ is based on Mozilla code. All Mozilla-based browsers are free to download.

MySQL   Fast, free, open-source database suitable for Web database functionality.

named anchor   An <a> anchor tag that uses the name attribute. Commonly, the named anchor is empty such as <a name="header"></a> where no content exists between the opening and closing <a> tags. Consider removing all named anchors and linking to tags with ids instead, such as <div id="header">.

named colors   A set of colors specifically designated for reference by name, rather than by RGB or hexadecimal values.

named target   A frame that has a designated name, allowing links to specify that content should be displayed within that frame.

nested frameset   A frameset that is the content of the frame of another frameset.

nested tag   A tag contained within another tag.

no frames section   Content provided for browsers that do not support frames contained within a noframes element.

obsolete   (X)HTML tags that have been removed from a specified standard.

opening tag   The indication of the start of an element containing the name of the element and any attributes.

Opera   Popular, advanced browser for Windows, Macintosh, Linux/UNIX, and cell phones from Opera.com: now available for free.

operating system (OS)   The software that allows your computer to function. An example of an operating system is Mac OS X, Microsoft Windows, or UNIX/Linux.

orphaned files   Files that exist below the root of the site but that are not linked or used in any pages in the Web site.

page properties In Web design, the characteristics of a layout page, including default background and text colors, page width, and background image.

page weight The total number of bytes required to download the HTML document and all associated assets such as images, CSS, and JavaScript files. Dreamweaver's Download indicator identifies the page weight — try to keep the page weight below 60 KB for pages of general interest on the Internet.

palette As derived from the term in traditional art, a collection of selectable colors.

PHP An open-source server-side Web-programming language capable of running on UNIX, Linux, Windows, and Macintosh Web servers. Easy to learn, free, and capable of powerful and sophisticated functionality.

PNG Portable Network Graphics. PNG is a new graphics format similar to GIF. It is a relatively new file format and is not yet fully supported by all browsers.

presentational HTML HTML tags and attributes that provide only style. The <b> (bold) tag and the align attribute are examples of presentational HTML. When designing a Web page, avoid using presentational HTML and use CSS instead.

progressive display A characteristic of JPEG files, in which the file will be displayed in increasingly greater detail as it is downloaded.

protocol A set of rules and conventions that describe the behavior computers must follow in order to understand each other.

raster image A type of picture created and organized in a rectangular array of bitmaps. Often created by paint software, scanners, or digital cameras.

refresh To reload.

relative path The location of a file or Web page that uses the location of the current file or page as a reference. In the case of a Web page, called "relative URL." See *absolute path*.

reload To re-retrieve and redisplay a Web page in the browser.

resample The process of rebuilding the pixels in a raster image after it has been resized. Resampling will occur if the image is increased or decreased in size.

RGB Red Green Blue. A means of specifying a color by indicating the amount of each of these components (channels) of the color.

RGBa Red Green Blue alpha. Similar to RGB plus a fourth channel to specify transparency. Used in PNG graphics to allow individual pixels to have different levels of transparency.

root Top-level directory from which all other directories branch out.

royalty-free Content that you may purchase and use in your published Web pages without having to pay a royalty to the creator of the content each time you use it. The content may be text- or image-based.

sans serif Fonts that do not have serifs. See *serif.*

screen reader Software that captures the onscreen content, stores it into a buffer, then passes it onto the user either through computerized speech processor or refreshable Braille displays.

search engine A Web site that allows users to search for keywords on Web pages. Every search engine has its own strategy for collecting data.

search engine optimization (SEO) Judicious incorporation of various methods and techniques to maximize the likelihood that sites will be ranked highly in search engine results. Given that search engines constantly fine-tune the methods by which they rank pages, SEO techniques also will change.

serif A line or curve projecting from the end of a letterform. Typefaces designed with such projections are called "serif faces."

server-side Pertaining to functions that are run at the computer that operates as a server before the results are sent to the client.

SGML Standard Generalized Markup Language. The predecessor to Hypertext Markup Language; a means for creating universally available content using tagging.

shareware Software you can test for a certain amount of time to determine whether or not you want to buy it.

site map A list of pages in a Web site. Commonly, the page names are links to the pages.

site root directory The parent folder that contains all other files and directories for a Web site.

Strict DTD A version of (X)HTML that does not include any presentational tags or attributes.

source code The actual text that makes up the Web page received by the browser, including HTML/XHTML, client-side scripting, and other information.

spam Unsolicited commercial e-mail sent to millions of e-mail addresses at the same time. Spam messages are solicitations for online gambling, pharmaceuticals, or pornography. The name comes from a Monty Python song and is considered to be a serious violation of netiquette.

SQL Structured Query Language. SQL is a standardized query language for requesting information from a database. SQL also supports database updates, inserts and deletes, and user management.

storyboard A small sketch that represents each page in a Web site.

structural tags Tags that provide information about content.

style The look or appearance of a Web site. Properly done, style is created using CSS, leaving HTML for structure only.

style sheet A defined set of formatting instructions for font and paragraph attributes, tabs, and other properties of text.

SVG Scalable Vector Graphics. An XML language for the creation of vector graphics using only tags. SVG may also incorporate raster images, ECMAscript, and animation.

syntax highlighting A method of distinguishing different components of code (such as tags, attributes, comments, and text) by coloring the code or background differently or applying bold, italic, or normal styling.

template   A document file containing layout, styles, and repeating elements (such as logos) from which a series of new documents can be built so as to maintain the same look and feel.

thumbnails   Small images used to represent their larger versions. Thumbnails in photo gallery Web sites are often linked to their larger versions. Ideally, the thumbnail images and large images are different image files and not simply the large images resized using the width and height attributes of the image tag.

title attribute   An attribute that may be used to expand an acronym and an abbreviation with the full term. It may also be used in the anchor tag to provide more information about the destination of the link.

transparency   An attribute of an image that allows background elements to partially or entirely show through. Index transparency allows one color to be 100% transparent, whereas alpha transparency allows each pixel to have its own transparency setting from 0% to 100%.

Transitional DTD   The most common version of (X)HTML. Includes all tags and attributes that are part of (X)HTML including deprecated tags and attributes but not those involving frames.

UNIX   Multiuser computer operating system. The Internet and the Web matured on UNIX, and these days UNIX is still the most common operating system for servers on the Internet.

uploading   The process of sending a file from a local client computer to a remote server.

URL   Uniform Resource Locator. Address of any resource on the Web.

usability   The ease with which a user can access, navigate, and interact with a Web site.

validate   To analyze the (X)HTML or XML code to ensure the structure, tag names, and attributes are correct, according to the DTD selected. CSS may also be validated, although there is no DTD.

VBScript   A Microsoft scripting language used both for client-side scripting and within ASP.

vector graphics   Graphics defined using coordinate points and mathematically drawn lines and curves, which may be freely scaled and rotated without image degradation of the final output.

W3C   World Wide Web Consortium.

WAI   Web Accessibility Initiative. A committee of the W3C struck to create guidelines for actions that developers should take to increase the accessibility of their sites and applications.

watermark   An impression incorporated into paper during manufacturing showing the name of the paper and/or the company logo. A watermark can be applied digitally to printed output as a very light screened image. A watermark background image attempts to achieve the same effect in a Web page.

WCAG   Web Content Accessibility Guidelines. A list of guidelines for Web page designers identifying what they must do to ensure their Web sites are accessible to everyone. WCAG is the result of the work of the WAI. WCAG 1.0 is the most recent version, but WCAG 2.0 is in development and expected to be released 2006.

Web designer   An individual who is the aesthetic and navigational architect of a Web site, determining how the site looks, how it is designed, and what components it contains.

Web developer   A person who builds the technical architecture of Web sites, providing the programming required for a particular Web product to work.

Web host   A company that provides access to a server on which you can place your Web site content. This server is connected to the Internet, allowing the general public to access your Web site.

Webmaster   In the past, this term usually described the person who was in charge of all aspects of a Web site, including HTML, CSS (design), graphic designer, programmer (client- and server-side), content developer, and server manager. More often these days, these tasks are divided up between many people.

Web page   A single file or Web address containing HTML or XHTML information. Web pages typically include text and images but may include links to other pages and other media.

Web-safe color   Color palette used for images that will be displayed on the Internet in which the colors must be consistent, whatever operating system may be in use.

Web site   A collection of HTML files and other content that visitors can access by means of a URL and view with a Web browser.

World Wide Web   Client/server hypertext system for retrieving information across the Internet.

World Wide Web Consortium (W3C)   The group responsible for definition and maintenance of (X)HTML Standards (http://www.w3c.org).

WYSIWYG   What You See Is What You Get.

XHTML   eXtensible HyperText Markup Language. The reformulation of HTML 4.01 in XML.

INDEX